LOGIC PROGRAM SYNTHESIS FROM INCOMPLETE INFORMATION

THE KLUWER INTERNATIONAL SERIES IN ENGINEERING AND COMPUTER SCIENCE

LOGIC PROGRAM SYNTHESIS FROM INCOMPLETE INFORMATION

by

Pierre Flener

Bilkent University

KLUWER ACADEMIC PUBLISHERS
Boston / Dordrecht / London

Distributors for North America:
Kluwer Academic Publishers
101 Philip Drive
Assinippi Park
Norwell, Massachusetts 02061 USA

Distributors for all other countries:
Kluwer Academic Publishers Group
Distribution Centre
Post Office Box 322
3300 AH Dordrecht, THE NETHERLANDS

Library of Congress Cataloging-in-Publication Data

A C.I.P. Catalogue record for this book is available
from the Library of Congress.

Printed on acid-free paper.

Printed in the United States of America

Table of Contents

Lists of Logic Algorithms, Figures, and Tables ix

Foreword xi

Preface xiii

I STATE OF THE ART

1 Automatic Programming 3

1.1 The Grand Aim of Automatic Programming 3
1.2 Specification, Algorithm, and Programming Languages 6
1.3 A Classification of Synthesis Mechanisms 10
1.4 Requirements and Promises of Automatic Programming 11
1.5 Sample Problems 13

2 Deductive Inference in Automatic Programming 15

2.1 Specifications by Axioms 15
2.2 Deductive Inference 18
2.2.1 Transformational Synthesis 18
2.2.2 Proofs-as-Programs Synthesis 19
2.2.3 Schema-Guided Synthesis 21
2.3 Functional Program Synthesis from Axioms 21
2.3.1 Transformational Synthesis of LISP Programs 21
2.3.2 Proofs-as-Programs Synthesis of LISP Programs 22
2.3.3 Schema-Guided Synthesis of LISP Programs 23
2.4 Logic Program Synthesis from Axioms 23
2.4.1 Transformational Synthesis of Prolog Programs 24
2.4.2 Proofs-as-Programs Synthesis of Prolog Programs 26
2.4.3 Schema-Guided Synthesis of Prolog Programs 27
2.5 Conclusions on Program Synthesis from Axiomatizations 28

3 Inductive Inference in Automatic Programming **29**

3.1 Specifications by Examples 29
3.2 Inductive Inference 32
3.2.1 Components of a Learning System 33
3.2.2 Rules of Inductive Inference 33
3.2.3 Empirical Learning from Examples 34
3.2.4 Algorithm Synthesis from Examples as a Niche of Learning . . 39
3.2.5 Pointers to the Literature 41
3.3 Functional Program Synthesis from Examples 42
3.3.1 Synthesis from Traces 42
3.3.2 Trace-Based Synthesis from Examples 42
3.3.3 Heuristic Synthesis from Examples 45
3.4 Logic Program Synthesis from Examples 46
3.4.1 Shapiro's *Model Inference System* 46
3.4.2 Other Model-Based Synthesis Systems 51
3.5 Conclusions on Program Synthesis from Examples 52

4 A Logic Program Development Methodology **55**

4.1 Elaboration of a Specification 56
4.2 Design of a Logic Algorithm 56
4.3 Transformation of a Logic Algorithm 61
4.4 Derivation of a Logic Program 61
4.5 Transformation of a Logic Program 62

5 Objectives **63**

5.1 Precise Statement of the Objective 63
5.2 Motivating Examples 64
5.2.1 Sample Logic Algorithms 64
5.2.2 Some Comments on Logic Algorithms 71
5.3 Challenges 75

II BUILDING BLOCKS

6 A Specification Approach **79**

6.1 Specifications by Examples and Properties 79
6.2 Sample Specifications by Examples and Properties 80
6.3 Future Work 83
6.4 Related Work 83
6.5 Conclusion 84

7 A Framework for Stepwise Logic Algorithm Synthesis 85

7.1 Correctness of Logic Algorithms 85
7.1.1 Logic Algorithm and Intentions 87
7.1.2 Logic Algorithm and Specification 89
7.1.3 Specification and Intentions 90
7.2 Comparison of Logic Algorithms 90
7.2.1 Semantic Generalization .91
7.2.2 Syntactic Generalization .91
7.3 Stepwise Logic Algorithm Synthesis Strategies 93
7.3.1 An Incremental Synthesis Strategy 93
7.3.2 A Non-Incremental Synthesis Strategy 94
7.4 Future Work 99
7.5 Related Work 99
7.6 Conclusion 100

8 Algorithm Analysis and Algorithm Schemata 101

8.1 Introduction to Algorithm Schemata 101
8.2 A Divide-and-Conquer Logic Algorithm Schema 103
8.2.1 Divide-and-Conquer Logic Algorithm Analysis 104
8.2.2 Integrity Constraints on Instances 107
8.2.3 Justifications 108
8.2.4 Discussion 109
8.3 Stepwise, Schema-Guided Logic Algorithm Synthesis 110
8.4 Future Work 111
8.5 Related Work 112
8.6 Conclusion 114

9 The Proofs-as-Programs Method 115

9.1 The Problem 115
9.2 A Method 116
9.3 Correctness 122
9.4 Illustration 123
9.5 Future Work 130
9.6 Related Work 130
9.7 Conclusion 132

10 The Most-Specific-Generalization Method 133

10.1 Most-Specific-Generalization of Terms 133
10.2 Objective and Terminology 134
10.3 The Ground Case 136
10.4 The Non-Ground Case 139
10.5 Future Work 142
10.6 Related Work 143
10.7 Conclusion 144

III A LOGIC ALGORITHM SYNTHESIS MECHANISM

11 Overview of the Synthesis Mechanism **147**

11.1 Desired Features 147
11.2 Preliminary Restrictions 151
11.3 A Sample Synthesis 152

12 The Expansion Phase **159**

12.1 Step 1: Syntactic Creation of a First Approximation 160
12.2 Step 2: Synthesis of *Minimal* and *NonMinimal* 161
12.3 Step 3: Synthesis of *Decompose* 166
12.4 Step 4: Syntactic Introduction of the Recursive Atoms 171

13 The Reduction Phase **175**

13.1 Step 5: Synthesis of *Solve* and the $SolveNonMin_k$ 175
13.2 Step 6: Synthesis of the $Process_k$ and $Compose_k$ 181
13.3 Step 7: Synthesis of the $Discriminate_k$ 186

14 Conclusion **191**

14.1 Summary 191
14.2 Extensions 196
14.2.1 Negation 196
14.2.2 Auxiliary Parameters 197
14.2.3 Supporting Other Schemata 198
14.2.4 The Synthesis Method 198
14.3 A Methodology for Choosing "Good" Examples and Properties . . . 204
14.4 The SYNAPSE System 206
14.4.1 The Architecture of SYNAPSE 206
14.4.2 Target Scenarios for SYNAPSE 207
14.5 Evaluation 211
14.5.1 Insights 211
14.5.2 Comparison with Related Systems 213

Appendix: Conventions, Abbreviations, and Symbols **215**

References **219**

Subject Index **235**

List of Logic Algorithms

Logic Algorithm 4-1: *LA(compress)* 57
Logic Algorithm 4-2: *LA(firstPlateau)* 57
Logic Algorithm 4-3: *LA(compress-int-L)* 61
Logic Algorithm 5-1: *LA(compress-ext-L)* 64
Logic Algorithm 5-2: *LA(compress-int-C)* 65
Logic Algorithm 5-3: *LA(compress-ext-C)* 65
Logic Algorithm 5-4: *LA(delOddElems-L)* 66
Logic Algorithm 5-5: *LA(efface-L)* 66
Logic Algorithm 5-6: *LA(firstN-L)* 66
Logic Algorithm 5-7: *LA(firstN-N)* 67
Logic Algorithm 5-8: *LA(insert-L)* 67
Logic Algorithm 5-9: *LA(insert-R)* 67
Logic Algorithm 5-10: *LA(member-L)* 68
Logic Algorithm 5-11: *LA(merge-<A,B>)* 68
Logic Algorithm 5-12: *LA(parity-L)* 69
Logic Algorithm 5-13: *LA(partition-L)* 69
Logic Algorithm 5-14: *LA(permutation-L)* 69
Logic Algorithm 5-15: *LA(plateau-N)* 70
Logic Algorithm 5-16: *LA(sort-int-L)* {Insertion-Sort} 70
Logic Algorithm 5-17: *LA(sort-ext-L)* {Quick-Sort} 70
Logic Algorithm 5-18: *LA(sort-ext-L)* {Merge-Sort} 70
Logic Algorithm 5-19: *LA(split)* 71
Logic Algorithm 12-1: LA_1*(firstPlateau)* 161
Logic Algorithm 12-2: *exp(*LA_1*(firstPlateau))* 161
Logic Algorithm 12-3: LA_2*(firstPlateau)* 166
Logic Algorithm 12-4: *exp(*LA_2*(firstPlateau))* 166
Logic Algorithm 12-5: LA_3*(firstPlateau)* 170
Logic Algorithm 12-6: *exp(*LA_3*(firstPlateau))* 170
Logic Algorithm 12-7: LA_4*(firstPlateau)* 174
Logic Algorithm 12-8: *exp(*LA_4*(firstPlateau))* 174
Logic Algorithm 13-1: LA_5*(firstPlateau)* 180
Logic Algorithm 13-2: *exp(*LA_5*(firstPlateau))* 180
Logic Algorithm 13-3: LA_6*(firstPlateau)* 185
Logic Algorithm 13-4: *exp(*LA_6*(firstPlateau))* 185
Logic Algorithm 13-5: LA_7*(firstPlateau)* 190
Logic Algorithm 13-6: *exp(*LA_7*(firstPlateau))* 190

List of Figures

Figure 1-1: The traditional software life-cycle 4
Figure 1-2: A new software life-cycle 5
Figure 1-3: A practical view of program development 6
Figure 3-2: Part of the specialization graph for the *member*/2 predicate 48
Figure 4-1: *Spec(compress)* 56
Figure 4-2: *Spec(firstPlateau)* 57
Figure 4-3: *LP(compress-int-L)* 62
Figure 4-4: A transformed version of *LP(compress-int-L)* 62
Figure 7-1: Upward and downward progression 94
Figure 10-1: MSG Method (ground case): The first two steps 137
Figure 10-2: MSG Method (ground case): Example 139

List of Tables

Table 3-1: Algorithm synthesis from examples as a niche of learning 40
Table 5-1: Summary of the features of some sample relations 73
Table 5-2: Summary of the features of some sample logic algorithms 74
Table 12-1: Database of instances of *Minimal*/1 and *NonMinimal*/1 163
Table 12-2: Database of intrinsic instances of *Decompose*/1+*h*+*t* 168
Table 12-3: Database of extrinsic instances of *Decompose*/1+*h*+*t* 168
Table 12-4: Database of logarithmic instances of *Decompose*/1+*h*+*t* 168
Table 14-1: Summary of the synthesis steps and tasks 192
Table 14-2: Summary of the features of the synthesized logic algorithms 193

Foreword

Computer programming is an incredibly ubiquitous activity; but it seems to be what we must do to get machines to carry out our wishes. We must state in considerable detail each step that is to be carried out and hope that we get the instructions correct. Automatic programming is the field in which we try to break away from conventional programming methods and find new more convenient and more reliable ways to create programs. This book is a contribution to the field of automatic programming, and it is an extremely important one in that it brings together two previously divergent approaches to the field and shows how to assemble them into one efficient and self-consistent architecture.

The first approach emphasizes the automatic derivation of programs from their specifications. The idea is that the user should specify *what* is to be computed, not *how*. The machine then is to create the algorithm using deductive mechanisms from logic and implement the necessary code. This has been an extremely important series of studies because they have clarified the nature of the connections between the specifications and the program. One cannot claim to understand computer science without coming to grips with these ideas. But this approach has problems when viewed as a practical programming scheme. The main objection is that it is hard for people to write down complete and correct specifications to a program. It may be easier for a user to write the program than to get the logic notations correct that would be adequate for a formal derivation. A second problem is the execution time. The cost of synthesizing a program from specifications may be too high.

A second approach emphasizes the synthesis of programs from examples of their behaviors. In this case, the user is to provide only examples of the input-output behaviors for the target program and the system is to create the program from this weak source of information. The attractiveness of the model is tremendous; it is like magic. If you want a program to reverse a LISP expression, you might type $(A \bullet (B \bullet C))$ yields $((C \bullet B) \bullet A)$ and possibly a few more examples. Soon you should have a general program for reversal automatically created for you. The major problem here is the execution time to find the answer. Methodologies have been found to do this kind of synthesis, but the cost is high.

The main contribution of this book is to show how to combine the two methodologies, synthesis from specifications and from examples, into a single system and to get them to work together efficiently. The idea from the user's point of view is that *both* kinds of information are desirable. The formal specifications give precise information as to what is to be computed but they may not be complete. The examples disambiguate the specifications where they are incomplete and show how to handle special cases. This has been a long needed contribution and it has not come easily. The author has had to push the state of the art in a variety of ways to achieve the combination.

The central methodology is to assume the target program can be created by instantiating a particular schema and to concentrate resources on finding how to fill in the associated fields. In this work, a divide-and-conquer schema is used which can be instantiated to do a wide variety of computations. Once the schema is selected, one can provide a number of specialized strategies for instantiating its parts and the associated costs can be kept under control. All of these ideas and many more are incorporated into the Flener system and covered here.

This book gives an excellent introduction to many of the best ideas from the field of automatic programming, an interesting coverage of some new ideas developed by the author, and a description of an ambitious synthesis system that utilizes them for practical automatic program synthesis.

Alan W. Biermann
Chapel Hill, North Carolina, U.S.A.

Preface

Automatic programming (also called automatic program synthesis) is an often suggested solution to the software crisis, which has been haunting commercial software production for over two decades now. Indeed, if we could write a program that develops correct programs from specifications, with as much (or as little) interaction as the specifier wants, then the program validation and maintenance stages would disappear from the software life-cycle, and one could instead focus on the more creative tasks of specification elaboration, validation, and maintenance, because replay of program development would become less costly.

This book describes a novel approach to the rapidly growing new field of Inductive Logic Programming (ILP), where logic programming and machine learning are being cross-fertilized. Aiming at the synthesis of recursive logic programs only, we take a software engineering approach that seems more appropriate for this class than the artificial intelligence approach of "standard" ILP. This is reflected in the structured provision of knowledge to the synthesizer, and in the resulting cross-fertilization, namely of ILP and deductive techniques for automatic program synthesis.

This material thus constitutes an interesting complement to the field of ILP, as well as a new boost to program synthesis from examples, which is generally believed to be a necessary component of large automatic programming systems.

Understanding the Title of this Book

The framework of this book is algorithm synthesis from "incomplete" specifications. More precisely, we tackle the problem of "*logic algorithm synthesis from specifications by examples and properties.*" This formulation implies several things. First, the chosen programming paradigm is *logic* programming. Second, we are here only interested in synthesizing recursive logic programs, which we call logic *algorithms*. Moreover, the focus is on the actual algorithm *synthesis*, and on the declarative semantics of such logic algorithms, but not on their transformation, optimization, or implementation. Third, synthesis starts from incomplete *specifications*, in the sense that one deliberately admits a lack of information in the specification with respect to the intentions: synthesis is meant to extrapolate these intentions. The chosen specification formalism is a compromise between specifications by examples and axiomatic specifications: *examples* of the intended relation are given, as well as *properties*, which are a specialized form of axioms, but also a generalized form of examples. Properties are meant to disambiguate examples. This approach allows more efficient and more effective synthesis than from examples alone, but also more natural and understandable specifications than first-order logic axiomatizations.

The Claim of this Book

These specification and programming paradigms have been chosen to illustrate our claim that "*program synthesis can be effectively performed by successively filling in the place-holders of some algorithm schema, each such instantiation being done by deploying the best-suited method of a generic tool-box of (inductive, deductive, ...) methods.*" Again, this formulation implies several things. First, we want a firm theoretical grip on the *effectiveness* of the synthesis: the development and application of suitable correctness criteria is a central theme in this book. Second, we want to decompose synthesis into a *succession* of well-defined software engineering tasks: this is where the notion of *algorithm schema* comes in. We here exclusively focus on the divide-and-conquer schema and define its *place-holders*. Schema-guidance is a very powerful way to inject algorithm design knowledge into synthesis, and thus reduce search spaces. Third, we suggest that synthesis need not be done by a unique mechanism in one fell swoop, nor by a decomposition into tasks that are performed using a single kind of reasoning: indeed, a *generic tool-box* of methods can be developed, each *method* being able to *instantiate* place-holders of schemas. We develop such a tool-box: some methods perform *inductive* reasoning, other methods perform *deductive* reasoning, yet other methods simply retrieve instances from knowledge bases.

We illustrate our claim of effective stepwise algorithm synthesis via schema-guidance and tool-box usage by finding a convenient mapping between the identified place-holders of the divide-and-conquer schema and the methods of the developed tool-box. This mapping is at the heart of our mechanism for synthesizing logic algorithms from specifications by examples and properties.

Compared to related systems, such as those of ILP, our synthesis mechanism features a smaller scope (recursive logic programs rather than any logic programs), but also a much more "disciplined" approach, due to its schema-guidance, well-structured knowledge provision, augmented specifications, and its use of the best-suited method of a tool-box for each task. In other words, the pragmatic restriction of scope allows us to achieve better results on the class of recursive logic programs.

Readership

This book is very much self-contained, and accessible to non-specialists of logic programming, inductive logic programming, or automatic programming. Its readership ranges from novices who want an introduction to automatic programming, to researchers in software engineering or artificial intelligence who want to know about current techniques in automatic program synthesis, to practitioners of logic programming, inductive logic programming, or automatic programming, who want to broaden their perspectives.

Using this Book

This book contains extensive background material and references on most aspects of automatic programming, and can thus be at the basis of a graduate (or senior) level introduction to that field.

Other developed aspects, such as logic program correctness and logic program schemata, are of general interest to the logic programming community, and can be studied independently of the overall objective of this book.

After the survey chapters on automatic programming, every technical chapter with new material concludes with sections on related work and future work. Two small, but non-trivial, algorithms are gradually being synthesized all across the text, providing the reader with a feel for the overall synthesis mechanism. Numerous other examples illustrate every newly introduced concept. A comprehensive list of algorithms, figures, and tables, and a subject index facilitate navigation within the book.

Organization of this Book

This book is divided into three parts: Part I is about the state-of-the-art in automatic programming, Part II provides some building blocks for a synthesis mechanism, and Part III describes our synthesis mechanism in terms of these building blocks.

Part I: State of the Art

In Part I, we present the *state-of-the-art* of the topics underlying this book, and introduce the relevant terminology along the way. The idea is to gradually introduce the objectives of this research by narrowing in from more general aims. Note, however, that Chapters 2 to 4 may be read in any order. This state-of-the-art is unusually long, because this book is at the intersection of numerous domains, such as software engineering, deductive inference and automated theorem proving, inductive inference and machine learning, and algorithm design methodologies.

In Chapter 1, we give a general introduction to the field of *automatic programming*. After a presentation of the grand aim of program synthesis research, we discuss the languages used for expressing specifications, algorithms, and programs. We then propose a classification scheme for synthesis mechanisms, and conclude with our personal viewpoint on the requirements and promises of automatic programming research.

In Chapter 2, we survey the use of *deductive inference in automatic programming*. Axiomatic specifications are expected to be complete and non-ambiguous, but are usually also quite lengthy and artificial. Deductive synthesis from axiomatic specifications can be classified into transformational synthesis, proofs-as-programs synthesis (or constructive synthesis), and schema-guided synthesis. We survey the achievements of deductive synthesis of LISP functions and Prolog predicates.

In Chapter 3, we survey the use of *inductive inference in automatic programming*. Specifications by examples are concise and natural, but are usually also incomplete and ambiguous, due to the insufficient expressive power of examples. As inductive inference is much less known than deductive inference, we first survey this field. Inductive synthesis from specifications by examples can be classified into trace-based synthesis and model-based synthesis. We survey the achievements of inductive synthesis of LISP functions and Prolog predicates.

In Chapter 4, we summarize a *methodology of logic program development* [Deville 87, 90]. It aims at programming-in-the-small, and is meant for algorithmic problems. It is divided into three stages: elaboration of an informal specification; design of a logic algorithm (an algorithm expressed in logic), and possibly its transformation; and derivation of a logic program, and possibly its transformation. The most creative second stage is based only on the declarative semantics of logic, and is independent of the target logic programming language used at the third stage.

In Chapter 5, we formulate the *objective* of this book in more detail, namely (semi-) automated logic algorithm synthesis. A series of motivating sample scenarios allows us to identify the challenges of this objective.

Part II: Building Blocks

In Part II, we provide the *building blocks* that are used later for the development of a logic algorithm synthesis mechanism. These building blocks are a new language for expressing incomplete specifications (Chapter 6), a complete theoretical framework for the formulation of stepwise synthesis strategies (Chapter 7), an introduction to the notion of algorithm schemas and their usage in algorithm synthesis (Chapter 8), a method for deductively synthesizing parts of logic algorithms (Chapter 9), and another method for inductively synthesizing parts of logic algorithms (Chapter 10). Note that Chapters 7 to 10 may be read in any order.

In Chapter 6, we define a *specification approach* that is based on the notions of *examples* and *properties*. It requires examples that are chosen in a consistent way by a specifier who knows the intended relation. The presence of properties (whose actual language is application-specific, and thus left unspecified for a while) is meant to overcome the problems of ambiguity and limited expressive power of examples, while still preserving their virtues of naturalness and conciseness. Such specification languages are quite expressive and readable. Specifications by examples and properties are usually incomplete, and hence ambiguous, but minimal. This specification approach holds the promise of more efficient and more effective synthesis than from examples alone.

In Chapter 7, we develop a *theoretical framework for stepwise synthesis of logic algorithms from specifications by examples and properties*. Three layers of correctness criteria relating intentions, specifications, and logic algorithms are introduced. Comparison criteria relating logic algorithms in terms of semantic or syntactic generality are then proposed. All these criteria provide an adequate structure for the formulation of stepwise synthesis strategies, be they incremental (examples and properties are presented one-by-one) or non-incremental (all-at-once presentation). A particular non-incremental strategy is developed in greater detail for use in the sequel.

In Chapter 8, we discuss *algorithm schemas* as a support for algorithm design. One of the major ideas of this book is that schema-independent methods can be developed for the synthesis of instances of the place-holders of schemas. Such methods may be merely based on databases of useful instances, but more sophisticated methods would perform actual computations for inferring such instances, based on the specification and the algorithm designed so far. Several methods might be applicable at each step, thus yielding opportunities for interaction with the specifier. We thus advocate a very disciplined approach to algorithm synthesis: rather than using a uniform method for instantiating all place-holders of a given schema (possibly without any awareness of such a schema), one should deploy the best-suited method for each place-holder. In other words, we propose to view research on automatic programming as: (1) the search for adequate schemas; (2) the development of useful methods of place-holder instantiation; and (3) the discovery of interesting mappings between these methods and the place-holders of these schemas. Our grand view of algorithm synthesis systems is thus one of a workbench with a generic tool-box of specialized methods and a set of schemas that covers (as much as possible of) the space of all possible algorithms.

In Chapter 9, we develop the *Proofs-as-Programs Method*, which deductively adds atoms to a logic algorithm so that it satisfies a given set of properties. The added atoms are extracted from the proof that the given logic algorithm is complete with respect to these properties. This method is part of our tool-box for instantiating place-holders of an algorithm schema.

In Chapter 10, we develop the *Most-Specific-Generalization Method*, which inductively synthesizes a logic algorithm from a set of examples. The intended relation, though unknown as a whole, is however known to feature a given data-flow pattern between its parameters. The synthesized logic algorithm is correct with respect to a "natural extension" of the given examples. Note that this method is also part of our tool-box for instantiating place-holders of an algorithm schema, but not a solution to the overall problem of synthesis from specifications by examples.

Most of these building blocks are not necessarily new (to algorithm synthesis), but they are here combined in a novel way, if not extended and associated with some new results.

Part III: A Logic Algorithm Synthesis Mechanism

In Part III, we develop an actual *logic algorithm synthesis mechanism* from specifications by examples and properties, as seen in Chapter 6. It fits the particular non-incremental synthesis strategy presented in Chapter 7, is guided by the divide-and-conquer algorithm schema seen in Chapter 8, and uses the tool-box of methods developed in Chapters 9 and 10.

In Chapter 11, we motivate the desired *features* of the mechanism (such as the actual language for the properties), and argue for a series of preliminary *restrictions*, so as to keep the presentation simple until the discussion of its extensions. We also give an intuitive *overview* of the entire synthesis mechanism by illustrating it on a sample execution, so as to give the reader the feel for its working.

In Chapter 12, we give full detail about the *expansion phase of synthesis*, that is the first four steps of the mechanism. These steps are rather straightforward, and do not require any sophisticated methods.

In Chapter 13, we give full detail about the *reduction phase of synthesis*, that is the remaining three steps of the mechanism. These steps are the truly creative and challenging ones, and thus require the sophisticated methods of the tool-box developed in Chapters 9 and 10.

In Chapter 14, we provide a detailed *evaluation* of the obtained synthesis mechanism with respect to the identified challenges. We also discuss some *extensions* to the synthesis mechanism. Then, we outline a *methodology for choosing "good" examples and properties*, which, when followed, increases reliability and speed of synthesis, and decreases the need for interaction with the specifier. A prototype *implementation* of this synthesis mechanism is being developed. It is called SYNAPSE (*SYNthesis of logic Algorithms from PropertieS and Examples*), and is written in portable Prolog. We briefly discuss its architecture, and list a few target scenarios of interaction between the specifier and the synthesizer. Finally, we give an *evaluation* of the power of the proposed synthesis mechanism, and compare it to related work.

Acknowledgments
This book is based on my Ph.D. dissertation, and I hereby express my deepest gratitude to Prof. Yves Deville (Université Catholique de Louvain). His expertise and advice were invaluable during the development of some theoretical aspects of this research, and his relentless pursuit of excellence drove me to improvements and generalizations I would never have dreamt of.

My warmest thanks also to Prof. Alan W. Biermann (Duke University), who hosted me during various leaves-of-absence at his department. His faith in my approach kept my spirit alive during many months of darkness, and as my mentor on program synthesis research, he distilled a lot of his wisdom during our numerous discussions.

I furthermore acknowledge extraordinary assistance by Prof. Baudouin Le Charlier (Université de Namur) whose spiritual patronage on this work is unmistakable and is the fruit of many fascinating conversations.

Many thanks also to Prof. Norbert Fuchs (Universität Zürich) and Prof. Klaus Peter Jantke (TH Leipzig) for their interest in my research. Prof. Laurent Fribourg (ENS Paris) kindly assisted me during the development of some aspects that are based on his own research. Moreover, I'm indebted to Luboš Popelínský (Masaryk University) for many productive discussions.

The research for this book was done at four universities: as a research scientist at the Université de Namur (FUNDP) and at Duke University, under grants by the Services de Programmation de la Politique Scientifique of the Government of Belgium; as a Ph.D. candidate at the Université Catholique de Louvain (UCL), under a grant by the Ministry of Scientific Research of the Government of Luxembourg; and at Bilkent University.

I very much appreciated the perceptive comments made on earlier drafts of this book by Dr. Naji Habra, Dr. Jean-Marie Jacquet, Prof. Pierre-Yves Schobbens (all at FUNDP), Prof. Don W. Loveland, Prof. Gopalan Nadathur, Tim Gegg-Harrison, Richard Hipp (all at Duke), Prof. Elie Milgrom, Prof. Michel Sintzoff, Prof. Axel van Lamsweerde, Bruno Charlier (all at UCL), Prof. Francesco Bergadano (Università di Torino), and Prof. Jimmy H. M. Lee (The Chinese University of Hong Kong).

I'm also grateful to Kluwer Academic Publishers, especially to Scott Delman. Finally, extra credit goes to my parents, siblings, relatives, colleagues, and friends, for encouraging me throughout this project.

Pierre Flener
Ankara, Turkey

I STATE OF THE ART

In this first part, the state of the art of the topics underlying this book is presented, and a lot of relevant terminology is introduced along the way. The idea is to gradually introduce the objective of this research by narrowing in from more general aims. Thus, in Chapter 1, a general introduction to the field of automatic programming (program synthesis) is given. Chapter 2 contains a survey of the use of deductive inference in automatic programming, while Chapter 3 surveys the use of inductive inference in automatic programming. In Chapter 4, we summarize the methodology of systematic logic program development of [Deville 87, 90], which underlies this research. Chapters 2 to 4 may be read in any order. Finally, in Chapter 5, we formulate the objectives of this book.

1 AUTOMATIC PROGRAMMING

There will certainly be many differences between the input to future automatic programming systems and what is currently called a program. However, programming is best typified not by what programs are but by what programming tasks are like. Undoubtedly these inputs will still have to be carefully crafted, debugged, and maintained according to changing needs. Whether or not one chooses to call these inputs programs, the tasks associated with them will be strongly reminiscent of programming.

— Charles Rich and Richard C. Waters.

In this chapter, a general introduction to the field of automatic programming (program synthesis) is given. In Section 1.1, the grand aim of this field is presented, together with its major issues. Then, in Section 1.2, we discuss some topics around the languages used in program synthesis, and in Section 1.3, we classify the different synthesis mechanisms that have appeared so far. In Section 1.4, we outline our viewpoint on the requirements and promises of automatic programming. Finally, in Section 1.5, we specify a series of sample problems that are used throughout this book.

1.1 The Grand Aim of Automatic Programming

Programming is hard! Indeed, programs are highly complex mathematical objects reflecting many inter-dependent decisions. For instance, in the imperative programming paradigm, initial instructions, loops and their invariants, and final instructions have to be carefully crafted; convenient data structures have to be selected; and operational correctness with respect to the specification and suitable time or space efficiency have to be achieved. It turns out that human beings are often inept at managing these difficulties. Even after intensive training, errors such as one-too-many iteration still occur.

This contributes to the so-called *software crisis*, which has been haunting commercial *software production* for over two decades now. A common symptom is the inability to deliver correct programs on time and to budget. Growing needs for more and more complex software have made the crisis outpace the academic results, known as *software engineering*, for dealing with it.

Note that, at this level of the discourse, we are not interested in the languages used for writing specifications and programs. The main issue is that there should be criteria for assessing the correctness of a specification with respect to the non-formal intentions, and criteria for assessing the operational correctness of a program with respect to its specification. Sample criteria are partial correctness, completeness, and termination (the latter being meaningless for specifications).

Actually, a classification of problems is needed for further clarification. On the one hand, there are *data-processing problems*, where the specification is almost tantamount to an actual program. On the other hand, there are *algorithmic problems*, where the specification is at best some kind of a naive (inefficient) program. The focus in this

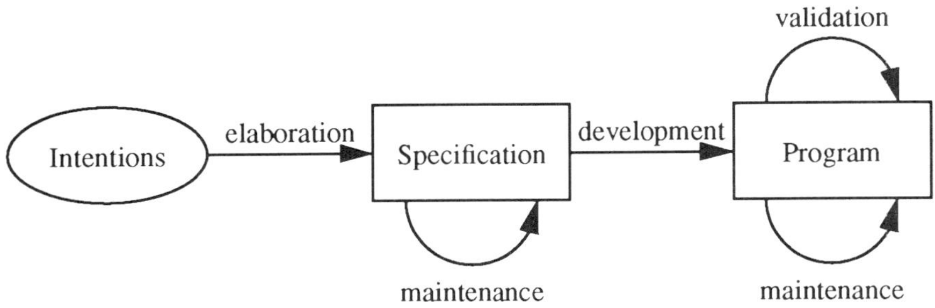

Figure 1-1: The traditional software life-cycle

book is exclusively on the more challenging algorithmic problems. Moreover, this implies that we are here only concerned with programming-in-the-small.

Let's perceive, in a first approximation, the actual *programming task* of the *software life-cycle* as being divided into two stages:

(1) *elaboration* of a specification from non-formal intentions;

(2) *development* of a program that is correct with respect to the specification.

However, this view assumes that stage (2) is "easy". In practice, the phrase "is correct" of that stage is often replaced by "seems correct", and a third stage is added:

(3) *validation* of the program so that it is correct with respect to the specification.

There are basically two approaches to validation. A first approach is *retrospective program verification*, where one checks the correctness of a given program with respect to its specification. This turns out to be extremely hard by hand, not to mention automation. The other approach is *program testing*, where the program is debugged so that it no longer fails on some test-cases. However, and despite the still wide-spread usage of this approach, this is not satisfactory because program debugging often amounts to patchwork, and because program testing amounts to verification only in the limit.

Moreover, specifications are sometimes perceived to be incorrect, and they need thus to be changed. And specifications sometimes evolve over time, as the intentions change. A fourth stage is then added:

(4) *maintenance* of the specification, and *maintenance* of the program so that it is correct with respect to the new specification.

Figure 1-1 summarizes this perception of the programming task of the software life-cycle. However, program maintenance sometimes operates directly on the old program. While justifiable for some minor changes to the specification, this approach is dangerous in general. A replay of stage (2) is definitely a better approach, even in case of inability to guarantee correctness.

So, how can the ideal formulation of stage (2) be achieved? A first solution is *constructive program verification*, where the program is developed in a way that guarantees its operational correctness with respect to the specification. This makes sense as program development actually requires the same kind of formal thinking as program verification. The programming methodologies proposed by Dijkstra, Floyd, Hoare, Naur, Wirth, ... since the late 1960s belong to this category. However, there is little concern about automating these methodologies.

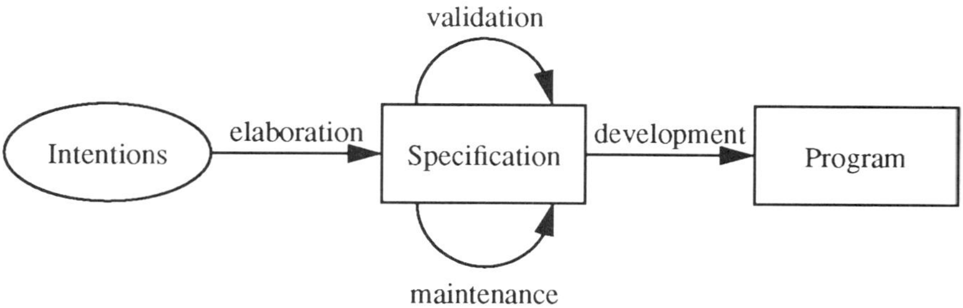

Figure 1-2: A new software life-cycle

The second solution is *automatic programming* (*program synthesis*), where some program develops correct programs from specifications, with as much (or as little) interaction as the specifier wants. This idea is as old as computer science itself, but is often dismissed as the automa-g-ic programming dream. A more general approach than program verification is indeed to prove that some program synthesis mechanism is sound, and that it thus always synthesizes correct programs. The benefits of such a solution would be the disappearance of the program validation and program maintenance stages from the programming task, and instead a focus on specification elaboration, validation (via prototyping, paraphrasing, ...), and maintenance, because replay of program development becomes less costly. Figure 1-2 shows the resulting paradigm shift and its new perception of the programming task of the software life-cycle.

Let's for a while still keep from actually surveying the achievements of program synthesis research. Instead, we first aim at restricting the scope of such research. Indeed, many people believe it is beneficial to decompose the program development stage into two sub-stages (see Figure 1-3):

(1) *design* of an abstract algorithm, with prime concern about its logical correctness with respect to the specification, but not so much concern about its time or space complexity;

(2) *implementation* of the algorithm as a concrete program written in some programming language, with concern about achieving operational correctness with respect to the specification and about maximizing time or space efficiency.

The advantages of this approach are twofold. First, the algorithm is not subjected to the computational model of the target programming language, nor to its deficiencies or even to its intended underlying machine architecture. Note that, at this level of the discourse, we are not interested in the language used for writing algorithms. The main issue is that there should be criteria for assessing the logical correctness of an algorithm with respect to its specification. Second, the algorithm implementation stage, now that it is clearly separated, may explicitly reuse the huge body of existing and on-going research in *algorithm transformation*, algorithm implementation, and *program transformation*. The disadvantage of this approach is however that algorithm complexity considerations cannot always be clearly dissociated from the algorithm design process: sometimes, at the transformation time, it is "too late" to improve an

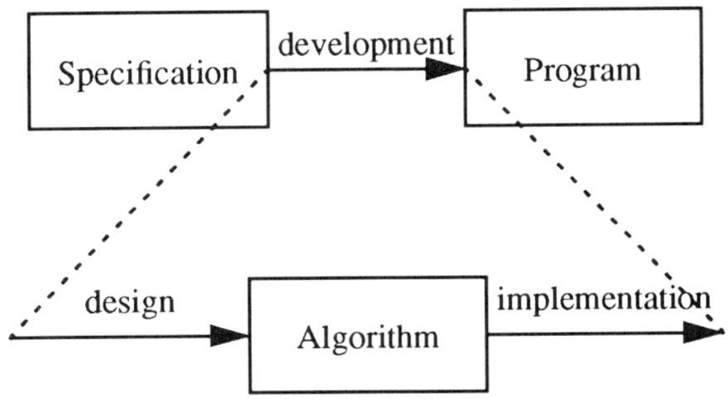

Figure 1-3: A practical view of program development

algorithm. Special attention needs thus to be paid to make the synthesis of low-complexity algorithms possible, if not likely, rather than a mere pot-shot.

There is a growing awareness since the early 1980s (see [Kant 85] or [Bauer *et al.* 89], for instance) of the necessity to separate these concerns, but such hasn't always been the case. At best, some projects focussed on the so-called "pure" aspects of programming languages such as LISP and Prolog. In this book, except for the surveys in Chapter 2 and Chapter 3, we thus focus on algorithm design rather than on program development. We also adopt the following terminology for distinguishing design approaches: *algorithm construction* stands for (completely) manual algorithm design (usually from non-formal specifications), whereas *algorithm synthesis* stands for (partly) automatic algorithm design (usually from formal specifications).

Even if the original scope of automatic programming is stripped down to sub-stage (1) only, we may still paraphrase our initial statement: Algorithm design is hard! Indeed, algorithms are highly complex mathematical objects reflecting many inter-dependent design decisions: initial instructions, loops and their invariants, and final instructions have to be carefully crafted; logical correctness with respect to the specification has to be achieved. It turns out that human beings are often inept at managing these difficulties. Even after intensive training, design errors such as one-too-many iteration still occur.

The root of the difficulty resides in the huge gap in content and formality between the *intentions* (informal description of *what* problem is to be solved) and the *program* (formal description of *how* that problem can be solved). Even though algorithm synthesis research restricts its focus to bridging the smaller gap between the *specification* (description of *what* a program does) and the *algorithm* (description of *how* the program does it), this is still a quite formidable task.

1.2 Specification, Algorithm, and Programming Languages

In this section, we first briefly discuss issues related to the choice of specification languages, algorithm languages, and programming languages in automatic programming research. We then take a cynical look at the history of automatic programming, and draw some conclusions about formal languages.

Specification Languages

Ideally, a *specification* is only a description of *what* a program does, and an explanation of *how to use* that program. A specification should faithfully capture the informal intentions. Such specifications are totally declarative in that they don't express how the program actually works, and they thus don't bias the programmer in her/his task. Specifications have been alternately required to be not (necessarily) executable [Hayes and Jones 89], (preferably) executable [Fuchs 92ab], and so on

Desirable qualities of a specification language are *expressiveness* (provision of constructs that are natural to human thinking in the application domain) and *readability*.

A crucial aspect of a specification is its *total correctness* with respect to the informal intentions. Total correctness is often divided into *partial correctness* (absence of contradictions with the intentions) and *completeness* (absence of under-specification). While partial correctness of a specification with respect to the intentions is often only assumed (even if this is often far from obvious), such is not the case with completeness, and hence with total correctness.

Other desirable qualities of a specification are *minimality* (absence of over-specification), *internal consistency* (absence of internal contradictions), *non-ambiguity* (existence of a single interpretation), and *non-redundancy* (absence of synonymy, homonymy, and so on).

A specification language should offer abstract data-types, so that specifications do not bias the algorithm design or implementation processes. However, abstract data-types and the issue of their reification are not addressed anywhere in this book.

Specifications may be written in a formal language or in a non-formal language. A *formal specification language* has a well-defined syntax and semantics. A *non-formal specification language* is not to be confused with pure natural language: just like proofs in mathematics textbooks, non-formal specifications use natural language constructs, but jointly with formal constructs that are introduced as the need arises [Le Charlier 85]. There are thus no predefined syntax and semantics.

There seems to be no doubt that automated algorithm synthesis can only start from formal specifications, but we'll get back to this issue later in this section. A host of formal specification languages has been proposed, some especially for synthesis purposes. The best-known formal specification languages are very-high-level languages such as GIST, *Refine*, SETL, Z, and so on. Other formal specification languages are first-order logic (sometimes in the guise of frames or semantic nets), algebraic formalisms, examples, execution traces, state transition diagrams, and so on.

Programming Languages and Algorithm Languages

The most popular programming languages used as target languages of synthesizers are, by far, LISP and Prolog. These languages are also the most-used languages for writing the synthesizers themselves. This is not surprising, due to the ease of reasoning about programs in these languages. However, due to the recent trend to synthesize algorithms rather than programs, the first aspect of this "domination" seems over, as the algorithm implementation stage may target virtually any programming language.

So what algorithm languages can be used? The so-called pseudo-code languages used in many algorithms textbooks are candidates, but they have received little attention so far, and probably won't ever. Indeed, the bulk of the algorithm language definition effort goes to the pure foundations of functional and logic programming, again because of the ease of reasoning about algorithms written in such languages.

A Cynical View on Formal Languages

Let's now lean back and take a look at the language aspect of the history of automatic programming. In computer science, description languages are traditionally classified as being more or less "high-level". At the "high" end of the continuum is natural language, such as we use it everyday. At the "low" end of the continuum are the most basic machine languages, as they are actually directly interpreted by computers. Low-level languages are very informative in describing *how* a problem is actually solved, whereas (very-)high-level languages only allow a description of *what* the problem is.

Every new generation of programming languages makes a quantum leap towards the high end of the language continuum. For instance, assembly languages relieved programmers from tedious on/off switching. *Fortran* provided evaluation of formulas. *Algol* supplied abstractions of control structures. Structured programming languages such as *Pascal* brought abstractions of data-structures. Functional and logic programming languages such as LISP and *Prolog* introduced declarative programming. And so on. Simultaneously, formal specification languages have also been moving towards the high end of the language continuum.

By observing the history of program synthesis research [Rich and Waters 88a], we can see that the first assemblers and compilers were seen as automatic programmers, as they relieved the programmers from many of the burdens of binary programming. Some programmers felt like they were only writing some form of specifications, and that the compilers (or interpreters) took care of the rest. But after a while, the new "specification languages" were perceived as programming languages! The same is happening over and over again with each new programming paradigm. One of the latest examples is *Prolog*: initially perceived by many as a specification language (and still being perceived as such by some people), the consensus now seems that it is a programming language. So how come that one-time specification languages are sooner or later perceived as programming languages, or that there never is a consensus about the difference between formal specifications and programs? The formal specifications of some people are indeed often very close to what other people would call programs. Moreover, formal specifications are often as difficult to elaborate and to maintain as the corresponding programs. Synthesis research is thus constantly trying to keep pace with formal specification languages (or, equivalently, to be one step ahead of the state-of-the-art in programming), but, in retrospect, it is nothing else but the quest for new programming paradigms. To paraphrase Tesler's theorem: automatic programming is whatever hasn't been compiled yet! Of course, as our notion of programs evolves, our understanding of compilation has to evolve as well: it is not because today's compilers are largely deterministic and automatic that tomorrow's compilers (today's synthesizers) are not allowed to have search spaces or to be semi-automatic.

Now, considering that programming languages and formal specification languages are moving over time to the high end on the language continuum, it is easy to see that, *in the limit*, they will both converge to natural language. In other words, programming and specifying-in-a-formal-language are the same processes *in the limit*! The very fact that there are occasionally periods of confusion about what formal specifications and programs actually are, already hints at this. So programming actually amounts, *in the limit*, to a formalization process [Flener and Popelínský 94] [Flener *et al.* 94].

Indeed, the problem with formal specifications is that there is no way to construct them so that we have a formal proof that they capture our intentions. So an informal proof is needed *somewhere* (at worst by testing a prototype, although testing never amounts to proving), as the purpose of software engineering is after all to obtain programs that implement our informal intentions. Writing formal specifications just shifts the obligation of performing an informal proof from the program *vs.* specification verification to the specification *vs.* intentions verification, but it doesn't rid us of that obligation. So specifications could just as well be informal, to prevent a delaying of an informal proof that has to be done anyway. So we are actually hoping for somebody to write a new paper stating that specifications ought to be informal!

In our opinion, the solution to all these problems with formality is thus that formal specifications and programs are intrinsically the same thing! The inevitable intertwining between the formal specification elaboration process and the programming process has already been pointed out by [Swartout and Balzer 82]. As algorithm synthesis research aims at raising the level of language in which we can interact with the computer, synthesizers and compilers perform intrinsically the same process. In other words, the "real" programming is being done during the formalization process while going from an informal specification to a formal specification/program (which is then submitted to a synthesizer/compiler). In logic programming, there is little research about this formalization process, a laudable exception being the work of [Deville 90] on hand-constructing logic algorithms from informal specifications (see Chapter 4).

Note that we are not saying that formal specifications are useless: of course it is important to be able to check whether a formal specification is internally consistent, and to generate prototypes from executable specifications, because this allows early error detection and hence significant cost-cutting. At any given time, formal specifications, even if written in a programming language, will have different purposes (validation, prototyping, contracts, ...) and attributes (readability, efficiency, ...) than programs [Fuchs 94]. We here just say that formal/executable specifications are already programs, though not in a conventional sense. But conventions change in time, and the specifications of today may well be perceived tomorrow as programs. To understand this, it helps to define programming from a process-theoretic viewpoint (that is, as an activity of carefully crafting, debugging, and maintaining a formal text) rather than from a product-theoretic viewpoint (programming yields a formal text).

Most of the early program synthesis projects actually did aim at starting from natural language specifications. A survey on very early projects was made by [Heidorn 76]. The SAFE project [Balzer 85] at the Information Sciences Institute of the University of Southern California initially went to great efforts to start from natural language specifications [Balzer *et al.* 77], but then eventually switched to defining GIST, a very-high-level specification language. The PSI project at Stanford University [Green *et al.* 79] included a strand of research on synthesis from natural language specifications. At MIT, the *Protosystem I* project [Ruth 78] aimed at generating programs for data-processing problems. At Duke University, there was the *Natural Language Computer* project [Biermann 83].

The aim of these projects is called *natural language programming*, and it still constitutes the ultimate goal of program synthesis research. Because of the limited success of these early projects, this strand of research seems more or less dormant nowadays.

1.3 A Classification of Synthesis Mechanisms

A huge variety of synthesis mechanisms have been developed, reflecting at least the variety of specification languages. These mechanisms could be classified according to whether they start from formal or non-formal specifications, or according to whether they start from complete or incomplete specifications, or according to whether they are completely automatic or only semi-automatic, or according to whether they perform *algorithmic synthesis* (no usage at all of heuristics) or *heuristic synthesis* (at least partial usage of heuristics). But such classifications tend to be very lopsided, and thus uninformative. Instead, we classify the mechanisms according to the predominant kind of reasoning:

- inductive synthesis:
  - trace-based synthesis;
  - model-based synthesis;
- deductive synthesis:
  - transformational synthesis;
  - proofs-as-programs synthesis;
  - schema-guided synthesis;
- abductive synthesis;
- analogical synthesis;
- knowledge-based synthesis:
  - empirical synthesis;
  - synthesis by inspection;
  - synthesis from natural language.

Actually, knowledge-based reasoning is not really a separate kind of reasoning to the same degree as inductive, deductive, abductive, or analogical reasoning. And synthesis mechanisms of the first four categories never perform their kind of inference in an entirely pure way from just the specifications, to the exclusion of all possible sources of other knowledge. But it certainly helps to view knowledge-based synthesis, with a predominant usage of knowledge, as a separate category, even if other kinds of reasoning are used as well. Of course, this classification is not strict: many mechanisms would actually fit into more than one category.

A graph confronting the specification languages with the synthesis mechanisms would be very sparse, because some mechanisms are unique to specification languages. The achievements of inductive and deductive synthesis are surveyed in Chapter 2 and Chapter 3, respectively.

The history of research in automatic programming has pretty much followed the pattern set by problem solving research in artificial intelligence. Indeed, the original quest for a completely general, fully automatic, end-user-oriented automatic programming system has gradually been replaced by more realistic objectives. Following [Rich and Waters 88a], there have been three major trends, each sacrificing one of these objectives in order to attain the other two:

- the *expert-specifier trend* sacrifices end-user orientation in view of attaining domain generality and full automation; in vogue until the late 1960s due to the good results in compiler design for high-level languages, this trend has reappeared in the early 1980s when the technology for handling very-high-level languages became available;
- the *narrow-domain trend* sacrifices domain generality in view of attaining end-user orientation and full automation; this trend was mainly a fallback during the 1970s while progress in the expert-specifier trend was stalled; however, this trend is slowly emerging again, as the idea of collections of narrow-domain synthesizers arises;
- the *software-assistant trend* sacrifices full automation in view of attaining domain generality and end-user orientation; this trend has been very popular since the 1980s, although the focus is sometimes more on having a calculus of algorithm design, than on actually using it for synthesis.

Of course, these trends are not as clear-cut as their descriptions might suggest. Indeed, many systems sacrifice a little bit of every objective.

1.4 Requirements and Promises of Automatic Programming

In this last introductory section to automatic programming, we list a few requirements for research in program synthesis, and outline the promises of this research. Finally, pointers to introductory literature are given.

First, there is a great need for incorporating knowledge into automatic programming systems, in order to overcome the old "sins" of general problem solving. There are essentially three kinds of useful synthesis knowledge:

- *algorithm design knowledge* is needed [Soloway and Ehrlich 84] for re-using human expertise in algorithm design, and thus for making synthesis a "disciplined" search process; such knowledge can be codified in various ways: as transformation rules (see the PECOS sub-system [Barstow 79, 84a] of PSI), as algorithm schemas (see the systems of [Smith 85, 90a]), as clichés (see the *Programmer's Apprentice* project at MIT [Rich and Waters 88b]), ...;
- *domain knowledge* (*application knowledge*) is equally crucial, for the same reasons (see the PHINIX system of [Barstow 84b, 85]);
- *meta-knowledge* is knowledge about how and when to use the previous two knowledge kinds (see the *Designer* project at CMU [Kant 85] [Steier and Kant 85]).

Furthermore, there is a need for *efficiency knowledge* (useful for algorithm transformation and implementation), but this carries us beyond our focus on actual synthesis. As usual, there is the knowledge acquisition bottleneck, but current machine learning techniques (see Chapter 3) seem a promising step towards overcoming this.

Next, there is a need for *evolutionary specifications*, where one deliberately omits some functionalities in a first specification, and then relies on replay facilities [Wile 83] when adding the missing functionalities in subsequent versions of the specification. This form of *exploratory programming* promises an answer to the endemic difficulty of providing partially correct and complete formal specifications.

A synthesis system should be able to design a whole family of algorithms from a single specification. The different design decisions taken at the choice-points during synthesis then provide an interesting *algorithm classification*. A popular idea is to benchmark the ability of a synthesis system on the sorting problem, whose specification is deceptively simple, and yet gives rise to a tremendous variety of different algorithms. Classification through synthesis of sorting algorithms has indeed been done by [Green and Barstow 78], [Clark and Darlington 80], [Broy 83], [Follet 84], [Smith 85], [Lau 89], and [Lau and Prestwich 91]. Moreover, the ability to find new algorithms might be considered another benchmark of the ability of a synthesizer.

Following [Kant 90], the "economics" of automatic program synthesis are as follows. The potential *benefits* are an increased productivity of software engineers (focus on creative aspects, automation of tedious routine, replay facilities, ...) and an increased quality of the developed software (correctness, efficiency, reusability, ...). The *costs* are the necessary acquisition of algorithm design knowledge and domain knowledge, the development of the synthesis system and its maintenance across various platforms, and the training of expert users. From this cost-benefit analysis, it appears that the use of a program synthesis system is worthwhile if either many similar programs need to be written, or a given program is changed sufficiently often, and if the application domain lends itself to natural and concise specifications, features well-understood problem solving techniques, and is complex enough for promising a payoff. The *break-even point* is thus attained when the usage of a program synthesis system is more economical than manual program development by an expert.

Regarding the promises, there is general optimism that program synthesis systems will eventually scale up to realistic tasks, especially now that some systems are already in commercial or pre-commercial use. Due to its very focus on programming-in-the-small, it is obvious that automatic programming will not supplant the need for programming-in-the-large, nor will it assist in project management issues. Also, the essentially evolutive nature of software cannot be prevented by program synthesis systems, though they will certainly help in coping with changing specifications. Programming jobs will not disappear, but our understanding of what the programming task is will definitely change. There will always be a need for validation and maintenance, but the promise is to do this on texts that are at today's specification level.

Pointers to the Literature

A thought experiment by [Green *et al.* 83] has led to the definition of the ideal architecture and functionalities of the software engineering environment of the future, namely the so-called KBSA (*Knowledge-Based Software Assistant*).

General introductions to program synthesis have been published by [Rich and Waters 86b, 88a] and [Kant 90].

A growing number of surveys of existing synthesis mechanisms and systems is being published: let's just mention those of [Barr and Feigenbaum 82], [Biermann *et al.* 84b], [Partsch and Steinbrüggen 83], [Smith 84], [Goldberg 86], [Feather 87], [Lowry and Duran 89], [Steier and Anderson 89], [Biermann 92], [Bundy 92], [Sammut 93], and [Deville and Lau 94].

Compilations of landmark papers on program synthesis have been edited by [Biermann and Guiho 83], [Biermann *et al.* 84a], [IEEE-TSE 85], [Rich and

Waters 86a], and [JSC 93]. The journal *Automated Software Engineering* (Kluwer Academic Publishers) is entirely dedicated to program synthesis and its related areas.

Artificial intelligence conferences typically have sessions or workshops on program synthesis. Especially in the logic programming area, there are specialized publications, such as [Jacquet 93] and the proceedings of the LOPSTR (*LOgic Program Synthesis and TRansformation*) workshops [Clement and Lau 92] [Lau and Clement 93] [Deville 94] [Fribourg and Turini 94].

1.5 Sample Problems

Here follow the specifications of a series of sample problems that are used throughout this book. For the sake of conciseness, we adopt the following format:

<procedure declaration> iff *<relation definition>*,
where *<domain description>*.

Note that this specification format is restricted to the purposes of algorithm design, as no non-functional requirements are given.

For some specifications, we need the following new notions. Informally speaking, a *plateau* is a non-empty list of identical elements. A *compact list* is a list of couples, where the first term of a couple, called the *value* of the couple, is different in two consecutive couples, and the second term of a couple, called the *counter* of the couple, is a positive integer. For convenience, we often drop the couple delimiters "<" and ">".

add(X,Y,S) iff *S* is the sum of *X* and *Y*,
where *X*, *Y*, *S* are integers.

append(A,B,C) iff *C* is the concatenation of *B* to the end of *A*,
where *A*, *B*, *C* are lists.

compress(L,C) iff *C* is a list of $<v_i,c_i>$ couples,
such that the ith plateau of *L* has c_i elements equal to v_i,
where *L* is a list and *C* is a compact list.

delOddElems(L,R) iff *R* is *L* without its odd elements,
where *L*, *R* are integer lists.

efface(E,L,R) iff *R* is *L* without its first (existing) occurrence of *E*,
where *E* is a term, *L* is a non-empty list, and *R* is a list.

firstN(N,L,R) iff *R* is the first *N* elements of *L*,
where *N* is an integer, *L* is a list of at least *N* elements,
and *R* is a list of *N* elements.

firstPlateau(L,P,S) iff *P* is the first maximal plateau of *L*,
and *S* is the corresponding suffix of *L*,
where *L* is a non-empty list, *P* is a plateau, and *S* is a list.

flatTree(T,L) iff *L* is the infix traversal of *T*,
where *L* is a list and *B* is a binary tree.

insert(E,L,R) iff *R* is *L* with *E* inserted at the "right" place,
where *E* is an integer, *L* is an non-descending integer list,
and *R* is a non-empty non-descending integer list.

length(L,N) iff N is the length of L,
where N is an integer and L is a list.

list(L) iff L is a list,
where L is a term.

member(E,L) iff E is an element of L,
where E is a term and L is a list.

merge(A,B,C) iff C is the merger of A and B,
where A, B, C are non-descending integer lists.

minimum(L,M) iff M is the minimum of L,
where M is an integer and L is a non-empty integer list.

mult(X,Y,P) iff P is the product of X and Y,
where X, Y, P are integers.

odd(N) iff N is odd,
where N is an integer.

ordered(S) iff S is non-descendingly ordered,
where S is a list of integers.

parity(L,R) iff R is *even* when L is of even length, and *odd* otherwise,
where L is a list and R is a term.

partition(L,P,S,B) iff S (respectively B) contains the elements of L that are smaller than (respectively bigger than or equal to) the pivot P,
where L, S, B are integer lists and P is an integer.

permutation(L,P) iff P is a permutation of L,
where L, P are lists.

plateau(N,E,P) iff P is a plateau of N elements equal to E,
where N is a positive integer, E is a term,
and P is a non-empty list.

reverse(L,R) iff R is the reverse of L,
where L, R are lists.

sort(L,S) iff S is an non-descendingly ordered permutation of L,
where L, S are integer lists.

split(L,F,S) iff F is the first half of L, and S is the second half of L,
where L, F, S are lists.

stuff(E,L,R) iff R is L with E inserted at a random place,
where E is a term, L is a list, and R is a non-empty list.

sum(L,S) iff S is the sum of the elements of L,
where S is an integer and L is an integer list.

2 DEDUCTIVE INFERENCE IN AUTOMATIC PROGRAMMING

Deductive inference is omnipresent in automatic programming. We first define, in Section 2.1, the underlying specification formalism, namely axiomatizations. In Section 2.2, we classify the various approaches to using deductive inference in automatic programming. Then, in Section 2.3 and Section 2.4, we survey synthesis of functional programs from axioms, and synthesis of logic programs from axioms, respectively. Finally, in Section 2.5, we draw some conclusions on the use of deductive inference in automatic programming.

2.1 Specifications by Axioms

We first define a possible language for specifications by axioms, and this in the logic programming framework. Later in this section, we list alternative approaches.

Definition 2-1: An *axiomatic specification* (or *specification by axioms*) of a procedure for predicate *r*/*n* consists of the union of a set of first-order axioms about *r*/*n* and the axiomatic specifications of all the non-primitive predicates used in these axioms.

We consider at least =/2, ≠/2, and ≤/2 to be primitives. Others are added whenever the need for simplification arises. Let's illustrate this on a few sample specifications.

Example 2-1: A possible axiomatic specification of the *member*/2 problem is:

```
∀E ∀L member(E,L) ⇔ append(_,[E|_],L)
```

with *append*/3 considered to be a primitive. ♦

Example 2-2: A possible axiomatic specification of the *firstPlateau*/3 problem is:

```
∀L ∀P ∀S firstPlateau(L,P,S) ⇔
   plateau(P) ∧ ¬sameFirst(P,S) ∧ append(P,S,L)
∀P plateau(P) ⇔ ∃U ∀E member(E,P) ⇒ E=U
∀P ∀L sameFirst(P,L) ⇔ ∃E ∃F P=[E|_] ∧ L=[F|_] ∧ E=F
```

with *append*/3 and *member*/2 as in the previous example. ♦

Example 2-3: A possible axiomatic specification of the *compress*/2 problem is:

```
∀L ∀C compress(L,C) ⇔ ∃E ∃P ∃S ∃T ∃N
      L=[]     ∧ C=[]
   ∨  L=[E|_]  ∧ firstPlateau(L,P,S)
               ∧ compress(S,T)
               ∧ length(P,N)
               ∧ C=[<E,N>|T]
∀L ∀N length(L,N) ⇔ ∃T ∃M
      L=[]     ∧ N=0
   ∨  L=[_|T]  ∧ length(T,M)
               ∧ N=s(M)
```

with *firstPlateau*/3 as in the previous example. ♦

Example 2-4: A possible axiomatic specification of the *sum*/2 problem is:

```
∀L ∀S sum(L,S) ⇔ ∃H ∃T ∃N
        L=[]    ∧ S=0
     ∨  L=[H|T] ∧ sum(T,N)
                ∧ add(H,N,S)
```

with *add*/3 considered to be a primitive. ♦

Example 2-5: A possible axiomatic specification of the *sort*/2 problem is:

```
∀L ∀S sort(L,S) ⇔ permutation(L,S) ∧ ordered(S)

∀L ∀P permutation(L,P) ⇔ ∀U member(U,L) ∨ member(U,P)
                ⇒ ∃N count(L,U,N) ∧ count(P,U,N)

∀L ordered(L) ⇔ ∀U ∀V ∀A ∀B
    append(A,B,L) ∧ member(U,A) ∧ member(V,B) ⇒ U≤V

∀L ∀E ∀N count(L,E,N) ⇔ ∃H ∃T ∃M
        L=[]    ∧ N=0
     ∨  L=[E|T] ∧ count(T,E,M)
                ∧ N=s(M)
     ∨  L=[H|T] ∧ H≠E
                ∧ count(T,E,N)
```

with *append*/3 and *member*/2 as in the previous examples. ♦

It should be noted that these sample specifications do not reflect the only possible way of expressing axioms. Specification approaches vary according to the following criteria:

- *language*: axioms may be given as statements in (some subset of) first-order logic (with or without equality), or in an algebraic formalism, and so on;
- *directionality*: axioms may be in *relational form* (where there is no bias about whether parameters are input parameters or output parameters), or in *functional form*; for instance, in the case of logic as specification language, relational form axioms take form (1), whereas functional form axioms take form (2) hereafter:

$$\forall Parameters\ Pre(Parameters) \Rightarrow (\ p(Parameters) \Leftrightarrow Post(Parameters)\ ) \quad (1)$$

$$\forall Inputs\ \exists Outputs\quad Pre(Inputs) \Rightarrow Post(Inputs, Outputs) \quad (2)$$

  where *Pre* is an optional *pre-condition* (constraints on the parameters), *Post* is a *post-condition* (relation between the parameters), and *p* is the specified predicate;
- *recursion*: axioms are sometimes constrained to be non-recursive, but most often, recursion is allowed in axioms;
- *connectives*: logic axioms are sometimes constrained to be implication statements, or equivalence statements; sometimes, both are allowed.

The *specifying agent* is usually assumed to be a human being, who is in turn assumed to know—even if only informally—the intentions. Moreover, it is usually assumed that the given axioms are consistent with these intentions.

Anyway, whatever the actual setting, the major potential advantage of axiomatic specifications is the following:

+ *completeness* and *non-ambiguity*: a correct axiomatic specification completely and unambiguously defines the intended relation, which is thus equal to the specified relation;

The disadvantages of axiomatic specifications are:

- *artificiality*: human beings rarely resort to axioms in order to explain some concept; moreover, reading such axioms is very difficult, even to experts; finally, elaborating such axioms is also tough, and potentially as error-prone as directly writing a corresponding program; especially the satisfaction of the completeness requirement is very hard to ensure;
- *length*: axioms are a quite lengthy way of intensionally specifying some concept, even if a large set of powerful primitives is available, because the axiomatic specifications of these primitives are technically part of the specification of the top-level predicate.

Approaches for tackling these drawbacks include evolutionary specifications, where one deliberately omits some functionalities in a first specification, and then relies on replay facilities when adding these functionalities in subsequent specifications.

Since the inception of logic programming, the line between specifications and programs has somewhat disappeared, if one considers that specifications ought to be formal, that is. See [Le Charlier 85] for an argumentation why specifications should be non-formal. We also adhere to that point of view [Flener and Popelínsky 94] [Flener *et al.* 94]. The placement of this line is historically controversial anyway.

For instance, the sample specifications above of *compress*/2, *length*/2, *sum*/2, and *count*/3 are actually already some kind of first-order logic programs, and are easily transformable into, say, Prolog programs. Indeed, these specifications are recursive and exhibit induction over some parameter; avoiding this leads to clumsy specifications. These specifications thus seem to bias the actual programming process because they already show a way of *how* to solve the problem, rather than only stating *what* the problem is.

Sometimes, the line between "what" and "how" is non-existent: for instance, the specification of *sameFirst*/2 is non-recursive, but it nevertheless also incorporates a way of *how* to solve the problem.

The other sample specifications above *seem* more descriptive, because they are non-recursive, and thus only *seem* to state *what* the problem is. We write "seem" twice in the previous sentence, because one tends to look at such specifications through glasses tainted by the current state-of-the-art of (logic) programming. Indeed, it is not because we don't (yet) consider implications and universal quantifiers in the right-hand sides of equivalence statements to have some computational contents that they do not do so. In a sense, even such specifications are actually logic programs, though they (usually) embody very inefficient ways of *how* to solve the problems.

The objective of deductive synthesis research is to find mechanisms of translating such possibly inefficient "programs-of-tomorrow" into efficient "programs-of-today", and this unbiased by any possibly existing recursion in the specification. This amounts to changing our current understanding of what formal specifications and programs are, and to viewing synthesis as a translation (compilation, transformation) process.

2.2 Deductive Inference

Deductive inference is the process of obtaining new sentences (called *theorems*) from a set (called *theory*) of given sentences (called *axioms*), by application of rules of deductive inference. Theorems are also called logical consequences of the theory. We assume that the reader is familiar with deductive inference, and thus just repeat the basic definition.

Definition 2-2: Given a theory $\mathcal{A}$, a sentence G is a *logical consequence* of $\mathcal{A}$ iff every model of $\mathcal{A}$ is a model of G. This is denoted $\mathcal{A} \models G$.

Note that deductive inference is always sound. Typical rules of deductive inference are *modus ponens*, *universal instantiation*, *resolution*, *mathematical induction*, and so on. The branch of artificial intelligence research that is bent on automating deductive inference is called *automated theorem proving*.

Since deductive inference is generally a familiar notion, we do not survey it here. We rather directly propose a taxonomy of the different ways of applying deductive inference to program synthesis from axiomatic specifications. Thus, Sections 2.2.1 to 2.2.3 respectively contain general introductions to transformational synthesis, proofs-as-programs synthesis, and schema-guided synthesis.

2.2.1 Transformational Synthesis

In transformational synthesis, a sequence of meaning-preserving transformation rules is applied directly to a specification, until a program is obtained. This kind of stepwise forward reasoning is akin to constructing a derivation tree, and is feasible with axiomatic specifications that link their parameters in a relational way:

$$\forall Parameters \quad Pre(Parameters) \Rightarrow (\ p(Parameters) \Leftrightarrow Post(Parameters)\ )$$

where Pre is an optional pre-condition (constraints on the parameters), $Post$ is a post-condition (relation between the parameters), and p is the specified predicate.

Applicability conditions are often attached to the transformation rules. Transformational synthesis is obviously an outgrowth of program transformation (optimization) research. And, as hinted before, there is only a fine line—if any—between program synthesis and program transformation.

There are *atomic transformation rules*, such as *unfolding* (which mimics the execution mechanism of the target language), *folding* (which performs the reverse transformation of unfolding), *universal instantiation*, *abstraction*, *predicate definition*, and various (possibly conditional) rewrite rules for the target language and the lemmas of the application domain.

The objective of applying transformations is to filter out a new version of the specification where recursion (or a loop) may be introduced by a folding step. This usually involves a sequence of unfolding steps, then some rewriting, and finally a folding step.

These atomic transformation rules constitute a correct and complete set for exploring the search space. However, they lead to very tedious and lengthy syntheses, which are myopic in the sense that there is no real plan about where to go, except for the above-mentioned objective of introducing recursion. The "eureka" about when and how to define a new predicate is difficult to find automatically. It is also hard to decide when to stop unfolding. There is a need for loop-detection techniques to avoid infinite synthesis through symmetric transformations.

The idea for overcoming these drawbacks is of course to define *macroscopic transformation rules* that are higher-level in the sense that they are closer to actual programming decisions, such as introducing an accumulator parameter. Such macroscopic rules could be inferred by learning from sample syntheses based on the atomic rules. The major problem is of course to provide such a set of macroscopic rules that is still correct and complete. In view of facilitating the understanding of a synthesis, and allowing its replay in case a specification changes, the usage of transformation rules should be recorded.

Note that transformational synthesis (and program transformation) is closely related to EBL (*Explanation-Based Learning*), an analytic branch of machine learning (see Chapter 3). Indeed, the sequence of transformations from a specification (seen as a non-operational description) to a program (seen as an operational description) amounts to an explanation of the specification. Cross-fertilization between these two areas has led to EBPT (*Explanation-Based Program Transformation*) [Bruynooghe and De Schreye 89], where sample concrete transformations are used to guide the overall abstract transformation process.

2.2.2 Proofs-as-Programs Synthesis

The proofs-as-programs approach to program synthesis—also classified as *constructive synthesis*—is based on the Curry-Howard isomorphism [Howard 80], which states that there is a one-to-one relationship between a (constructive) proof of an existence theorem and a program that actually computes witnesses of the existentially quantified variables of the theorem. Given a specification in the functional form:

$$\forall Inputs\ \exists Outputs \quad Pre(Inputs) \Rightarrow Post(Inputs, Outputs)$$

the idea is to proceed in two steps:

(1) (constructively) prove the satisfiability of a statement expressing that a realization of this specification exists;

(2) obtain the method, embodied in the proof, of realizing the specification.

For the second step, one distinguishes between two approaches:

- the *interpretative approach* directly interprets the proof as a program, by means of an operational semantics defined on proofs;
- the *extractive approach* mechanically extracts ("compiles") a program, in a given target language, from the proof.

The two approaches have complementary advantages and drawbacks: interpretation is not as efficient as the execution of a compiled version, but the choice of a target language might obscure computational properties of proofs.

In any case, the crux is of course the state-of-the-art in theorem proving: the key issues are soundness of the synthesis (entailing correctness, completeness, and possibly termination of the resulting programs), deductive power (provability for an entire class of statements, extractability of whole families of programs for the same specification), and efficiency (need for proof planning in order to control the huge search space). Traditional theorem provers, such as the one of [Boyer and Moore 79], are inadequate due to their inability to reason constructively about existential quantifications. A common grudge is that the used specification form naturally leads only to the synthesis of total functions, but not of full-fledged relations (partial, multi-valued, possibly non-terminating predicates, that is). Solutions to this problem have been worked out (see Section 2.4.2).

The idea of exploiting (constructive) proofs as programs is actually way older than its naming as the Curry-Howard isomorphism in 1980: the idea is inherent to intuitionistic logic (see the work of Kleene in the 1940s), and the oldest synthesis systems that we could definitely identify as being part of this paradigm are those developed in the late 1960s by [Green 69] and [Waldinger and Lee 69]. The terminology itself seems to have been coined by Robert Constable in the early 1970s, according to [Bates and Constable 85].

There is an obvious interest in proofs-by-induction, because these allow the synthesis of recursive programs. Note that there often is a similar "proof" content in transformational synthesis and proofs-as-programs synthesis, and it seems that the same proof construction techniques should be applicable to both. This may suggest that these approaches are probably two facets of the same process. For instance, the work of [Neugebauer 93] shows how the specification forms of these approaches may be reconciled.

Just as there is a need for higher-level transformation rules in transformational synthesis, there here is a need for proof planning in order to incorporate expert knowledge. This meta-synthesis issue is usually tackled by the use of tactics. Following [Bundy 88], a *proof tactic* is a meta-program within a theorem prover that guides the application of the inference rules. For instance, a tactic could set up a proof-by-induction. Tactics should operate at the level of proof ideas such as those that are typically used by human provers. For synthesis, there should be tactics that embody actual programming knowledge (design strategies, efficiency considerations, and so on), and not just tactics that embody proof knowledge. Since tactics are programs, they can probably also be synthesized, and the correctness of tactics must be proven. In view of facilitating the understanding of a proof, and allowing its replay in case a specification changes, the usage of tactics should be recorded. Tactics may be bundled together to form *proof strategies*. A *proof method* is then a meta-level specification of a tactic, and a *proof plan* is a meta-level specification of a strategy.

Compared to transformational synthesis, there is no problem here about when to stop: synthesis halts when the proof is completed. Transformational synthesis seems more appropriate for synthesis from specifications that are almost programs (in which case synthesis is more like an optimizing transformation), whereas proofs-as-programs synthesis seems more appropriate for synthesis from highly descriptive specifications. Note that program transformation may actually be performed by the transformation of synthesis proofs.

However, there seems [Sintzoff 93] to be some pessimism of late regarding the wellfoundedness of pursuing this strand of research: it appears indeed that obtaining constructive proofs is an order of magnitude harder than writing programs. It would thus be preferable to write programs directly, rather than going through the tedium of proving their specifications first and then extracting programs therefrom. Moreover, if the conjectured isomorphism between the proofs-as-programs approach and the transformational approach holds, then the latter seems "doomed" as well.

2.2.3 Schema-Guided Synthesis

Programs can be classified according to their design strategies, such as divide-and-conquer, generate-and-test, top-down decomposition, and so on. Informally, a *program schema* is a template program with a fixed control flow, but without specific indications about the parameters or the actual computations. A program schema thus represents a whole family of particular programs that can be obtained by instantiating the place-holders to particular parameters or code. It is therefore interesting to guide program design by a schema that captures the essence of some strategy: a program is obtained by successively instantiating the place-holders of that schema, using the specification, the program synthesized so far, and the integrity constraints of the schema. This usually involves a lot of deductive inference sub-tasks, hence the justification for viewing this as deductive synthesis. Schemas are discussed in more detail in Chapter 8.

Schema-guided synthesis is likely to involve deductive inference, hence its classification in this category. Moreover, it is actually an answer to the complexity and size problems of both proofs-as-programs synthesis and transformational synthesis. Indeed, the application of a schema may be seen as the application of a macroscopic transformation rule that embodies very-high-level design decisions. And the application of a schema may also be seen as a proof tactic that embodies very-high-level programming knowledge, rather than just proof knowledge. However, we consider that schema-guided synthesis deserves its own sub-category, especially because, as hinted above, the previous two sub-categories might be similar anyway.

2.3 Functional Program Synthesis from Axioms

The synthesis of functional programs (LISP programs, say) has received wide-spread attention since the late 1960s, due to the ease of reasoning about functional programs. The surveys of [Barr and Feigenbaum 82], [Biermann *et al.* 84b], [Partsch and Steinbrüggen 83], [Goldberg 86], [Feather 87], [Lowry and Duran 89], [Steier and Anderson 89], and [Biermann 92] include discussions of the landmark systems. Similarly for the compilations edited by [Biermann and Guiho 83], [Biermann *et al.* 84a], [IEEE-TSE 85], [Rich and Waters 86a], and [JSC 93].

This survey is organized as follows: Sections 2.3.1 to 2.3.3 respectively survey the achievements of transformational synthesis, proofs-as-programs synthesis, and schema-guided synthesis of functional programs from axiomatic specifications.

2.3.1 Transformational Synthesis of LISP Programs

The pioneering work in LISP program transformation is the research of [Burstall and Darlington 77], who present a strategy and a semi-automated system for transforming (optimizing) recursive equations into tail-recursive ones, using folding, unfolding, universal instantiation, abstraction, and eureka-guided predicate definition. The developed system was also used for LISP program synthesis [Darlington 81].

The same results, though directly aimed at program synthesis, were obtained simultaneously, but independently, by [Manna and Waldinger 79]. However, their DEDALUS system (the *DEDuctive ALgorithm Ur-Synthesizer*, which is the successor of SYNSYS [Manna and Waldinger 77]) is automated. Moreover, particular care is taken to check input and termination conditions before introducing recursion by folding. Heuristics are used, but at the expense of possibly missing a better algorithm.

The field of *transformational implementation* is about synthesis of programs from specifications in very-high-level languages. This requires very large sets of transformation rules that redefine the very-high-level constructs of the specification language in terms of the programming language.

The 15-year SAFE project [Balzer 85] at the Information Sciences Institute of the University of Southern California aimed at transformational synthesis from specifications written in the GIST language. Some of the used transformation rules are explained by [London and Feather 82]. Ways of mechanizing the application of transformation rules are embodied by the GLITTER sub-system of [Fickas 85].

The PSI project at Stanford University [Green *et al.* 79] was built around a transformational engine, called PECOS [Barstow 79, 84a]. The incorporated programming knowledge is further discussed by [Green and Barstow 78]. Tight heuristic-based interaction [Kant and Barstow 81] of PECOS with the efficiency expert LIBRA [Kant 83] ensures efficient synthesis of efficient programs. A successor system, called CHI [Smith *et al.* 85], was partly developed at Kestrel Institute. The system was shown to be able to synthesize its own rule-compiler [Green and Westfold 82].

The role of domain knowledge codified as transformation rules has been advocated in the context of the PHINIX system [Barstow 84b, 85] at Schlumberger-Doll Research.

2.3.2 Proofs-as-Programs Synthesis of LISP Programs

As mentioned above, the probably first proofs-as-programs synthesis systems are QA3 (*Question-Answering system*) of [Green 69], and the *PROgram Writer* (PROW) of [Waldinger and Lee 69]. In the latter, a post-proof processor extracts LISP programs from constructive existence proofs.

The theoretical foundations have then been laid out by numerous people, such as [Martin-Löf 79], [Howard 80], [Beeson 85], [Constable *et al.* 86], [Hayashi 86], and so on. An actual program synthesis systems is the one of [Mohring 86], which is based on Coquand and Huet's calculus of construction. More recent achievements can be found in [Nordström *et al.* 90] and in [Huet and Plotkin 91].

The DEDALUS mechanism (see the previous section) has been rephrased in the proofs-as-programs paradigm [Manna and Waldinger 80, 91]. The so-called *deductive tableau method* is used for the proofs. There is no loss of synthesis power, but the mechanism is expressed in a considerably more elegant manner. An interesting insight is that constructive logics are not necessarily required for proofs-as-programs synthesis: indeed, many derivation steps during synthesis actually are only verification steps, and thus need thus not be constructive at all. Classical logic seems thus sufficient, provided it is "sufficiently" constructive when needed. The main focus seems to be on having a calculus of program synthesis, showing the derivability of many (hopefully all, that is) algorithms, including very intricate ones such as unification [Manna and Waldinger 81], and interesting new ones that haven't been hand-constructed yet [Manna and Waldinger 87]. But there is no mention yet of proof planning.

2.3.3 Schema-Guided Synthesis of LISP Programs

The use of deduction in the schema-guided synthesis paradigm is pretty much the brainchild of Douglas R. Smith. A technique for the derivation of pre-conditions (which is a generalization of theorem proving and of formula simplification) constitutes the deductive corner-stone of this approach [Smith 82]. Indeed, schema-guided synthesis often requires deriving pre-conditions of a formula constructed by instantiation of a schema with information extracted from the specification and the partially designed algorithm. Such pre-conditions are used to either strengthen or instantiate some part of the algorithm.

The *Cypress* system [Smith 85] is based on a divide-and-conquer schema. Specifications of sub-problems are derived from the adaptation of a schema to the top-level specification, and recursively so on, until primitive problems are reached. This top-down problem reduction is then followed by a bottom-up composition of the synthesized sub-algorithms into the top-level algorithm, according to the schema. The system is interactive, yields totally correct algorithms, and is even able to cope with partial specifications.

The successor system, called KIDS (*Kestrel Interactive Development System*) [Smith 88, 90ab, 93, 94], handles schemas for design strategies such as divide-and-conquer, local search, and global search (an enumerative search strategy that generalizes many known search strategies, such as binary search, backtracking, branch-and-bound, constraint satisfaction, and so on). Much effort has been put into transformation techniques for optimizing the synthesized algorithms: this subsequent transformation process gives this system the flavor of transformational synthesis. KIDS is believed to be very close to the break-even point where its usage is more economical than manual algorithm construction by an expert.

2.4 Logic Program Synthesis from Axioms

The synthesis of logic programs (Prolog programs, say) is an area of intense research since the late 1970s. Since the synthesized program is a logic program, the axioms are presented in the relational form. An introduction to reasoning about logic programs is [Bundy 92]. A detailed survey was prepared by [Deville and Lau 94], and compilations of papers are available [Jacquet 93]. Specialized workshops are held annually within the LOPSTR (*LOgic Program Synthesis and TRansformation*) series [Clement and Lau 92] [Lau and Clement 93] [Deville 94] [Fribourg and Turini 94]. Other meeting grounds are the biannual META (*Meta-programming in logic programming*) workshops, and (workshops at) the various logic programming conferences. Correctness issues of logic programming are addressed by [Clark and Tärnlund 77], [Clark 79], [Hogger 81, 84], and [Deville 90], among others. This present survey is organized as follows: Sections 2.4.1 to 2.4.3 respectively survey the achievements of transformational synthesis, proofs-as-programs synthesis, and schema-guided synthesis of logic programs from axiomatic specifications.

2.4.1 Transformational Synthesis of Prolog Programs

In order to give a rough feel for transformational synthesis of logic programs, we first present the pioneering mechanism in some detail. Then, we cite the achievements of some of the more recent mechanisms.

Synthesis by Symbolic Execution

Some of the early efforts were conducted at Imperial College of Science and Technology in London (UK). The developed synthesis mechanisms, called *symbolic execution*, were inspired by the foundational work on LISP program transformation of [Burstall and Darlington 77].

Under the first approach [Clark and Sickel 77] [Clark 79, 81], the specification is "executed" with symbolic values that cover all possible forms of the type of some chosen induction parameter. For instance, if that parameter is a list, then the specification is "executed" with the symbolic values [] and $[H|T]$. "Execution" is a transformational process, based on a predefined set of transformation rules, whose aim is to obtain a variant of the specification that is recursive and under the form of a definite clause procedure. The transformation rules include *folding* (replacing a sub-formula by an atom), *unfolding* (replacing an atom by its definition; this mimics the execution mechanism of Prolog), logical rewrite and simplification rules, domain-specific rewrite and simplification rules, *specification introduction*, and many others. Recursion is obtained by folding part of a new version of the body of the specifying axiom into a recursive call.

A similar approach was taken by [Hogger 78, 81, 84], though with slight differences. Unfolding is referred to as *resolution*, which is perfectly adequate and underlines the operational flavor of symbolic execution. More importantly, the induction on some parameter is only introduced as the need arises, and this by strengthening an implicant with a form-identifying atom, such as $L = [H|T]$.

We now illustrate all this on a sample synthesis.

Example 2-6: The synthesis of a logic program for *member*/2 goes as follows. As a reminder, the top-level specification is (for convenience, we omit quantifiers):

$$member(E,L) \Leftrightarrow append(P,[E|S],L) \quad (1)$$

Suppose that *append*/3 is defined as follows:

```
append(A,B,C) ⇔
      A=[]    ∧ C=B
    ∨ A=[H|T] ∧ append(T,B,V)
              ∧ C=[H|V]
```

Suppose now that parameter L is chosen as the induction parameter. It is a list, so let's perform a symbolic execution for the mutually exclusive symbolic values [] and $[H|T]$. Let's start with the base case, and apply the substitution $\{L/[]\}$ to (1):

$$member(E,[]) \Leftrightarrow append(P,[E|S],[])$$

Unfolding the *append*/3 atom yields, after some logical simplifications:

$$member(E,[]) \Leftrightarrow (false) \vee (false) \quad (2)$$

Let's now pursue with the structure case, and apply the substitution $\{L/[H|T]\}$ to (1):

$$member(E,[H|T]) \Leftrightarrow append(P,[E|S],[H|T])$$

Unfolding the *append*/3 atom yields:

$$member(E,[H|T]) \Leftrightarrow (P=[] \wedge [H|T]=[E|S]) \vee$$
$$(P=[Q|U] \wedge append(U,[E|S],V) \wedge [H|T]=[Q|V])$$

Folding the *append*/3 atom according to (1) introduces the wanted recursion:

$$member(E,[H|T]) \Leftrightarrow (H=E) \vee (P=[Q|U] \wedge member(E,V) \wedge [H|T]=[Q|V])$$

Some logical simplifications yield:

$$member(E,[H|T]) \Leftrightarrow H=E \vee member(E,T) \quad (3)$$

The obtained statements (2) and (3) are easily transformed into definite clause form:

```
member(E, [H|T]) ← H=E
member(E, [H|T]) ← member(E,T)
```

This completes the synthesis. It is admittedly a little bit contrived because its linearity skips the issues of transformation rule selection and backtracking, but the point is here to get a feel for this kind of synthesis mechanism. ♦

Synthesis by symbolic execution obviously features the usual advantages and drawbacks of transformational synthesis.

Other Approaches

Folding/unfolding transformations were the object of a first formal study in logic programming by [Tamaki and Sato 84], although these transformations were already present in the above-mentioned symbolic execution synthesis approaches.

A highly structured top-down strategy for applying folding and unfolding, guided by a recursion schema provided by the specifier, is proposed by [Lau 89] [Lau and Prestwich 90, 91]. This approach is amenable to mechanization.

The theoretical foundations to transformational synthesis are being laid out by [Lau and Ornaghi 93, 94ab] [Lau *et al.* 94]. (Note that their "deductive synthesis" corresponds to what we here call transformational synthesis.) This work introduces a realistic specification elaboration scenario, based on specification frameworks, where the synthesis process may provide feedback to the specification elaboration process.

The research for *Periwinkle* [Kraan *et al.* 93ab] takes a novel approach: a logic program is synthesized as a by-product of the planning of a verification proof of the specification. This proof is performed, at the object level, in a sorted, first-order logic with equality. The proof is planned, at the meta-level, while initially having the actual body of the extracted program represented by a second-order variable (this is called *middle-out reasoning*). As the planning proceeds by applying tactics to a conjecture (this is tantamount to applying transformation rules), the program becomes gradually instantiated. This requires an extension of the used *Clam* proof planner (see Section 2.4.2). This technique may also be classified into the proofs-as-programs paradigm.

The LOPS (*LOgical Program Synthesis*) system [Bibel 80] [Bibel and Hörnig 84], though originally described within the proofs-as-programs synthesis paradigm, actually performs transformational synthesis [Neugebauer 93]. A very small set of hardwired heuristics (which could be seen as algorithm design strategies) leads to the uniform synthesis of a recursive re-formulation of the specification. Another originality of this system is that, guided by the syntax of the specification, it tries to discover itself the crucial knowledge about how to solve the base case of a proof-by-induction, and about how to compose partial results in the structure case of such a proof.

Several researchers have tried to make synthesis a deterministic process, akin to compilation. For instance, implication formulas with arbitrary bodies may be normalized into normal clauses by the so-called *Lloyd-Topor translation process* (see [Lloyd 87]). This is, however, a non-deterministic translation. Moreover, it does not always yield useful logic programs, due to the deficiencies of SLDNF resolution, such as floundering. Sometimes, the obtained programs are hopelessly inefficient. The work of [Sato and Tamaki 84] shows how to combine the folding/unfolding rules [Tamaki and Sato 84] with their so-called *negation technique* in order to perform an almost deterministic synthesis of definite logic programs from non-recursive specifications. However, the search space is way too large due to the generate-and-test flavor of the mechanism. The same team eventually did come up with a completely deterministic and automatic synthesizer [Sato and Tamaki 89], which is based this time on the notion of universal continuation forms, as well as the folding/unfolding rules. This "compiler" starts from a specification written as a set of clauses whose bodies are conjunctions of atoms or universally quantified implications. Either it finitely produces a definite clause program that is guaranteed to be partially correct with respect to the specification, or it aborts for lack of logical power.

The work of [Waldau 92] is a first step towards proving the validity of transformation rules for logic programs.

2.4.2 Proofs-as-Programs Synthesis of Prolog Programs

Various systems exist for doing constructive synthesis of logic programs. We simply enumerate them here, but give no insights into their underlying mechanisms, nor do we illustrate them on sample syntheses.

First, a large-scale effort was conducted by the UPMAIL group at the University of Uppsala (Sweden). The development of a logic programming calculus [Clark and Tärnlund 77] [Tärnlund 78] [Hansson *et al.* 82], which is based on Prawitz' natural deduction system for intuitionistic logic, led to a nice unified framework for logic program synthesis, verification, transformation, and execution. [Hansson 80] shows how to extract logic programs from constructive proofs-by-induction performed within this system. [Eriksson 84] used this mechanism for one of the first syntheses of a unification algorithm, which is considered one of the ultimate benchmarks of automatic programming. A proof development system, *NatDed* [Eriksson and Johansson 82], was developed for assisting in the proof process. This editor was subsequently optimized to successfully recognize symmetry [Johansson 84] and transitivity in proofs.

Then, there is *Nuprl* [Constable *et al.* 86], a proof development system that is based on the intuitionistic second-order type theory of [Martin-Löf 79], and that has been used for the synthesis of deterministic logic programs by [Bundy 88]. A first-order subset of the *Oyster* proof development system—a re-implementation of *Nuprl* in Prolog—was used for logic program synthesis by [Bundy *et al.* 90], with special focus on the synthesis of logic programs that compute full-fledged relations, and not just total functions. In view of automating proofs, a proof-planner called *Clam* was adjoined to *Oyster*. That overall effort was further pursued by the same group from Edinburgh, and resulted in the *Whelk* proof development system [Wiggins 92] [Wiggins *et al.* 92], which is based on a first-order constructive logic with equality, performs proofs in the Gentzen sequent calculus, and extracts logic programs written in Prolog or *Gödel* [Hill and Lloyd 94], a logic programming language that is much closer to the true ideals of logic programming than Prolog.

The system *ExExE* described by [Fribourg 90] synthesizes deterministic logic programs by coupling program extraction rules to a subset of the inference rules of extended Prolog execution [Kanamori and Fujita 86] [Kanamori and Seki 86]. The synthesized program is defined in a primitive recursive way; moreover, it is guaranteed to be correct with respect to the specification, and to terminate. Tail-recursive programs may be synthesized at the expense of the termination guarantee. Little knowledge seems required for the proofs, and the search space seems of manageable size. The automatic generation of simplification lemmas [Fribourg 91] for syntheses involving proofs-by-induction seems a promising step towards full automation of the mechanism.

Another approach is proposed by [Takayama 87], namely doing the constructive proofs in the typed logical system *QJ*, and then extracting programs in some intermediate code that is then compiled into Prolog.

2.4.3 Schema-Guided Synthesis of Prolog Programs

As of now, we are not aware of any full-fledged schema-guided synthesis systems for logic programs. The work of [Fuchs and Fromherz 92] and [Kraan *et al.* 93ab] is definitely schema-based, but their logic program schemas are not finegrained enough to more effectively *guide* the synthesis.

We thus quickly enumerate here a few approaches to using schemas for assisting the manual construction of logic programs.

In the field of *logic programming tutors* (for beginners), [Gegg-Harrison 89] proposes a hierarchy of fourteen logic program schemas. These are set in a second-order logic framework. They reflect a divide-and-conquer design strategy, but are already partly instantiated for certain data-structures and classes of programs.

In the area of *manual or computer-aided program construction* (for experts), [Deville and Burnay 89] and [Deville 87, 90] suggest a divide-and-conquer schema. They also discuss interesting transformation schemas, based on (structural or computational) generalization.

A similar study is made by [O'Keefe 90], who uses algebraic specifications. The predicates of such specifications can be directly plugged into given logic program schemas. Several schemas may be applicable according to the properties (associativity, commutativity, existence of left identities, and so on) of the identified predicates.

Alternatively, [Lakhotia 89] experiments with what he calls "incorporating programming techniques into Prolog programs". Similarly, [Barker-Plummer 90] discusses a system based on clichés that assists experienced programmers in the construction of Prolog programs. These approaches could be seen as transformation rather than design approaches.

2.5 Conclusions on Program Synthesis from Axiomatizations

The use of deductive inference in program synthesis from axiomatic specifications has given rise to two major approaches: transformational synthesis and proofs-as-programs synthesis. As suggested several times above, these approaches are probably only two facets of the same process. This claim can be substantiated by the ability of several researchers to classify their systems in both sub-categories [Manna and Waldinger 79, 80] [Smith 85] [Kraan *et al.* 93ab]. Moreover, we have felt the need to name a third sub-category, namely schema-guided synthesis, which is rather a common extension to the two other approaches.

A first major problem of deductive approaches to program synthesis is the enormous size of the search spaces, and the lack of power of current automated theorem provers. For the proving aspects, the use of rippling [Bundy *et al.* 93] and automatic lemma generation [Fribourg 91] has been suggested for speeding up and further automating proofs-by-induction. For the search space aspects, macroscopic transformation rules and proof-planning via proof tactics [Bundy 88] have been proposed. Moreover, a lot of theoretical effort is being directed at building *theories of algorithms* that may underlie synthesis. Almost any algorithm can be synthesized using these approaches. What is needed *also* is a *theory of algorithm design* in order to allow even more efficient traversal of these huge search spaces. We believe that the key lies in schema-guided synthesis, so that algorithm design knowledge may be included in synthesizers.

The other major problem with deductive synthesis is related to the formality of the specifications. Where do the formal specifications come from? If deductive synthesizers guarantee total correctness of the resulting algorithms with respect to their specifications, what guarantee do we have that these specifications correctly capture our *intentions*? These questions are often either dismissed as irrelevant or considered as intractable issues that are left for future research. But what use are these synthesizers if we don't even know whether they solve our problems or not? See [Le Charlier 85] and [Flener and Popelínský 94] for a detailed discussion of this controversial topic.

Finally, another problem is, as already said in Chapter 1, that too much emphasis is often put on the synthesis of actual programs in some programming language, which entails taking into account the execution mechanism (and its known deficiencies) and other extra-algorithmic issues. Sometimes, too much emphasis is even put on the synthesis of efficient programs. A clear separation of correct-algorithm synthesis, algorithm transformation, algorithm implementation (into programs), and program transformation (optimization) helps in overcoming the ensuing problems. Fortunately, more and more researchers focus on algorithm synthesis, leaving transformation and implementations issues to separate research. For instance, the LOPS system of [Bibel 80] and the systems of [Smith 85, 90a] and [Bauer *et al.* 89] clearly mention algorithms. The notion of *logic algorithm* (an algorithm expressed in logic) was introduced by [Deville 87, 90] in the context of a methodology for logic program development. This idea has also been advocated and used later for the *Oyster/Clam* synthesis system of [Bundy *et al.* 90] and the *Whelk* system of [Wiggins 92] [Wiggins *et al.* 92].

3 INDUCTIVE INFERENCE IN AUTOMATIC PROGRAMMING

Inductive inference[1] is not so common in automatic programming. We first define, in Section 3.1, the underlying specification formalism, namely examples. In Section 3.2, we present the major results about inductive inference. Then, in Section 3.3 and Section 3.4, we survey the synthesis of functional programs from examples, and the synthesis of logic programs from examples, respectively. Finally, in Section 3.5, we draw some conclusions on the use of inductive inference in automatic programming.

3.1 Specifications by Examples

We first define a possible language for specifications by examples. Later in this section, we list alternative approaches.

Definition 3-1: A *specification by examples* of a procedure for predicate r/n consists of a finite set $\mathcal{E}(r)$ of ground examples of r/n, split into:

- a set $\mathcal{E}^+(r)$ of *positive examples* of r/n (that is, ground atoms whose n-tuples are supposed to belong to the intended relation $\mathcal{R}$);
- a set $\mathcal{E}^-(r)$ of *negative examples* of r/n (that is, ground negated atoms whose n-tuples are supposed not to belong to the intended relation $\mathcal{R}$).

Negative examples are also called *counter-examples*. The phrase "an example" stands for "a positive example or a negative example".

We illustrate[2] all this on a few sample specifications.

Example 3-1: A possible specification by examples of the *member*/2 problem is:

```
E+(member) = {  member(a,[a])              (E1)
                member(b,[b,c])            (E2)
                member(c,[b,c])            (E3)
                member(d,[d,e,f])          (E4)
                member(e,[d,e,f])          (E5)
                member(f,[d,e,f]) }        (E6)

E-(member) = {  ¬member(a,[])              (C1)
                ¬member(d,[b,c]) }         (C2)
```

Counter-example C_1 suggests that empty lists have no members. C_2 suggests that members must belong to L. ♦

Example 3-2: A possible specification by examples of the *firstPlateau*/3 problem is:

```
E+(firstPlateau)= {firstPlateau([a],[a],[])         (E1)
                   firstPlateau([b,b],[b,b],[])     (E2)
                   firstPlateau([c,d],[c],[d])      (E3)
                   firstPlateau([e,f,g],[e],[f,g])  (E4)
```

1. Attention! Inductive inference is not to be confused with deductive proofs-by-induction.
2. Attention! There is a potential ambiguity between "examples of a problem" and "examples that illustrate our purpose". To announce examples of the latter category, we often use the verb "to illustrate" and the adjective "sample". The intended category of examples should however always be clear from context.

```
                               firstPlateau([h,i,i],[h],[i,i])      (E5)
                               firstPlateau([j,j,k],[j,j],[k])      (E6)
                               firstPlateau([m,m,m],[m,m,m],[])}    (E7)
ℰ⁻(firstPlateau)= {¬firstPlateau([a],[],[a])                        (C1)
                   ¬firstPlateau([b,b],[b],[b])                     (C2)
                   ¬firstPlateau([c,d],[c,d],[])                    (C3)
                   ¬firstPlateau([e,f,e],[e,e],[f])                 (C4)
                   ¬firstPlateau([h,i,i],[i,i],[h])}                (C5)
```

Counter-example C_1 suggests that plateaus are non-empty. C_2 suggests that maximal plateaus need to be extracted. C_3 suggests that plateaus are lists of identical elements. C_4 suggests that the first plateau of L is not the list of all occurrences of its first element. C_5 suggests that the first plateau of L is not necessarily a maximal plateau. ♦

Example 3-3: A possible specification by examples of the *compress*/2 problem is:

```
ℰ⁺(compress)= {  compress([],[])                       (E1)
                 compress([a],[a,1])                   (E2)
                 compress([b,b],[b,2])                 (E3)
                 compress([c,d],[c,1,d,1])             (E4)
                 compress([e,e,e],[e,3])               (E5)
                 compress([f,f,g],[f,2,g,1])           (E6)
                 compress([h,i,i],[h,1,i,2])           (E7)
                 compress([j,k,m],[j,1,k,1,m,1]) }     (E8)
ℰ⁻(compress)= {  ¬compress([b,b],[b,1,b,1])            (C1)
                 ¬compress([d,c],[c,1,d,1])            (C2)
                 ¬compress([j,k,j],[j,2,k,1]) }        (C3)
```

Counter-example C_1 suggests that maximal plateaus need to be compressed. C_2 suggests that the left-to-right order of appearance of the plateaus in L determines the order of appearance of the couples in C, and not, say, the alphabetical order. C_3 suggests that non-adjacent plateaus of the same value are compressed separately. ♦

Example 3-4: A possible specification by examples of the *sum*/2 problem is:

```
ℰ⁺(sum)  = { sum([],0)                 (E1)
             sum([7],7)                (E2)
             sum([4,5],9)              (E3)
             sum([2,3,1],6) }          (E4)
ℰ⁻(sum)  = { ¬sum([],32767)            (C1)
             ¬sum([7],9) }             (C2)
```

Counter-example C_1 suggests that the sum of the empty list is not different from 0, and C_2 suggests that the sum of a singleton list is not different from its first element. ♦

Example 3-5: A possible specification by examples of the *sort*/2 problem is:

```
ℰ⁺(sort)= { sort([],[])                (E1)
            sort([1],[1])              (E2)
            sort([3,2],[2,3])          (E3)
            sort([6,4,5],[4,5,6]) }    (E4)
```

```
ℰ⁻(sort)= { ¬sort([3,2],[3,2])                 (C1)
            ¬sort([6,4,5],[4,6,5])             (C2)
            ¬sort([6,4,5],[5,6])               (C3)
            ¬sort([6,4,5],[4,5,6,7]) }         (C4)
```

Counter-example C_1 suggests that a sorted list is not always equal to the unsorted list. C_2 suggests that it doesn't always suffice to permute the first two elements. C_3 and C_4 suggest that the elements of a sorted list are exactly those of the unsorted list. ♦

It should be noted that Definition 3-1 is not the only possible definition for specifications by examples. It is too much geared towards the synthesis of algorithms. So let's generalize it to the larger framework of *empirical learning* from examples. Specification approaches vary according to the following criteria:

- *multiplicity of examples*: sometimes, only one example is required, but most often, more than one example is expected;
- *multiplicity of concepts*: most often, examples of only one concept are required, but sometimes multiple related concepts can be specified together;
- *language of examples*:
  - *groundness*: examples are mostly ground literals, but one could also consider any kinds of literals; for instance, $sum([X],X)$ would be a useful example;
  - *multiplicity of predicates*: often, a single literal with predicate r/n constitutes an example; alternatively, examples are conjunctions of literals (called *instance descriptions*) with predicates other than r/n that describe the attributes of an *instance* of a relation r/n (called a *concept*, where usually $n = 1$); for example, the instance *Tweety* of the concept *bird*/1 could be described as follows:

$$mouth(tweety,beak) \wedge legs(tweety,2) \wedge skin(tweety,feathers) \wedge utterance(tweety,sings) \wedge color(tweety,yellow)$$

  - *directionality*: examples are often given in a relational form, but the functional form (which lists *input/output examples*) is also very common; for instance, $compress([c,d]) = [c,1,d,1]$ is an input/output example leading to a function that can only compress lists, but not decompress compact lists;
- *sign of examples*: the presence of positive *and* negative examples is commonly expected, but sometimes only one of these two kinds of examples is required.

Other criteria classify the learning mechanism (learner), rather than specifications:

- *moment of presentation of examples*: the two extreme approaches are presenting all the examples before the learning, respectively presenting all the examples on-the-fly during the learning, as the need for more examples arises;
- *formulation of examples*: examples are formulated either directly as examples by the specifier, or indirectly as classification queries by the learner; in the latter case, the specifier has to classify an example as a positive or negative example.

Finally, some criteria depend on the circumstances under which examples are chosen:

- *specifying agent*: the specifier is either a human being, or some automated device, such as a robot, a sonde, a catheter, and so on;
- *status of intended concept*: at the moment of choosing the examples, the intended concept is either known or unknown; "knowing a concept" means that one can *act* as a decision procedure for answering classification queries for that concept [Angluin 88], but it doesn't necessarily imply the ability to actually *write* such a

decision procedure; for instance, the *compress*/2 problem was known for the elaboration of the specification in Example 3-3, but the protein structure of a molecule may be unknown during the generation of its examples;
- *consistency of examples*: either examples are known or assumed to be consistent with the intended concept, or examples are known or assumed to be possibly inconsistent with the intended concept.

All these criteria allow a precise classification of settings for learning from examples.

Anyway, whatever the actual setting, the advantages of specifications by examples are the following:

+ *naturalness*: human beings often resort to examples in order to explain some concept; moreover, examples are easy to elaborate and easy to understand;
+ *conciseness*: examples are a concise[3] way of intensionally specifying some concept, because the actual computations are abstracted by a black-box model.

The major disadvantage of specifications by examples is:

– *incompleteness* and *ambiguity*: a finite set of examples cannot completely and unambiguously specify an infinite relation; in practice, one even expects the number of given examples to be orders of magnitude less than the number of all possible examples; for instance, the total ordering underlying the *sort*/2 problem is mentioned nowhere; the same holds for the summation operator underlying the *sum*/2 problem; the kind of determinism of a relation is notoriously hard to convey by examples; in Example 3-2, the sub-concept of plateau is not entirely clear from the examples, as nothing explicitly says that it is only the difference between two successive elements of L that determines where the break into P and S occurs, and not some other criterion that is based, say, on the notions of vowels, consonants, or positions within the alphabet.

From this drawback, it is obvious that, given a specific learner and a human specifier, there is a definite need for a methodology for choosing "good" examples.

3.2 Inductive Inference

Inductive inference is the process of formulating a general rule from incomplete information, such as examples. This ability is a fundamental component of human intelligence. *Learning* is the process of increasing one's knowledge or skill. This is a broader problem than inductive inference, though techniques of the latter are often used in learning. The branch of artificial intelligence research that is about learning is called *machine learning*. In this section, we only concentrate on the sub-branch of machine learning that focuses on the so-called *empirical learning from examples*, which relies heavily on inductive inference.

In Section 3.2.1, we suggest a terminology for the components of an empirical learning system. Then, in Section 3.2.2, we define rules of inductive inference, and survey their usage in empirical learning from examples in Section 3.2.3. Finally, in

3. This needs to be relativized, though. First, large-size data-structures go against conciseness. For instance, specifying 3D-matrix-multiplication by examples is not really concise, not to mention the tediousness of doing so (assuming a human specifier). Second, large numbers of examples also go against conciseness. Expansion factors are very small in such cases, but one should not forget that such large and/or numerous examples are sometimes all that is available for learning.

Section 3.2.4, we define the niche of algorithm synthesis from examples within empirical learning from examples, and give pointers to the literature in Section 3.2.5.

3.2.1 Components of a Learning System

We first propose a terminology for the components of an empirical learning system.

A *teacher* (*trainer, instructor*) chooses *instance descriptions* (*examples*) of instances of the *intended concept*, and *presents* them to a *learner*. There are different ways of presenting examples: *all-at-once* and *chunk-wise* (for instance, *one-by-one*).

Sometimes, the learner asks or queries an *oracle* (*informant*) for classification of examples it invents itself. The oracle is usually the teacher, but it is sometimes automated via reliance on other information, such as *background knowledge*.

The learner periodically produces *hypotheses* (*conjectures*).

This terminology is sufficient for our purposes. But note that a complete and general learning system would have many more components, such as a *blackboard*, an *example selector*, and so on. An ideal architecture is described by [van Lamsweerde 91].

3.2.2 Rules of Inductive Inference

Logical formulations of inductive inference rules were developed by [Genesereth and Nilsson 88] and by [van Lamsweerde 91]. This chapter is based on these papers, as well as on [Angluin and Smith 83].

Definition 3-2: Given background knowledge $\mathcal{B}$ and a set of examples $\mathcal{E}$, a hypothesis H is an *inductive conclusion* of $\mathcal{B}$ and $\mathcal{E}$ iff the following four conditions hold:

(1) $\mathcal{B} \cup \{H\} \models \mathcal{E}$ (the hypothesis "explains" the examples);

(2) $\mathcal{B} \cup \mathcal{E} \not\models \neg H$ (the hypothesis is consistent with the given data);

(3) $\mathcal{B} \not\models H$ (the hypothesis is not a consequence of the background knowledge);

(4) $\mathcal{B} \not\models \mathcal{E}$ (the examples are not redundant with the background knowledge).

Note that inductive inference is not necessarily sound: $\mathcal{B} \cup \mathcal{E} \models H$ does not hold in general. But, on the other hand, not every induction is unsound.

A list of atomic inductive inference rules includes *standard generalization*, *deleting-a-conjunct*, *adding-a-disjunct*, *replacing-a-constant-by-a-variable*, *splitting-a-variable-into-several-variables*, *weakening-an-implicant*, *extending-the-domain-of-a-variable*, *closing-an-interval*, and *climbing-a-specialization-tree*. More elaborate inductive inference rules for complex formulas are based on the fundamental notions of *generalization* and *msg* (*most-specific-generalization*): these are surveyed in detail in Chapter 7 and Chapter 10.

Since there are many possible inductive conclusions for any background knowledge and example set, it is necessary to prune the generalization search space so as to get "useful" inductive conclusions. Interesting approaches are based on *induction biases*:

- *semantic bias* restricts the vocabulary available for hypotheses; for instance, the *model maximization technique* prefers hypotheses that have a maximal number of models, and *conceptual bias* restricts the vocabulary to a predefined set of predicates, called the *basis set*; in this context, in a *selective rule* of inductive inference the conclusion only uses predicates appearing in the premiss, whereas in a *constructive rule* the conclusion "invents" predicates not appearing in the premiss;

- *syntactic bias* restricts the language of hypotheses; for instance, (existential) conjunctive hypotheses and disjunctive normal form hypotheses represent very common search spaces, both in propositional calculus and in first-order logic.

Other approaches are based on preference criteria for utility or efficiency measures.

We here only focus on *instance-to-class* generalization. Other kinds of generalization are *class-to-class* generalization and *part-to-whole* generalization.

3.2.3 Empirical Learning from Examples

The aim of empirical learning from examples is the elaboration of a concept description from multiple positive and negative examples, when little—or no—background knowledge is available. The inferred hypothesis must be satisfied by all the positive examples, but by none of the negative examples. In the following, "learning" stands for "empirical learning". In this section, we discuss concept classes, examples, presentations, hypotheses, possible identification criteria, a classification of learning mechanisms, and actual learning mechanisms. We actually simultaneously summarize both the more theoretical concerns (such as learnability) of the inductive inference community, and the more practical concerns (such as actual mechanisms) of the machine learning community. Hence, "learning" also stands for "identification".

Concept Classes, Examples, and Presentations

There are many classes of concepts: functions, relations, sequences, (stochastic) languages, and so on. The language of examples used for illustrating these concept classes, the nature of *admissible presentations* of these examples, and the kinds of hypotheses for describing elements of these concept classes vary accordingly.

Example 3-6: The concept class aimed at by Definition 3-1 is the set of relations over any domain. Examples of a relation are elements of its graph, and any (possibly infinite) sequence of such examples constitutes an admissible presentation iff this sequence lists all and only the elements of the graph of the relation. Hypotheses could be expressed as algorithms, programs, Turing machines, automata, and so on.

Example 3-7: In *grammatical inference*, the concept class aimed at is the set of languages over some alphabet. Examples of a language are sentences of that language. Hypotheses may be expressed as grammars, acceptors, regular expressions, and so on.

Restrictions on admissible presentations may have to be imposed, such as computability (below some complexity threshold), or ordering according to some total order. A *positive presentation* lists all and only the positive examples, whereas a *complete presentation* lists all the positive and negative examples. A *presentation by informant* queries an oracle for classification of examples as positive or negative examples. A *mixed presentation* combines complete presentation and presentation by informant. Repetition is usually allowed in admissible presentations.

Hypotheses

Learning can be abstracted as the search through a state space, where states correspond to hypotheses, and operators correspond to rules of inductive inference.

Various constraints may be imposed on the hypothesis space.

Example 3-8: The hypothesis space is often supposed to be constrained by a conceptual bias and a syntactic bias: an *acceptable hypothesis* satisfies both biases. A hypothesis is *characteristic* for a set $\mathcal{E}$ of examples iff it is satisfied by all the positive examples of $\mathcal{E}$. A hypothesis is *discriminant* for $\mathcal{E}$ iff its negation is satisfied by all the negative examples of $\mathcal{E}$. An acceptable hypothesis is *admissible* (*consistent*) for $\mathcal{E}$ iff it is characteristic for $\mathcal{E}$ and discriminant for $\mathcal{E}$. The *version space* for a set of examples $\mathcal{E}$ is the set of all admissible hypotheses (versions) for $\mathcal{E}$.

Moreover, *goodness orderings* may be defined for comparing hypotheses. Such orderings usually are partial orders, and are often required to be computable. A goodness ordering is *sample-independent* iff the order between two hypotheses is preserved for any example set. Other goodness orderings are based on some measure of the *size* or *simplicity* of hypotheses, or on probabilistic measures, and so on.

* **Example 3-9:** A version space is usually organized according to a partial order under which hypothesis H_1 is *less general* than H_2 iff H_1 implies H_2. This is a sample-independent ordering, but decidable only in specific settings. The set of *minimal* (*maximally specific*) hypotheses (no hypothesis in $\mathcal{V}$ is less general than these) of $\mathcal{V}$ is called the *lower boundary set* of $\mathcal{V}$, and the set of *maximal* hypotheses (every hypothesis in $\mathcal{V}$ is less general than these) of $\mathcal{V}$ is called the *upper boundary set* of $\mathcal{V}$. A version space $\mathcal{V}$ is *well-formed* iff every ascending chain of maximal length in $\mathcal{V}$ starts from a hypothesis that is minimal in $\mathcal{V}$ and ends in a hypothesis that is maximal in $\mathcal{V}$.

The size of the search space is typically exponential, even when constrained and partially ordered. However, the size of a search space never prejudices the existence of efficient learning mechanisms for that space. Of course, the most efficient mechanism is usually very specific to its search space, and hence difficult to adapt into a more general mechanism.

* **Example 3-10:** Version spaces are of a size exponential in the size of the basis set, not to mention the syntactic bias. Fortunately, well-formed version spaces (for instance, when the basis set is finite) have the interesting property that they are indeed bound by their boundary sets, which provides for an admissibility check that is independent of the examples. See below for an application of this property.

Identification Criteria

An *identification criterion* is a criterion that defines under what circumstances learning is successful in identifying the intended concept (that is, in producing a hypothesis that is correct wrt the intended concept). There are two main identification criteria.

First, the seminal work by [Gold 67] has introduced the criterion of *identification-in-the-limit*. Learning is viewed as an infinite process of example presentations and hypothesis productions whose limiting behavior is used as a criterion of success.

Definition 3-3: A learner L correctly *identifies* an intended concept C *in the limit* iff the infinite sequence of hypotheses produced by L, say $H_1, H_2, \ldots$, is such that there exists some number n such that $H_n = H_m$ for every $m > n$, and such that H_n is correct wrt C.

Note that there is no way that L can tell that it actually has identified C, because the next example might or might not provoke a revision of the last hypothesis. An important limiting result is that the class of total recursive functions is not identifiable-in-the-limit: this means that there can't be a universal mechanism of program synthesis from incomplete information. However, the class of primitive recursive functions is identifiable-in-the-limit. Moreover, given positive examples only, the class of finite languages is identifiable-in-the-limit, but no class containing all finite languages and at least one infinite language is identifiable-in-the-limit [Gold 67].

A possible way of achieving identification-in-the-limit is the *identification-by-enumeration* learning mechanism: after each presentation of a new example, one systematically traverses the entire search space until a hypothesis is found that is satisfied by all the examples presented so far. This requires computability of the enumeration and of the satisfiability checking of hypotheses wrt examples. This is however an extremely impractical mechanism because of the (typically exponential) size of the search space. Improvements usually consist in defining a partial order on the search space, which then allows pruning of uninteresting branches, and sometimes even suggesting plausible replacements for rejected hypotheses. Other improvements are based on heuristic measures of the goodness of hypotheses.

Years later, Leslie G. Valiant has introduced *PAC* (*probably-approximately-correct*) *identification* [Valiant 84] [Pitt and Valiant 88], which is today's most-used learning model. The idea is to weaken the tight constraints of identification-in-the-limit by allowing the final hypothesis to be "nearly correct" wrt the intended concept. Moreover, the actual learning process is usually based on a finite presentation, although admissible presentations are mostly infinite. Other motivations are the need for polynomial-time learning, and the need for tolerance to noise: hence a probabilistic approach.

Definition 3-4: A learner *PAC-identifies* an intended concept iff an arbitrary hypothesis that is consistent with the examples presented so far can be guaranteed with high probability to be consistent with most of the examples that are yet to be presented.

The main result is that whatever the probability distributions from which the examples are drawn, a hypothesis distinguishing the positive examples from the negative examples with controllable error can be inferred easily, except if the hypothesis language is too expressive.

Many other identification criteria have been defined. An *identification type* is the class of all the sets of hypotheses that are identifiable according to some given identification criterion. A wealth of learnability results order the identification types by set-inclusion into a partially-ordered set. Example presentation has a major impact on these results. Positive presentation seems to be afflicted with negative results for identification-in-the-limit.

Finally, note that identification is not the only inductive inference problem. Another problem is *prediction* (*extrapolation*), where the nth value of a sequence is to be predicted from the $n - 1$ first values of that sequence. Criteria of successful prediction have been defined, but we do not discuss this topic here.

Classification of Learning Mechanisms

We here focus on stepwise learning, whose purpose is to have monitoring points where the learning process can be assessed in terms of correctness and progression.

Definition 3-5: *Stepwise learning* is performed by a sequence of steps, each producing a hypothesis that is designed from the previous hypothesis and from (some of) the examples presented so far.

Note that this definition does not preclude the sequence of steps to be (partly) defined by a loop over the same step. This definition also does not mention how and when examples are presented. Stepwise learning can be divided into two complementary sub-categories:

Definition 3-6: *Incremental learning* is stepwise learning where each hypothesis may be the final one. *Non-incremental learning* is stepwise learning where only the last hypothesis is supposed to be the final one, the other hypotheses being temporary.

Incremental learning is often used in conjunction with a one-by-one presentation of the examples (prior to each step, a single example is presented), and a single step that is iterated over after each presentation. In the following, we equate incremental learning with this particular case. Non-incremental learning is often used in conjunction with an all-at-once presentation of the examples (prior to the first step, all the examples are presented), and multiple steps that are each executed only once. In the sequel, we equate non-incremental learning with this particular case. These two approaches have complementary pros and cons:

- considering that an example embodies several kinds of information, incremental learning has to extract all these kinds of information from the examples presented so far, whereas non-incremental learning may extract only one kind of information from every example at each step;
- incremental learning is prone to be sensitive to the presentation order of the examples, in the sense that different hypotheses may emerge from different presentation orders, whereas non-incremental learning is usually insensitive to the presentation order of the examples, thus turning the latter into a fully declarative specification; non-incremental learners usually first perform example ordering;
- incremental learning only consumes as many examples as are needed, because it relies on an example stream, whereas non-incremental learning requires all the examples to be ready prior to learning, which may result in a useless computational overhead, or in teacher inflexibility.

Choosing one of these strategies is obviously a very delicate design decision.

Other useful characterizations of learning mechanisms are as follows:

Definition 3-7: *Algorithmic learning* is performed by the sole execution of a learning algorithm. *Heuristic learning* is at least partially based on heuristics.

Definition 3-8: *Interactive learning* involves experiment generation and classification queries to an oracle. *Passive learning* is non-interactive learning.

We now establish a list of useful classification criteria for stepwise learning mechanisms. They amount to restricting identification types, but the reward is tight knowledge about, and control over, the evolution of the learning process:

- *iterative learning* is incremental learning where every new hypothesis is designed only from the most recently presented example and from the previous hypothesis;
- *monotonic learning* is stepwise learning where every new hypothesis covers no less conclusions than the previous hypothesis;

- *consistent learning* is stepwise learning where every new hypothesis is consistent with all the examples presented so far;
- *conservative learning* is incremental learning where a hypothesis is different from its predecessor only if the latter is inconsistent with the last presented example;
- *reliable learning* is stepwise learning that converges to the correct hypothesis, whenever it does converge;
- *finite learning* is stepwise learning that stops (has converged) iff two successive hypotheses are the same (this removes the uncertainty about the convergence of identification-in-the-limit);

Combinations of these criteria are of course possible.

Some concepts are learnable only via non-monotonic learning [Jantke 91]. Other concepts are learnable only via inconsistent learning [Lange and Wiehagen 91]. A host of learnability results inserts the corresponding refined identification types into the partially-ordered set of identification types [Jantke 89, 91].

Learning mechanisms may be compared in terms of various criteria. Possible comparison criteria are as follows:

- given an identification criterion I and an example presentation method P, a learning mechanism is *more powerful* than another one wrt I and P iff its class of hypotheses that can be correctly identified wrt I and P properly contains the corresponding class of the other mechanism;
- a learning mechanism is *(strictly) more data-efficient* than another one iff it converges (strictly) "faster" than the other one, whenever that one converges; a learning mechanism is *optimally data-efficient* iff no mechanism is strictly more data-efficient than it;
- the overall *number of distinct hypotheses* and the *number of mind changes* (whenever two successive hypotheses are distinct) are other measures;

and so on.

Example 3-11: Identification-by-enumeration is an incremental, consistent, conservative, and optimally data-efficient learning mechanism [Gold 67].

Learning Mechanisms

Empirical learning research has basically taken two approaches [van Lamsweerde 91]:

- the *data-driven approach* starts from examples only; the examples are assumed consistent wrt the intended concept;
- the *approximation-driven approach* (also called the *model-driven approach*) starts from examples and a set of approximate hypotheses about the intended concept; approximate hypotheses are incorrect, or incomplete, or both;

Let's briefly discuss these approaches.

* The data-driven approach features incremental learning, with (by definition) an iteration over the set $\mathcal{E}$ of given examples, where each presentation of an example leads to an update of the current hypothesis (set) wrt that example. There are three main strategies for reducing the version space to a hypothesis (set) that is admissible for $\mathcal{E}$:

- *depth-first search*: at each presentation of an example, the search for an admissible hypothesis considers only one hypothesis, which is adapted according to the presented example. The drawbacks are the need for managing backtracking, and the need for re-checking the admissibility of the new hypothesis wrt all examples presented so far that are of a sign opposite to the one of the last-presented example;

- *breadth-first search*: at each presentation of an example, the search for an admissible hypothesis considers several hypotheses in parallel, which are adapted according to the presented example. The considered hypotheses are those of the lower boundary set. The successive hypotheses are monotonically increasing in generality, so there is no need for re-checking whether the new hypothesis is characteristic wrt all positive examples presented so far. The drawback is the need for re-checking whether the new hypothesis is discriminant wrt all negative examples presented so far. A variant of this strategy, for well-formed version spaces only, achieves symmetry between the handling of positive and negative examples by simultaneously considering the lower *and* upper boundary sets at each presentation: this leads to the *candidate-elimination mechanism* of [Mitchell 81]. Convergence of the ascending and descending hypothesis series to the same unique limit is guaranteed, and admissibility re-checking is useless;
- *heuristic search*: in order to cope with extremely large version spaces, heuristic preference functions may be introduced; Michalski's *star algorithm* is a sample application of this idea, but we do not develop this here.

These three strategies differ by the representative subset of the version space they build. Ultimately, the minimal hypotheses of the inferred hypothesis (set) are retained, because they are satisfied by the potentially smallest possible set of examples unrelated to the intended concept. The data-driven approach has a low tolerance to noise.

* The approximation-driven approach features non-incremental learning, with an iteration over the given approximations. There are two strategies for doing so:

- *bottom-up search*: if the given approximations are not general enough, then use any data-driven learning algorithm for generalizing an approximation into a set of maximally specific hypotheses that are admissible wrt *all* the given examples;
- *top-down search*: if the given approximations are too general, then use the dual of any data-driven learning algorithm for specializing an approximation into a set of maximally specific hypotheses that are admissible wrt *all* the given examples.

The inferred hypotheses are collected into a hopefully representative subset of the version space. The approximation-driven approach has some tolerance to noise.

Empirical learning from examples usually requires a sufficient number of examples for successful learning of the intended concept. Moreover, the shown approaches are very sensitive to the quality and ordering of examples. Investigated optimization techniques include the localization and pruning of forbidden features, hill-climbing for searching locally optimal hypotheses, jumping-to-conclusions based on plausible features, and so on.

3.2.4 Algorithm Synthesis from Examples as a Niche of Learning

The synthesis of algorithms from examples is a machine learning task as it falls into the category of empirical learning from examples. Indeed, let's state the objectives of both fields:

- the aim of empirical learning from examples is the elaboration of a concept description from multiple positive and negative examples of the intended concept;

- the aim of synthesis from examples is the design of an algorithm from multiple positive and negative examples of its intended relation.

The renaming substitutions to pass from one objective to the other one are obvious.

But algorithm synthesis from examples is a highly specialized niche within empirical learning from examples. Table 3-1 summarizes the differences between the concerns of algorithm synthesis (as we view it) and the mainstream concerns (so far) of empirical learning.

Table 3-1: Algorithm synthesis from examples as a niche of learning

	Empirical learning	Algorithm synthesis
Intentions	any concept class	relations
Class of hypotheses	any	recursive algorithms
Specifying agent	human or machine	often a human being
Status of intentions	sometimes unknown	always known
Consistency of examples	any attitude	assumed consistent
Nb. of examples	any	a few
Nb. of pred.s in examples	at least 1	exactly 1
Rules of inductive inference	mostly selective	necessarily constructive
Correctness of hypotheses	any attitude	total correct. is crucial
Existence of hyp. schemas	hardly any	yes, many
Nb. of correct hypotheses	usually only a few	always many

Indeed, for algorithm synthesis, we are here only interested in recursive algorithms for relations, whereas most concept descriptions are non-recursive. Moreover, we are here mostly interested in human specifiers who know—even if only informally—the intended relation, and who are assumed to choose only examples that are consistent with the intended relation. Moreover, such a specifier cannot be expected to be willing to give more than just a few examples. But this setting constitutes only a particular case of empirical learning. Then, as in Definition 3-1, examples of an intended relation only involve one predicate, whereas instance descriptions usually involve several predicates. Algorithm synthesis from examples thus necessarily has to focus on constructive rules of inductive inference, whereas empirical learning can explore vast research areas by just using selective rules. Also, a synthesized algorithm is only useful if it is totally correct wrt its intended relation, whereas a learned concept description may be useful despite some deficiencies. Finally, algorithms are highly structured, complex entities that are designed according to some strategy (such as divide-and-conquer, generate-and-test, ...), whereas concept descriptions can have virtually any format (unless constrained by some induction bias): algorithm synthesis can thus be effectively guided by a schema (see Chapter 8) reflecting some design strategy. The existence of many such schemas, and the existence of many choices within the corresponding design strategies, entail the existence of many correct algorithms (even if they have vastly different complexities) for a given intended relation. For instance, the sorting problem may be solved by algorithms such as Insertion-Sort,

Merge-Sort, Quick-Sort, and so on. Such a multiplicity of correct solutions is unusual elsewhere.

In other words, algorithms are a highly specialized kind of concept descriptions. We believe that algorithm synthesis thus deserves a highly specialized set of mechanisms, rather than off-the-shelf ones from empirical learning. For algorithm synthesis, we thus adopt the following terminology: we say "specifier" instead of "teacher", "synthesizer" instead of "learner", "example" instead of "instance description", "relation" instead of "concept", "algorithm" instead of "concept description", and "synthesis" instead of "learning".

3.2.5 Pointers to the Literature

An excellent historical overview of the role of inductive inference in scientific discovery is given by [Muggleton 91]. Comprehensive introductions to, and surveys of, inductive inference research are those of [Angluin and Smith 83], [Angluin 84], [Biermann 86], and [Jantke 89]. In this theoretical field, there are highly specialized workshops such as AII (*Analogical and Inductive Inference*), ALT (*Algorithmic Learning Theory*), and COLT (*COmputational Learning Theory*). Journals for inductive inference results are *Machine Learning* (Kluwer Academic Publishers) and *New Generation Computing*.

A comprehensive survey of machine learning techniques is proposed by [van Lamsweerde 91]. In this more practical field, there are conferences such as ICML (*International Conference on Machine Learning*), ECML (*European Conference on Machine Learning*, formerly EWSL: *European Working Session on Learning*), and the various artificial intelligence conferences. Journals for machine learning results are basically the same as above.

Unfortunately, there seems to be little cross-fertilization between these two communities: "abstract results proliferate uselessly, while the concrete results produce little or nothing of significance beyond their very narrow domains" [Angluin and Smith 83]. Moreover, terminologies often diverge. Closer collaboration and unification of the frameworks seem thus highly desirable. Especially the incorporation of domain knowledge into the theoretical results seems a must, because the exponential complexities of the learning mechanisms suggested by these results make them unusable in practice, and because such knowledge is after all available to human learners.

Applications of inductive inference and machine learning are numerous. A most promising application of the technology is the accelerated bootstrapping of expert systems by automated acquisition of rules from example sets, rather than by interviewing human experts. Also, advanced user-interfaces allow non-expert computer users to specify by examples what they want the computer to do. For instance, the *Query-by-Example* system of [Zloof 77] allows easy database querying. Or the *EP* systems of [Waterman *et al.* 84] assist at the operating system level. Finally, as shown in Section 3.2.4, algorithm (or program) synthesis is an application, too.

The next two sections survey the synthesis of functional programs from examples, and the synthesis of logic programs from examples, respectively.

3.3 Functional Program Synthesis from Examples

The synthesis of functional programs (LISP programs, say) was an area of intense research during the 1970s. Since the inferred concept description is a functional program, it suffices to present the examples in the functional form: examples are then called *input/output examples*, and abbreviated *I/O-examples*, or simply examples for the purpose of this section. Recall the important limiting result of [Gold 67], which says that the class of total recursive functions is not identifiable-in-the-limit: this means that there can't be any universal mechanism of program synthesis from incomplete information. However, [Gold 67] also shows that a function can be inferred from examples if it belongs to a class of enumerable functions with a decidable halting problem. A detailed and insightful survey was made by [Smith 84]. The general synthesis surveys of [Biermann *et al.* 84b] [Biermann 92] also include sections on synthesis from examples. This present survey is organized as follows. First, Section 3.3.1 surveys synthesis from traces, which appears later to be a useful component of synthesis from examples. Then, we survey the trace-based and heuristic approaches to synthesis from examples in Section 3.3.2 and Section 3.3.3, respectively.

3.3.1 Synthesis from Traces

A *trace* is a sequence of instructions executed by a program on some given input data. Traces are often used by human beings to explain an existing algorithm. For instance, the protocol of using a telephone is easily described by sample traces.

Biermann has developed a general algorithmic mechanism of synthesis from traces (the *Trainable Turing Machine*) [Biermann 72], and has applied it to program synthesis, such as the trainable desk calculator of [Biermann and Krishnaswamy 76], which identifies the intended program in the limit. The given traces are equal to the traces the synthesized program produces on the same input data. A sample synthesis appears in Example 3-12 below. Other research on synthesis from traces includes the work of [Bauer 79] on extending Biermann and Krishnaswamy's results.

Traces are however a very tedious and error-prone specification formalism. Worse, traces oblige the specifier to already know the desired algorithm, which often goes counter the setting of algorithm synthesis. All this somewhat discredits synthesis from traces as an approach to automatic programming, but see below.

3.3.2 Trace-Based Synthesis from Examples

All the surveyed mechanisms proceed in two steps:

(1) *trace generation*: trace(s) are generated from the input/output example(s);

(2) *trace generalization*: the trace(s) are generalized into a recursive program.

This approach gives new value to synthesis from traces. The idea of two-step decomposition seems to stem from [Siklóssy and Sykes 75]. Their problem solver, called LAWALY, generates traces from multiple examples, in a heuristic way. The synthesizer proper, called SYN, fully automatically generalizes the traces into LISP-like recursive programs. There is however no concern about correctness, nor about the targeted class of programs.

We here discuss the two best-developed approaches to this idea, namely Biermann's function merging mechanism, and Summers' recurrence relation detection mechanism. Both reflect passive, non-incremental, two-step, consistent synthesis from positive, ground, pre-synthesis I/O-example(s) that are selected by an agent who knows the intended function.

Biermann's Function Merging Mechanism

Biermann has applied this two-step approach, but he used his own synthesis from traces mechanism [Biermann 72] for the second step. The resulting synthesis mechanism for so-called regular LISP programs (with only one parameter, and where the only predicate, if any, is *atom*) is described by [Biermann 78, 84a]. Let's first illustrate it on a simple synthesis (taken from [Biermann 92]).

Example 3-12: Suppose we want a LISP function for reversing S-expressions. The following example specifies this:

```
reverse(((a•b)•c)) = (c•(b•a))
```

The synthesis goes as follows.

First, the output *Y* of the example is uniquely decomposed—in an algorithmic way—by applying the basic functors *car*, *cdr*, *cons* on the input *X* of the example:

```
Y = cons(cdr(X),cons(cdr(car(X)),car(car(X))))
```

This decomposition can be re-expressed as the following trace:

```
Y = f1(X)
f1(X) = cons(f2(X),f3(X))
f2(X) = f4(cdr(X))
f3(X) = f5(car(X))
f4(X) = X
f5(X) = cons(f6(X),f7(X))
f6(X) = f8(cdr(X))
f7(X) = f9(car(X))
f8(X) = X
f9(X) = X
```

Second, the synthesis from traces mechanism proceeds by merging the obtained functions into a minimal number of functions that preserve the original computations. If a merged function is multiply defined, then a predicate generator searches for discriminants. This works here as follows. The functions f_1, f_4, f_5, f_8, f_9 may be merged into a function *reverse*. The predicate generator infers that the body of f_4, f_8, f_9 is applicable iff the parameter is an atom. Hence the following definition of *reverse*:

```
reverse(X) = cond( (atom(X) X) (T cons(f2(X),f3(X))) )
```

Similarly, function f_6 may be merged (unconditionally) into f_2, and function f_7 may be merged (unconditionally) into f_3:

```
f2(X) = reverse(cdr(X))
f3(X) = reverse(car(X))
```

The functions *reverse*, f_2, f_3 constitute the synthesized program. ♦

This function merging mechanism usually works from any single "significant" positive example. It is however very costly in computations (namely of a complexity that is exponential on the size of the target program), because of its identification-by-enumeration approach. It finitely identifies the intended program in the limit. It thus performs consistent, conservative, and optimally data-efficient synthesis. Moreover, it can synthesize any program in the class of regular LISP programs.

As [van Lamsweerde 91] observes, this kind of synthesis from examples actually is a precursor to EBL (*Explanation-Based Learning*), another branch of machine learning. Indeed, the goal of EBL in general [DeJong and Mooney 86], and EBG (*Explanation-Based Generalization*) in particular [Mitchell *et al.* 86], is the elaboration of a concept description from a very small number of examples (typically a single one), in the presence of much background knowledge. EBL proceeds by first seeking an explanation of why the example describes an instance of the intended concept (using the background knowledge), and then generalizing that explanation. Rules of deductive, abductive, and analogical inference are typically used in EBL, in contrast to the rules of inductive inference used in empirical learning: EBL reflects thus *analytic learning*.

Summers' Recurrence Relation Detection Mechanism

The THESYS system of [Summers 77] reflects another solution to the two-step approach that is based on traces. Let's first illustrate it on a simple synthesis.

Example 3-13: Suppose we want a LISP function for reversing S-expressions. This may be specified as follows:

```
reverse(a) = a                                (E1)
reverse((b•c)) = (c•b)                        (E2)
reverse(((d•e)•f)) = (f•(e•d))                (E3)
reverse((((g•h)•i)•j) = (j•(i•(h•g)))         (E4)
```

The synthesis goes as follows.

First, each sample output is uniquely decomposed—in an algorithmic way—by applying the basic functors *car*, *cdr*, *cons* on the corresponding input: [4]

$$f_1(X) = X$$

$$f_2(X) = cons(cdr(X), car(X))$$

$$f_3(X) = cons(cdr(X), cons(cdar(X), ca^2r(X)))$$

$$f_4(X) = cons(cdr(X), cons(cdar(X), cons(cda^2r(X), ca^3r(X))))$$

where function f_i corresponds to example E_i. Similarly, predicates are generated to recognize terms of the same structure as each sample input:

$$p_1(X) = atom(X)$$

$$p_2(X) = atom(car(X))$$

4. The function cd^nr denotes the composition of n applications of the function *cdr*. The function cd^na^mr denotes the composition of n applications of the function *cdr* composed to the composition of m applications of the function *car*.

$$p_3(X) = atom(ca^2r(X))$$

$$p_4(X) = atom(ca^3r(X))$$

where predicate p_i recognizes terms of the same structure as the input term of E_i.

Second, recurrence relations are sought among the decompositions:

$$f_1(X) = X$$

$$f_i(X) = cons(cdr(X), f_{i-1}(car(X))) \qquad (i>1)$$

Similarly, recurrence relations are sought among the structure recognition predicates:

$$p_1(X) = atom(X)$$

$$p_i(X) = p_{i-1}(car(X)) \qquad (i>1)$$

These recurrence relations are then plugged by the so-called *Basic Synthesis Theorem* into a LISP program schema that reflects a divide-and-conquer design strategy. This yields the following LISP program:

```
reverse(X) = cond(  (atom(X) X)
                    (T cons(cdr(X),reverse(car(X)))) )
```

This completes the synthesis. Note that this program is not doubly recursive like the one in Example 3-12: the reasons are that the examples given here incorrectly suggest that the input S-expressions are always left-linear trees, and that Biermann's mechanism looks for the smallest possible merger of the decomposition trace. Indeed, Biermann's mechanism would find the above program by merging f_4 and f_8 not into *reverse*, but into each other, which however doesn't yield the smallest merger. ♦

This recurrence relation detection mechanism requires multiple positive examples, which overcomes the potential ambiguity problems of single-example approaches. It is more efficient than Biermann's, but less robust as the examples must be carefully chosen. A striking difference with Biermann's approach is that recursion is here detected by folding parts of several traces obtained from different examples, whereas Biermann's mechanism detects recursion by folding a single trace onto itself.

The mentioned Basic Synthesis Theorem constitutes a major breakthrough, as it provides a firm theoretical foundation to synthesis from examples. Summers also describes a technique that automatically introduces accumulator parameters when no recurrence relations can be found: this amounts to descending generalization [Deville 90]. The results of Summers have spawned considerable efforts for generalization and improvement, especially by [Jouannaud and Kodratoff 83] [Kodratoff and Jouannaud 84]. Their achievements are very encouraging as the developed sequence matching algorithms are very efficient.

3.3.3 Heuristic Synthesis from Examples

Heuristic synthesis from examples involves more or less heavy use of heuristics in order to prune the search space.

Heuristic synthesis from examples is performed by the systems of [Hardy 75], [Shaw *et al.* 75], [Siklóssy and Sykes 75], and [Biggerstaff 84], in the sense that they fill in the place-holders of a LISP divide-and-conquer schema (see Chapter 8) in a plausible way according to the given examples.

A more disciplined usage of heuristics is advocated by [Biermann 84]: astronomically-sized search spaces and poorly-understood pruning techniques can be avoided by developing synthesis mechanisms for restricted program classes that are well-understood. Such synthesis mechanisms are very efficient and reliable, and could be components of a large synthesis tool-box. A hierarchical decomposition schema and a production rule mechanism are used by [Biermann and Smith 79] to speed-up the algorithmic synthesis mechanism of [Biermann 78], and this for the so-called scanning LISP programs. The resulting mechanism is fairly algorithmic, except for the selection of the used production rules. This approach achieves a neat separation of the synthesis control structure from the programming knowledge that is encoded in the production rules. Efficiency of synthesis is thus gained at the expense of generality.

3.4 Logic Program Synthesis from Examples

The synthesis of logic programs (Prolog programs, say) is an area of intense research since the early 1980s. Since the inferred concept description is a logic program, the examples are presented in the relational form. Muggleton has recently named this field ILP (*Inductive Logic Programming*) [Muggleton 91], because it is at the intersection of empirical (inductive) learning and logic programming. We prefer to call this *model-based synthesis* (see below for our reasons). The main objectives are to upgrade the results of empirical learning (which are largely restricted to the propositional calculus) to the computational first-order logic framework of logic programming, and to inject (more) background knowledge into empirical learning from examples.

Unfortunately, there is a potential confusion due to the designation "inductive logic programming". Indeed, one could partition the class of (logic) programs into *algorithms* (which usually involve some iterating mechanism, such as loops or recursion), and *concept descriptions* (which do not involve some iterating mechanism). But ILP research seems to focus mostly on learning concept descriptions, with the hope that the developed learning mechanisms also work for algorithms. However, we believe that the class of all possible logic programs, recursive or non-recursive, is way too large to be efficiently synthesizable by a uniform mechanism. For the purpose of this survey, we accept this broad view of ILP regarding logic programs, but the remainder of this book is only concerned with the synthesis of recursive logic programs.

The foundations of ILP are laid out by [Muggleton 95], and surveys [Sammut 93] [Muggleton and De Raedt 94] and a compilation [Muggleton 92] are available. Moreover, special ILP workshops exist. This present survey is organized as follows. First, in Section 3.4.1, we present Shapiro's *Model Inference System*, the pioneering learner of ILP. Then, in Section 3.4.2, we briefly discuss other relevant model-based systems.

3.4.1 Shapiro's *Model Inference System*

The foundational work for ILP was laid by the research on subsumption and generalization in the early 1970s by [Plotkin 70, 71] and [Reynolds 70]. Their results, as well as the efforts on extending them, are surveyed in Chapter 7. Then, in the early 1980s, Ehud Y. Shapiro started experimenting with his MIS (*Model Inference System*) as a mechanism for synthesizing Prolog programs from ground (positive and negative)

Prolog facts. He later discovered that program synthesis from examples is a particular case of program debugging from test-cases (namely when the initial program is empty), and subsequently called his thesis *Algorithmic Program Debugging* [Shapiro 82]. However, in this discussion, we only focus on the synthesis aspects of MIS. This section is organized as follows. After presenting the synthesis mechanism, we list research on extensions, and finally evaluate MIS.

The Synthesis Mechanism

The (positive and negative) examples are presented one-by-one, and the incremental synthesis mechanism debugs its current program accordingly.

A program (hypothesis) is a finite set of definite clauses. The program search space is ordered by a clause subsumption relation, a particular case of generalization and an extension of Plotkin's θ-subsumption. This allows intelligent pruning of the search space, and thus an improvement over basic identification-by-enumeration:

- *incompleteness*: if a program *P* fails on some positive example, then no program more specific than *P* need be considered;
- *incorrectness*: dually, if a program *P* succeeds on some negative example, then no program more general than *P* need be considered.

The resulting synthesis mechanism is then as follows (we here omit aspects related to the detection of potential non-termination, which may arise due to the semi-decidability of subsumption checking).

Algorithm 3-1: Incremental synthesis of logic programs from examples.
Input: a (possibly infinite) sequence of positive and negative examples.
Output: a sequence of logic programs covering all the presented positive examples, but none of the presented negative examples.
Algorithm:

set the program *P* to the empty set of clauses;
repeat
  read the next example;
  repeat
    if *P* finitely fails on a known positive example {*P* is incomplete}
      then find an atom *A* that is not covered by *P*
        and add to *P* a new clause that covers *A*;
    if *P* succeeds on a known negative example {*P* is incorrect}
      then remove from *P* a clause found to be wrong;
  until *P* is complete wrt all positive examples and correct wrt all negative examples;
  write *P*
forever *or* *until* no examples are left.

A key feature is the *clause generator* used in case of incompleteness (*bug correction*). It is parameterized on a specialization operator, and thus easily adaptable to different clause languages. We here focus on the operator that enumerates definite clauses, and which is thus used for logic program synthesis. Other operators would enumerate definite clause grammars, and so on. The enumeration of definite clauses may be carefully designed so as to achieve the objective of intelligent pruning of the search space. The clauses are partially ordered by the subsumption relation into a

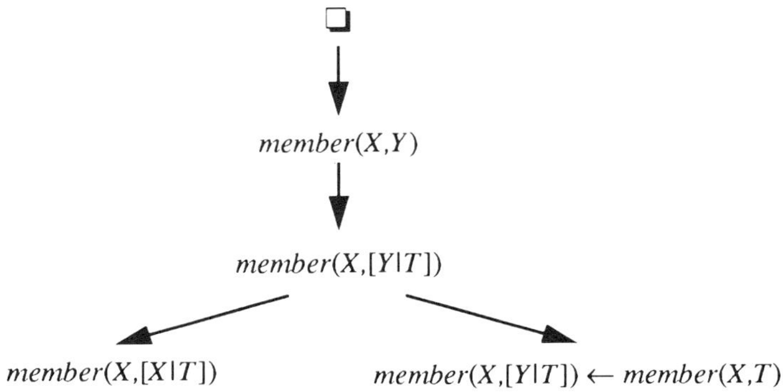

Figure 3-2: Part of the specialization graph for the *member*/2 predicate

specialization graph. Thus, if a clause is found to be wrong, then it need never be considered again, and its immediate descendants in the specialization graph are considered plausible replacements. This is an accurate technique for locating and avoiding forbidden features, and definitely a better technique than backtracking. In order to be realistic, this operator however needs a declaration of the basis set of all the predicates that may appear in clauses. The specialization graph is searched breadth-first.

Example 3-14: Part of the specialization graph for the *member*/2 predicate is in Figure 3-2 (where the vertical arrows denote subsumption). For convenience, the specialization operator was also given the type information that the first parameter of *member*/2 is a term, and that its second parameter is a list. ♦

The *bug location* diagnoses in case of incompleteness and incorrectness are performed by experiment generation and classification queries to an *oracle*. Shapiro has experimented with three different search strategies to find a clause that covers a given atom (in case of incompleteness):

- the *eager strategy* is the most powerful as it always succeeds, but this is at the expense of many (often superfluous) queries to the oracle;
- the *lazy strategy* is less powerful, but formulates no queries at all, because it relies on the already presented positive examples;
- the *adaptive strategy* is a compromise in power between the first two strategies; it formulates no queries at all, because it relies on the already presented positive examples and on the currently hypothesized program.

The classes of programs that can be obtained via these strategies are different. Identification-in-the-limit is guaranteed by all three strategies under some well-defined preconditions. See the evaluation section below for further comments on these strategies.

Let's illustrate all this on a simple synthesis.

Example 3-15: During the synthesis of a program for the *member*/2 problem, the (here heavily annotated) dialog between MIS and the user goes basically as follows:

MIS: Declare the predicate to be synthesized.

User: *member*/2.

MIS: What are the predicates used by *member*/2? (That is: what is the basis set?)

User: *member*/2. (The user here anticipates that the target logic program is recursive, and that no other predicates will be useful.)

MIS: The initial program P_0 is { }. First example?

User: *member*(*a*,[*a*]).

MIS: P_0 is incomplete, because *member*(*a*,[*a*]) is not covered. After a call to the clause generator, the revised program P_1 is {*member*(*X*,*Y*)}, which is correct wrt the examples presented so far. Next example?

User: $\neg$*member*(*a*,[*b*]).

MIS: P_1 is incorrect, because *member*(*a*,[*b*]) is covered. The first, and only, clause of P_1 is removed. The resulting empty program is incomplete, because *member*(*a*,[*a*]) is not covered. After a call to the clause generator, the revised program is {*member*(*X*,[*Y*|*T*])}. This program is incorrect, because *member*(*a*,[*b*]) is covered. Its first, and only, clause is removed. The resulting empty program is incomplete, because *member*(*a*,[*a*]) is not covered. After a call to the clause generator, the revised program P_2 is {*member*(*X*,[*X*|*T*])}, which is correct wrt the examples presented so far. Next example?

User: *member*(*a*,[*b*,*a*]).

MIS: P_2 is incomplete, because *member*(*a*,[*b*,*a*]) is not covered. After a call to the clause generator, the revised program P_3 is {*member*(*X*,[*X*|*T*]); *member*(*X*,[*Y*|*T*]) $\leftarrow$ *member*(*X*,*T*)}, which is correct wrt the examples presented so far. Next example?

Suppose the user now stops presenting examples. MIS has synthesized a correct logic program for the *member*/2 predicate. This sample synthesis is admittedly a little bit contrived (and actually devoid of queries to the oracle), but the point is here to get a feel for this synthesis mechanism. ♦

Let's summarize: MIS starts from a mixed presentation of multiple, ground, single-predicate, relational, positive and negative examples that are selected by an agent (usually a human specifier) who knows the intended relation, and who is assumed to select only examples that are consistent with the intended relation. The hypotheses are definite programs. A conceptual bias on the program language is achieved by the declaration of a basis set of predicates that may appear in the bodies of clauses. The background knowledge consists of logic programs for some of the basis set predicates. The search space is ordered by the sample-independent subsumption relation, which is however undecidable in general: hence the need for resource-bounded subsumption checking. The used identification criterion is identification-in-the-limit. MIS however doesn't proceed by enumeration, because of its intelligent organization of the search space. Type, mode, and determinism information about the specified predicate is used for further restriction of the search space. MIS performs incremental (actually even iterative) synthesis, which is moreover breadth-first data-driven, algorithmic, interactive, non-monotonic, consistent, and conservative. Multiple related concepts are learned simultaneously.

Extensions

MIS has spawned a huge variety of efforts for improvement. Some immediate optimizations were proposed by [Huntbach 86].

Other researchers have tackled Shapiro's remarks on oracle mechanization [Shapiro 82, Section 3.7] via the incorporation of "constraints and partial specifications". The solutions by [Lichtenstein and Shapiro 88], [Drabent *et al.* 88], and [De Raedt and Bruynooghe 92a] are surveyed in Chapter 6. The solution by [Dershowitz and Lee 93] seems unrealistic in general, because it relies on a complete specification, which could thus rather be used to perform deductive synthesis.

The search for clauses goes from general-to-specific, using a most-general-specialization operator to descend a subsumption hierarchy. But subsumption is a weak model of generalization: it is insufficient because many "wanted" generalizations are not obtained, due to the lack of background knowledge, and inadequate because many "unwanted" generalizations are obtained. Background knowledge should thus be used for inferring more "interesting" generalizations. In Chapter 7, we survey the efforts of [Buntine 88] and [Muggleton 91] for introducing stronger models of generalization. The MARKUS system of [Bratko and Grobelnik 93] [Grobelnik 94] introduces other improvements of the clause generator. [Bergadano and Gunetti 94] suggest constraining and refining the hypothesis space (set of allowed clauses) so as to improve the scope and efficiency of learning.

Finally, the notion of logic program schema (see Chapter 8) allows a further organization of the search space. The system of [Tinkham 90] is based on the insight that synthesis need not start from the empty program, but could actually start from the most-specific schema that is believed to be applicable. The search space is thus extended to a second-order search space, at the bottom of which are logic programs, and at the top of which are logic program schemas. If synthesis starts from a "good" schema, then the improvement is exponential. A similar approach is taken by the MISST system of [Sterling and Kirschenbaum 93], who develop a new specialization operator, based upon a view of logic programs as skeletons (schemas) to which programming techniques (standard programming practices) are applied.

Evaluation

The complexity and power of MIS compare favorably with the trace-based synthesis mechanisms of Biermann and Summers (see Section 3.3.2). Since it is parameterized on a specialization operator, it is much more adaptable than these other mechanisms. However, MIS is much less data-efficient than the latter.

The eager search-strategy is not sensitive to the order of presentation of the examples. However, the lazy search strategy is order-sensitive. [Shapiro 82, page 110] shows how an (inadvertent) adversary user might trick MIS (equipped with the lazy strategy) into synthesizing an arbitrarily large program: the example sequence *member*(*a*,[*a*]), *member*(*b*,[*a*,*b*]), *member*(*c*,[*a*,*b*,*c*]), ..., generates the infinite logic program {*member*(*X*,[*X*|*T*]); *member*(*X*,[*Y*,*X*|*T*]); *member*(*X*,[*Z*,*Y*,*X*|*T*]); ...}. This is clearly not a desirable behavior. But the research of [Jantke 89] [Jantke and Goldammer 92] seems a possible solution to this situation, as their synthesis mechanism starts from precisely such clause sequences.

The adaptive strategy is less order-sensitive, and said to be the most useful one in practice. However, it may result in dead code (clauses that always lead to failure), namely when it relies on a clause yet unknown to be incorrect. Again, this is not a desirable behavior.

Another consequence of order-dependence arises because MIS synthesizes Prolog programs, rather than some form of logic algorithms: an (inadvertent) adversary user might trick MIS into synthesizing the base-case clause after the recursive clause. While declaratively correct, such a program goes into infinite loops for certain call-modes.

Moreover, as reported by [Sterling and Kirschenbaum 93], MIS is likely to generate redundant clauses. Removing these seems too computationally expensive to be practical, although the work of [Buntine 88] gives promising ideas towards this.

All the predicates used by the clause generator must be declared prior to synthesis, and an oracle is assumed to be willing to answer questions about them. Multiple related concepts may be learned simultaneously, but this feature doesn't prevent MIS from being unable to invent its own predicates, not to mention implementing them.

Other weak spots are those addressed by the above-mentioned extensions. However, MIS should not be discredited, because it is after all a pioneering system.

3.4.2 Other Model-Based Synthesis Systems

The other ancestor system of ILP [Sammut 93], though much less influential, is CONFUCIUS (see [Cohen and Sammut 84]), which has been very much inspired by Banerji's research (see [Banerji 84]). From positive and negative examples, this system incrementally synthesizes a program by oscillating between over- and under-generalization. The mechanism is however largely heuristic-based. It has no background knowledge and no oracle. Recursion is discovered in a way similar to the trace-folding of [Biermann 78]. A successor system is MARVIN [Sammut and Banerji 86], which also uses only a single generalization rule in its specific-to-general search. But it uses background knowledge, and asks questions to an oracle in order to test its hypotheses. It is unable to invent its own predicates, but rather expects to be taught simple concepts before complex ones.

The INDUCE systems (see [Michalski 84]) were among the first to address the issues of using constructive rules of inductive inference. The learning mechanism is a bottom-up approximation-driven one, though heavily based on heuristics.

The CIGOL ("logic" backwards) system of [Muggleton and Buntine 88] performs interactive, incremental synthesis from a mixed presentation of multiple, ground, relational, positive and negative examples, in the presence of background knowledge. It also addresses constructive induction. The technique is based on the ingenious insight that if resolution of clauses (by unification of two literals of the same predicate p, but of opposite signs) may make disappear predicate p in the resolvent clause (namely if there are no other occurrences of p in the two resolved clauses), then inverse resolution (using anti-unification) may make appear a predicate, and its clausal definition. The system is restricted to generating unit clauses for the invented predicate, and the teacher is then asked to name the latter from these unit clauses (which are nothing else but non-ground examples). If the identified name is unknown to the system, then synthesis occurs from these unit clauses. The successor system, GOLEM [Muggleton and Feng 90], extends these ideas. Another descendant system is ITOU [Rouveirol 91], which is based on the inversion of logical entailment, rather than of resolution.

The CLINT (*Concept Learning in an INTeractive way*) system of [De Raedt 92] [De Raedt and Bruynooghe 92ab] incrementally learns multiple related concepts simultaneously, from a mixed presentation of multiple, ground, relational, positive and negative examples, in the presence of background knowledge and integrity constraints. The bug correction component is an adaptation of MIS. Identification-in-the-limit is guaranteed. The system automatically shifts its syntactic bias when needed. It generates itself almost all the examples it needs, and interacts with an oracle for the classification of these examples as positive or negative ones. It assimilates newly learned concepts by adding them to its knowledge base. Predicate invention is tackled by analogical inference wrt assimilated concepts. A successor system is CLAUDIEN [De Raedt and Bruynooghe 93].

The FOIL (*First-Order Inductive Learner*) system of [Quinlan 90] extends propositional attribute-value learners to the first-order formalism of relations and definite clauses, in view of benefitting from the additional expressive power. The system is very different from all others described here, in that it performs passive, non-incremental learning from positive and negative examples. Compared to MIS, it constructs clauses literal-by-literal, rather than using a clause-generator; the notions of proof, oracle, and background knowledge are absent; and the hypothesized program is the maximally-general one, rather than the maximally-specific one, as in MIS. On the negative side, its greedy, heuristic-based search for suitable literals to expand a clause prevents all backtracking. Recursive programs are considered, though at the expense of potential non-termination. There is no predicate invention. Moreover, extremely large example sets are needed for successful learning: for instance, 10,261 examples are reported to be needed for *append*/3, and 4,761 examples for *reverse*/2. All this shows that FOIL seems inadequate for recursive program synthesis.

The LINUS system of [Lavrač and Džeroski 94] learns relational concept descriptions, but works by first transforming the examples into propositional form, and then using propositional attribute-value learners (which may handle noisy examples).

A completely different approach is advocated by [Hagiya 90]. He re-formulates Summers' recurrence relation detection mechanism in a logic framework, using higher-order unification in a type theory with a recursion operator. The method is extended to synthesizing deductive proofs-by-induction from concrete sample proofs.

The work of [Jorge and Brazdil 94] is another attempt at trace-based synthesis of logic programs. Their specifications by examples are augmented with partial execution traces, called algorithm sketches.

3.5 Conclusions on Program Synthesis from Examples

In Section 3.2.4, we have defined algorithm synthesis from examples as a niche of empirical learning from examples. As a reminder, for algorithm synthesis, we are here only interested in the setting with *human* specifiers who *know* (even if only informally) the intended relation, and who are assumed to choose only examples that are *consistent* with the intended relation. Moreover, the intended relation is assumed to have a *recursive* algorithm. There is a general consensus that a synthesizer from examples would be a useful component of any larger synthesis system. So we now draw some conclusions about the approaches surveyed in the previous two sections.

The surveyed trace-based mechanisms of LISP program synthesis actually turn out to be pretty much orthogonal to those of model-based Prolog program synthesis. They were developed in different time-periods (until the late 1970s, and since the early 1980s, respectively), and the latter seem to have completely supplanted the former. This supersession is largely due to the "declaration of defeat" by the former (because of the mechanisms, not because of the target language), and to the ensuing search for new approaches. The growing awareness of the early 1980s that concept descriptions and logic programs may share the same formalism has even provoked a gradual absorption of program synthesis from examples by the field of empirical learning. This culminates in the designation *Inductive Logic Programming* (ILP), which is unfortunately a misleading name because it gives too much tribute to "programming", compared at least to the current trends of ILP research. The logic programming paradigm has blurred the distinction between learning-from-examples and programming-by-examples. While academically rewarding, this new perception seems very dangerous to us in practice: as Section 3.2.4 shows, the superclass relation between both fields is sufficiently "strict" to justify highly specialized mechanisms for the latter—at least now, where both fields are still young, though maturing. The future will tell whether there effectively is a unique and efficient learning mechanism for all classes of concepts. However, we strongly doubt this!

All the surveyed mechanisms perform pretty well on predicates that involve only structural manipulations of their parameters, such as list concatenation or list reversal. But as soon as the actual values of the parameters are relevant (such as for list sorting), problems arise due to the inherent incompleteness and ambiguity of specifications by examples. There is thus an important need for making more knowledge available to synthesis, because such knowledge is after all available to human algorithm designers. Knowledge may be given under the form of extended incomplete specifications, of background knowledge (domain knowledge, for instance), and of algorithm design knowledge. Whereas (some of) the 1970s approaches were pretty much on the analytic (EBL) side of machine learning (though without background knowledge, and thus necessarily enumerative), most of the 1980s-and-beyond approaches are definitely on the empirical side of machine learning. Today's trend seems fortunately to be towards an integration of analytic (knowledge-reliant) and empirical (user-reliant) learning, and this in view of cross-fertilization for overcoming drawbacks.

Although human learning is naturally incremental and non-monotonic, we believe that automated algorithm synthesis from examples should be non-incremental and monotonic. Indeed, incremental synthesizers tend to be very "undisciplined" due to their non-monotonic debugging (patchwork) approach. This need not always be the case, for instance if the examples (and their ordering) are "well-chosen". But one should bear in mind that the specifier is not always supervising the synthesis. And even if s/he were, putting the synthesizer (back) on the right track with a carefully crafted example goes counter the most frequent setting where the specifier doesn't know how to best define the intended relation by an algorithm, and is possibly even unable to understand an algorithm. The risks of infinite, redundant, or dead code due to the potential sensitivity to the order of the presented examples are symptomatic for some incremental mechanisms that have no understanding of what they are synthesizing. Considering that an example embodies several kinds of information, incremental synthesis has to extract all these kinds of information from the examples presented so far, whereas non-incremental synthesis may extract only one kind of information from every example at each step. The latter seems to us to be a much more reasonable approach. We thus believe that a synthesis mechanism should carefully design, just like an expert human designer (and unlike an inexpert human learner), a correct algorithm in a monotonic way from a fixed set of given examples.

The current trend of ILP research seems [Muggleton 91] to be towards handling noisy examples, and to PAC-identification, whose probabilistic approach to correctness is however inherently incompatible with the goals of algorithm synthesis. The most promising applications of ILP research seem [Muggleton 91] to be when the intended concept is unknown, which also does not fit our algorithm synthesis setting. There is general skepticism about the usefulness of program schemas, because these tend either to spell out the entire search space (which is fruitless), or to be too domain-specific (and hence difficult to obtain), if they exist at all. All this clearly indicates a desire to do empirical learning in general, rather than "only" algorithm synthesis. The achievements of ILP are already very impressive [Muggleton 91]. But this quest for a general mechanism is inevitably at the cost of a poor synthesis of recursive algorithms, because the developed learners often merely perform some kind of example-analysis in a pre-enumerated search space, whereas algorithm synthesis requires more complex operations such as generating logic quantifiers. We are here not interested in learning to recognize Michalski's trains or Winston's arches.

4 A LOGIC PROGRAM DEVELOPMENT METHODOLOGY

This research is set in the framework of the logic program development methodology described in [Deville 90]. In order to keep this book self-sufficient, we summarize that methodology, and put special focus on aspects directly related to our research. This summary mainly states results, and not always their motivations or proofs: refer to [Deville 90] when in need of further explanations.

The original promise of programming in (first-order) logic when using Prolog is impaired by the following facts:

- the Prolog inference engine is incomplete, unfair, and unsound;
- the Prolog inference engine approximates logical negation by negation-as-failure;
- the Prolog language embodies control predicates (!/0, ...), extra-logical predicates (side-effect predicates, *clause*/2, *assert*/1, *retract*/1, ...), meta-logical predicates (*ground*/1, *var*/1, *call*/1, ==/2, ...), and second-order predicates (*setof*/3, ...), which allow programming outside first-order logic;
- Prolog procedures are rarely multi-directional.

But all these features have been deliberately chosen so as to make Prolog a practical programming language.

So there is a need for a maximally language-independent logic programming methodology that reconciles this gap between the declarative and the procedural semantics. Alternative approaches would have been either to forget about declarative logic programming, or to design a new language not suffering from that gap, or to design a new logic filling that gap. But these approaches have not been judged to be very attractive.

Such a methodology has been formulated. It aims at programming-in-the-small, and is (mainly) meant for algorithmic problems. It is sub-divided into three stages: [5]

- Stage A: Elaboration of a specification;
- Stage B: Design of a logic algorithm (and possibly its transformation);
- Stage C: Derivation of a logic program (and possibly its transformation).

Stage B is based only on the declarative semantics of logic, and is independent of the target logic programming language used at Stage C.

An integrated logic programming environment, called *Folon*,[6] is being developed to support the entire methodology [Henrard and Le Charlier 92].

Note however that this book is independent of that methodology. We just use its framework because of its useful notations and its focus on the logical aspect of logic program development.

This chapter is organized as follows. In Section 4.1, we discuss the elaboration of specifications. Section 4.2 is about the design of logic algorithms, whereas Section 4.3 is about their transformation. Section 4.4 describes the derivation of logic programs, whereas Section 4.5 describes their transformation.

5. Note that we say "logic algorithm" where [Deville 90] says "logic description". This terminology was already used in [Deville 87], which was the starting point for [Deville 90].
6. The environment is named after Jean-Michel Folon, a famous contemporary Belgian painter.

```
Procedure
   compress(L,C)
Types
   L: list of term
   C: list of <term,integer>
Restrictions on Parameters
   compactList(C)
Directionalities
   in(ground,novar):out(ground,ground) <0-1>
   in(ground, var ):out(ground,ground) <1-1>
Relation
   C is the compression of L
```

Figure 4-1: *Spec(compress)*

4.1 Elaboration of a Specification

The first stage of the methodology is the elaboration of a specification. Informally, a specification of a procedure is a statement describing the problem that is to be implemented, as well as how to correctly use the resulting procedure. We here restrict the focus to side-effect-free problems.

Definition 4-1: A *specification* of a procedure for predicate r/n, denoted *Spec*(r), is composed of a procedure declaration, a type declaration for each parameter, a set of restrictions on parameters, a set of directionalities, and a relation definition.

We present the involved components only by means of a few sample specifications.

Example 4-1: A possible version of *Spec(compress)* is in Figure 4-1. Note that the first four entries are here written in a formal language, while the relation entry is non-formal. The first three entries are assumed to be self-explanatory. The first directionality says that given L ground and C a non-variable, there is at most one ground instance of C such that *compress*(L,C) succeeds. The second directionality says that given L ground and C a variable, there is exactly one ground instance of C such that *compress*(L,C) succeeds. Other directionalities could have been given (for instance for L non-ground), but we only want a procedure satisfying the two given ones.

Example 4-2: A possible version of *Spec*(*firstPlateau*) is given in Figure 4-2.

The different entries of a specification act as pre- and/or post-conditions.

4.2 Design of a Logic Algorithm

The second stage of the methodology is the design of an algorithm, independently of any logic programming language, starting from the specification of a procedure. Such an algorithm is expressed in first-order logic, and called a logic algorithm. The design is based solely on the declarative semantics of first-order logic. This implies that the directionality information from the specification is not used at this stage.

Definition 4-2: A *logic algorithm* defining a predicate r/n, denoted *LA*(r), is a closed well-formed formula of the form:

```
Procedure
  firstPlateau(L,P,S)
Types
  L,P,S: list of term
Restrictions on Parameters
  L≠[] ∧ P≠[]
Directionalities
  in(ground,novar,novar):out(ground,ground,ground) <0-1>
  in(ground, var , var ):out(ground,ground,ground) <1-1>
Relation
  P is the first maximal plateau of L,
   and S is the corresponding suffix of L
```

Figure 4-2: *Spec(firstPlateau)*

```
compress(L,C) ⇔
      L=[]               ∧ C=[]
    ∨ L=[HL]             ∧ C=[<HL,1>]
    ∨ L=[HL1,HL2|TL]     ∧ HL1≠HL2
                         ∧ compress([HL2|TL],TC)
                         ∧ C=[<HL1,1>|TC]
    ∨ L=[HL1,HL2|TL]     ∧ HL1=HL2
                         ∧ compress([HL2|TL],TC)
                         ∧ C=[<V,s(N)>|TTC] ∧ TC=[<V,N>|TTC]
```

Logic Algorithm 4-1: *LA(compress)*

```
firstPlateau(L,P,S) ⇔
      L=[HL]             ∧ P=L ∧ S=[]
    ∨ L=[HL1,HL2|TL]     ∧ HL1≠HL2
                         ∧ P=[HL1] ∧ S=[HL2|TL] ∧ list(TL)
    ∨ L=[HL1,HL2|TL]     ∧ HL1=HL2
                         ∧ firstPlateau([HL2|TL],TP,TS)
                         ∧ P=[HL1|TP] ∧ S=TS
```

Logic Algorithm 4-2: *LA(firstPlateau)*

$$\forall X_1 \ldots \forall X_n \quad r(X_1,\ldots,X_n) \Leftrightarrow B$$

where the X_i are distinct variables, and B is a well-formed formula. The atom $r(X_1,\ldots,X_n)$ is called the *head*, and B is called the *body* of the logic algorithm.

In the following, we drop the universal quantifications in front of the heads, as well as any existential quantifications at the beginnings of bodies of logic algorithms.

Example 4-3: A possible version of *LA(compress)* is Logic Algorithm 4-1.

Example 4-4: A possible version of *LA(firstPlateau)* is Logic Algorithm 4-2.

Note that logic algorithms take the "natural" form of what one would expect to be a logic program (that implements an algorithmic problem). Indeed, the equivalence symbol is necessary to state when *r*/*n* is *true*, as well as when *r*/*n* is *false*. Logic algorithms correspond in fact to the notion of completed logic programs [Clark 78]. Hence, reasoning on logic algorithms is equivalent to using logic programs, but reasoning on their completions.

The correctness of a logic algorithm wrt its specification is an important issue. All the predicates used in a logic algorithm are considered as primitives, and the existence of correct logic algorithms is thus assumed for all of them. Throughout this book, we adopt the following primitives: =/2, ≠/2, </2, >/2, ≤/2, ≥/2, *list*/1, and *odd*/1.

This allows a definition of logic algorithm correctness that is only in terms of the specifications of the used predicates. It establishes an equivalence between the specified relation and the set of Herbrand-logical consequences of the logic algorithm.

Definition 4-3: Let *Spec*(*r*) be a specification, *LA*(*r*) be a logic algorithm, and $\mathcal{A}$ be a finite set of logic algorithms containing *LA*(*r*). Then *LA*(*r*) is (*totally*) *correct* in $\mathcal{A}$ wrt *Spec*(*r*) iff, for any ground *n*-tuple ***t***, the following two conditions hold:

$$\mathcal{A} \models r(\boldsymbol{t}) \quad \text{iff} \quad \boldsymbol{t} \in \mathcal{R} \text{ and } \boldsymbol{t} \in dom(r)$$

$$\mathcal{A} \models \neg r(\boldsymbol{t}) \quad \text{iff} \quad \boldsymbol{t} \notin \mathcal{R} \text{ or } \boldsymbol{t} \notin dom(r)$$

The second condition is necessary because negation can be used in logic algorithms. Note that this definition is restricted to ground terms: this simplifies proofs and does not affect the existence of correct witnesses to existential queries. Also, this definition implies that a logic algorithm has to verify whether its parameters belong to the domain of the procedure. The opposite approach is taken at the logic program level.

A correct logic algorithm is Herbrand-satisfiable. The truth value of a ground atom *r*(***t***) is the same in every Herbrand model of a correct logic algorithm *LA*(*r*). A correct logic algorithm remains correct if a new logic algorithm is added.

There are of course many methodologies of logic algorithm design. Deville discusses three of them, namely construction by structural induction, top-down decomposition, and iteration through universal quantification. We here only have a look at the first of these methodologies, because it is the most important one. It is based on structural induction. The *principle of well-founded induction* suggests constructing a logic algorithm by induction over the structure of some parameter. The value of that *induction parameter* is reduced to something smaller according to some *well-founded relation*, and a partial result is recursively computed. If no reduction is possible, then the problem is solved directly. There are four steps to this design methodology:

- Step 1: Selection of an induction parameter;
- Step 2: Selection of a well-founded relation;
- Step 3: Selection of the structural forms of the induction parameter;
- Step 4: Construction of the structural cases.

Let's explain these four steps one by one. Note that this method is proven to yield correct logic algorithms. A tool, called *Logist*, is being developed for the *Folon* environment to assist a designer in following these steps [Deville and Burnay 89].

Step 1: Selection of an Induction Parameter

The first step is the selection of an induction parameter. Only parameters of inductive types (such as integers, lists, trees, sets, strings,...) are eligible as induction parameters. For simplicity, throughout this book, we assume that no parameters are tuples.

Definition 4-4: A *simple induction parameter* is composed of only one parameter. A *compound induction parameter* is composed of at least two parameters.

Most problems can be implemented by logic algorithms with induction over a simple induction parameter.

The selection of a suitable induction parameter is straightforward, but two useful heuristics have been identified:

Heuristic 4-1: *Functionality Heuristic*
Select an induction parameter such that, given a ground instance of it, the specified relation holds for at most one ground instance of the other parameters.

This heuristic usually simplifies the remainder of the design process.

Heuristic 4-2: *Directionality Heuristic*
Select an induction parameter that is ground in the *in*-parts of all the directionalities.

This heuristic only reveals its advantages when one looks ahead: at the logic program derivation stage (Section 4.4), domain checking and termination proofs are simplified, and the derived logic programs usually are more efficient. One could thus argue that this heuristic is the best.

Example 4-5: For the *compress*/2 problem, both heuristics lead towards selecting *L* as the induction parameter.

In the sequel, when talking about a logic algorithm *LA*(*r*), we sometimes write *LA*(*r*-*X*) to show that *X* was selected as induction parameter. Note however that the predicate defined by *LA*(*r*-*X*) still is *r*, and not *r*-*X*.

Step 2: Selection of a Well-Founded Relation

The second step is the selection of a well-founded relation (wfr) over the type of the induction parameter. Two heuristics have been identified:

Heuristic 4-3: *Intrinsic Heuristic*
Select a wfr reflecting the definition of the type of the induction parameter.

This is easy since the definition itself of an inductive type already suggests a wfr.

Example 4-6: For the *compress*/2 problem, the intrinsic heuristic leads towards selecting "is the tail of" as well-founded relation over the type of *L*. Weaker relations such as "has less elements than" or "is a suffix of" are also suitable, but it is best to start with strong relations, and relax them as needed.

Heuristic 4-4: *Extrinsic Heuristic*
Select a well-founded relation that reflects the definition of the type of some other parameter, or that reflects the structure of the specified relation.

Applying this heuristic is often more complicated, but the ensuing construction steps can then often be simplified.

Example 4-7: For the *compress*/2 problem, the extrinsic heuristic leads towards selecting "has one plateau less than" as well-founded relation over the type of *L*, because it reflects the structure of the *C* parameter. But we retain the well-founded relation suggested by the Intrinsic Heuristic for the remainder of this section, and come back to this decision in Section 5.2.1.

None of these two heuristics is superior to the other. In the sequel, when talking about a logic algorithm *LA(r)*, we sometimes write *LA(r-int-X)*, or *LA(r-ext-X)*, to show that *X* was selected as induction parameter, and that the intrinsic (respectively extrinsic) heuristic was applied. Again, the predicate defined by *LA(r-int-X)* still is *r*, and not *r-int-X*.

An interesting exercise is to compare logic algorithms designed by induction on different parameters, or using different well-founded relations. Considering the heuristics above, it is no surprise that, for a binary predicate *r* having *X* and *Y* as parameters, *LA(r-int-X)* and *LA(r-ext-Y)* are structurally similar, or that *LA(r-int-Y)* and *LA(r-ext-X)* are structurally similar.

Step 3: Selection of the Structural Forms of the Induction Parameter

The third step is the selection of the structural forms of the induction parameter. *Structural forms* are terms. This step consists of finding at least one minimal form and at least one non-minimal form for the induction parameter, such that they partition the domain of the induction parameter. A *non-minimal form* is a structure case of the domain of the induction parameter. A *minimal form* is a base case of the domain of the induction parameter, that is a form to which at least one sample computation starting from a non-minimal form eventually reduces the induction parameter.

Example 4-8: For the *compress*/2 problem, we select [] as the minimal form, and $[HL_1|TL]$ as the non-minimal form of the induction parameter *L*.

Step 4: Construction of the Structural Cases

The fourth and last step is the construction of the structural cases. This amounts to formalizing how the other parameters relate to the induction parameter, for each of its structural forms. The results are *structural cases*. A structural case is a *minimal case* if the induction parameter is of a minimal form, and a *non-minimal case* if the induction parameter is of a non-minimal form. This step is the most creative one, and requires a lot of skill. It is actually divided into two sub-steps:

- Step 4-1: Construction of the structural cases, independently of domains;
- Step 4-2: Introduction of domain-checking literals.

The second sub-step is important in view of achieving correctness of the designed logic algorithm. Indeed, the logic algorithm must evaluate to *false* in case the parameters do not belong to the domain. With a domains-as-preconditions approach, domain checking literals would have to be added to ensure that the used predicates are correctly used. In most situations, Step 4-2 reduces to doing nothing at all.

Example 4-9: For the *compress*/2 problem, we proceed as follows:

- if *L* is of the selected minimal form (*L* = []), then *C* must be empty, too (*C* = []);
- if *L* is of the selected non-minimal form ($L = [HL_1|TL]$), then:
  - either *TL* is empty, and *C* must then be $[<HL_1,1>]$;
  - or *TL* is non-empty and starts with a term identical to HL_1, and *C* must then be $[<HL_1,s(N)>|TC]$, where $compress(TL,[<HL_1,N>|TC])$ holds;
  - or *TL* is non-empty and starts with a term different from HL_1, and *C* must then be $[<HL_1,1>|TC]$, where *compress(TL,TC)* holds.

```
compress(L,C) ⇔
      L=[]              ∧ C=[]
    ∨ L=[HL1|TL]        ∧ TL=[]
                        ∧ C=[<HL1,1>]
    ∨ L=[HL1|TL]        ∧ TL=[HL2|TTL] ∧ HL1=HL2
                        ∧ compress(TL,[<HL1,N>|TC])
                        ∧ C=[<HL1,s(N)>|TC]
    ∨ L=[HL1|TL]        ∧ TL=[HL2|TTL] ∧ HL1≠HL2
                        ∧ compress(TL,TC)
                        ∧ C=[<HL1,1>|TC]
```

Logic Algorithm 4-3: *LA(compress-int-L)*

No domain-checking literals need to be added. We obtain Logic Algorithm 4-3, which is equivalent to Logic Algorithm 4-1. ♦

4.3 Transformation of a Logic Algorithm

Correctness-preserving transformations of logic algorithms aim at allowing the derivation of more efficient logic programs at Stage C. The truly creative effort thus goes into the design of a first, correct logic algorithm, without any concern for its form and complexity. Moreover, the ensuing transformation is often easier to perform than the design from scratch of an optimized algorithm.

A set of correctness-preserving transformation rules (such as folding, unfolding, ...) has been developed, but we don't list them here. They allow the syntactic simplification of logic algorithms, the transformation of a logic algorithm into another one that reflects induction on a different parameter, the transformation of a logic algorithm into another one that reflects a computational generalization of the original problem, the merging of several predicates sharing some parameter(s) into one predicate, and so on. These transformations only deal with the declarative semantics of logic.

4.4 Derivation of a Logic Program

The third and last stage of the methodology is the derivation of a logic program, starting from the designed logic algorithm. This is a language-specific task and has thus to take into account all aspects that make logic programming different from programming in a specific language (Prolog, say). These aspects are the features of the underlying inference engine (such as incompleteness, unsoundness, and unfairness due to the search rule, the computation rule, the negation-as-failure rule, the absence of an occur-check), as well as some primitives of the programming language (extra-logical, meta-logical, second-order, and control predicates). The procedural semantics of logic is now considered, and the directionality information of specifications is now used.

A straightforward syntactic translation of a logic algorithm into a pure logic program already achieves partial correctness and completeness wrt the specification, whatever the used SLDNF refutation procedure. This translation amounts to a "decompletion" process, as the completion of the pure logic program resulting from the syntactic translation of a logic algorithm is logically equivalent to that logic algorithm.

```
compress(L,C)  ←  L=[],
                  C=[]

compress(L,C)  ←  L=[HL1|TL],TL=[],
                  C=[<HL1,1>]

compress(L,C)  ←  L=[HL1|TL],TL=[HL2|TTL],
                  HL1=HL2,
                  compress(TL,[<HL1,N>|TC]),
                  C=[<HL1,s(N)>|TC]

compress(L,C)  ←  L=[HL1|TL],TL=[HL2|TTL],
                  not(HL1=HL2),
                  compress(TL,TC),
                  C=[<HL1,1>|TC]
```

Figure 4-3: *LP(compress-int-L)*

```
compress([],[])
compress([HL1],[<HL1,1>])
compress([HL1,HL2|TTL],[<HL1,s(N)>|TC]) ←
                       HL1=HL2,!,
                       compress([HL2|TTL],[<HL1,N>|TC])
compress([HL1,HL2|TTL],[<HL1,1>|TC]) ←
                       compress([HL2|TTL],TC)
```

Figure 4-4: A transformed version of *LP(compress-int-L)*

The remaining, rather technical correctness criteria are specific to every SLDNF refutation procedure. These aspects are usually a simple manual task. They can also be handled by data-flow analysis or abstract interpretation techniques that reveal, for each directionality, a correct permutation of the program clauses, and a correct permutation of the literals in the body of each clause, and sometimes the addition or deletion of literals. Multi-directionality is usually difficult to achieve. The corresponding tool of the *Folon* environment is described by [De Boeck and Le Charlier 90].

Example 4-10: For the *compress*/2 problem, the pure logic program derived from Logic Algorithm 4-3 is given in Figure 4-3.

4.5 Transformation of a Logic Program

Correctness-preserving transformations of logic programs aim at optimizing the derived pure logic program into a time/space-efficient Prolog program. They are based on the procedural semantics (computation rule, search rule), the control predicates and the implementation features (anonymous variables, tail recursion optimization, clause indexing, ...) of Prolog systems, as well as on partial evaluation, the properties of equality, and so on. These transformation rules are irrelevant in our context.

Example 4-11: For the *compress*/2 problem, Figure 4-4 gives a transformed version of the logic program in Figure 4-3.

5 OBJECTIVES

The objective of this book is (semi-)automatic logic algorithm synthesis. First, in Section 5.1, we define this objective in more detail and clearly state its boundaries. In order to motivate this research, we develop a series of sample problems in Section 5.2 and show that non-trivial issues have to be solved. This allows us to identify, in Section 5.3, the challenges of logic algorithm synthesis.

5.1 Precise Statement of the Objective

The objective of this book is (semi-)automatic logic algorithm synthesis. This means that our research is set in a logic programming framework, and that there is exclusive concern about the synthesis of correct logic algorithms, but no concern at all about algorithm complexity, algorithm transformation, algorithm implementation, program transformation, or data structure reification. This modular approach achieves reuse of existing and forthcoming research on (logic) algorithm transformation and implementation. Indeed, the design of correct (logic) algorithms is already sufficiently hard, so there is no need to complicate matters with simultaneous considerations about time/space complexity or implementability. The so-called "naive" version of the *reverse* algorithm is thus a perfectly convenient result, because it is correct, it can be automatically transformed into a more efficient algorithm, and it can be automatically implemented into an executable form.

Moreover, the focus is on the synthesis of algorithms for the so-called algorithmic problems, and actually, to be even more precise, on the synthesis of recursive algorithms, where the intentions may correspond to a full-fledged relation (and not just to a total function). The following two assumptions are made. First, we assume that the specifier knows the intended relation, even if s/he doesn't have a formal definition of it. Second, we assume that the actually specified relation is a subset of the intended relation. This means that there is assumed to be no noise in specifications. Other aims are that the developed synthesis mechanism be able to synthesize entire families of algorithms from a single specification, and that a fair amount of algorithm design knowledge and domain knowledge be available to it.

A first question that naturally comes to mind is: What specification language to use? As the relation entry in the specification language of [Deville 90] is non-formal, it is obvious that this language is only appropriate for manual construction of logic algorithms, but not for (semi-)automatic synthesis thereof. There are then basically three solutions: either augment the existing specification language with suitable entries, or develop a language that allows the writing of intermediate descriptions that are good starting points for automated synthesis, or develop a new specification language. In Chapter 6, we opt for the latter solution. The actually chosen language is irrelevant at this point, but the first two stages of the overall methodology now are:

- Stage A': Elaboration of a specification (in the new formalism);
- Stage B': Synthesis of a logic algorithm.

Once the new specification formalism developed, this book is mainly concerned with Stage B', and only marginally with Stage A'.

5.2 Motivating Examples

In order to motivate this research, in Section 5.2.1, we give sample logic algorithms solving some of the problems posed in Section 1.5. Then, in Section 5.2.2, we give some comments on these logic algorithms.

5.2.1 Sample Logic Algorithms

We now list sample logic algorithms in order to illustrate the variety of difficulties that arise. No domain checking literals have been added. The given logic algorithms may look somewhat contrived, and are definitely subject to many simplifying transformation opportunities, but these versions make subsequent analysis much easier. Also, these logic algorithms do not always exactly result from an application of the construction methodology of [Deville 90], as outlined in the previous chapter.

We first construct a few alternative logic algorithms for the *compress*/2 problem. Then we list some logic algorithms for some of the problems posed in Section 1.5.

Alternative Logic Algorithms for the compress/2 Problem

In order to give some more insights into Stage B of the existing methodology, we first construct a few alternative logic algorithms for the *compress*/2 problem.

Let's first reconsider Step 2 (Selection of a Well-Founded Relation), and follow the Extrinsic Heuristic when selecting a well-founded relation over the type of the induction parameter *L*. This means that we want to decompose *L* into something smaller in a way reflecting the structure of parameter *C*. Every element of *C* represents a "summary" of a plateau of *L*, so the idea is to decompose *L* by extracting its first maximal plateau as head of *L*, and the corresponding suffix as tail of *L*. This decomposition is non-trivial, but considerably facilitates the rest of the construction. Step 3 is unaffected by this decision, and after Step 4, the result is:

```
compress(L,C) ⇔
      L=[]      ∧ C=[]
   ∨  L=[_|_] ∧ firstPlateau(L,HL,TL)
                ∧ compress(TL,TC)
                ∧ plateau(N,E,HL) ∧ HC=<E,N>
                ∧ C=[HC|TC]
```

Logic Algorithm 5-1: *LA*(*compress-ext-L*)

Let's now reconsider Step 1 (Selection of an Induction Parameter), and select the other parameter, *C*, as induction parameter. At Step 2 (Selection of a Well-Founded Relation), we first follow the Intrinsic Heuristic, and select "is the tail of" as well-founded relation over the type of the induction parameter. Step 3 is straightforward, and after Step 4, the result is:

```
compress(L,C) ⇔
      C=[]      ∧ L=[]
   ∨  C=[_|_] ∧ C=[HC|TC]
                ∧ compress(TL,TC)
```

```
                ∧ HC=<E,N> ∧ plateau(N,E,HL)
                ∧ firstPlateau(L,HL,TL)
```

Logic Algorithm 5-2: *LA(compress-int-C)*

Let's finally reconsider Step 2 (Selection of a Well-Founded Relation), and follow the Extrinsic Heuristic when selecting a well-founded relation over the type of induction parameter *C*. This means that we want to decompose *C* into something smaller in a way reflecting the structure of parameter *L*. Every element of *L* represents an increment by 1 of the counter in an element of *C*, so the idea is to decompose *C* by decrementing, if possible, the counter of its first element by 1. Step 3 is unaffected by this decision, and after Step 4, the result is:

```
compress(L,C) ⇔
      C=[]     ∧ L=[]
   ∨  C=[_|_]  ∧ decompose(C,HC,TC)
               ∧ compress(TL,TC)
               ∧ HL=HC
               ∧ L=[HL|TL]
decompose(C,HC,TC) ⇔
      C=[<E,s(N)>|T]  ∧ N=0  ∧ HC=E  ∧ TC=T
   ∨  C=[<E,s(N)>|T]  ∧ N>0  ∧ HC=E  ∧ TC=[<E,N>|T]
```

Logic Algorithm 5-3: *LA(compress-ext-C)*

Logic Algorithm 5-1 and Logic Algorithm 5-2 are almost identical. Also, Logic Algorithm 4-3 and an unfolding of Logic Algorithm 5-3 would be almost identical.

Logic Algorithms for Other Problems

Here follow, in alphabetical order on the predicates, some logic algorithms for some problems posed in Section 1.5. We do not explain their design processes, but give some useful comments on the results. The reader is invited to check that they are correct wrt their specifications. Unless otherwise noted, they have all been designed with the Intrinsic Heuristic.

Example 5-1: The following logic algorithm for *delOddElems(L,R)* has been designed with *L* as induction parameter. A design with *R* as induction parameter would yield a quite similar logic algorithm.

```
delOddElems(L,R) ⇔
      L=[]     ∧ R=[]
   ∨  L=[_|_]  ∧ L=[HL|TL]
               ∧ odd(HL)
               ∧ delOddElems(TL,TR)
               ∧ HR=_
               ∧ R=TR
   ∨  L=[_|_]  ∧ L=[HL|TL]
               ∧ ¬odd(HL)
               ∧ delOddElems(TL,TR)
```

```
                    ∧ HR=HL
                    ∧ R=[HR|TR]
```

Logic Algorithm 5-4: *LA*(*delOddElems-L*)

Example 5-2: The following logic algorithm for *efface*(*E*,*L*,*R*) has been designed with *L* as induction parameter. A design with *R* would yield a quite similar logic algorithm. Note that the non-minimal form gives rise to two cases, one of them without recursion. Also note that *E* could have been used instead of *TE* in the recursive atom, because both are unified with *HE*. Such a parameter is called an *auxiliary parameter*, because it has nothing to do with the inductive nature of the problem. Induction on an auxiliary parameter obviously is a bad idea.

```
efface(E,L,R) ⇔
      L=[_]              ∧ L=[HL] ∧ E=HL ∧ R=[]
    ∨ L=[_,_|_]          ∧ L=[HL|TL]
                         ∧ HL=E
                         ∧ E=HL ∧ R=TL
    ∨ L=[_,_|_]          ∧ L=[HL|TL]
                         ∧ HL≠E
                         ∧ efface(TE,TL,TR)
                         ∧ HE=_ ∧ HR=HL
                         ∧ E=TE ∧ R=[HR|TR]
```

Logic Algorithm 5-5: *LA*(*efface-L*)

Example 5-3: The following logic algorithm for *firstN*(*N*,*L*,*R*) has been designed with *L* as induction parameter. A design with *R* as induction parameter would yield a quite similar logic algorithm. The non-minimal form gives rise to two cases, one of them without a recursive atom. Note the relevant redundancy between the N=0 atoms.

```
firstN(N,L,R) ⇔
      L=[]      ∧ N=0 ∧ R=[]
    ∨ L=[_|_] ∧ L=[HL|TL]
                ∧ N=0
                ∧ N=0 ∧ R=[]
    ∨ L=[_|_] ∧ L=[HL|TL]
                ∧ N>0
                ∧ firstN(TN,TL,TR)
                ∧ HN=_ ∧ HR=HL
                ∧ N=s(TN) ∧ R=[HR|TR]
```

Logic Algorithm 5-6: *LA*(*firstN-L*)

The following other logic algorithm for *firstN*(*N*,*L*,*R*) has been designed with *N* as induction parameter. Note the interesting variable sharing between *HL* and *HR*: their value is “invented”, but common. Also note the relevant presence of a `true` atom.

```
firstN(N,L,R) ⇔
      N=0       ∧ L=_ ∧ R=[]
```

```
    ∨ N>0       ∧ N=s(TN) ∧ HN=N
                ∧ true
                ∧ firstN(TN,TL,TR)
                ∧ HL=A ∧ HR=A
                ∧ L=[HL|TL] ∧ R=[HR|TR]
```

Logic Algorithm 5-7: *LA(firstN-N)*

Example 5-4: The following logic algorithm for *insert(E,L,R)* has been designed with *L* as induction parameter. Parameter *E* is an auxiliary parameter. Note that the non-minimal form gives rise to two cases, one of them without a recursive atom.

```
insert(E,L,R) ⇔
      L=[]      ∧ E=_ ∧ R=[E]
    ∨ L=[_|_] ∧ L=[HL|TL]
                ∧ HL≥E
                ∧ E=_ ∧ R=[E|L]
    ∨ L=[_|_] ∧ L=[HL|TL]
                ∧ HL<E
                ∧ insert(TE,TL,TR)
                ∧ HE=_ ∧ HR=HL
                ∧ E=TE ∧ R=[HR|TR]
```

Logic Algorithm 5-8: *LA(insert-L)*

The following other logic algorithm for *insert(E,L,R)* has been designed with *R* as induction parameter. Note that the non-minimal form gives rise to two cases, one of them without a recursive atom.

```
insert(E,L,R) ⇔
    R=[_]           ∧ R=[A] ∧ E=A ∧ L=[]
  ∨ R=[_,_|_]       ∧ R=[HR|TR]
                    ∧ HR=E
                    ∧ E=HR ∧ L=TR
  ∨ R=[_,_|_]       ∧ R=[HR|TR]
                    ∧ HR<E          {HR≠E would do as well}
                    ∧ insert(TE,TL,TR)
                    ∧ HE=_ ∧ HL=HR
                    ∧ E=TE ∧ L=[HL|TL]
```

Logic Algorithm 5-9: *LA(insert-R)*

Example 5-5: The following logic algorithm for *member(E,L)* has been designed with *L* as induction parameter. Parameter *E* is an auxiliary parameter. Note that the non-minimal form gives rise to two cases, one of them without a recursive atom. Also note how the desired non-determinism is achieved.

```
member(E,L) ⇔
    L=[_]           ∧ L=[A] ∧ E=A
  ∨ L=[_,_|_]       ∧ L=[HL|TL]
```

```
                  ∧ true
                  ∧ E=HL
∨ L=[_,_|_]       ∧ L=[HL|TL]
                  ∧ true
                  ∧ member(TE,TL)
                  ∧ HE=_
                  ∧ E=TE
```

Logic Algorithm 5-10: *LA(member-L)*

Example 5-6: The following logic algorithm for *merge(A,B,C)* has been designed with the couple *<A,B>* as compound induction parameter. Note the different decomposition patterns. Parameter *A* or *B* alone as induction parameter does not lead to a successful design. This is however possible with *C* alone, but we do not list that logic algorithm here.

```
merge(A,B,C) ⇔
      A=[]      ∧ C=B
    ∨ B=[]      ∧ C=A
    ∨ A=[_|_] ∧ B=[_|_]
                ∧ A=[HA|TA] ∧ B=[HB|TB]
                ∧ HA=HB
                ∧ merge(TA,TB,TC)
                ∧ HC=HA ∧ HC=HB
                ∧ C=[HC,HC|TC]
    ∨ A=[_|_] ∧ B=[_|_]
                ∧ A=[HA|TA] ∧ B=TB
                ∧ HA<HB ∧ B=[HB|_]
                ∧ merge(TA,TB,TC)
                ∧ HC=HA
                ∧ C=[HC|TC]
    ∨ A=[_|_] ∧ B=[_|_]
                ∧ A=TA ∧ B=[HB|TB]
                ∧ HA>HB ∧ A=[HA|_]
                ∧ merge(TA,TB,TC)
                ∧ HC=HB
                ∧ C=[HC|TC]
```

Logic Algorithm 5-11: *LA(merge-<A,B>)*

Example 5-7: The following logic algorithm for *parity(L,R)* has been designed with *L* as induction parameter. Note that there are two minimal forms, and that the non-minimal form is decomposed by taking two elements away from *L*.

```
parity(L,R) ⇔
      L=[]              ∧ R=even
    ∨ L=[_]             ∧ R=odd
    ∨ L=[_,_|_]         ∧ L=[HL1,HL2|TL]
                        ∧ true
```

```
                    ∧ parity(TL,TR)
                    ∧ HR=_
                    ∧ R=TR
```

Logic Algorithm 5-12: *LA(parity-L)*

Example 5-8: The following logic algorithm for *partition(L,P,S,B)* has been designed with *L* as induction parameter. Parameter *P* is an auxiliary parameter.

```
partition(L,P,S,B) ⇔
      L=[]       ∧ P=_ ∧ S=[] ∧ B=[]
    ∨ L=[_|_]    ∧ L=[HL|TL]
                 ∧ HL≥P
                 ∧ partition(TL,TP,TS,TB)
                 ∧ HP=_ ∧ HS=_ ∧ HB=HL
                 ∧ P=TP ∧ S=TS ∧ B=[HB|TB]
    ∨ L=[_|_]    ∧ L=[HL|TL]
                 ∧ HL<P
                 ∧ partition(TL,TP,TS,TB)
                 ∧ HP=_ ∧ HS=HL ∧ HB=_
                 ∧ P=TP ∧ S=[HS|TS] ∧ B=TB
```

Logic Algorithm 5-13: *LA(partition-L)*

Example 5-9: The following logic algorithm for *permutation(L,P)* has been designed with *L* as induction parameter. Because of the symmetry of the underlying relation, a design with *P* as induction parameter would yield the same logic algorithm. Note that the use of *efface(HP,P,TP)* rather than *stuff(HP,TP,P)* avoids redundant solutions at the logic program level.

```
permutation(L,P) ⇔
      L=[]       ∧ P=[]
    ∨ L=[_|_]    ∧ L=[HL|TL]
                 ∧ permutation(TL,TP)
                 ∧ HP=HL
                 ∧ efface(HP,P,TP)
```

Logic Algorithm 5-14: *LA(permutation-L)*

Example 5-10: The following logic algorithm for *plateau(N,E,P)* has been designed with *N* as induction parameter. A design with *P* as induction parameter would yield a quite similar logic algorithm. Note the intricate way in which *HP* is unified with the correct value. Parameter *E* is an auxiliary parameter.

```
plateau(N,E,P) ⇔
      N=1        ∧ E=_ ∧ P=[E]
    ∨ N>1        ∧ N=s(TN) ∧ HN=N
                 ∧ plateau(TN,TE,TP)
```

```
∧ HE=A ∧ HP=A
∧ E=TE ∧ E=HE ∧ P=[HP|TP]
```

Logic Algorithm 5-15: *LA(plateau-N)*

Example 5-11: The following logic algorithm for *sort(L,S)* has been designed with *L* as induction parameter, following the Intrinsic Heuristic. The result is the Insertion-Sort algorithm.

```
sort(L,S) ⇔
      L=[]      ∧ S=[]
    ∨ L=[_|_] ∧ L=[HL|TL]
                ∧ sort(TL,TS)
                ∧ HS=HL
                ∧ insert(HS,TS,S)
```

Logic Algorithm 5-16: *LA(sort-int-L)* {Insertion-Sort}

The following other logic algorithm for *sort(L,S)* has been designed with *L* as induction parameter, following the Extrinsic Heuristic by partitioning *L* according to some pivot element. The result is the Quick-Sort algorithm.

```
sort(L,S) ⇔
      L=[]      ∧ S=[]
    ∨ L=[_|_] ∧ L=[HL|T] ∧ partition(T,HL,TL1,TL2)
                ∧ sort(TL1,TS1) ∧ sort(TL2,TS2)
                ∧ HS=HL
                ∧ append(TS1,[HS|TS2],S)
```

Logic Algorithm 5-17: *LA(sort-ext-L)* {Quick-Sort}

The following other logic algorithm for *sort(L,S)* has been designed with *L* as induction parameter, following the Extrinsic Heuristic by splitting *L* into two halves. The result is the Merge-Sort algorithm.

```
sort(L,S) ⇔
      L=[]      ∧ S=[]
    ∨ L=[_|_] ∧ split(L,TL1,TL2)
                ∧ sort(TL1,TS1) ∧ sort(TL2,TS2)
                ∧ merge(TS1,TS2,S)
```

Logic Algorithm 5-18: *LA(sort-ext-L)* {Merge-Sort}

Example 5-12: The following logic algorithm for *split(L,F,S)* has been designed by a totally different method, namely introduction of an additional parameter, plus logic algorithm design by structural induction for the new problem.

```
split(L,F,S) ⇔
    split(L,L,F,S)

split(L,M,F,S) ⇔
    M=[]              ∧ F=[] ∧ S=L
  ∨ M=[_]             ∧ F=[] ∧ S=L
```

```
∨ M=[_,_|_]        ∧ M=[HM1,HM2|TM] ∧ L=[HL|TL]
                   ∧ true
                   ∧ split(TL,TM,TF,TS)
                   ∧ HF=HL ∧ HS=_
                   ∧ F=[HF|TF] ∧ S=TS
```

Logic Algorithm 5-19: *LA(split)*

5.2.2 Some Comments on Logic Algorithms

Several aspects of logic algorithm design can be discussed now. We first propose a useful terminology for logic algorithm classification, and then show in what sense minimal cases and non-recursive non-minimal cases, though syntactically similar, are totally different concepts.

Logic Algorithm Classification

Logic Algorithms can be classified along five dimensions, namely according to how the induction parameter is decomposed, according to how much of the induction parameter is actually traversed, according to how many times the induction parameter is traversed, according to the determinism of the defined relation given a ground value of the induction parameter, and according to the kind of manipulations performed on the constituents (constants and variables) of the parameters.

Regarding the decomposition of the induction parameter, we distinguish between the following three categories of logic algorithms:

- *intrinsic-decomposition logic algorithms*: X is decomposed into $h \geq 1$ heads and $t \geq 1$ tails in a manner reflecting the definition of the type of X; for instance, decompose a list L into its head HL and tail TL;
- *extrinsic-decomposition logic algorithms*: X is decomposed into $h \geq 0$ heads and $t \geq 1$ tails in a manner reflecting the definition of the type of some other parameter than X, or reflecting the intended relation; for instance, partition an integer-list L according to a pivot P into a list S of elements smaller than P and a list B of elements bigger than or equal to P;
- *logarithmic-decomposition logic algorithms*: X is decomposed into $h = 0$ heads and $t \geq 2$ tails of about equal size; for instance, split a list L into 2 halves A and B.

An intrinsic decomposition reflects a well-founded relation selected via the Intrinsic Heuristic, and an extrinsic or logarithmic decomposition reflects a well-founded relation selected via the Extrinsic Heuristic (see Chapter 4). Sample classifications are given below.

Regarding the scope of the traversal of the induction parameter, we here distinguish between the following two categories of logic algorithms:

- *complete-traversal logic algorithms*: all elements of the induction parameter are visited;
- *prefix-traversal logic algorithms*: only the first few elements of the induction parameter are visited.

Other categories could be added here. Sample classifications are given below.

Regarding the number of times the induction parameter is actually traversed, we distinguish between the following two categories of logic algorithms:

- *single-loop logic algorithms*: only one traversal of the induction parameter is being performed at any moment;
- *multiple-loop logic algorithms*: at least two nested traversals of the induction parameter are performed at some moment.

Sample classifications are given below.

Regarding the determinism of a logic algorithm given ground values of the induction parameter and the auxiliary parameter(s), we define the following notions.

Definition 5-1: A *scalar* is either an integer, or the special symbol $*$ (representing any finite integer), or the special symbol ∞ (representing infinity).

Definition 5-2: Let *min* and *max* be two scalars. Let $LP(r)$ be the logic program derived from a logic algorithm $LA(r)$. Let $r(\boldsymbol{t})$ be an atom where the induction parameter and the auxiliary parameter(s) are ground, and all other parameters are variables. We say that $LA(r)$ is *min – max deterministic* iff there are between *min* and *max* ground instances of $r(\boldsymbol{t})$ for which there exists an SLDNF refutation using $LP(r)$.

The following terminology is then useful for classifying logic algorithms according to their determinism:

- *deterministic logic algorithms* are 0 – 1 deterministic;
- *fully-deterministic logic algorithms* are 1 – 1 deterministic;
- *non-deterministic logic algorithms* are *min – max* deterministic, where *min* is a positive integer, and *max* is either an integer greater than *min*, or $*$, or ∞;
- *finite logic algorithms* are *min – max* deterministic, where *min* is an integer, and *max* is either an integer greater than *min*, or $*$;
- *infinite logic algorithms* are *min* – ∞ deterministic, where *min* is any scalar.

Sample classifications are given below.

Finally, regarding the kind of manipulations performed on the constituents of the parameters, we distinguish between the following two categories of logic algorithms:

- *structural-manipulation logic algorithms*: some—if not all—constituents of the induction parameter are shuffled around unconditionally, because their values are irrelevant, for the construction of the other parameters;
- *semantic-manipulation logic algorithms*: some—if not all—constituents of the induction parameter are shuffled around conditionally, as their values *are* relevant, or even new constituents are used for the construction of other parameters.

This last dimension is actually also applicable for classifying relations, as no design choice affects into which category the resulting logic algorithms fall.

Example 5-13: Table 5-1 charts the features of the relations for which logic algorithms have been given so far. The columns list (from left to right):

- the arity of the relation;
- the presence of auxiliary parameters (denoted by their names), or the absence (denoted *no*) of auxiliary parameters;
- the kind of the manipulations on the parameters. ♦

But this ambivalence does not hold for the first four dimensions, because a relation might give rise to several logic algorithms that are classified differently along them.

Table 5-1: Summary of the features of some sample relations

	Arity	AP	Manipulation
compress	2	no	semantic
delOddElems	2	no	semantic
efface	3	*E*	semantic
firstN	3	no	structural
firstPlateau	3	no	semantic
insert	3	*E*	semantic
member	2	*E*	structural
merge	3	no	semantic
parity	2	*R*	structural
partition	4	*P*	semantic
permutation	2	no	structural
plateau	3	*E*	semantic
sort	2	no	semantic
split	4	no	structural

Example 5-14: Table 5-2 charts the features of the logic algorithms given so far. The columns list (from left to right):

- the name of the selected induction parameter;
- the kind of the selected induction parameter (where *s* stands for simple induction parameter, and *c* stands for compound induction parameter);
- the kind of traversal performed on the induction parameter (where *c* stands for complete-traversal, and *p* stands for prefix-traversal);
- the determinism of the logic algorithm given ground values of the induction parameter and the auxiliary parameter(s);
- the number of structural forms of the induction parameter, represented as $a + b$, where a is the number of minimal forms, and b the number of non-minimal forms;
- the selected strategy of decomposition of the induction parameter (where *int* stands for intrinsic decomposition, *ext* stands for extrinsic decomposition, and *log* stands for logarithmic decomposition);
- the number of cases of the logic algorithm, represented as $u + v + w$, where u is the number of minimal cases, v is the number of non-minimal non-recursive cases, and w is the number of non-minimal recursive cases;
- the number of loops performed by the logic algorithm (where 1 indicates that it is a single-loop logic algorithm, and integers greater than 1 indicate that it is a multiple-loop logic algorithm);
- the number of the logic algorithm in this book, and the page where it can be found.

The first four features are independent of the selected decomposition strategy. The numbers of cases and loops depend on the selected decomposition strategy. ♦

Table 5-2: Summary of the features of some sample logic algorithms

	IP	K	T	Det.	Fms	Dec	Cases	Lps	LA #, page #
compress	*L*	s	c	1 – 1	1+1	int	1+0+2	1	4-3, page 61
						ext	1+0+1	2	5-1, page 64
	C	s	c	1 – 1	1+1	int	1+0+1	2	5-2, page 65
						ext	1+0+1	1	5-3, page 65
delOddElems	*L*	s	c	1 – 1	1+1	int	1+0+2	1	5-4, page 66
efface	*L*	s	p	1 – 1	1+1	int	1+1+1	1	5-5, page 66
firstN	*L*	s	p	1 – *	1+1	int	1+1+1	1	5-6, page 66
	N	s	c	1 – 1	1+1	int	1+0+1	1	5-7, page 67
firstPlateau	*L*	s	p	1 – 1	1+1	int	1+1+1	1	4-2, page 57
insert	*L*	s	p	1 – 1	1+1	int	1+1+1	1	5-8, page 67
	R	s	p	1 – 1	1+1	int	1+1+1	1	5-9, page 67
member	*L*	s	c	1 – *	1+1	int	1+1+1	1	5-10, page 68
merge	*A*, *B*	c	c	1 – 1	2+1	int	2+0+3	1	5-11, page 68
parity	*L*	s	c	1 – 1	2+1	int	2+0+1	1	5-12, page 69
partition	*L*	s	c	1 – 1	1+1	int	1+0+2	1	5-13, page 69
permutation	*L*	s	c	1 – *	1+1	int	1+0+1	2	5-14, page 69
plateau	*N*	s	c	1 – 1	1+1	int	1+0+1	1	5-15, page 70
sort	*L*	s	c	1 – 1	1+1	int	1+0+1	2	5-16, page 70
						ext	1+0+1	2	5-17, page 70
						log	1+0+1	2	5-18, page 70
split	*M*	s	c	1 – 1	2+1	int	2+0+1	1	5-19, page 71

Minimal Cases and Non-Recursive Non-Minimal Cases

As the logic algorithms of this book exhibit, not all non-minimal cases are recursive. Indeed, prefix-traversal logic algorithms have non-recursive non-minimal cases. But some structural cases of logic algorithms in Chapter 4, or [Deville 90], seem hard to classify. There are several potential reasons to this.

A first reason is that non-recursive non-minimal cases of prefix-scan logic algorithms can often be merged with their minimal cases. The resulting algorithm looks like it has no minimal case. It exhibits cases whose structural forms are not mutually exclusive, and is thus easy to detect as being a rewriting of the "canonical" version.

Example 5-15: Logic Algorithm 5-5 could be rewritten as follows:

```
efface(E,L,R) ⇔
     L=[_|_]          ∧ L=[HL|TL]
                      ∧ HL=E
```

```
                          ∧ E=HL  ∧ R=TL
  ∨  L=[_,_|_]            ∧ L=[HL|TL]
                          ∧ HL≠E
                          ∧ efface(TE,TL,TR)
                          ∧ HE=_  ∧ HR=HL
                          ∧ E=TE  ∧ E=HE  ∧ R=[HR|TR]
```

The form $L = [\_|\_]$ is not minimal, as it overlaps with the other form. It rather results from a merger of the minimal case and the non-recursive non-minimal case. ♦

Another reason for non-recursive non-minimal cases is recursion elimination by partial evaluation. The result is a non-minimal case that looks like a minimal case. This is hard to detect, since the cases still exhibit mutually exclusive structural forms. There is no limit to creating non-recursive non-minimal cases by partial evaluation.

Example 5-16: Logic Algorithm 4-1 is actually a rewriting of:

```
compress(L,C) ⇔
      L=[]      ∧ C=[]
   ∨  L=[_|_]   ∧ L=[HL|TL]
                ∧ (TL=[]) ∨ (L=[HL1,HL2|_] ∧ HL1≠HL2)
                ∧ compress(TL,TC)
                ∧ HC=<HL,1>
                ∧ C=[HC|TC]
   ∨  L=[_|_]   ∧ L=[HL|TL]
                ∧ L=[HL1,HL2|_] ∧ HL1=HL2
                ∧ compress(TL,TC)
                ∧ HC=_
                ∧ C=[<V,s(N)>|TTC] ∧ TC=[<V,N>|TTC]
```

Indeed, we have that $TL = []$ iff $TC = []$, so the rewriting is correct. But it is also misleading as the fact that there really is only one minimal case and only one non-minimal form is not apparent at all. ♦

It is important to understand that such logic algorithms with non-recursive, non-minimal cases are the result of re-writing "canonical" logic algorithms, rather than unpleasant aberrations.

5.3 Challenges

Looking at the sheer variety of possible logic algorithms, some of them in the preceding section, the automatic synthesis of logic algorithms looks like quite a formidable task. Indeed, the following difficulties need to be tackled:

- *What induction parameter to select? How to discover compound induction parameters? According to what well-founded relation to decompose the induction parameter?* Ideally, a synthesis mechanism should be able to design a whole family of possible logic algorithms for a given problem. For instance, given the sorting problem, at least the three logic algorithms above should be designed.
- *How many structural forms are there?* The number of minimal and non-minimal structural forms is specific to each logic algorithm. While most logic algorithms

seem to have one minimal and one non-minimal form, this does not always hold, as illustrated by the logic algorithms for *parity*/2 and *split*/4.

- *What are the structural forms?* The type of the induction parameter is not sufficient to infer its structural forms: these are actually dependent on the domain of the induction parameter, and are thus a problem-specific issue.
- *Into how many sub-cases is each structural case divided? How to discriminate between these sub-cases?* Many of the logic algorithms listed above fork their non-minimal case into two sub-cases.
- *How to detect that recursion is useless in some non-minimal sub-cases?* Sometimes, the desired result is obtained before reducing the induction parameter to a minimal form, and no recursion is then needed: this happens for instance in the logic algorithms for *efface*/3 and *insert*/3. The existence or not of useless recursion is dependent on the selected induction parameter, as illustrated by the two logic algorithms for *firstN*/3.
- *How to "invent" or reuse appropriate predicates? How to implement "invented" predicates?* The combination of partial results often is a full-scale problem by itself, as illustrated by the logic algorithms for *compress*/2 (induction on *C*), *permutation*/2, and *sort*/2. The same holds for a decomposition following the Extrinsic Heuristic. This is known as the *predicate invention problem.*
- *How to discover which parameters are auxiliary parameters?* Problems such as *efface*/3, *insert*/3, *member*/2, *partition*/4, and *plateau*/3 have auxiliary parameters: unless this is stated somewhere, considerable design effort may go into detecting this. The logic algorithms listed above for these problems actually are versions for which the detection was not done.
- *How to synthesize logic algorithms that are non-deterministic*, such as those for *member*/2 and *permutation*/2? As seen in Section 2.4, this is known to be a hard problem for deductive synthesis approaches.
- *How to achieve a synthesis that yields logic algorithms that are correct wrt their intentions?* This is another tough problem.

and so on. This list of challenges is impressive. The answers depend of course a lot on the chosen specification language. Once that language defined, and a synthesis mechanism developed for it, we evaluate the results to see to what extent we have brought answers to these challenges.

II BUILDING BLOCKS

In this second part, we provide the building blocks for a solution to our objective. Thus, in Chapter 6, we define a generic specification approach that is based on examples and properties. Next, in Chapter 7, we develop a theoretical framework for stepwise synthesis of logic algorithms from such specifications, and address the aspects of correctness and comparison of logic algorithms. In Chapter 8, we introduce logic algorithm schemata as an important support for logic algorithm design. Chapter 9 is about the Proofs-as-Programs Method, which deductively enhances a logic algorithm such that it satisfies certain correctness criteria wrt a given set of properties. Finally, Chapter 10 is about the Most-Specific-Generalization Method, which inductively infers a logic algorithm from a given set of examples. Chapters 7 to 10 may be read in any order.

6 A SPECIFICATION APPROACH

The first building block is the actual specification formalism used to elaborate the input to algorithm synthesis. An arbitrary choice has been made here to investigate synthesis from incomplete specifications. Starting from the pros and cons of specifications by examples, and of specifications by axioms, as outlined in Part I, we define, in Section 6.1, a specification approach that is based on examples and properties. Then, in Section 6.2, we illustrate this approach on a few sample problems. Future work and related work are discussed in Section 6.3 and Section 6.4, respectively, before drawing some conclusions in Section 6.5.

6.1 Specifications by Examples and Properties

When contrasting the pros and cons of specifications by axioms (as seen in Section 2.1) and specifications by examples (as seen in Section 3.1), it turns out that these specification approaches are quite complementary, each alleviating the drawbacks of the other by its own advantages. This gives rise to the idea of combining these two specification approaches so as to preserve only their benefits, while diminishing their disadvantages. But we must bear in mind the fundamental difference between the two approaches, namely specification completeness and specification incompleteness.

Merely amalgamating the two formalisms into specifications by axioms and examples is thus not a good idea, as the incomplete example-set would only play an illustrative side-role to the complete axiom-set.

But, on the other hand, one could aim at incomplete specifications and add some stronger form of axioms to the examples so as to overcome the weaknesses of specifications by examples only. We call *properties* [Flener and Deville 92, 93ab] such a strong form of axioms, and only require them to be written in (some subset of) logic. Indeed, until Part III, we do not restrict ourselves to any syntax or required computational content of properties. We only assume that properties are an incomplete source of information. Actually, in case properties were a complete source of information, most of the results hereafter would remain valid, but not always be relevant.

Let $\mathcal{R}$ be the relation one has in mind when elaborating a specification of a procedure for predicate *r*. We call $\mathcal{R}$ the *intended relation*, in contrast to the relation actually specified, called the *specified relation*. This distinction is very important in general, but crucial with incomplete specifications, where one *deliberately* admits a gap between the two.

The following three assumptions are crucial in the sequel. First, we only aim at specifying relations that give rise to recursive algorithms. This excludes many of the concept descriptions aimed at by the machine learning community. Second, we assume the specifier knows $\mathcal{R}$, even if s/he doesn't have a formal definition of it. This also precludes some scenarios envisaged by the machine learning community. Third, we assume that the specified relation is a subset of the intended relation. This means that there is assumed to be no noise in specifications. These assumptions define a highly specialized niche within the learning problem, and allow hence some specific choices in the following.

Definition 6-1: A *specification by examples and properties* of a procedure for predicate r/n, denoted $EP(r)$, consists of:

- a set $\mathcal{E}(r)$ of ground examples of r/n, partitioned into:
  - a set $\mathcal{E}^+(r)$ of positive examples of r/n (that is, ground atoms whose n-tuples are supposed to belong to $\mathcal{R}$);
  - a set $\mathcal{E}^-(r)$ of negative examples of r/n (that is, negated ground atoms whose n-tuples are supposed not to belong to $\mathcal{R}$);
- a set $\mathcal{P}(r)$ of properties (first-order logic statements) of r/n.

The (unique) specified relation is defined as follows:

Definition 6-2: The *specified relation* of a specification by examples and properties is the set of tuples extracted from the set of its Herbrand-logical consequences.

It is interesting to note that, very often, examples are properties, because the example language is a subset of the property language. In these cases, one could then simply talk about specifications by properties. But a specification language doesn't prejudice on how the specification information is actually used in algorithm design: indeed, an algorithm designer might use examples in a way that is totally different from the way non-example properties are used. This is why, in case the language subset relationship holds, we still prefer to talk about specifications by examples and properties. The assumption then is that the word "property" refers to properties that are not examples.

6.2 Sample Specifications by Examples and Properties

Let's illustrate the notion of specifications by examples and properties by a few sample specifications (others may be found in Section 14.4.2). The chosen language for properties is, strictly for the sake of illustration, non-recursive normal clauses that have a head with the predicate of the examples. Universal quantifiers are usually dropped for convenience. Also, negative examples are not allowed. Note that most of this Part II is independent of such choices. Our claim is that such properties and examples, if carefully chosen, embody the minimal knowledge that doesn't give away the solution, but is sufficient for successful algorithm design.

Example 6-1: A sample version of $EP(compress)$ is:

```
ℰ(compress) = { compress([],[])                        (E1)
                compress([a],[a,1])                    (E2)
                compress([b,b],[b,2])                  (E3)
                compress([c,d],[c,1,d,1])              (E4)
                compress([e,e,e],[e,3])                (E5)
                compress([f,f,g],[f,2,g,1])            (E6)
                compress([h,i,i],[h,1,i,2])            (E7)
                compress([j,k,m],[j,1,k,1,m,1]) }      (E8)

𝒫(compress) = { compress([X],[X,1])                    (P1)
                compress([X,Y],[X,2]) ⇐ X=Y            (P2)
                compress([X,Y],[X,1,Y,1]) ⇐ X≠Y }      (P3)
```

Note that, for ease of syntax, we have changed the format of compact lists to lists whose elements alternately are values and counters.

How to elaborate these properties?

Note that properties P_1 to P_3 generalize examples E_2 to E_4, respectively. Example E_1 can't be generalized. So what about generalizing examples E_5 to E_8? The clause:

$$compress([X, Y, Z], [X, 2, Z, 1]) \Leftarrow X = Y \wedge Y \neq Z$$

generalizes example E_6, and is a legal property. But it doesn't introduce any predicates the three properties above don't already introduce: it could thus be considered a superfluous property. Similarly, properties generalizing examples E_5, E_7, or E_8 wouldn't provide any new information either.

But one could also think about writing properties that generalize more than the given examples, say with the first parameter being a list of any length. Rather than only generalizing the problem-specific constants *a*, *b*, ... of the examples into variables *X*, *Y*, ..., this consists in also generalizing the predefined constant *nil* into a variable, say *T*. The clauses:

$$compress([X \mid T], [X, 1 \mid U]) \Leftarrow T \neq [X \mid \_] \wedge compress(T, U)$$
$$compress([X \mid T], [X, s(N) \mid U]) \Leftarrow compress(T, [X, N \mid U])$$
$$compress([X, Y \mid T], [X, 2 \mid U]) \Leftarrow X = Y \wedge T \neq [Y \mid \_] \wedge compress(T, U)$$
$$compress([X, Y \mid T], [X, 1 \mid U]) \Leftarrow X \neq Y \wedge compress([Y \mid T], U)$$
$$compress([X, Y \mid T], [X, 1, Y, 1 \mid U]) \Leftarrow X \neq Y \wedge T \neq [Y \mid \_] \wedge compress(T, U)$$

state constraints on compressing lists of at least one, or at least two, elements. But, for our sample language, they are not properties because of the non-recursion restriction. Indeed, these statements are already almost identical to clauses of a logic program that correctly implements the given problem. Moreover, the elaboration of correct recursive properties is almost as difficult as designing the logic algorithm itself. This is clearly not what one would expect from an incomplete specification, and thus speaks in favor of disallowing recursive properties. If one is given such statements where the gap to a correct logic program is quite small, then the techniques advocated in this book are not adequate, and a purely deductive approach would be more reasonable.

Evaluation of this specification

When studying this first sample specification, it becomes easily apparent how it improves on its examples-only counterpart: properties allow the specifier to make explicit what s/he perfectly knows, but can't express by examples alone. Especially the last two properties in the given property-set embody such additional knowledge: it is equality or disequality of the first two elements of the non-compressed list that discriminate between having the first counter of the compact list being 1 or larger than 1. This knowledge has otherwise to be guessed by the algorithm designer, which is dangerous (risk of wrong guesses) and time-consuming (enumeration of all possible guesses). The addition of disambiguating properties thus holds the promise of more effective and more efficient algorithm synthesis. ♦

Example 6-2: A sample version of *EP*(*firstPlateau*) is:

```
ℰ(firstPlateau) = {
            firstPlateau([a],[a],[])                (E1)
            firstPlateau([b,b],[b,b],[])            (E2)
```

```
                firstPlateau([c,d],[c],[d])                  (E3)
                firstPlateau([e,f,g],[e],[f,g])              (E4)
                firstPlateau([h,i,i],[h],[i,i])              (E5)
                firstPlateau([j,j,k],[j,j],[k])              (E6)
                firstPlateau([m,m,m],[m,m,m],[]) }           (E7)
𝒫(firstPlateau) = {
                firstPlateau([X],[X],[])                     (P1)
                firstPlateau([X,Y],[X,Y],[]) ⇐ X=Y           (P2)
                firstPlateau([X,Y],[X], [Y]) ⇐ X≠Y }         (P3)
```

How to elaborate these properties?

Properties P_1 to P_3 generalize examples E_1 to E_3, respectively. As in the preceding sample specification, there is no real motivation to explicitly generalize the other examples. But, this time, it *is* possible to generalize the *nil* constant into a variable without *always* having to introduce recursion. The resulting allowed properties are:

$$firstPlateau([X \mid T], [X], T) \Leftarrow T \neq [X \mid \_] \quad (1)$$

$$firstPlateau([X, Y \mid T], [X, Y], T) \Leftarrow X = Y \wedge T \neq [Y \mid \_] \quad (2)$$

$$firstPlateau([X, Y \mid T], [X], [Y \mid T]) \Leftarrow X \neq Y \quad (3)$$

and the disallowed properties are:

$$firstPlateau([X \mid T], [X \mid U], V) \Leftarrow T = [X \mid \_] \wedge firstPlateau(T, U, V)$$

$$firstPlateau([X, Y \mid T], [X, Y \mid U], V) \Leftarrow X = Y \wedge T = [Y \mid \_] \wedge firstPlateau(T, U, V)$$

Each property (i) is more informative than its counterpart P_i, for i = 1, 2, 3. Also, property (1) actually subsumes property (3). So the probably most useful set of properties would be {(1), (2)}. But the property-set above should also be convenient for algorithm design, even though it is less informative. The same holds for any subset of properties chosen among the six above, as long as the predicates ≠/2 and =/2 occur in them (the latter may actually be hidden through variable sharing). ♦

Example 6-3: A sample version of *EP*(*efface*) is:

```
ℰ(efface) = {   efface(a,[a],[])                      (E1)
                efface(b,[b,c],[c])                   (E2)
                efface(e,[d,e],[d])                   (E3)
                efface(f,[f,g,h],[g,h])               (E4)
                efface(j,[i,j,k],[i,k])               (E5)
                efface(p,[m,n,p],[m,n]) }             (E6)
𝒫(efface) = {   efface(X,[X|T],T)                     (P1)
                efface(X,[Y,X|T],[Y|T]) ⇐ X≠Y }       (P2)
```

Note that, in property P_2, the conclusion actually also holds if $X = Y$. In other words, property P_2 could be rewritten as follows:

$$efface(X, [Y, X \mid T], [Y \mid T])$$

But this new version no longer contains the predicate ≠/2, which is so crucial for disambiguating the examples. This is a useful illustration of the following observation: properties are implications (even though most of them could be recast as equivalences and still be correct), but nothing prejudices that their bodies must be as general as possible: properties are meant to be informative, rather than maximally general.

Also note that the following clause:

$$efface(X, [Y|T], U) \Leftarrow X \neq Y$$

is incorrect, because $X \neq Y$ doesn't imply that $X \in [Y|T]$, which is required by the informal specification. The only way to correct this is to add the atom *efface(X,T,U)* to the body, but the resultant recursive clause is a disallowed property. ♦

Example 6-4: A sample version of *EP(permutation)* is:

```
ℰ(permutation) = { permutation([],[])                          (E1)
                   permutation([a],[a])                        (E2)
                   permutation([b,c],[b,c])                    (E3)
                   permutation([b,c],[c,b])                    (E4)
                   permutation([d,e,f],[d,e,f])                (E5)
                   permutation([d,e,f],[d,f,e])                (E6)
                   permutation([d,e,f],[e,d,f])                (E7)
                   permutation([d,e,f],[e,f,d])                (E8)
                   permutation([d,e,f],[f,d,e])                (E9)
                   permutation([d,e,f],[f,e,d]) }              (E10)

𝒫(permutation) = { permutation([X],[X])                        (P1)
                   permutation([X,Y],[X,Y])                    (P2)
                   permutation([X,Y],[Y,X]) }                  (P3)
```

Example 6-5: A sample version of *EP(sum)* is:

```
ℰ(sum) = {  sum([],0)                                          (E1)
            sum([7],7)                                         (E2)
            sum([4,5],9)                                       (E3)
            sum([2,3,1],6) }                                   (E4)

𝒫(sum) = {  sum([X],X)                                         (P1)
            sum([X,Y],R) ⇐ add(X,Y,R) }                        (P2)
```

6.3 Future Work

Regardless of the actually chosen language for properties, it is quite likely that the latter are some form of a generalization of examples. It would therefore be interesting to investigate more formally how properties can be elaborated from examples. We even conjecture that this process might be partially automated.

6.4 Related Work

In terms of related work, specifications by examples are surveyed in Section 3.1. Also, the notion of specifying property can be traced back to the notion of specifying axiom, and specifications by axioms are surveyed in Section 2.1. In this section, we only survey research on extending example-based specifications by another incomplete information source.

Shapiro pointed out that the oracle of his *Model Inference System* (MIS, see Section 3.4.1) could be partly mechanized by the incorporation of "constraints and partial specifications" [Shapiro 82, page 79]. The idea is investigated by [Lichtenstein and Shapiro 88], whose system asks non-ground queries to an oracle.

Shapiro's idea has also been picked up by [Drabent *et al.* 88]: they define four kinds of *assertions* that may be added to a specification by examples. These assertions describe approximate knowledge about the intended model of the specified program. These assertions are used for partly mechanizing the oracle of Shapiro's MIS. They constitute a possible instantiation of our notion of properties.

Another interesting idea is proposed by [De Raedt and Bruynooghe 92a]: in view of cross-fertilization, they represent the problems of intensional knowledge-base updating and incremental concept-learning as particular cases of the more general problem of belief updating from *integrity constraints* and queries. Indeed, intensional knowledge-base updating can benefit from the possibility of asserting non-unit clauses in the knowledge-base. And incremental concept-learning can benefit from the generalization of examples into integrity constraints. The language for integrity constraints is range-restricted functor-free clauses. However, some integrity constraints are slightly different from our properties in the sense that they are not meant to (partially) specify the problem, but rather to verify the behavior of the designed program. This is then reflected in the possible presence of predicate(s) other than the one(s) of the examples in the conclusions of integrity constraints.

Similarly, note that properties are totally different from *background knowledge*, as often used in concept-learning from examples. Indeed, properties partially define the predicate(s) that is (are) incompletely specified by the examples, whereas background information defines predicate(s) that is (are) different from the one(s) found in the examples.

6.5 Conclusion

In this chapter, we have developed an approach for incomplete specifications that is based on the notions of examples and properties.

It requires multiple, ground, single-predicate, relational, positive and negative, pre-synthesis examples that are chosen in a consistent way by a human specifier who knows the intended relation.

The presence of properties (whose actual language is application-specific, and thus left unspecified in this part) is meant to overcome the problems of ambiguity and limited expressive power of specifications by examples, while still preserving the virtues of naturalness and conciseness of such specifications. The predicates used in the properties constitute a partial basis set, and thus a partial conceptual bias for synthesis.

Overall, the specification language is quite expressive and readable. Specifications by examples and properties are usually incomplete, and hence ambiguous, but minimal. There is a danger of internal inconsistency and redundancy in such specifications, though.

This specification approach holds the promise of more effective and more efficient synthesis of algorithms than from specifications by examples alone.

7 A FRAMEWORK FOR STEPWISE LOGIC ALGORITHM SYNTHESIS

In this chapter, we develop a theoretical framework for stepwise synthesis of logic algorithms from examples and properties. Thus, in Section 7.1, we elaborate correctness criteria for logic algorithms, and in Section 7.2, we develop comparison criteria for logic algorithms. This provides an adequate structure for the formulation, in Section 7.3, of stepwise logic algorithm synthesis strategies. Future work and related work are discussed in Section 7.4 and Section 7.5, respectively, before drawing some conclusions in Section 7.6.

7.1 Correctness of Logic Algorithms

It is important to measure a logic algorithm against its intentions and its specification, as well as to measure a specification against its intentions. Indeed, such correctness criteria allow us to have a grip on any software engineering activity, be it specification elaboration, manual algorithm construction from informal specifications, semi-automatic algorithm synthesis from formal specifications, algorithm transformation, algorithm verification, and so on.

We here consider three levels of objects, namely the *intended relation*, the *specified relation* (by the specification), and the *computed relation* (by the logic algorithm). This means that we restrict our attention to relations, and not to any kind of intentions. Moreover, we assume that the intended relation is known, even if there only is an informal description of it: no fixed language is imposed for expressing the intentions. So if the intended relation is informally defined, then the correctness criteria cannot be automatically verified. They may however be used to guide software engineering activities. By specifications, we here implicitly mean specifications by examples and properties. This may be generalized to any kind of logic specifications, as in [Deville and Flener 94]. A fourth level, the *actually-computed relation* (by a logic program) could also be considered here, but we here put the focus exclusively on the logical part of software engineering activities. Comparing these three levels of relations one-by-one gives rise to three sets of correctness criteria. After completing this introduction with more formal definitions of the three levels of relations, this section is divided into three sub-sections, each dedicated to one of the three sets of correctness criteria.

Since we are only concerned with the declarative semantics of logic statements, we define model-theoretic criteria, rather than proof-theoretic ones. The used logic framework is a Herbrand-based first-order logic. This means that we are here only interested in Herbrand interpretations. For simplicity and uniformity, we assume an (infinite) language underlying our specifications and logic algorithms. Some correctness criteria have already been given in Chapter 4, but they do not handle examples and properties. We thus start from scratch for the elaboration of a suitable set of criteria.

Let $\mathcal{R}$ be the n-ary intended relation. The final objective is to obtain a logic program that succeeds on the n-tuples of $\mathcal{R}$, and fails on the n-tuples of $\overline{\mathcal{R}}$ (which is the complement of $\mathcal{R}$ in the set of all ground n-tuples over the universe $\mathcal{U}$ of terms).

We now formally define the notion of specified relation. It consists of the set of n-tuples for which the specified predicate r/n is *true* according to the specification, and of the set of n-tuples for which r/n is *false* according to the specification:

Definition 7-1: The *specified relation* of a specification by examples and properties $EP(r)$ consists of the following two sets:

$$EP^+(r) = \{\boldsymbol{t} \mid EP(r) \models r(\boldsymbol{t})\}$$

$$EP^-(r) = \{\boldsymbol{t} \mid EP(r) \models \neg r(\boldsymbol{t})\}.$$

It is clear that the specified relation is usually different from the intended relation. It is usually expected to be a subset of the intended relation, though. It is also clear that $EP^-(r)$ is not always the complement of $EP^+(r)$. We however assume that $EP(r)$ is internally consistent, that is that the intersection between $EP^+(r)$ and $EP^-(r)$ is empty.

A logic algorithm induces a computed relation. It also consists of two sets:

Definition 7-2: The *computed relation* of a logic algorithm $LA(r)$ consists of:

$$LA^+(r) = \{\boldsymbol{t} \mid LA(r) \models r(\boldsymbol{t})\}$$

$$LA^-(r) = \{\boldsymbol{t} \mid LA(r) \models \neg r(\boldsymbol{t})\}.$$

Let $LA(r)$ be $r(\boldsymbol{X}) \Leftrightarrow B[\boldsymbol{X}]$. In the following, we assume that the body B contains only primitive predicates and possibly the r/n predicate. This restriction amounts to assuming that the sub-problems involved in $LA(r)$ have been—or will be—correctly implemented, and can thus be seen as primitives for $LA(r)$. This restriction is only for ease of understanding, and can be overcome by simultaneously considering $LA(r)$ and its non-primitive predicates, as in [Deville 90].

In order to stress the differences between a specification and a logic algorithm, we further restrict logic algorithms to those designed by structural induction (as in [Deville 90]). This means that some well-founded relation can be defined between the recursive literals and the head of the logic algorithm. This emphasizes the algorithmic aspect of the formula. This also expresses that the obtained logic algorithm "terminates" (for ground queries). If such a requirement is not fulfilled, then, according to our framework, the logic algorithm is considered a specification.

When a logic algorithm is designed by structural induction on some parameter (as in Chapter 4), then predicate r/n can be interpreted in *any* Herbrand model of $LA(r)$.

Theorem 7-1: *If $LA(r)$ is designed by structural induction, then the interpretation of r/n is the same in all the Herbrand models of $LA(r)$.*

* **Proof 7-1:** *Base case.* In a design by structural induction of B, there are disjuncts in B that are without recursion. Since all predicates other than r/n have a fixed interpretation in all the Herbrand models of $LA(r)$, so does every instance of r/n that satisfies the non-recursive disjuncts. *Structure case.* Since $LA(r)$ is designed by structural induction, in any disjunct with recursion, the recursive literals involve parameters that are smaller, according to some well-founded relation, than those in the head. More precisely, for every ground instance of the logic algorithm such that the non-recursive literals in the disjunct are *true*, the recursive literals have smaller parameters than the head. Hence, by the induction hypothesis, the recursive instances of r/n have a fixed interpretation in all the Herbrand models. Since the other, non-recursive literals also have a fixed interpretation, so does r/n for the recursive disjuncts. ❑

Corollary 7-2: *If $LA(r)$ is designed by structural induction, then $LA^+(r)$ is the complement of $LA^-(r)$.*

In the following, we thus only consider recursive logic algorithms where some well-founded relation can be defined between the recursive literals and the head. We thus have to enforce that a synthesis mechanism doesn't design non-terminating recursion (for ground queries).

For convenience, correctness criteria are here defined wrt a Herbrand interpretation $\mathfrak{I}$, called the *intended interpretation*, which is such that the following conditions hold:

- $r(t)$ is *true* in $\mathfrak{I}$ iff $\mathcal{R}(t)$ holds,
- $\mathfrak{I}$ is a model of all primitive predicates.

Note that $\mathfrak{I}$ captures the intended relation $\mathcal{R}$, since the interpretation of r/n in $\mathfrak{I}$ is $\mathcal{R}$. So $\mathcal{R}$ does not have to be explicitly considered in the correctness criteria.

Example 7-1: Here are four logic algorithms for *sum*/2:

```
LA1(sum): sum(L,S) ⇔      L=[]            ∧ S=0

LA2(sum): sum(L,S) ⇔      L=[]            ∧ S=0
                        ∨ L=[HL|TL]       ∧ sum(TL,TS)
                                          ∧ add(HL,TS,S)

LA3(sum): sum(L,S) ⇔      L=[]            ∧ S=0
                        ∨ length(L,N)     ∧ N>0
                                          ∧ sub(S,TS,HL)

LA4(sum): sum(L,S) ⇔      L=[]            ∧ S=0
                        ∨ L=[HL|TL]
```

where *sub(X,Y,D)* holds iff *add(Y,D,X)* holds. The intended relation is denoted $\mathcal{S}um$. We use these logic algorithms in the following to illustrate our purpose. ♦

Three levels of correctness criteria can now be identified [Flener and Deville 92, 93ab]: measuring a logic algorithm against its intentions, measuring a logic algorithm against its specification, and comparing a specification and its intentions. We discuss these three levels in Sections 7.1.1 to 7.1.3, respectively.

7.1.1 Logic Algorithm and Intentions

The idea behind correctness of a logic algorithm wrt its intentions is to state that the intended relation $\mathcal{R}$ is identical to the relation computed by $LA(r)$:

$$\mathcal{R} = LA^+(r) \text{ and } \overline{\mathcal{R}} = LA^-(r)$$

Correctness thus states an identity, in the Herbrand models of $LA(r)$, between the intended relation $\mathcal{R}$ and the interpretation of predicate r/n. The second condition, which in general is not a consequence of the first one, is necessary to handle logic algorithms with negation (also see [Deville 90]).

Since we only consider logic algorithms that are designed by structural induction, correctness reduces, by Corollary 7-1, to $\mathcal{R} = LA^+(r)$. Moreover, partial correctness is achieved iff $\mathcal{R} \supseteq LA^+(r)$ (that is, iff the atoms "computed" by $LA(r)$ are correct), and completeness is achieved iff $\mathcal{R} \subseteq LA^+(r)$ (that is, iff all the correct atoms are "computed" by $LA(r)$). These criteria are in the sequel called the *intuitive criteria*.

The total correctness of a logic algorithm wrt its intended relation can however be re-expressed more conveniently, yielding what we call the *actual criteria*:

Definition 7-3: $LA(r)$ is *totally correct wrt* $\mathcal{R}$ iff $r(X) \Leftrightarrow B[X]$ is *true* in $\mathfrak{I}$.

We now show that this actual criterion is equivalent to its intuitive counterpart:

Theorem 7-3: *$r(X) \Leftrightarrow B[X]$ is true in $\mathfrak{I}$ iff $\mathcal{R} = LA^+(r)$.*

* **Proof 7-3:** Let's prove the involved implications one by one:

(1) Suppose that $r(X) \Leftrightarrow B[X]$ is *true* in $\mathfrak{I}$. $\mathfrak{I}$ is thus a Herbrand model of $LA(r)$. By Theorem 7-1, the interpretation of r/n is $\mathcal{R}$ in all the Herbrand models of $LA(r)$. Hence $\mathcal{R} = LA^+(r)$.

(2) Suppose that $\mathcal{R} = LA^+(r)$. By the definition of $LA^+(r)$, $r(t)$ is *true* in all the Herbrand models of $LA(r)$ iff $t \in \mathcal{R}$, or, equivalently, iff $r(t)$ is *true* in $\mathfrak{I}$. Hence $\mathfrak{I}$ is also a model of $LA(r)$, that is $r(X) \Leftrightarrow B[X]$ is *true* in $\mathfrak{I}$. ❑

Total correctness is as usual decomposed into partial correctness and completeness:

Definition 7-4: $LA(r)$ is *partially correct wrt* $\mathcal{R}$ iff $r(X) \Leftarrow B[X]$ is *true* in $\mathfrak{I}$.

Definition 7-5: $LA(r)$ is *complete wrt* $\mathcal{R}$ iff $r(X) \Rightarrow B[X]$ is *true* in $\mathfrak{I}$.

Example 7-2: $LA_2(sum)$ is totally correct wrt $\mathcal{S}um$. $LA_1(sum)$ is only partially correct wrt $\mathcal{S}um$. $LA_3(sum)$ and $LA_4(sum)$ are only complete wrt $\mathcal{S}um$.

These actual criteria are slightly stronger than their intuitive counterparts:

Theorem 7-4: *Assuming $B[X]$ is in disjunctive normal form and without recursion through negation, the following assertions hold:*

(1) *If $r(X) \Leftarrow B[X]$ is true in $\mathfrak{I}$, then $\mathcal{R} \supseteq LA^+(r)$;*

(2) *If $r(X) \Rightarrow B[X]$ is true in $\mathfrak{I}$, then $\mathcal{R} \subseteq LA^+(r)$.*

* **Proof 7-4:** See [Flener 93].

* Note that Theorem 7-4 does not hold when there is recursion through negation. We show this by constructing adequate counter-examples:

- Regarding partial correctness, let $\mathcal{R} = \{[],[1]\}$, and let $LA(r)$ be:

```
r(L) ⇔ L=[]
     ∨ L=[_,_|_] ∧ ¬r([1])
```

  In the Herbrand models of $LA(r)$, the interpretation of r/n is the set $\{r(t) \mid t$ is any non-singleton list$\}$, and thus $\mathcal{R} \not\supseteq LA^+(r)$. However, $r(L) \Leftarrow B[L]$ is *true* in $\mathfrak{I}$, as $B[L]$ is *true* in $\mathfrak{I}$ only for $L = []$, and as $r([])$ is *true* in $\mathfrak{I}$. Assertion (1) thus doesn't hold when there is recursion through negation.

- Regarding completeness, let $\mathcal{R}$ be the set of lists of 1s, and let $LA(r)$ be:

```
r(L) ⇔ L=[]
     ∨ L=[0|T] ∧ r(T)
     ∨ L=[1|T] ∧ ¬r([0|T])
```

  No Herbrand model of $LA(r)$ contains $r([1])$, and thus $\mathcal{R} \not\subseteq LA^+(r)$. However, $r(L) \Rightarrow B[L]$ is *true* in $\mathfrak{I}$. Assertion (2) thus doesn't hold when there is recursion through negation.

* Also note that the converse assertions of (1) and (2) do not hold. We show this by constructing adequate counter-examples:

- Regarding partial correctness, let $\mathcal{R} = \{[],[1]\}$, and let $LA(r)$ be:

```
r(L) ⇔ L=[]
     ∨ L=[_,_|_] ∧ r([1])
```

The only Herbrand model of $LA(r)$ is $\{r([])\}$, and thus $LA^+(r) = \{[]\} \subseteq \mathcal{R}$. Hence $LA(r)$ fulfills the intuitive criterion of partial correctness. However, $r(L) \Leftarrow B[L]$ is *false* in $\mathfrak{I}$, because $B[[1,1,1]]$ is *true* in $\mathfrak{I}$, but $r([1,1,1])$ is *false* in $\mathfrak{I}$. Hence $LA(r)$ does not fulfill the actual criterion of partial correctness. The converse of assertion (1) thus doesn't hold.

- Regarding completeness, let $\mathcal{R}$ be the set of lists of 1s, and let $LA(r)$ be:

```
r(L) ⇔ L=[]
     ∨ L=[0|T] ∧ r(T)
     ∨ L=[1|T] ∧ r([0|T])
```

$LA^+(r)$ is the set of lists of 0s and 1s, and thus a superset of $\mathcal{R}$. Hence $LA(r)$ fulfills the intuitive criterion of completeness. However, $r(L) \Rightarrow B[L]$ is *false* in $\mathfrak{I}$, because $r([1])$ is *true* in $\mathfrak{I}$, but $B[[1]]$ is *false* in $\mathfrak{I}$. Hence $LA(r)$ does not fulfill the actual criterion of completeness. The converse of (2) thus doesn't hold.

These last two counter-examples clearly show why the actual criteria are "better" than their intuitive counterparts: they prevent logic algorithms that are partially correct (respectively complete) in a "bad" way, namely in that they cannot easily be "extended" to totally correct algorithms.

7.1.2 Logic Algorithm and Specification

Next come criteria for measuring a logic algorithm against its specification. Given a set of examples $\mathcal{E}(r) = \mathcal{E}^+(r) \cup \mathcal{E}^-(r)$, a logic algorithm $LA(r)$ is complete wrt $\mathcal{E}(r)$ iff the positive examples are contained[7] in the relation computed by $LA(r)$, but the negative ones are not (that is, iff $\mathcal{E}^+(r) \subseteq LA^+(r)$ and $\mathcal{E}^-(r) \subseteq LA^-(r)$). And $LA(r)$ is partially correct wrt $\mathcal{E}(r)$ iff the positive examples contain the computed relation (that is, iff $\mathcal{E}^+(r) \supseteq LA^+(r)$; it would be meaningless to include here the partial correctness of the negative examples, because $\mathcal{E}^+(r)$ is not usually the complement of $\mathcal{E}^-(r)$ in $\mathcal{U}^n$).

Similar criteria can be expressed for a set of properties $\mathcal{P}(r)$. In the versions above, the sets $\mathcal{E}^+(r)$ and $\mathcal{E}^-(r)$ then have to be replaced by the following two sets:

$$\mathcal{P}^+(r) = \{t \mid \mathcal{P}(r) \models r(t)\}$$
$$\mathcal{P}^-(r) = \{t \mid \mathcal{P}(r) \models \neg r(t)\}$$

Again, these criteria are in the following called the *intuitive criteria*. Their formalization is defined in terms of the intended interpretation $\mathfrak{I}$. Although slightly stronger than the intuitive criteria, the following *actual criteria* are more adapted to a framework of logic algorithm synthesis [Deville and Flener 94]:

Definition 7-6: $LA(r)$ is *complete wrt* $\mathcal{E}(r)$ iff the following two conditions hold:

- $r(t) \in \mathcal{E}^+(r) \Rightarrow B[t]$ is *true* in $\mathfrak{I}$;
- $\neg r(t) \in \mathcal{E}^-(r) \Rightarrow B[t]$ is *false* in $\mathfrak{I}$.

Definition 7-7: $LA(r)$ is *partially correct wrt* $\mathcal{E}(r)$ iff the next condition holds:

- $r(t) \in \mathcal{E}^+(r) \Leftarrow B[t]$ is *true* in $\mathfrak{I}$.

---

7. For ease of notation, the set $\mathcal{E}^+(r)$ of positive examples is here also considered to denote the corresponding set of tuples. Similarly for the set $\mathcal{E}^-(r)$ of negative examples.

Definition 7-8: $LA(r)$ is *complete wrt* $\mathcal{P}(r)$ iff the following two conditions hold:

- $\mathcal{P}(r) \models r(t) \Rightarrow B[t]$ is *true* in $\Im$;
- $\mathcal{P}(r) \models \neg r(t) \Rightarrow B[t]$ is *false* in $\Im$.

Definition 7-9: $LA(r)$ is *partially correct wrt* $\mathcal{P}(r)$ iff the next condition holds:

- $\mathcal{P}(r) \models r(t) \Leftarrow B[t]$ is *true* in $\Im$.

Definition 7-10: $LA(r)$ is *totally correct wrt* $\mathcal{E}(r)$ (respectively $\mathcal{P}(r)$) iff $LA(r)$ is complete and partially correct wrt $\mathcal{E}(r)$ (respectively $\mathcal{P}(r)$).

Any of these criteria holds between a logic algorithm $LA(r)$ and a specification $EP(r)$ iff it holds between $LA(r)$ and *both* the example set and the property set of $EP(r)$.

Total correctness thus means that what is computed (positively or negatively) by the logic algorithm must be consistent with its (part of the) specification. For a tuple t where the considered (part of the) specification is undecidable (that is, where $t \notin EP^+(r)$ and $t \notin EP^-(r)$), $r(t)$ can be either *true* or *false* in the logic algorithm.

Example 7-3: $LA_2(sum)$, $LA_3(sum)$, and $LA_4(sum)$ are complete wrt $EP(sum)$.

7.1.3 Specification and Intentions

Finally, there is consistency of a specification wrt the intentions. For instance, consistency of the examples $\mathcal{E}(r)$ wrt the intended relation $\mathcal{R}$ means that the positive examples are contained in $\mathcal{R}$, and that the negative examples are contained in its complement $\overline{\mathcal{R}}$.

Definition 7-11: $\mathcal{E}(r)$ is *consistent with* $\mathcal{R}$ iff the following two conditions hold:

- $r(t) \in \mathcal{E}^+(r) \Rightarrow r(t)$ is *true* in $\Im$ (that is, iff $\mathcal{E}^+(r) \subseteq \mathcal{R}$);
- $\neg r(t) \in \mathcal{E}^-(r) \Rightarrow r(t)$ is *false* in $\Im$ (that is, iff $\mathcal{E}^-(r) \subseteq \overline{\mathcal{R}}$).

Definition 7-12: $\mathcal{P}(r)$ is *consistent with* $\mathcal{R}$ iff the next condition holds:

- $p \in \mathcal{P}(r) \Rightarrow p$ is *true* in $\Im$ (that is, iff $\mathcal{P}^+(r) \subseteq \mathcal{R}$ and $\mathcal{P}^-(r) \subseteq \overline{\mathcal{R}}$).

Definition 7-13: A specification $EP(r)$ is *consistent with* $\mathcal{R}$ iff *both* the example set and the property set of $EP(r)$ are consistent with $\mathcal{R}$.

Example 7-4: $EP(sum)$ is consistent with $\mathcal{S}um$.

The specified relation of a consistent specification is thus a subset of the intended relation. Moreover, if $LA(r)$ is partially or totally correct wrt $\mathcal{E}(r)$ (respectively $\mathcal{P}(r)$), and $\mathcal{E}(r)$ (respectively $\mathcal{P}(r)$) is consistent with $\mathcal{R}$, then $LA(r)$ is partially correct wrt $\mathcal{R}$.

If there is no formal definition of the intended relation $\mathcal{R}$, then some correctness criteria cannot be applied in a formal way. But they can be used to state features and heuristics of a synthesis mechanism.

7.2 Comparison of Logic Algorithms

It is also important to compare logic algorithms for the same intended relation $\mathcal{R}$. Indeed, this is useful in stepwise synthesis to compare intermediate logic algorithms, and to establish progression criteria.

Let $\mathcal{L}(r)$ be the set of all possible logic algorithms of r/n, where the bodies only involve some fixed set of primitive predicates and the r/n predicate, and where $X_1,\ldots,X_n$ are the distinct variables used in the heads. Let:

- $LA_1(r)$: $r(X_1,\ldots,X_n) \Leftrightarrow B_1[X_1,\ldots,X_n]$
- $LA_2(r)$: $r(X_1,\ldots,X_n) \Leftrightarrow B_2[X_1,\ldots,X_n]$

be two logic algorithms in $\mathcal{L}(r)$.

In Section 7.2.1, we define a criterion for comparing logic algorithms in terms of generality. Since verifying this criterion is only semi-decidable, we introduce, in Section 7.2.2, a sound approximation of it, namely syntactic generalization.

7.2.1 Semantic Generalization

Intuitively, $LA_1(r)$ is less general than $LA_2(r)$ iff B_1 is "less often" true than B_2. More formally:

Definition 7-14: $LA_1(r)$ is *(semantically) less general than* $LA_2(r)$ (denoted $LA_1(r) \leq LA_2(r)$) iff $\forall X_1 \ldots \forall X_n \, (B_1 \Rightarrow B_2)$ is *true*.

Being *semantically more general* ($\geq$) is defined dually. Two logic algorithms, each more general than the other, are *semantically equivalent* ($\cong$). We use $<$ for $\leq$ and $\not\cong$.

Example 7-5: We have $LA_1(sum) < LA_2(sum) < LA_3(sum) < LA_4(sum)$.

Note that a semantic generalization relationship between two logic algorithms does not amount to a logical implication relationship between them.

* The set $\mathcal{L}(r)$ modulo $\cong$ (denoted $\mathcal{L}(r)^{\cong}$) is partially ordered under $\leq$. It includes as least element $\bot_r$ (defined as $r(X_1,\ldots,X_n) \Leftrightarrow false$, and called *bottom*) and as greatest element $\top_r$ (defined as $r(X_1,\ldots,X_n) \Leftrightarrow true$, and called *top*). In order to have an upper bound to any ascending sequence of logic algorithms, let's extend $\mathcal{L}(r)$ to $\mathcal{M}(r)$ by allowing an infinite number of literals in the body of a logic algorithm. We obviously have that $(\mathcal{M}(r)^{\cong}, \leq)$ is isomorphic to $(\mathcal{P}(\mathcal{U}^n), \subseteq)$, where $\mathcal{P}(\mathcal{S})$ denotes the set of subsets of set $\mathcal{S}$. Hence $(\mathcal{M}(r)^{\cong}, \leq)$ is also a complete lattice, whose lub operator is the logical *or* connective (denoted $\vee$), and whose glb operator is the logical *and* connective (denoted $\wedge$) over the bodies of logic algorithms.

Comparing logic algorithms in terms of semantic generality can be a difficult task, and is only semi-decidable anyway. We thus define a particular case of this generality relation in terms of purely syntactic criteria.

7.2.2 Syntactic Generalization

In view of defining syntactic criteria for generalization, we need to constrain the logic algorithm language. Thus, in this section, we assume that logic algorithms have bodies that are in disjunctive normal form. We represent formulas by multisets, so as to avoid ordering problems. A similar development, though for second-order expressions, but without negation, has been made by [Tinkham 90].

Definition 7-15: Let F be a conjunction of literals (respectively a disjunction of conjunctions of literals). Then *elems*(F) is $\varnothing$ iff F is *true* (respectively *false*), and the multiset of literals of F (respectively the multiset of the conjunctions of literals of F), otherwise.

Let's first define syntactic generalization over conjunctions of literals, and then over logic algorithms:

Definition 7-16: A conjunction C_1 is *syntactically less general than* a conjunction C_2 *with* a substitution θ (denoted $C_1 \ll C_2$) iff $elems(C_2\theta) \subseteq elems(C_1)$.

Example 7-6: $p(a,X) \wedge q(Y) \ll p(V,W)$ with $\{V/a, W/X\}$.

This definition is different from classical θ-subsumption for clauses [Plotkin 70], because the used substitution is here *given*, rather than only constrained to exist. This variant is useful for comparing sets of clauses, as captured in the next definition.

Definition 7-17: $LA_1(r)$ is *syntactically less general than* $LA_2(r)$ (denoted $LA_1(r) \ll LA_2(r)$) iff there is a total function *fct* from $elems(B_1)$ to $elems(B_2)$, such that, for every disjunct D in $elems(B_1)$, there is a substitution θ that only binds existential variables of $LA_2(r)$, such that $D \ll fct(D)$ with substitution θ.

Note that θ cannot bind a universal variable of $LA_2(r)$ since this could actually lead to a specialization. For instance: $r(X,Y) \Leftrightarrow q(Z) \;\; > \;\; r(X,Y) \Leftrightarrow q(X)$.

Example 7-7: We have $LA_1(sum) \ll LA_2(sum) \ll LA_4(sum)$. However, $LA_2(sum)$ and $LA_3(sum)$ are incomparable under «, as they involve different predicates.

Being *syntactically more general* (») is defined dually. Two logic algorithms, each syntactically more general than the other, are *syntactically equivalent* (≈). Syntactical equivalence is more general than alphabetic variance, because of the irrelevance of the ordering of disjuncts within logic algorithms, and of literals within disjuncts.

The set $\mathcal{L}(r)^{\approx}$ is partially ordered under «. The following proposition is a direct consequence of the definitions:

Proposition 7-5: *The relations «, », ≈ are sub-relations of ≤, ≥, ≅, respectively.*

We now define an atomic refinement operator, after making two preliminary observations. A *most-general literal* in a disjunct D of $LA(r)$ is of the form $p(Z_1,\ldots,Z_m)$ or $\neg p(Z_1,\ldots,Z_m)$, where p is an m-ary predicate, and $Z_1,\ldots,Z_m$ are existential variables occurring exactly once in D. And a *most-general term* in a disjunct D of $LA(r)$ is of the form $f(Z_1,\ldots,Z_m)$, where f is an m-ary functor, and $Z_1,\ldots,Z_m$ are existential variables occurring exactly once in D.

Definition 7-18: The refinement operator *gen*/1 is such that $LA_2(r) \in gen(LA_1(r))$ iff exactly one of the following holds:

- $LA_2(r)$ is derived from $LA_1(r)$ by adding a disjunct to $LA_1(r)$; [8]
- $LA_2(r)$ is derived from $LA_1(r)$ by replacing a disjunct D_1 by a disjunct D_2, so that:
  - D_2 is D_1 without a most-general literal in D_1; [9]
  - D_2 is D_1 where one or more occurrences of a variable V are replaced by a new existential variable W;
  - D_2 is D_1 where one or more occurrences of a most general term in D_1 are replaced by a new existential variable W.

The ability to add a disjunct of course often overrides the need to modify a disjunct, as it suffices to add the modified disjunct in the first place, for instance when creating a logic algorithm from $\perp_r$. However, this is not always possible, for instance when modifying an existing logic algorithm into another one.

8. By convention, adding a disjunct D to $\perp_r$ amounts to replacing *false* by D.
9. By convention, deleting the unique literal of a singleton disjunct D amounts to replacing D by *true* if there is no *true* disjunct yet in $LA_1(r)$, and to discarding D, otherwise.

Example 7-8: $LA_2(sum) \in gen(LA_1(sum))$, and $LA_4(sum) \in gen^3(LA_2(sum))$.

Let us now relate the refinement operator *gen* to the syntactic generality relation «:

Theorem 7-6: *The following three assertions hold:*

(1) *gen is a syntactic generalization operator:*
$\forall LA'(r) \in gen(LA(r)) \quad LA(r) \ll LA'(r)$;

(2) *gen can generate any syntactic generalization:*
$LA_1(r) \ll LA_2(r) \Leftrightarrow \exists n\ \exists LA_2'(r) \in gen^n(LA_1(r)) \quad LA_2'(r) \approx LA_2(r)$;

(3) *gen can generate all logic algorithms of $\mathcal{L}(r)$ from $\bot_r$:* $gen^*(\bot_r) = \mathcal{L}(r)$.

Proof 7-6: Analogous to the proofs in [Tinkham 90]. ❑

An inverse operator *spec*/1 of *gen*/1 is similarly defined, such that *spec*/1 is a syntactic specialization operator that can generate all logic algorithms of $\mathcal{L}(r)$ from $\top_r$.

7.3 Stepwise Logic Algorithm Synthesis Strategies

It is interesting to decompose a synthesis process into a series of steps, each designing an intermediate logic algorithm. Indeed:

- this allows different methods to be deployed at each step, thus enforcing a neat separation of concerns;
- this yields monitoring points where correctness and comparison criteria can be applied, hence measuring the effectiveness and progression of synthesis.

Stepwise synthesis can be:

- *incremental*: examples or properties are presented one-by-one, each presentation yielding a run through all synthesis steps;
- *non-incremental*: examples or properties are presented all-at-once, yielding a single run through all synthesis steps;
- *increasing*: each logic algorithm is more general than its predecessor;
- *decreasing*: each logic algorithm is less general than its predecessor;
- *monotonic*: synthesis is either increasing or decreasing;
- *non-monotonic*: synthesis is neither increasing, nor decreasing;
- *consistent*: each intermediate logic algorithm is complete wrt the examples and properties presented so far;
- *inconsistent*: each intermediate logic algorithm is not necessarily complete wrt the examples and properties presented so far.

Using the criteria defined in the two previous sections, a huge variety of stepwise synthesis strategies can be defined, fitting any valid combination of the features enumerated above. In Section 7.3.1, we briefly sketch a strategy for incremental synthesis, and in Section 7.3.2, we fully describe a strategy for non-incremental synthesis.

* 7.3.1 An Incremental Synthesis Strategy

In the case of incremental synthesis, let's view the steps of one synthesis increment as a macro-step performing a transformation *trans*. Synthesis is then the design of a series of logic algorithms:

$$LA_0(r), LA_1(r), \ldots, LA_i(r), \ldots$$

from a series of specifications $\mathcal{S}_i(r)$ that are sets of examples and properties:

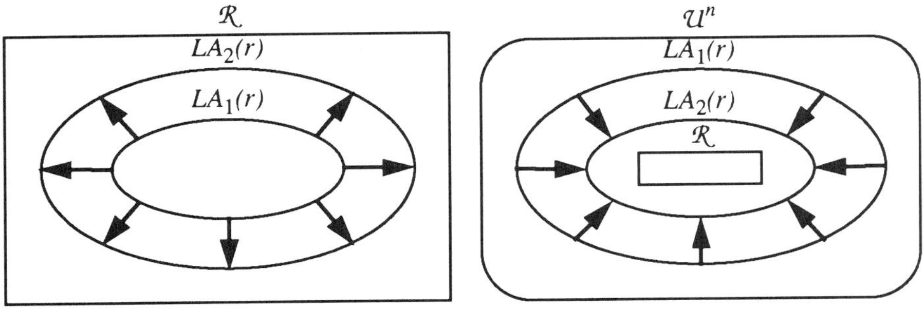

Figure 7-1: (a) Upward and (b) downward progression

$$\mathcal{S}_1(r), \ldots, \mathcal{S}_i(r), \ldots$$

with:

$$\mathcal{S}_i(r) \subseteq \mathcal{S}_{i+1}(r), \text{ for } i \geq 0$$

such that the following two conditions hold:

- $LA_0(r) = \perp_r$,
- $LA_i(r) = trans(LA_{i-1}(r), \mathcal{S}_i(r))$, for $i > 0$.

This covers *iterative synthesis*, where only the last presented example or property is actually used by *trans*. If *trans* is monotonic and continuous (wrt the ≤ order on logic algorithms), then $trans^{\omega}(\perp_r)$ is its least fixpoint. So if *trans* preserves partial correctness wrt $\mathcal{R}$, then the fixed point is also partially correct wrt $\mathcal{R}$. Note that completeness wrt $\mathcal{R}$ is not necessarily achieved, and that the resulting logic algorithm can involve infinitely many literals. This incremental strategy yields increasing (hence monotonic) synthesis; it may yield consistent or inconsistent synthesis.

7.3.2 A Non-Incremental Synthesis Strategy

Let's first give a criterion for upward (or partial-correctness preserving) progression:

Definition 7-19: (See Figure 7-1a.) If the following two conditions hold:

- $LA_2(r) \geq LA_1(r)$,
- $LA_2(r)$ is partially correct wrt $\mathcal{R}$,

then $LA_2(r)$ is a *better partially correct approximation of* $\mathcal{R}$ *than* $LA_1(r)$.

Dually, there is a criterion for downward (or completeness preserving) progression:

Definition 7-20: (See Figure 7-1b.) If the following two conditions hold:

- $LA_2(r) \leq LA_1(r)$,
- $LA_2(r)$ is complete wrt $\mathcal{R}$,

then $LA_2(r)$ is a *better complete approximation of* $\mathcal{R}$ *than* $LA_1(r)$.

Example 7-9: $LA_3(sum)$ is a better complete approximation of $\mathcal{Sum}$ than $LA_4(sum)$.

A first idea of a non-incremental stepwise synthesis strategy (with a fixed, finite number f of predefined steps) is to achieve downward progression:

At **Step 1**, "create" $LA_1(r)$ such that:

- $LA_1(r)$ is complete wrt $\mathcal{R}$.

At **Step *i*** ($2 \leq i \leq f$), transform $LA_{i-1}(r)$ into $LA_i(r)$ such that:

- $LA_i(r)$ is a better complete approximation of $\mathcal{R}$ than $LA_{i-1}(r)$.

An obvious way to do Step 1 is to make $LA_1(r)$ equal to T_r.

But this strategy doesn't take care of the partial-correctness aspects. We thus want to define a specialization operator that allows the transformation of the series of intermediate logic algorithms into another series of intermediate logic algorithms that actually reflects upward progression. The idea is to expand the disjuncts of a logic algorithm with equality atoms, each such atom unifying one of the variables of a disjunct with some constant(s) obtained by "evaluating", in $\Im$, that disjunct on some example of the specification.

Example 7-10: Let $LA_5(sum)$ be as follows:

```
sum(L,S) ⇔
      L=[]
  ∨   L=[HL|TL]        ∧  sum(TL,TS)
```

Its expansion according to the examples of $EP(sum)$, as in Example 6-5, is:

```
sum(L,S) ⇔
      L=[]             ∧     L=[] ∧ S=0
  ∨   L=[HL|TL]        ∧  sum(TL,TS)
                       ∧     L=[7]∧HL=7∧TL=[]∧TS=0∧S=7
                          ∨  L=[4,5]∧HL=4∧TL=[5]∧TS=5∧S=9
                          ∨  L=[2,3,1]∧HL=2∧TL=[3,1]∧TS=4∧S=6
```

where the boldface atoms are synthesized atoms, and the others are trailing atoms. ♦

In such a non-incremental synthesis, the series of expanded logic algorithms can be shown to progress upwards (see below). To achieve this expansion, we here only consider logic algorithms whose bodies are in disjunctive normal form. The used predicates are assumed to be either primitives or the predicate r/n that is defined by the logic algorithm. Let's start with a few basic definitions.

Definition 7-21: Let $D[\boldsymbol{X}]$ be a disjunct of a logic algorithm $LA(r)$, such that the only free variables of D are the n universal variables $\boldsymbol{X}$ in the head of $LA(r)$. We say that $D[\boldsymbol{X}]$ *covers* atom $r(\boldsymbol{t})$ iff $\exists D[\boldsymbol{t}]$ is *true* in $\Im$.

Example 7-11: The first disjunct of $LA_5(sum)$ covers the example $sum([],0)$. Its second disjunct covers the example $sum([7],7)$, but it doesn't cover $sum([],0)$.

* **Definition 7-22:** Let disjunct $D[\boldsymbol{X}]$ of a logic algorithm $LA(r)$ cover atom $r(\boldsymbol{t})$. The *expansion of* $D[\boldsymbol{X}]$ *wrt* $r(\boldsymbol{t})$ is $D[\boldsymbol{X}] \wedge \boldsymbol{X} = \boldsymbol{t} \wedge wit(\boldsymbol{Y})$, where $\boldsymbol{Y}$ are the existential variables of $D[\boldsymbol{X}]$, and $wit(\boldsymbol{Y})$ is a formula that is *true* in $\Im$ only for (ground) witnesses $\boldsymbol{w}$ of $\boldsymbol{Y}$ in $\exists D[\boldsymbol{t}]$ (that is, $D[\boldsymbol{t}]\{\boldsymbol{Y}/\boldsymbol{w}\}$ is *true* in $\Im$ iff $wit(\boldsymbol{w})$ is *true* in $\Im$).

Example 7-12: The expansion of the second disjunct of $LA_5(sum)$ wrt $sum([7],7)$ is:

$$L = [HL|TL] \wedge sum(TL,TS) \wedge (L = [7] \wedge S = 7) \wedge (HL = 7 \wedge TL = [] \wedge TS = 0)$$

The expansion of the second disjunct of $LA_5(sum)$ wrt $sum([1,2,A],6)$ is:

$$L = [HL|TL] \wedge sum(TL,TS) \wedge$$
$$(L = [1,2,A] \wedge S = 6) \wedge (HL = 1 \wedge TL = [2,A] \wedge TS = B \wedge add(2,A,B)).$$ ♦

Obviously, $wit(\boldsymbol{Y})$ can always be expressed as a possibly infinite disjunction of equality atoms. In the sequel, we here only consider the situation where $wit(\boldsymbol{Y})$ can be expressed as a *finite* disjunction of equality atoms (whose left-hand sides are Y). Moreover, we then rewrite $wit(Y)$ as $Y = w$ (iff $wit(Y)$ is a single equality atom whose right-hand side is the term-tuple w), or as $Y \in \underline{w}$ (iff $wit(Y)$ is a disjunction of equality atoms whose right-hand sides are the term-tuples w_i). We call w, or $\underline{w}$, the *witnesses* of Y, even though they are not necessarily ground.

For non-recursive literals, since they are assumed to be primitives, it is possible to compute the witnesses $\underline{w}$ *without* knowing $\mathcal{R}$. We thus only need an oracle for the specified predicate r/n. A candidate mechanized oracle is one that performs deduction using the specification $EP(r)$ as knowledge about r/n. Such a *deductive oracle* is sound[10] provided $EP(r)$ is consistent with $\mathcal{R}$. Other oracles can be imagined, performing analogical reasoning, say. In the sequel we just assume the existence of such an oracle, but do not require it to be sound or complete. A more practical version of the previous definition is thus:

* **Definition 7-23:** Let $O(r)$ be an oracle for predicate r/n. Let disjunct $D[X]$ of a logic algorithm $LA(r)$ cover atom $r(t)$. The *expansion of* $D[X]$ *wrt* $r(t)$ *and* $O(r)$ is $D[X] \wedge X = t \wedge Y \in \underline{w}$, where Y are the existential variables of $D[X]$, and $\underline{w}$ are the witnesses of Y, using $O(r)$, in $\exists D[t]$.

Example 7-13: Take $EP(permutation)$ as in Example 6-4, and $LA(permutation)$ as:

```
permutation(L,P) ⇔
       L=[]
   ∨  L=[HL|TL]          ∧ permutation(TL,TP)
```

The expansion of the second disjunct of $LA(permutation)$ wrt $permutation([a,b,c],[c,a,b])$ and the deductive oracle based on $EP(permutation)$ is:

$$L = [HL|TL] \wedge permutation(TL,TP) \wedge$$
$$(L = [a,b,c] \wedge P = [c,a,b]) \wedge (HL = a \wedge TL = [b,c] \wedge TP \in \{[b,c],[c,b]\})$$

If $TL = [b,c]$, then the deductive oracle infers that either $TP = [b,c]$ or $TP = [c,b]$, according to properties P_2 and P_3, respectively. ♦

Example 7-14: Take $EP(efface)$ as in Example 6-3, and let $LA(efface)$ be:

```
efface(E,L,R) ⇔
       R=[]
   ∨  R=[HR|TR]          ∧ efface(TE,TL,TR)
```

The expansion of the second disjunct of $LA(efface)$ wrt $efface(b,[b,c],[c])$ and the deductive oracle based on $EP(efface)$ is:

$$R = [HR|TR] \wedge efface(TE,TL,TR) \wedge$$
$$(E = b \wedge L = [b,c] \wedge R = [c]) \wedge (HR = c \wedge TR = [] \wedge \langle TE,TL\rangle \in \{\langle a,[a]\rangle,\langle X,[X]\rangle\})$$

Indeed, if $TR = []$, then the deductive oracle infers that either $\langle TE,TL\rangle = \langle a,[a]\rangle$ or $\langle TE,TL\rangle = \langle X,[X]\rangle$, according to example E_1 and property P_1, respectively. This illustrates three things. First, some of the existential variables may have to be regrouped into tuples in order to avoid losing some relationships. Second, the availability of the examples to the oracle provokes the appearance of an answer that is totally unrelated to any computation of $efface(b,[b,c],[c])$, namely $\langle TE,TL\rangle = \langle a,[a]\rangle$.

10. An oracle is *sound* iff all its answers are correct. An oracle is *complete* iff it gives all correct answers.

We explain in Section 12.4.2 how such freak answers may be eliminated. Third, variables may appear in answers given by the oracle, such as in <*TE*,*TL*> = <*X*,[*X*]>. It is important to realize that these are existential variables. ♦

Let's now extend the previous definition to entire sets of covered atoms:

* **Definition 7-24:** Let $O(r)$ be an oracle for predicate r/n. Let disjunct $D[\boldsymbol{X}]$ of a logic algorithm $LA(r)$ cover all the atoms of an atom set $\mathcal{A}(r) = \{r(\boldsymbol{t}_i)\}$. The *expansion of* $D[\boldsymbol{X}]$ *wrt* $\mathcal{A}(r)$ *and* $O(r)$ is $D[\boldsymbol{X}] \wedge \vee_i (\boldsymbol{X} = \boldsymbol{t}_i \wedge \boldsymbol{Y} \in \underline{\boldsymbol{w}}_i)$, where $\boldsymbol{Y}$ are the existential variables of $D[\boldsymbol{X}]$, and $\underline{\boldsymbol{w}}_i$ are the witnesses of $\boldsymbol{Y}$, using $O(r)$, in $\exists D[\boldsymbol{t}_i]$.

Finally, let's extend this definition to the expansion of an entire logic algorithm:

* **Definition 7-25:** Given an atom set $\mathcal{A}(r)$, an oracle $O(r)$, and a logic algorithm $LA(r)$, the operator *exp*/3 is a total function into $\mathcal{L}(r)$, such that $exp(LA(r), \mathcal{A}(r), O(r))$ is $LA(r)$ where each disjunct has been replaced by its expansion wrt the largest subset of $\mathcal{A}(r)$ that it covers and $O(r)$.

Example 7-15: We effectively have that $exp(LA_5(sum), \mathcal{E}^+(sum), EP(sum))$ is as depicted in Example 7-10. ♦

It is obvious that *exp*/3 can be expressed as a sequence of applications of *spec*. So *exp* is a syntactic specialization function: $exp(LA(r)) \ll LA(r)$, thus $exp(LA(r)) \leq LA(r)$.

In the following, once a specification $EP(r)$ has been clearly mentioned, we assume that $O(r)$ is the deductive oracle based on $EP(r)$, and that $\mathcal{A}(r)$ is the positive example set of $EP(r)$. This allows a more compact notation for the *exp*/3 operator.

Definition 7-26: In an expanded logic algorithm, the literals can be partitioned into two categories: the *synthesized literals* are those that are already present before the expansion process, and the *trailing atoms* are those added by the expansion process.

For syntactic brevity, the trailing atoms of a logic algorithm are often summarized into an annotation to the disjunct of synthesized literals they are logically attached to. Such an annotation consists of a set of identifiers of positive examples.

Example 7-16: For instance, $exp(LA_5(sum))$ could also be written as:

```
sum(L,S) ⇔
      L=[]                                           {E1}
   ∨  L=[HL|TL]        ∧  sum(TL,TS)            {E2,E3,E4}
```

The non-incremental synthesis strategy above can now be refined as follows, so as to achieve simultaneous upward and downward progressions [Flener and Deville 92, 93ab]:

At **Step 1**, "create" $LA_1(r)$ such that:

- $LA_1(r)$ is complete wrt $\mathcal{R}$,
- $exp(LA_1(r))$ is partially correct wrt $\mathcal{R}$.

At **Step *i*** ($2 \leq i \leq f$), transform $LA_{i-1}(r)$ into $LA_i(r)$ such that:

- $LA_i(r)$ is a better complete approximation of $\mathcal{R}$ than $LA_{i-1}(r)$,
- $exp(LA_i(r))$ is a better partially correct approximation of $\mathcal{R}$ than $exp(LA_{i-1}(r))$.

This strategy is very general.

We now state and prove a generic theorem showing how steps 2 to f of the generic strategy above can be refined in order to yield a practical framework.

Theorem 7-7: *Let $LA(r)$ be $r(X) \Leftrightarrow \vee_{1 \le j \le m} A_j$ and $LA'(r)$ be $r(X) \Leftrightarrow \vee_{1 \le j \le m} A_j \wedge B_j$, where A_j, B_j are any formulas. The following two assertions hold:*

(1) *If $LA(r)$ is complete wrt $\mathcal{R}$ and $\mathcal{R}(X) \wedge A_j \Rightarrow B_j$ $(1 \le j \le m)$ then $LA'(r)$ is a better complete approximation of $\mathcal{R}$ than $LA(r)$.*

(2) *If $LA(r)$ is partially correct wrt $\mathcal{R}$ and $A_j \Rightarrow B_j$ $(1 \le j \le m)$ then $LA'(r)$ is a better partially correct approximation of $\mathcal{R}$ than $LA(r)$.*

* **Proof 7-7:** Let's prove these assertions one by one:

(1) By Definition 7-5, the first hypothesis reads:

$$r(X) \Rightarrow \vee_{1 \le j \le m} A_j.$$

By definition of $\mathfrak{I}$, the second hypothesis reads $(1 \le j \le m)$:

$$r(X) \wedge A_j \Rightarrow B_j, \text{ or, equivalently: } r(X) \Rightarrow \neg A_j \vee B_j$$

Combined with the first hypothesis, we get:

$$r(X) \Rightarrow (\vee_{1 \le j \le m} A_j) \wedge (\wedge_{1 \le j \le m} \neg A_j \vee B_j)$$

The right-hand side can be rearranged as:

$$\vee_{1 \le j \le m} A_j \wedge B_j \wedge C_j$$

where C_j is a formula involving $\neg A_i$ and B_i $(1 \le i \le m, i \ne j)$. Hence:

$$r(X) \Rightarrow \vee_{1 \le j \le m} A_j \wedge B_j$$

that is: $LA'(r)$ is complete wrt $\mathcal{R}$. By construction, we have: $LA'(r) \ll LA(r)$, that is, by Theorem 7-5: $LA'(r) \le LA(r)$. Thus: $LA'(r)$ is a better complete approximation of $\mathcal{R}$ than $LA(r)$.

(2) Obviously, we have:

$$\vee_{1 \le j \le m} A_j \wedge B_j \Rightarrow \vee_{1 \le j \le m} A_j$$

Moreover, the second hypothesis implies:

$$\vee_{1 \le j \le m} A_j \Rightarrow \vee_{1 \le j \le m} A_j \wedge B_j$$

Thus: $LA'(r) \cong LA(r)$, that is, in particular: $LA'(r) \ge LA(r)$. Using the first hypothesis, we obtain: $LA'(r)$ is partially correct wrt $\mathcal{R}$. Thus: $LA'(r)$ is a better partially correct approximation of $\mathcal{R}$ than $LA(r)$. ❑

The second hypothesis of assertion (2) ensures that the introduced literals are redundant with the already existing ones. In other words, as the proof shows, we then actually have $LA'(r) \cong LA(r)$. The second hypothesis of assertion (1) ensures that the introduced literals are "redundant" with the intended relation $\mathcal{R}$.

In practice, assertion (1) is applied to the logic algorithms $LA_i(r)$, whereas assertion (2) is applied to the logic algorithms $exp(LA_i(r))$, where $i > 1$. The first hypotheses of both assertions need not be proved if they are established by Step 1 and then preserved by application of Theorem 7-7 to all previous steps. Proving the second condition of assertion (1) can't be done in a formal way in case of a lack of a formal definition of $\mathcal{R}$. However, this can be used to guide a synthesis mechanism, for instance by means of interaction with the specifier, hence increasing the confidence in the synthesis.

Also note that the $exp(LA_i(r))$ actually do not strictly *pro*gress upwards at all, and that there is hence no possible upwards convergence. This is not a disaster, because the $LA_i(r)$ may actually strictly progress downwards, and hence possibly converge to a correct logic algorithm. But the $exp(LA_i(r))$ do not *re*gress either, and may be used to show that completeness wrt the examples is preserved (provided this is initially achieved by Step 1). Moreover, the $exp(LA_i(r))$ are useful in that they provide the input data for steps $i + 1$.

7.4 Future Work

This chapter doesn't address *learnability*. This issue is very important for inductive inference, and has mainly been studied for incremental approaches. The definition of the class of algorithms that can be identified from examples and properties, and the characterization of how this identification can be attained (finitely, in-the-limit,...), are open questions so far.

Regarding *generalization models*, the main focus here is on syntactic generalization, because of its usage and adequacy in later chapters. But our framework of comparing logic algorithms in terms of generality can of course be further generalized by incorporating stronger, semantic generalization criteria, such as those of [Buntine 88], which exploit background knowledge.

7.5 Related Work

The here presented criteria for *correctness* of logic algorithms are a direct consequence of the results by [Deville 90], which are also outlined in Chapter 4. A comprehensive survey of correctness criteria for logic programs can be found in the background sections of chapters 4 and 8 of [Deville 90]. Some researchers of the machine learning community, and almost all authors of the ILP community (see Chapter 3), have addressed the correctness issue. The resulting criteria are specific to the chosen specification languages, but very similar (also to ours) once the differences in terminology are abstracted away. A consensus is about to emerge, though. These works usually also address learnability issues.

Many artificial intelligence tasks involve a search space of hypotheses. A *model of generalization* of hypotheses then comes in handy to organize that search space. This allows a more intelligent search than pure enumeration, for instance by pruning uninteresting branches of the search space.

One of the first studies on syntactic generalization was made by [Plotkin 70, 71]. His generalization criterion for clauses, known as *θ-subsumption*, is that clause C θ-subsumes clause D iff there exists a substitution σ such that $C\sigma \subseteq D$. In other words, only the deleting-a-conjunct and replacing-a-constant-by-a-variable rules are used by θ-subsumption. But this criterion is purely syntactic, and thus doesn't exploit possibly existent background knowledge. So he developed another criterion, called *relative subsumption*, which says that clause C generalizes clause D relative to the set of clauses P iff there exists a substitution σ such that $P \models \forall(C\sigma \Rightarrow D)$. He also introduced an induction mechanism for computing the *relative least-general generalization* (*rlgg*) of two clauses relative some other clauses. His search for an *rlgg* goes from specific-to-general. The drawback of this technique is that, in general, the *rlgg* of two clauses is not finite. This severely restricts the applicability of these results.

The concept of θ-subsumption was picked up again by [Shapiro 82], who only considers definite clauses. His search for hypotheses goes from general-to-specific, using a *most-general specialization* operator to explore a specialization hierarchy. The technique has been applied to logic program synthesis and debugging: specialization of a too general program occurs by discarding too general clauses, and generalization of a too specific program occurs by adding specializations of previously discarded clauses.

This *Model Inference System* (MIS, see Section 3.4.1) has spawned a lot of renewed interest in generalization models. For instance, [Tinkham 90] extends Shapiro's results to a second-order search space. Simultaneously, but independently, [Gegg-Harrison 89] also suggests generalization operators within a second-order logic, though for an entirely different application.

But these models of syntactic generalization are insufficient (because many "wanted" generalizations are not covered), and inadequate (because they cover many "unwanted" generalizations). [Buntine 88] introduces *generalized subsumption* as a stronger model of semantic generalization, of which θ-subsumption is a particular case. Background knowledge is used for inferring more "interesting" generalizations. As we don't exploit such background knowledge in the sequel, these stronger models have not been further investigated here: refer to [Buntine 88] for more details, for a comparison with other generalization models and logical implication, and for applications for inductive inference and redundancy control.

Building upon the "limited success due to the complexity of constructed clauses" of Buntine's proposal to circumvent Plotkin's negative result, [Muggleton 91] introduces another model of generalization, with more restrictions on hypotheses.

Regarding *stepwise synthesis*, the immense majority of research goes into incremental approaches, with much focus on monotonic and consistent techniques. Other incremental approaches are, for instance, non-monotonic synthesis [Jantke 91] and inconsistent synthesis [Lange and Wiehagen 91].

The non-incremental, stepwise synthesis strategy presented in Section 7.3.2 features the same idea as the incremental *version spaces* strategy of [Mitchell 81], namely simultaneous bottom-up and top-down search, but is after all totally different from it.

7.6 Conclusion

In this chapter, we have developed a general framework for stepwise synthesis of logic algorithms from specifications by examples and properties. It includes correctness criteria for relating the intended, specified, and computed relations, as well as comparison criteria for relating logic algorithms in terms of their generality. As part of a framework, these sets of criteria are modular, as new criteria can be added. The main issue is that such criteria can be used to state strategies of stepwise synthesis, be they incremental or not, monotonic or not, consistent or not. A particular, non-incremental, monotonic, and consistent strategy has been developed in greater detail for use in the following.

8 ALGORITHM ANALYSIS AND ALGORITHM SCHEMATA

Algorithm schemata are a popular research topic. In Section 8.1, we introduce algorithm schemata and argue that they are an important support for guiding algorithm design. Then, in Section 8.2, we introduce a logic algorithm schema reflecting a divide-and-conquer design strategy. This allows us, in Section 8.3, to refine the framework of Chapter 7 to stepwise and schema-guided synthesis of logic algorithms from examples and properties. Future work and related work are discussed in Section 8.4 and Section 8.5, respectively, before drawing some conclusions in Section 8.6.

8.1 Introduction to Algorithm Schemata

Algorithms can be classified according to their design strategies, such as divide-and-conquer, generate-and-test, global search, local search, top-down decomposition, and so on. Informally, an *algorithm schema* is a template algorithm with a fixed control flow, but without specific indications about the actual parameters or the actual computations. An algorithm schema thus represents a whole family of particular algorithms that can be obtained by instantiating its place-holders to particular parameters or calls. It is therefore interesting to guide algorithm design by a schema that captures the essence of some strategy.

In order to be more precise, we have to settle for a specific algorithm language. Our focus goes to logic algorithms. Informally, in a first approximation, a *logic algorithm schema* is a second-order logic algorithm. A particular logic algorithm, called an *instance* of the schema, is then obtained by instantiating the variables of the schema.

Example 8-1: Here is a logic algorithm schema for the generate-and-test strategy:

```
R(X,Y) ⇔ Generate(X,Y) ∧ Test(Y)
```

The following logic algorithm for the *sort*/2 problem is also known as Naive-Sort:

```
sort(L,S) ⇔ permutation(L,S) ∧ ordered(S)
```

This algorithm is an instance of the generate-and-test schema, namely via the second-order substitution {*R/sort, Generate/permutation, Test/ordered, X/L, Y/S*}. ◆

Reality is more complex, however. Function-variables and predicate-variables may have any arity, and this calls for schema-variables to denote these arities. Conjunctions, disjunctions, or quantifications of any length may appear, and this calls for schema-variables to denote the ranges of such ellipses. Permutations of parameters, conjuncts, disjuncts, or quantifications may have to be performed in order to see why a logic algorithm is an instance of some schema. Unfold transformations may have to be performed in order to see why a logic algorithm is an instance of some schema.

Example 8-2: Given the logic algorithm schema:

$$
\begin{array}{lll}
R(X_1, \ldots, X_n, Y) \Leftrightarrow & & \\
 & & P(Y, Z_1, \ldots, Z_n) \\
 & \wedge\ \bigwedge_{1 \le i \le n} & Q_i(X_i, Z_i)
\end{array}
$$

it is not immediately clear why the logic algorithm *LA*(*foo*):

```
foo(S,B,A) ⇔
      permutation(A,SA)
    ∧ reverse(B,RB)
    ∧ append(SA,RB,S)
    ∧ ordered(SA)
```

is an instance of it. Indeed, a possible schema substitution is $\{R/foo,\ n/2,\ X_1/B,\ X_2/A,\ Y/S,\ P/append,\ Z_1/RB,\ Z_2/SA,\ Q_1/reverse,\ Q_2/sort\}$. But the *sort*/2 atom must also be unfolded into the conjunction of the *permutation*/2 and *ordered*/1 atoms (as in Example 8-1), and a series of permutations of parameters and conjuncts are furthermore required to obtain this instance. ♦

A wff schema language is thus needed to write realistic logic algorithm schemas. The formal definition of such a language and of its semantics is beyond the scope of this book, so we do not develop it. But we know from experience that the intuitive understanding of our schemata is sufficient.

Definition 8-1: A *logic algorithm schema* is a closed wff schema of the form:

$$\forall R \ \ \forall X_1 \ldots \forall X_n \quad R(X_1, \ldots, X_n) \Leftrightarrow F$$

where n is a schema-variable or a constant, the X_i are distinct variables, R is a predicate-variable, and F is a wff schema. The atom schema $R(X_1, \ldots, X_n)$ is called the *head*, and F is called the *body* of the logic algorithm schema.

Hereafter, we drop the universal quantifications in front of the heads, as well as any existential quantifications at the beginning of the bodies of logic algorithm schemas.

It is evident that a logic algorithm schema without function-variables, predicate-variables, and schema-variables is a logic algorithm.

Definition 8-2: An *instance* of a logic algorithm schema is a logic algorithm obtained by the following sequence of operations:

(1) permutation of parameters, conjuncts, disjuncts, and quantifications of the schema;
(2) application of a schema substitution to the resulting schema, such that all function-, predicate-, and schema-variables are instantiated to first-order objects;
(3) application of unfold transformations.

This process is called *instantiation* of a schema. The reverse process is called *classification* of the logic algorithm, and yields a schema called a *cover* of that algorithm.

The process of classifying several algorithms into a same schema is called *algorithm analysis*. It may also be seen as *schema synthesis*, because it amounts to schema learning. Similarly, the process of instantiating a given schema into several algorithms is called *algorithm synthesis*, but may also be seen as *schema analysis*.

In order to facilitate "visual" classification of logic algorithms, we introduce the following purely syntactic criterion for the writing of logic algorithms.

Definition 8-3: A *canonical representation* of a logic algorithm wrt a covering schema exactly matches the layout of that schema.

Example 8-3: A possible canonical representation of *LA*(*foo*) wrt the schema of the previous example is:

```
foo(S,B,A) ⇔
     append(SA,RB,S)
  ∧ reverse(B,RB) ∧ ( permutation(A,SA) ∧ ordered(SA) ) ♦
```

Note that a canonical representation is not unique, because of the possible permutations of parameters. The permutations of parameters as in the schema can't be imposed at the instance level, because there is no possible control over how problems, and hence predicates, are defined. We can't thus introduce a concept such as *the* normalized representation of a logic algorithm.

Almost all logic algorithms of this book are canonical representations wrt some schema in this chapter.

Note that one may distinguish between design schemas and transformation schemas: the former are useful for guiding algorithm design, whereas the latter are useful for guiding algorithm transformation. But as nothing prevents the use of transformation schemas for guiding algorithm design, the boundary between these two kinds of schemas seems to be a subjective one. Our views on the differences between design and transformation extend to the differences between design schemas and transformation schemas. Good examples of transformation schemas are the generalization schemas of [Deville 90].

8.2 A Divide-and-Conquer Logic Algorithm Schema

As algorithm design strategies are fairly orthogonal, there is apparently little opportunity for re-use between design steps for different strategies. In this book, we focus on the divide-and-conquer strategy, for the following reasons (also see [Smith 85]):

- *diversity*: a wide variety of relations can be implemented by such algorithms;
- *complexity*: the resulting algorithms often have good time/space complexities;
- *simplicity*: the simplicity of this strategy makes it particularly convenient for (semi-)automated algorithm design.

The support of other strategies is discussed in Section 14.2.3.

In essence, the divide-and-conquer design strategy solves a problem by the following sequence of three steps:

(1) *divide* a problem into sub-problems, unless it can be trivially solved;

(2) *conquer* the sub-problems by solving them recursively;

(3) *combine* the solutions to the sub-problems into a solution to the initial problem.

Hence the name of the strategy. In the sequel, we focus on applying this strategy to data-structures, rather than to states of partial computations.

This strategy description is a little rough, and calls for further details. In Section 8.2.1, we proceed by successive refinements to incrementally infer various versions of a divide-and-conquer logic algorithm schema. Then, in Section 8.2.2, we list the integrity constraints that instances of these schemas have to satisfy in order to be divide-and-conquer algorithms. In Section 8.2.3, we justify the choices that have been made during this algorithm analysis. Finally, in Section 8.2.4, we discuss some other issues related to divide-and-conquer schemas.

```
R(X,Y) ⇔
            Minimal(X)     ∧ Solve(X,Y)
  ∨         NonMinimal(X)  ∧ Decompose(X,HX,TX)
                           ∧ R(TX,TY)
                           ∧ Process(HX,HY)
                           ∧ Compose(HY,TY,Y)
```

Logic Algorithm Schema 8-1: Divide-and-conquer (version 1)

8.2.1 Divide-and-Conquer Logic Algorithm Analysis

We now incrementally infer four different versions of a divide-and-conquer logic algorithm schema, starting from the logic algorithms of Section 5.2. Each new version covers a larger set of logic algorithms. We hypothesize that no parameter is a tuple, that is that procedure declarations are "flattened" out.

First Version

Let's first restrict ourselves to binary predicates, and present a most basic strategy that already yields solutions to many problems.

A *divide-and-conquer algorithm* for a binary predicate r over parameters X and Y works as follows. Let X be the induction parameter. If X is minimal, then Y is (usually) easily found by directly solving the problem. Otherwise, that is if X is non-minimal, decompose X into a vector $\boldsymbol{HX}$ of heads of X and a vector $\boldsymbol{TX}$ of tails of X, the tails being of the same type as X, as well as smaller than X according to some well-founded relation. The tails $\boldsymbol{TX}$ recursively yield tails $\boldsymbol{TY}$ of Y. The heads $\boldsymbol{HX}$ are processed into a vector $\boldsymbol{HY}$ of heads of Y. Finally, Y is composed from its heads $\boldsymbol{HY}$ and tails $\boldsymbol{TY}$.

For further discussion, we quantify the vectors as follows. There are h heads of X, and h' heads of Y, and t tails of X, hence t tails of Y. Thus:

$$\#\boldsymbol{HX} = h$$
$$\#\boldsymbol{HY} = h'$$
$$\#\boldsymbol{TX} = \#\boldsymbol{TY} = t$$

Note that h, h', t are schema-variables, not constants.

Logic algorithms designed by this basic divide-and-conquer strategy are covered by Schema 8-1, where $\boldsymbol{R(TX,TY)}$ stands for $\wedge_{1 \leq j \leq t} R(TX_j,TY_j)$, and j is a notation-variable.

Note that we prefer the verb "decompose" to "divide", and that the "combine" operation is actually split into a "process" operation and a "compose" operation.

Example 8-4: Logic algorithms that are covered by Schema 8-1 are *LA(compress-ext-L)* (LA 5-1), *LA(compress-int-C)* (LA 5-2), *LA(compress-ext-C)* (LA 5-3), *LA(permutation-L)* (LA 5-14), *LA(sort-int-L) {Insertion-Sort}* (LA 5-16), *LA(sort-ext-L) {Quick-Sort}* (LA 5-17), and *LA(sort-ext-L) {Merge-Sort}* (LA 5-18).

Second Version

Many logic algorithms are not covered by Schema 8-1 because the non-minimal case is further partitioned into sub-cases, each featuring a different way of combining partial solutions. The enhanced strategy is as follows.

A *divide-and-conquer algorithm* for a binary predicate r over parameters X and Y works as follows. Let X be the induction parameter. If X is minimal, then Y is (usually)

```
R(X,Y) ⇔
                Minimal(X)     ∧ Solve(X,Y)
  ∨ ∨1≤k≤c      NonMinimal(X)  ∧ Decompose(X,HX,TX)
                               ∧ Discriminatek(HX,TX,Y)
                               ∧ R(TX,TY)
                               ∧ Processk(HX,HY)
                               ∧ Composek(HY,TY,Y)
```

Logic Algorithm Schema 8-2: Divide-and-conquer (version 2)

easily found by directly solving the problem. Otherwise, that is if X is non-minimal, decompose X into a vector ***HX*** of heads of X and a vector ***TX*** of tails of X, the tails being of the same type as X, as well as smaller than X according to some well-founded relation. The tails ***TX*** recursively yield tails ***TY*** of Y. The heads ***HX*** are processed into a vector ***HY*** of heads of Y. Finally, Y is composed from its heads ***HY*** and tails ***TY***. It may happen that sub-cases emerge with different processing and composition operators: discriminate between them according to the values of ***HX***, ***TX***, Y.

Of course, if non-determinism of the problem requires alternative solutions, then discriminants should evaluate to *true*. Logic algorithms designed by this enhanced divide-and-conquer strategy are covered by Schema 8-2.

A schema-variable c represents the number of different sub-cases of the non-minimal case. This new schema supersedes the previous schema if c is bound to 1, and the $Discriminate_1$ predicate-variable is bound to a predicate that always holds.

Example 8-5: A logic algorithm that is covered by Schema 8-2, but not by the previous schema, is *LA(delOddElems-L)* (LA 5-4).

Third Version

Many logic algorithms are not even covered by Schema 8-2 because the non-minimal case is partitioned into a recursive and a non-recursive case, each of which is in turn partitioned into sub-cases. In the non-recursive case, Y is (usually) easily found by directly solving the problem, taking advantage of the decomposition of X into ***HX*** and ***TX***. We assume there are v non-recursive sub-cases and w recursive sub-cases, such that $v + w = c$, where c, v, w are schema-variables. Logic algorithms designed by this enhanced divide-and-conquer strategy are covered by the following schema:

```
R(X,Y) ⇔
                 Minimal(X)     ∧ Solve(X,Y)
  ∨ ∨1≤k≤v       NonMinimal(X)  ∧ Decompose(X,HX,TX)
                                ∧ Discriminatek(HX,TX,Y)
                                ∧ SolveNonMink(HX,TX,Y)
  ∨ ∨c-w<k≤c     NonMinimal(X)  ∧ Decompose(X,HX,TX)
                                ∧ Discriminatek(HX,TX,Y)
                                ∧ R(TX,TY)
                                ∧ Processk(HX,HY)
                                ∧ Composek(HY,TY,Y)
```

But this schema is very lengthy, and doesn't sufficiently show the commonalities between the recursive and the non-recursive sub-cases. We thus syntactically merge

```
R(X,Y) ⇔
                 Minimal(X)     ∧ Solve(X,Y)
  ∨ ∨_{1≤k≤c}    NonMinimal(X)  ∧ Decompose(X,HX,TX)
                                ∧ Discriminate_k(HX,TX,Y)
                                ∧ (        SolveNonMin_k(HX,TX,Y)
                                       |
                                           R(TX,TY)
                                         ∧ Process_k(HX,HY)
                                         ∧ Compose_k(HY,TY,Y)         )
```

Logic Algorithm Schema 8-3: Divide-and-conquer (version 3)

```
R(X,Y) ⇔
                 Minimal(X)     ∧ Solve(X,Y)
  ∨ ∨_{1≤k≤c}    NonMinimal(X)  ∧ Decompose(X,HX,TX)
                                ∧ Discriminate_k(HX,TX,Y)
                                ∧ (        SolveNonMin_k(HX,TX,Y)
                                       |
                                           R(TX,TY)
                                         ∧ Process_k(HX,HY)
                                         ∧ Compose_k(HY,TY,Y)         )
```

Logic Algorithm Schema 8-4: Divide-and-conquer (version 4)

these cases by separating their differences by a second-order exclusive-or connective, denoted "|". The result is Schema 8-3.

Example 8-6: A logic algorithm that is covered by Schema 8-3, but not by the previous two schemas, is *LA(member-L)* (LA 5-10).

Fourth Version

Let's now relax the requirement that predicate r be binary. But we keep the (so far implicit) constraint that the induction parameter be simple. Supposing predicate r is n-ary (where n is a schema-variable), this new setting implies that Y becomes a vector $\boldsymbol{Y}$ of n–1 variables Y_j, and that vector $\boldsymbol{TY}$ becomes a vector $\underline{\boldsymbol{TY}}$ of n–1 vectors $\boldsymbol{TY}_j$, each of which is a vector of t variables TY_{jl} (where j, l are notation-variables). Similarly, $\boldsymbol{HY}$ becomes a vector $\underline{\boldsymbol{HY}}$ of n–1 vectors $\boldsymbol{HY}_j$, each of which is a vector of $h'(j)$ variables HY_{jl}, where $h'/1$ is a schema function-variable. Thus:

$$\#\boldsymbol{HX} = h$$
$$\#\boldsymbol{HY}_j = h'(j) \quad (1 \le j \le n-1)$$
$$\#\boldsymbol{TX} = \#\boldsymbol{TY}_j = t \quad (1 \le j \le n-1)$$
$$\#\boldsymbol{Y} = \#\underline{\boldsymbol{HY}} = \#\underline{\boldsymbol{TY}} = n - 1$$

Logic algorithms designed by this enhanced divide-and-conquer strategy are covered by Schema 8-4, where $\boldsymbol{R(TX,\underline{TY})}$ stands for $\wedge_{1 \le l \le t}\ R(TX_l, TY_{1l}, \ldots, TY_{n-1\,l})$.

Example 8-7: Logic algorithms that are covered by Schema 8-4, but not by the previous three schemas, are *LA(efface-L)* (LA 5-5), *LA(firstN-L)* (LA 5-6), *LA(firstN-N)* (LA 5-7), *LA(insert-L)* (LA 5-8), *LA(insert-R)* (LA 5-9), *LA(partition-L)* (LA 5-13), and *LA(plateau-N)* (LA 5-15).

Notations are already getting complicated with this fourth version. But covering *LA(parity-L)* (LA 5-12) calls for the support of arbitrary numbers of minimal and non-minimal cases (and not just 1), while covering *LA(merge-<A,B>)* (LA 5-11) calls for the support of compound induction parameters, and *LA(split)* (LA 5-19) would then still be uncovered [Flener 93]. Other possible extensions are outlined in Section 8.4. The remainder of this discussion is mostly about version 4.

8.2.2 Integrity Constraints on Instances

The schemas above can be instantiated in many ways. However, some constraints need to be verified by these instantiation processes in order to result in valid divide-and-conquer logic algorithms. The constraints on instances of version 4 are as follows.

The instance of X, that is the induction parameter, must be of an inductive type. Indeed, otherwise, its decomposition into tails $\boldsymbol{TX}$ that are each smaller than X according to some well-founded relation would be impossible.

The minimal and non-minimal forms must be mutually exclusive over the domain of the induction parameter. This means that the chosen instance of the formula:

$$X \in dom(\mathcal{R}) \Rightarrow Minimal(X) \veebar NonMinimal(X) \tag{1}$$

must be *true* in $\mathfrak{I}$, where $\veebar$ denotes the exclusive-or connective. This constraint considerably facilitates algorithm design. Of course, as seen earlier, a rewriting of the final logic algorithm may blur this distinction, which is thus only mandatory at the level of canonical representations of divide-and-conquer logic algorithms.

The instance of *NonMinimal* must be a precondition for the instance of *Decompose*. And the instance of *Decompose* must be deterministic if X is given. This means that the chosen instance of the formula:

$$X \in dom(\mathcal{R}) \wedge NonMinimal(X) \Rightarrow \exists! \boldsymbol{HX}\, \exists! \boldsymbol{TX}\;\; Decompose(X,\boldsymbol{HX},\boldsymbol{TX}) \tag{2}$$

must be *true* in $\mathfrak{I}$. This is a reasonable constraint, as it facilitates algorithm design, especially in conjunction with constraint (1). The determinism of *Decompose* is not necessary for correctness reasons, but is reasonable in view of efficiency of the synthesized algorithm.

The decomposition of X must yield tails TX_i that are each smaller than X according to some well-founded relation "<". This means that the formula:

$$\exists\text{“<”}\ \forall (Decompose(X,\boldsymbol{HX},TX_1,\ldots,TX_t) \Rightarrow \forall i \in \{1,\ldots,t\}\ TX_i \text{“<”} X) \tag{3}$$

must be *true* in $\mathfrak{I}$. This ensures "termination" of the algorithm in the all-ground mode. Note that a similar constraint need not be imposed on $\boldsymbol{TY}$.

The constraints on the instances of the schema-variables (all versions) are:

$$n \geq 1 \tag{4}$$

$$c \geq 1 \tag{5}$$

$$h \geq 0 \tag{6}$$

$$h' \geq 0, \text{ respectively } h'(j) \geq 0 \quad (1 \leq j \leq n-1) \tag{7}$$

$$t \geq 1 \tag{8}$$

Constraint (4) states that 0-ary relations cannot be solved by a divide-and-conquer approach. Constraint (5) says the each non-minimal case must have at least one sub-case. Constraints (6) to (8) state that every parameter must be decomposable into at least one tail and zero heads.

Note that there is no constraint that the primitive =/2 must be used in the definition of the instances of *Minimal* and *NonMinimal*. We used it throughout Section 5.2, but this is not necessary. For instance, if the minimal form is [], and the non-minimal form is [_|_], the following instances of *NonMinimal* could be used:

$$nonMinimal(L) \Leftrightarrow L = [\_|\_]$$

$$nonMinimal(L) \Leftrightarrow L \neq []$$

$$nonMinimal(L) \Leftrightarrow length(L,N) \wedge N > 0$$

Up to domain checking, these variants are equivalent.

It is also worth noting that the elements of ***HX*** (respectively ***HY***) may be of the same type as *X* (respectively *Y*). Indeed, there is no reason why, say, *HL* should be an integer when *L* is a list of integers. This is illustrated by *LA(compress-ext-L)* (LA 5-1), where *HL* is a list of integers.

8.2.3 Justifications

A series of deliberate decisions have been made during the algorithm analysis above. Let's justify them now.

Instances of *Solve* may be defined by fairly complex formulas, including divisions into sub-cases and the corresponding discriminating mechanisms, just as in non-minimal cases. But since this is relatively exceptional, we prefer to keep the schema simple, and always treat such a formula as the instance of a single predicate-variable.

Such is however not the case with the $SolveNonMin_k$, where *Decompose* and $Discriminate_k$ are explicitly present: this is for reasons of homogeneity with the recursive non-minimal case. This even implies that instances of the $SolveNonMin_k$ may use the variables ***HX*** and ***TX*** introduced by *Decompose*, rather than start from scratch with a non-decomposed *X*.

Instances of *Solve* and the $SolveNonMin_k$ are fundamentally different in nature from instances of the $Process_k \wedge Compose_k$ conjunctions: in the former, *Y* can be anything, even totally unrelated to *X*, ***HX***, ***TX***; in the latter, *Y must* be in terms of ***TY*** at least.

The distinction between *NonMinimal* and *Decompose* may seem artificial at first sight. Indeed, in many of the logic algorithms of Chapter 5, their instances can be unified, such as in *LA(firstN-L)* (LA 5-6). But the mission of *NonMinimal* only is to *detect* a non-minimal form, whereas the mission of *Decompose* is to *decompose* a form that is known to be non-minimal: these are two totally different missions, and the integrity constraint above on the relationship between their instances indeed is an implication, not an equivalence. This is also reflected in the different parameters to the corresponding predicate-variables. Sample logic algorithms that clearly illustrate these differences are *LA(compress-ext-L)* (LA 5-1), *LA(sort-ext-L) {Quick-Sort}* (LA 5-17), and *LA(efface-L)* (LA 5-5).

NonMinimal(X) can be rewritten as $\neg$*Minimal(X)* iff this preserves constraint (2). But there is no need for such an arbitrary restriction on possible instances of *NonMinimal*.

8.2.4 Discussion

Some issues about the divide-and-conquer strategy need to be discussed in order to show its generality, and to clearly distinguish it from some other approaches.

First, the divide-and-conquer strategy is often believed to be restricted to algorithms that involve some sophisticated design decisions. A famous example is the Quick-Sort algorithm, where the divide step partitions the given list into two sublists of elements that are greater (respectively smaller) than a pivot element. However, such design decisions only affect the complexity of the resulting algorithm, and are thus not strictly necessary for the design of correct algorithms. Hence, a divide step that simply decomposes a list into its head and tail is also acceptable. In the sorting problem, it leads to the Insertion-Sort algorithm.

Also, we mentioned that step (1) of a divide-and-conquer strategy consists of "dividing a problem into sub-problems, unless it can be trivially solved". We have here taken the option that the "unless it can be trivially solved" clause is applicable iff a minimal form of the domain of the induction parameter is attained. An alternative interpretation would be that the clause may be applicable in even other cases. A good illustration of this point of view is Sedgewick's enhancement of Hoare's original Quick-Sort algorithm: it switches to Insertion-Sort once the unsorted list has less than, say, 15 elements. Such sophisticated design-choices are beyond the scope of our study.

An apparent disadvantage of the divide-and-conquer strategy is that it seems to lead to logic algorithms, and hence logic programs, that are not tail-recursive, because of the very placement of recursion in the schema. This argument can however be disputed because (automatable) transformation techniques exist for obtaining tail-recursive versions of a program, and this in many cases [Deville 90].

The divide-and-conquer strategy should not be confused with the top-down decomposition strategy, despite their almost synonymic names and their overall problem reduction approaches. Indeed, the former is a very precisely defined strategy that always yields recursive algorithms, whereas the latter almost never yields recursive algorithms. Note however that the former may be applied recursively, yielding a top-down approach. This amounts to re-applying the divide-and-conquer strategy in order to instantiate some predicate-variables of the divide-and-conquer schema.

Finally, what is the relationship between the divide-and-conquer strategy and the methodology of algorithm construction by structural induction, as described in Chapter 4? Fundamentally, there is none: both strategies are based on the principle of well-founded induction. However, in practice, there are some differences. The divide-and-conquer strategy, especially its formalization as a schema, is much more prescriptive and more precisely defined than the other methodology. For instance, the first-order variables of a divide-and-conquer schema have well-defined scopes. A good illustration of this phenomenon is that the logic algorithms of Chapter 4 are designed by the structural induction methodology, but are not obtainable by simply instantiating some divide-and-conquer schema. Such schema instances usually look a little bit contrived compared to their more natural-looking hand-constructed counterparts. But it is precisely this extreme formalization that allows (partial) mechanization of the design process. The point thus merely is that both methodologies were formulated with different objectives in mind: hand-construction, respectively automation.

8.3 Stepwise, Schema-Guided Logic Algorithm Synthesis

Let's reconsider the strategies of stepwise synthesis of logic algorithms, seen in Section 7.3. An interesting idea, especially with non-incremental stepwise strategies, is then to establish a mapping between steps and the variables of a schema: each step synthesizes instance(s) of some predicate- or schema-variable(s) of a given schema.

Example 8-8: Given Schema 8-3, a possible stepwise strategy would be the following fixed sequence of steps [Flener and Deville 92, 93ab]:

Step 1: Syntactic creation of a first approximation;
Step 2: Synthesis of *Minimal* and *NonMinimal*;
Step 3: Synthesis of *Decompose*;
Step 4: Syntactic introduction of the recursive atoms;
Step 5: Synthesis of *Solve* and the $SolveNonMin_k$;
Step 6: Synthesis of the $Process_k$ and $Compose_k$;
Step 7: Synthesis of the $Discriminate_k$.

This sequence of predicate-variable instantiations is quite "natural". It can be justified as follows. Due to interdepencies within the schema, there is no discussion as to the mission of Steps 1, 2, 7. Also, Steps 5 and 6 have missions that can be accomplished in parallel. Finally, there is no prejudice about what happens first at Step 6: the predicates could be synthesized serially or in parallel. But an alternative sequence nevertheless emerges: one might first choose an adequate composition operator for parameter *Y*, and then reason backwards in order to infer the corresponding decomposition operator for parameter *X*. As a result, Step 3 would be interchanged with Steps 5 and 6. A similar analysis is made by [Smith 85]. However, due to the multi-directionality (or reversibility) of logic algorithms, we can here claim that the given sequence and its outlined alternative are isomorphic: choosing a composition operator *compose* for parameter *Y* amounts to actually selecting *Y* as the induction parameter and using *compose*, in its reversed directionality, as a decomposition operator for *Y*. In other words, the given sequence is probably the only one. ♦

One of the major ideas of this book is that schema-independent methods can be developed for the synthesis of predicate-variables. Such methods may be merely based on databases of useful instances of predicate-variables. More sophisticated methods would perform actual computations for inferring such instances. Possible modes of reasoning are inductive inference, deductive inference, analogical inference, abductive inference, and so on. Such reasoning would be based on the contents of the specifications, as well as the algorithm as designed so far. Several methods of such a tool-box might be applicable at each step, thus yielding opportunities for specifier interaction, or for the application of heuristics.

We thus advocate a more disciplined approach to algorithm synthesis: rather than use a uniform method for instantiating *all* variables of a given schema (possibly without any awareness of such a schema), one should deploy for each variable the *best*-suited method. We thus propose to view research on program synthesis as (1) the search for adequate schemas; (2) the development of useful methods of predicate-variable instantiation; and (3) the discovery of interesting mappings between these methods and the variables of these schemas.

As many methods would be schema-independent, and hence variable-independent, one could even investigate synthesis methodologies that are parameterized on schemas. In other words, a Step 0 would be to select an appropriate schema, and the subsequent steps would be either a hardwired sequence (specific to the selected schema) of applications of methods, or a specifier-guided selection of variables and methods. Our grand view of algorithm synthesis systems thus is one of a large workbench with a disparate set of highly specialized methods for a set of schemas that covers (as much as possible of) the space of all possible algorithms.

Note that this discussion is independent of the used specification formalism, and hence of their completeness or incompleteness. In this book, we investigate a particular niche of automatic algorithm synthesis: in the context of (incomplete) specifications by examples and properties, we develop methods of predicate-variable instantiation, and apply them to the step/variable mapping identified in Example 8-8.

8.4 Future Work

There are several directions for future research.

First, in view of having a *theory of logic algorithm schemas* and a formalization of the accompanying notions of instantiation and classification, a language for wff schemas needs to be developed, as well as its semantics defined.

Second, as we already have hinted when stopping the incremental inference of different versions of a divide-and-conquer schema, version 4 of that schema is far from covering all possible divide-and-conquer logic algorithms.

A possible enhancement is a schema that automatically introduces an additional parameter to the specified predicate, hence covering *LA(split)* (LA 5-19). Such an extension is discussed by [Summers 77]. This schema could still be considered a design schema, rather than a transformation schema, as it is not possible to design a logic algorithm for *split*/3 that is covered by one of the given versions.

Another observation is that no operator is applied to the final value of parameter *Y*. For instance, problems like:

average(*L*,*A*) iff *A* is the average value of *L*,
where *A* is an integer and *L* is a non-empty integer-list.

are beyond the scope of the given schemas, and must be solved via a different approach. For instance, it could be solved by a top-down decomposition:

```
average(L,A) ⇔ sum(L,S) ∧ length(L,N) ∧ div(S,N,A)
```

and possible optimization by loop-merging the algorithms for *sum*/2 and *length*/2. Another solution would be to extend the divide-and-conquer schemas accordingly.

Also, in Chapter 5, we have informally introduced the notion of *auxiliary parameter*. But in this chapter, we have completely ignored them. This is justifiable by the observation that the identification of auxiliary parameters is not necessary at all for correct algorithm design. Indeed, as the logic algorithms of Section 5.2 show, it *is* possible to write logic algorithms that don't distinguish between auxiliary parameters and "ordinary" parameters. However, the (de)composition of an auxiliary parameter from (into) its heads and tails may look cumbersome because an auxiliary parameter *Y* and its tail *TY* are eventually found to be identical: $Y = TY$. But it is precisely this composition pattern that allows the subsequent detection of auxiliary parameters, and their elimination from the decomposition machinery, so as transform the logic algorithm into a more "graceful" and "natural" version. For instance, *LA(efface-L)* (LA 5-5) could be rewritten as follows:

```
efface(E,L,R) ⇔
        L=[_]               ∧ L=[HL] ∧ E=HL ∧ R=[]
    ∨   L=[_,_|_]           ∧ L=[HL|TL]
                            ∧ HL=E
                            ∧ E=HL ∧ R=TL
    ∨   L=[_,_|_]           ∧ L=[HL|TL]
                            ∧ HL≠E
                            ∧ efface(E,TL,TR)
                            ∧ HR=HL
                            ∧ R=[HR|TR]
```

We should not forget that just a casual glance at a specification will not tell whether a parameter is an "ordinary" or an auxiliary one. Things are even more difficult with automated algorithm design, and the surest way is indeed to ignore the potential existence of auxiliary parameters until a transformation phase. But suppose now that knowledge about which parameters are auxiliary parameters *is* available *earlier* during the algorithm synthesis process (for instance because the specifier declares them as such, or because type heuristics detect them as such). It would certainly be helpful to pre-compile the needed subsequent transformations into a schema with an explicit consideration of auxiliary parameters.

Third, this chapter is exclusively concerned with the divide-and-conquer strategy. It would be interesting to investigate the development of schemas for other strategies, such as local search, global search, and so on.

8.5 Related Work

Algorithm (and program) schemas are an old, and ever popular, idea of computer science. They have been proposed for a huge variety of applications.

Some *properties of programs* can be proven independently of their actual computations. Hence the idea of abstracting away these details, and proving such properties for the resulting schemas. This makes proofs of properties at the instance level easier, as it suffices to show that the program is covered by a schema that is known to have the desired property. Sample properties are termination, divergence, equivalence, isomorphism, and so on. An early survey of this research can be found in [Manna 74]. Note that Manna's schemas are first-order schemas, and that their semantics is defined via (Herbrand) interpretations. This semantics-based approach is of course also perfectly acceptable. It is sufficient for the study of schemas, but not as a tool for algorithm design. Indeed, unlike our second-order approach, it doesn't permit the concept of instantiation of a schema, and is thus less "constructive" for design purposes.

In the field of *logic programming tutors* for beginners, [Gegg-Harrison 89] proposes a hierarchy of 14 logic program schemas. These are also set in a second-order logic framework, and embody the otherwise rare feature of arbitrary arities. They are specialized versions of our divide-and-conquer schemas, in the sense that they have less predicate-variables, and that they are already partly instantiated (induction parameter of type list, fixed forms, fixed decomposition, fixed number of cases, fixed discriminants, and so on).

In the area of manual or computer-aided *algorithm/program construction* for experts, [Deville 87, 90] and [Deville and Burnay 89] suggest an ancestor version of our divide-and-conquer schemas. It roughly corresponds to a highly instantiated version of our version 1 (no discriminants, and most schema-variables are bound to the constant 1). They also discuss interesting transformation schemas, based on structural or computational generalization.

A similar study is made by [O'Keefe 90], who rephrases specifications of problems in an algebraic way. The predicates of such specifications can be directly plugged into given logic program schemas. Several schemas may be applicable according to the properties (associativity, commutativity, existence of left identities, and so on) of the identified predicates.

Alternatively, [Lakhotia 89] experiments with what he calls "incorporating programming techniques into Prolog programs". Similarly, [Barker-Plummer 90] discusses a system based on clichés that assists experienced programmers in the construction of Prolog programs. These approaches could be seen as transformation rather than design approaches.

The field of automatic *algorithm/program synthesis* has naturally seen a lot of interest in schemas. The promise of schema-guidance is a more disciplined synthesis that exploits useful knowledge about algorithm design strategies.

In the sub-area of synthesis from incomplete specifications, schemas are often implicitly or explicitly present to guide the synthesis. Early systems based on divide-and-conquer schemas are described by [Shaw *et al.* 75], [Hardy 75], [Summers 77], and [Biermann and Smith 79].

Surprisingly, the new strand of research spawned by MIS [Shapiro 82] (see Section 3.4.1) has long ignored the virtues of schemas. It is only in these days that schemas have been found to be interesting for organizing search spaces for MIS-like systems. Sample approaches are described by [Tinkham 90] and [Sterling and Kirschenbaum 93].

In the sub-area of synthesis from complete specifications, the use of schemas seems much less established. The *Programmer's Apprentice* project is based on the notion of clichés, which are application-specific schemas [Rich and Waters 88b].

Some of the most fascinating research on using schemas for program synthesis is being reported by Douglas R. Smith. The synthesis of divide-and-conquer algorithms is described by [Smith 81, 85]: the underlying schema is quite similar to our version 4, except that the discriminants are merged into the form-identifying formulas. With the implemented system, called *Cypress*, one proceeds by arbitrarily choosing instances of two predicate-variables among <*Decompose, Process, Compose*>, and then infers the other ones deductively using a synthesis theorem.

The synthesis of global search algorithms is reported by [Smith 88, 90a]. Global search is an enumerative search strategy that generalizes many known search strategies, such as binary search, backtracking, branch-and-bound, constraint satisfaction, and so on. The resulting system, called KIDS, has an approach similar to *Cypress*.

As a conclusion of this survey, it must be observed that almost all of the research has gone into investigating divide-and-conquer schemas. This is not a bad thing, as the covered class of algorithms is very interesting and large. But these published schemas tend to be extremely simplified ones, namely often at best the equivalents of our version 2. In order to be really useful, we think that more sophisticated versions should also be supported.

8.6 Conclusion

In this chapter, we have given a brief semi-formal introduction to algorithm schemas, and argued for their usefulness in guiding algorithm design. Focusing on the divide-and-conquer strategy, we have incrementally inferred four increasingly powerful schemas from a series of divide-and-conquer logic algorithms. These schemas are data-structure independent. Finally, we have proposed a vision of stepwise, schema-guided algorithm synthesis mechanisms, where each variable of a schema is instantiated using the best-suited method from a tool-box of such methods.

Algorithm schemas are used in a widespread variety of areas, including automated algorithm synthesis. This is quite natural, as algorithm schemas are a powerful way of embodying our knowledge about algorithms. Surprisingly, though, schemas are not as broadly used across all existing synthesis mechanisms as we think they ought to be. For instance, in the branch of inductive synthesis, schemas had almost disappeared until recently. One of the reasons could be that Inductive Logic Programming (ILP) seems more focused on concept learning than on algorithm design, and it is little wonder that concept schemas are hardly existent, and thus considered only with skepticism. Similarly, in the branch of deductive synthesis, schemas have attracted ittle attention. We think that deductive synthesis paradigms such as proofs-as-programs synthesis, or transformational synthesis, would gain a lot from schema-guided approaches, as search spaces can then be significantly pruned.

9 THE PROOFS-AS-PROGRAMS METHOD

In this chapter, we develop the Proofs-as-Programs Method, which adds atoms to a logic algorithm so that some correctness criteria wrt a set of properties become satisfied. This method is part of our tool-box of methods for instantiating the predicate-variables of a schema. First, in Section 9.1, we state the problem. Then, in Section 9.2, we explain a method to solve this problem, and discuss its correctness in Section 9.3. In Section 9.4, we illustrate this method on a few sample problems. Future work and related work are discussed in Section 9.5 and Section 9.6, respectively, before drawing some conclusions in Section 9.7.

9.1 The Problem

Let's first illustrate the objectives on a sample problem.

Example 9-1: Intuitively, the first objective consists of adding atoms to a logic algorithm so that it becomes totally correct wrt a given set of properties. For instance, given the logic algorithm *LA(efface)*:

```
efface(E,L,R) ⇔
      L=[HL|TL]        ∧ R=TL
    ∨ L=[HL|TL]        ∧ efface(E,TL,TR)
                       ∧ R=[HL|TR]
```

and the set of properties *𝒫(efface)*:

```
efface(X, [X|T],T)
efface(X, [Y,X|T], [Y|T]) ⇐ X≠Y
```

one can see that *LA(efface)* is complete, but not totally correct, wrt *𝒫(efface)*. Indeed, some atoms are missing for deciding when *R* should be unified with *TL* (namely iff $HL = E$), respectively when *R* should be unified with $[HL \mid TR]$ (namely iff $HL \neq E$ and the first element of *TL* is *E*). The objective is thus to add the missing literals to *LA(efface)*, yielding *LA'(efface)*:

```
efface(E,L,R) ⇔
      L=[HL|TL]        ∧ HL=E  ∧ R=TL
    ∨ L=[HL|TL]        ∧ HL≠E  ∧ TL=[E|_]
                       ∧ efface(E,TL,TR)
                       ∧ R=[HL|TR]
```

which is indeed totally correct wrt *𝒫(efface)*. However, as properties are usually an incomplete source of information about the intended relation, we are not necessarily interested in achieving such a total correctness wrt the given property set. We are thus rather interested in achieving total correctness wrt the intended relation. The second objective is thus to generalize *LA'(efface)* into *LA''(efface)* so that it becomes "more complete" wrt *ℰfface*, and this with some reasonable certainty. In our case, this may be achieved by dropping one of the initially added conditions (namely that the first element of *TL* be *E*). So *LA''(efface)* is:

```
efface(E,L,R) ⇔
        L=[HL|TL]          ∧ HL=E ∧ R=TL
    ∨   L=[HL|TL]          ∧ HL≠E
                           ∧ efface(E,TL,TR)
                           ∧ R=[HL|TR]
```

which is indeed totally correct wrt $\mathcal{E}$*fface*. In general, the conditions to be dropped are determined by some application-specific generalization heuristics, whereas the initial addition of conditions seems feasible in an application-independent fashion. ♦

Formally, the problem can now be posed as follows.
Given:

- a logic algorithm $LA(r)$,
- a set of properties $\mathcal{P}(r)$,
- a set $\mathcal{H}$ of application-specific generalization heuristics,

such that:

- $LA(r)$ only contains primitive predicates, and the r/n predicate,
- $LA(r)$ is complete wrt $\mathcal{P}(r)$,

find:

- a logic algorithm $LA'(r)$,
- a logic algorithm $LA''(r)$,

such that:

- $LA'(r)$ is a syntactic specialization of $LA(r)$ that is totally correct wrt $\mathcal{P}(r)$,
- $LA''(r)$ is obtained by applying the heuristics of $\mathcal{H}$ to $LA'(r)$.

The latter task cannot be further explained here, as the heuristics are application-specific. A semantic specialization of $LA(r)$ would be $\mathcal{P}(r)$ re-expressed as a logic algorithm. The most "useful" specialization is however a syntactic specialization that only *adds* atoms to the existing disjuncts of $LA(r)$, and hence preserves the existing computations. Indeed, the ultimate objective is not that $LA'(r)$ be totally correct wrt $\mathcal{P}(r)$, but that $LA''(r)$ be totally correct wrt $\mathcal{R}$. So the construction of $LA'(r)$ is only a useful intermediate step.

9.2 A Method

First of all, let's remark that our Proofs-as-Programs Method is totally unlike classical proofs-as-programs approaches to algorithm synthesis (see Chapter 2). Indeed, we here adopt the liberal viewpoint that any technique that extracts some computational contents from a proof may be seen as a proofs-as-programs technique.

Intuitively, the Proofs-as-Programs Method specializes the given logic algorithm by adding atoms extracted from the proofs that the given properties are its logical consequences. After deciding on some concrete language issues, this section is organized as follows: Section 9.2.1 is about the proof aspects of the Proofs-as-Programs Method, whereas Section 9.2.2 is about its condition extraction aspects.

The concrete languages for logic algorithms and properties need to be fixed before actually developing a method for solving the problem at hand. We now assume that:

- logic algorithms have bodies in prenex disjunctive normal form, with no negation;
- properties are definite clauses with atoms of predicate r/n in their heads.

These choices are motivated by the theorem proving technology used below. Note that the language for properties is different from the language chosen in Section 6.2, because recursion *is* allowed here, while negation is disallowed here.

9.2.1 Proofs by Extended Execution

The idea is to perform a verification proof that $LA(r)$ is effectively complete wrt $\mathcal{P}(r)$. This should reveal, in case of success, a set of conditions explaining why, if at all, $LA(r)$ is not already totally correct wrt $\mathcal{P}(r)$.

If we want to perform this proof in a mechanized fashion, we cannot apply the actual criterion of completeness (namely Definition 7-8) of a logic algorithm wrt a property set, because this requires the knowledge of $\mathfrak{I}$. So we have to resort to the (weaker) intuitive criterion of completeness. The latter would be achieved if (but not only if) $LA(r) \models \mathcal{P}(r)$. But we rather want to prove, for each property $P_i \in \mathcal{P}(r)$, that:

$$\mathcal{T}_i \models P_i \tag{1}$$

where $\mathcal{T}_i$ is a theory composed of:

- the logic algorithm $LA(r)$,
- the specification $\mathcal{P}(r) \setminus \{P_i\}$,
- logic algorithms for all primitive predicates.

The reason why only the properties other than P_i are included in $\mathcal{T}_i$ is that the recursive calls of $LA(r)$ had better not be resolved using $LA(r)$ itself, as we have no guarantee yet of the total correctness of $LA(r)$ wrt the intended relation $\mathcal{R}$. So these other properties should be used for the resolution of these recursive calls, because properties are assumed to be a consistent, albeit incomplete, approximation of $\mathcal{R}$. This is reflected in the search rule described below.

These proofs have to be performed by an extension to SLD resolution, because the initial goals are here definite clauses, and not mere conjunctions of atoms. An existing such extension is the *extended execution* mechanism of [Kanamori and Seki 86] [Kanamori and Fujita 86], where theories are definite programs, and goals are so-called *S-formulas* (short for *specification formulas*). Note that most of the terminology (but not the notation) used hereafter is borrowed from these two original references. This passage only states results, but not their motivations or proofs: refer to these references when in need of further explanations.

We syntactically restrict S-formulas (which are not explained here) to *implicative goals* (as in [Fribourg 90, 93]), that is statements G of the form:

$$\forall \boldsymbol{X}\, \exists \boldsymbol{Y} \quad G^+(\boldsymbol{X},\boldsymbol{Y}) \Leftarrow G^-(\boldsymbol{X})$$

where *conclusion* G^+ and *hypothesis* G^- are conjunctions of atoms, and $\boldsymbol{X}$, $\boldsymbol{Y}$ are vectors of (*universal*, respectively *existential*) variables. For syntactic convenience, we write implicative goals in quantifier-free form:

$$G^+(\boldsymbol{X},?\boldsymbol{Y}) \Leftarrow G^-(\boldsymbol{X})$$

where $\boldsymbol{X}$, $?\boldsymbol{Y}$ are (now) vectors of (*free*, respectively *undecided*) variables. In the following, we often write "goal" instead of "implicative goal".

Properties are thus a particular case of implicative goals. Note that $?\boldsymbol{Y}$ is necessarily always empty for a property.

As a theory of extended execution is a definite program, a definite program version of $\mathcal{T}_i$ has to be generated: let's call it $\mathcal{D}_i$. In definite clauses, we use the connectives "$\leftarrow$" and "," for "if" and "and", respectively. This is straightforward due to the chosen languages for logic algorithms and properties. This is explained, for instance, in [Deville 90, pages 227–228] and [Lloyd 87, page 113]. Note that such a translation is deterministic in this case, and thus reversible. Objective (1) thus amounts to proving the following:

$$\mathcal{D}_i \vdash P_i \tag{2}$$

The variables of $\mathcal{D}_i$ are renamed at each use so that there is no conflict with the variable names of previous goals.

The *initial goal* is property P_i, translated into an implicative goal.

Due to our syntactic restriction to implicative goals, only three inference rules of extended execution are actually required in our context. [11]

Definition 9-1: The rule of *definite clause inference* (denoted *DCI*) is a natural extension of SLD resolution to implicative goals. Given a goal G, the selected atom is chosen within G^+, and the mgu may only bind undecided variables of G^+. All new variables introduced in the resolvent goal are undecided variables.

Definition 9-2: The rule of *negation-as-failure inference* (denoted *NFI*) is a natural extension of the NF rule [Clark 78] to implicative goals. Given a goal G, the selected atom A is chosen within G^-, and a conjunction of d resolvent goals is generated, namely $G\sigma_i$, where $A\sigma_i$ has been replaced by the conjunction $B_i\sigma_i$, with $H_i \leftarrow B_i$ being one of the d definite clauses whose head H_i unifies with A under mgu σ_i. All new variables introduced in the resolvent goals are free variables.

Definition 9-3: Given a goal G, the rule of *simplification* (denoted *Sim*) selects two atoms A and B, in G^+ and G^- respectively, that unify with an mgu σ that only binds undecided variables of G^+: the resolvent goal is obtained from $G\sigma$ by deleting A and B.

This subset of extended execution is sound and complete wrt the Clark completion semantics [Kanamori 86]. Hence, provability by extended execution is equivalent to truth. Moreover, since $\mathcal{T}_i$ is by construction the completion of $\mathcal{D}_i$, the proofs of (2) thus effectively do amount to the truths of (1).

SLD resolution is parameterized on a computation rule and a search rule [Lloyd 87]. For extended execution, these rules are, for the purpose of the Proofs-as-Programs Method, instantiated as follows:

- the *computation rules* for *DCI* and *NFI* satisfy the following condition: never select an atom with predicate *r/n* if there are atoms with primitive predicates. Indeed, while theoretically not required, delaying the selection of *r/n* atoms generally results in less search;
- the *search rule* for *DCI* is as follows:
  - an atom with a primitive predicate is resolved according to its semantics;

11. Note that we could have adapted extended execution to handle our original formalisms without translations. But we feel that re-using (subsets of) existing results (namely [Kanamori and Fujita 86] [Kanamori and Seki 86] for execution, and [Deville 90] for the necessary translations) is a better approach.

- *the* atom with predicate *r/n* originating from the initial goal of the proof tree is resolved using the clauses generated from *LA*(*r*);
- *an* atom with predicate *r/n* not originating from the initial goal of the proof tree is resolved using the clauses generated from $\mathcal{P}(r) \setminus \{P_i\}$.

Note that the search rule is context-dependent. For the resolution of the atom with predicate *r/n* originating from the initial goal, we use *LA*(*r*) rather than $\mathcal{P}(r) \setminus \{P_i\}$, because that wouldn't make sense: we are trying to prove *LA*(*r*) complete wrt $\mathcal{P}(r)$, not to prove $\mathcal{P}(r)$ internally consistent. For the resolution of atoms with predicate *r/n* not originating from the initial goal, we use $\mathcal{P}(r) \setminus \{P_i\}$ rather than *LA*(*r*), because the latter is in general not correct wrt $\mathcal{P}(r)$.

There is independence of the computation rules. But a fairness condition requires that no atom be indefinitely ignored by *NFI*. The completeness proof of extended execution [Kanamori 86] states that every logical consequence is provable by a so-called *normalized derivation*, in which a sequence of *NFI* inferences precedes a sequence of *DCI* inferences, which in turn precedes a sequence of *Sim* inferences. Hence the idea of a priority ordering between the inference rules, namely *NFI* > *DCI* > *Sim*.

Definition 9-4: A derivation via the *NFI*, *DCI*, *Sim* rules *succeeds* iff it ends in a goal whose conclusion is empty. Such a derivation *fails* iff it doesn't succeed.

Failure is not always detectable, except in specific settings. For instance, no infinite derivation can occur if all primitive predicates have finite proofs for all directionalities, and if there is a well-founded relation between the recursive atoms of a property and the head of that property.

Before proceeding with the theoretical considerations, let's illustrate all this on a sample derivation.

Example 9-2: Given the definite clause theory $\mathcal{D}_2$:

```
firstPlateau(L,P,S) ←     L=[_,_|_],
                          L=[HL|TL],
                          firstPlateau(TL,TP,TS),
                          P=[HL|TP],S=TS,TP=[HL|_]  (C3)

firstPlateau([X],[X],[])                            (P1)

firstPlateau([X,Y],[X],[Y]) ← X≠Y                   (P3)
```

and the implicative goal:

```
firstPlateau([X,Y],[X,Y],[]) ⇐ X=Y                  (P2)
```

here follows the proof that $\mathcal{D}_2 \vdash P_2$: [12]

firstPlateau([X,Y],[X,Y],[]) ⇐ **X=Y**

NFI: *LA*(=) ↓ {*Y*/*X*}

firstPlateau([X,X],[X,X],[]) ⇐

DCI: C_3 ↓ {}

12. In sample derivations, the selected atom(s) for the next inference(s) is (are) written in boldface (because there is no ambiguity with the vector convention).

```
[X,X]=[?_,?_|?_] ∧ [X,X]=[?HL|?TL] ∧
        firstPlateau(?TL,?TP,?TS) ∧
[X,X]=[?HL|?TP] ∧ []=?TS ∧ ?TP=[?HL|?_] ⇐
```

$5 \times DCI$: $LA(=)$ $\downarrow$ $\{HL/X, TL/[X], TP[X], TS/[]\}$

```
firstPlateau([X],[X],[]) ⇐
```

DCI: P_1 $\downarrow$ $\{\}$

❑

This derivation succeeds. ♦

For a non-recursive property P_i, a normalized successful derivation is an instance of the following derivation schema: [13]

$$\begin{array}{rcl} & & \mathtt{r(t)} \Leftarrow \underline{B} \\ NFI & \downarrow & \lambda \\ & & \underline{\mathtt{r(t)}\lambda} \Leftarrow Q \\ DCI\text{: clause } C_k \text{ from } LA(r) & \downarrow & \{\} \\ & & \underline{S} \wedge \mathtt{r(s)} \Leftarrow Q \\ DCI & \downarrow & \sigma \\ & & \underline{\mathtt{r(s)}\sigma} \Leftarrow Q\sigma \\ DCI\text{: } \mathcal{P}(r) \setminus \{P_i\} & \downarrow & \mu \\ & & \underline{T} \Leftarrow \underline{Q\sigma\mu} \\ DCI, Sim & \downarrow & \rho \\ & & \Leftarrow Q\sigma\mu\rho \end{array}$$

where:

- B, Q, S, T are (possibly empty) conjunctions of atoms with primitive predicates,
- $\boldsymbol{s}, \boldsymbol{t}$ are vectors of terms,
- λ, σ, μ, ρ are mgus.

The relevant part of the computed answer substitution, denoted φ, is $\sigma\mu\rho$.

If clause C_k is not recursive, then everything related to $\boldsymbol{r(s)}$ may simply be ignored. A slight variation of this schema can be established for recursive properties.

We are now able to state a theorem that shows a practical way of verifying the completeness of a logic algorithm wrt a property set.

Theorem 9-1: *A logic algorithm $LA(r)$ is complete (according to the new criterion (1)) wrt a property set $\mathcal{P}(r)$ iff, for every property P_i in $\mathcal{P}(r)$, there exists a successful derivation (via the NFI, DCI, Sim rules) of $\mathcal{D}_i \vdash P_i$, where theory $\mathcal{D}_i$ is as above.*

Proof 9-1: The theorem directly follows from the soundness and completeness of extended execution wrt the Clark completion semantics [Kanamori 86]. ❑

The problem statement of the Proofs-as-Programs Method requires that $LA(r)$ be complete wrt $\mathcal{P}(r)$, and this, in retrospective, according to the new criterion (1). Indeed, there wouldn't exist any complete syntactic specialization otherwise. But in practice, it is often impossible to know beforehand whether this constraint is satisfied

13. In derivation schemas, however, the selected atom(s) for the next inference(s) is (are) underlined.

or not. Theorem 9-1 thus shows a way of verifying this simultaneously with the attempts at enhancement, as captured in the following definition:

Definition 9-5: The Proofs-as-Programs Method *succeeds* iff $LA(r)$ is proven (by extended execution) to be complete wrt $\mathcal{P}(r)$. It *fails* otherwise.

So far for the proof aspects of the Proofs-as-Programs Method. Let's now turn to the condition extraction aspects.

9.2.2 The Extraction of Conditions

The fundamental observation of condition extraction is that the final goal of a successful derivation may have a non-empty hypothesis. So the idea is to use that hypothesis (even if it is empty, that is *true*) together with the computed answer substitution in order to build a condition that, if added to the original logic algorithm, would then give rise to an unconditionally successful derivation.

More precisely, let C_k be the kth clause generated from $LA(r)$. Assume C_k is:

$$\texttt{r}(\mathbf{U}) \leftarrow \exists \mathbf{W}\ \texttt{B}_k[\mathbf{U}]$$

where:

- U is the vector of universal variables in the kth disjunct of $LA(r)$,
- W is the vector of existential variables in the kth disjunct of $LA(r)$.

In case of a successful derivation whose first *DCI* resolution was based on C_k, a (new) predicate q_k is partially defined by the definite clause:

$$q_k(\boldsymbol{t},\boldsymbol{W})\varphi \leftarrow Q\varphi \tag{3}$$

where:

- $\boldsymbol{t}$ is the vector of terms in the head of P_i,
- φ is the computed answer substitution,
- $Q\varphi$ is the hypothesis of the last goal of the derivation.

Note that such a definite clause is defined in terms of primitive predicates only. Indeed, $Q\varphi$ originally is the body of property P_i (remember that properties are defined in terms of primitives only), and atoms can be deleted from it (by use of the *NFI* and *Sim* rules), and atoms with primitive predicates can be added to it (by use of the *NFI* rule). An important feature is thus that these definite clauses can't be recursive.

Before proceeding, let's illustrate all this on a sample condition extraction.

Example 9-3: The derivation of Example 9-2 succeeds, and a new predicate, say $discFirstPlateau_3$, is partially defined as follows:

```
discFirstPlateau₃(L,P,S,HL,TL,TP,TS) ←
                        L=[X,X],P=[X,X],S=[],
                        HL=X,TL=[X],TP=[X],TS=[]
```
◆

Once that *all* successful derivations of all formulas (2) have been computed, and provided the method succeeds, $LA'(r)$ is obtained from $LA(r)$ by adding an atom $q_k(\boldsymbol{U},\boldsymbol{W})$ to its kth disjunct, for every newly created predicate q_k.

Similarly, a set $\mathcal{Z}$ of logic algorithms $LA(q_k)$ is obtained by translating the definite procedures of the q_k into logic algorithms. The used translation rules are the reverse of those used for achieving the applicability of extended execution: they amount to computing the Clark completion of the definite procedures of the q_k. These logic algorithms are by construction non-recursive, so they may be unfolded into $LA'(r)$.

The Proofs-as-Programs Method is deterministic because the results of *all* successful derivations are collected before computing $\mathcal{Z}$ therefrom. The method is thus independent of any ordering of disjuncts within $LA(r)$, or of properties within $\mathcal{P}(r)$. The method may fail, as conveyed by Definition 9-5. However, nothing can be said about the synthesized logic algorithms in terms of determinism or finiteness, because nothing is known about the properties.

Establishing the complexity of the method is quite intricate, unless some assumptions are made. Thus, assume that properties are non-recursive, and that all primitives used in $\mathcal{P}(r)$ are deterministic, and let c be the number of disjuncts in $LA(r)$, p the number of properties of $\mathcal{P}(r)$, and t the number of recursive atoms in $LA(r)$. There are p proofs to be made. Each proof-tree has only two choice-points, namely the *DCI* resolution of the head of the initial goal, where there are c possibilities, and the *DCI* resolution of the t recursive atoms, where there are $p-1$ possibilities, all other proof steps being deterministic. Each proof tree thus has size $O(cp^t)$. Hence, the time complexity of the method is $O(cp^{t+1})$. This assumes that there is a fixed maximum number of atoms for the definitions of the used primitives. Indeed, if that number is a function of c, t, or p, then this complexity analysis doesn't hold.

9.3 Correctness

The following correctness theorem can now be established.

Theorem 9-2: $LA'(r)$ is a syntactic specialization of $LA(r)$ that is totally correct with respect to $\mathcal{P}(r)$.

* **Proof 9-2:** Let $\mathcal{T}_i'$ be defined like $\mathcal{T}_i$, but using $LA'(r)$ rather than $LA(r)$. Suppose we now prove that each property P_i is a logical consequence of its theory $\mathcal{T}_i'$. Without loss of generality, we can assume that the previous derivations of $\mathcal{D}_i \vdash P_i$ are prefixes of the new derivations of $\mathcal{D}_i' \vdash P_i$ (namely by a relaxation of the recommendations above for the computation rules and for the normalization of proofs). Each new derivation then eventually yields a goal whose conclusion only involves a $\mathtt{q}_k$ atom, as shown by the revised derivation schema:

$$
\begin{array}{rc}
 & \mathtt{r}(\mathbf{t}) \Leftarrow \underline{\mathtt{B}} \\
NFI & \downarrow \ \lambda \\
 & \underline{\mathtt{r}(\mathbf{t})\lambda} \Leftarrow \mathtt{Q} \\
DCI\text{: clause } C'_k \text{ from } LA'(r) & \downarrow \ \{\} \\
 & \underline{\mathtt{S}} \wedge \mathbf{r}(\mathbf{s}) \wedge \mathtt{q}_k(\mathbf{t},\mathbf{W}) \Leftarrow \mathtt{Q} \\
DCI & \downarrow \ \sigma \\
 & \underline{\mathbf{r}(\mathbf{s})\sigma} \wedge \mathtt{q}_k(\mathbf{t},\mathbf{W})\sigma \Leftarrow \mathtt{Q}\sigma \\
DCI\text{: } \mathcal{P}(r) \setminus \{P_i\} & \downarrow \ \mu \\
 & \underline{\mathtt{T}} \wedge \mathtt{q}_k(\mathbf{t},\mathbf{W})\sigma\mu \Leftarrow \underline{\mathtt{Q}\sigma\mu} \\
DCI, Sim & \downarrow \ \rho \\
 & \mathtt{q}_k(\mathbf{t},\mathbf{W})\sigma\mu\rho \Leftarrow \mathtt{Q}\sigma\mu\rho
\end{array}
$$

Replacing $\sigma\mu\rho$ by φ, this last goal may be rewritten more compactly, and the revised derivation schema continues as follows:

$$\begin{array}{rcl} \underline{\mathtt{q}_k\mathtt{(t,W)}\,\varphi} & \Leftarrow & \varrho\varphi \\ \mathit{DCI}\text{: clause (3)} & \downarrow & \{\} \\ \underline{\varrho\varphi} & \Leftarrow & \underline{\varrho\varphi} \\ \mathit{Sim} & \downarrow & \{\} \\ & \Box & \end{array}$$

Every new derivation thus succeeds as well. By soundness and completeness of extended execution wrt the Clark completion semantics [Kanamori 86], the property set $\mathcal{P}(r)$ is thus also a logical consequence of $LA'(r)$. Hence $LA'(r)$ is complete wrt $\mathcal{P}(r)$.

Note that $LA'(r)$ is certainly the most-specific syntactic specialization of $LA(r)$ that the Proofs-as-Programs Method can produce: starting from $LA'(r)$, a renewed application of that method would, as the proof above indicates, lead to a logic algorithm that is syntactically equivalent to $LA'(r)$. The Proofs-as-Programs Method is thus idempotent, and $LA'(r)$ is partially correct wrt $\mathcal{P}(r)$, that is syntactically equivalent to $\mathcal{P}(r)$ expressed as a logic algorithm.

By construction, $LA'(r)$ is a syntactic specialization of $LA(r)$. ❑

9.4 Illustration

Let's illustrate the described method on two sample problems.

Example 9-4: The logic algorithm *LA*(*compress*) to be specialized is:

```
compress(L,C) ⇔
       L=[]      ∧ C=[]
    ∨  L=[_|_] ∧ L=[HL|TL]
                 ∧ compress(TL,TC)
                 ∧ C=[HL,1|TC]
    ∨  L=[_|_] ∧ L=[HL|TL]
                 ∧ compress(TL,TC)
                 ∧ C=[HL,s(s(N))|TTC]  ∧ TC=[HL,s(N)|TTC]
```

The corresponding definite program is:

```
compress(L,C) ←   L=[],C=[]                          (C1)
compress(L,C) ←   L=[_|_],
                  L=[HL|TL],
                  compress(TL,TC),
                  C=[HL,1|TC]                        (C2)
compress(L,C) ←   L=[_|_],
                  L=[HL|TL],
                  compress(TL,TC),
                  C=[HL,s(s(N))|TTC],
                  TC=[HL,s(N)|TTC]                   (C3)
```

Finally, let the properties be:

```
compress([],[])                                    (E1)
compress([X],[X,1])                                (P1)
compress([X,Y],[X,2]) ⇐ X=Y                        (P2)
compress([X,Y],[X,1,Y,1]) ⇐ X≠Y                    (P3)
```

The objective is to attempt to prove, by extended execution, that each property P_i is a logical consequence of theory $\mathcal{T}_i$.

We skip the proof of property E_1, as it is trivial, and as it leads to the extraction of a condition that is redundant wrt the existing atoms.

Let's pursue with P_1, and use clause C_1 for the first *DCI* resolution:

```
compress([X],[X,1]) ⇐
    DCI: C1  ↓  {}
[X]=[] ∧ [X,1]=[] ⇐
```

This derivation fails, and no extraction is performed.

We continue with clause C_2 for the first *DCI* resolution:

```
compress([X],[X,1]) ⇐
    DCI: C2  ↓  {}
[X]=[?_|?_] ∧ [X]=[?HL|?TL] ∧
compress(?TL,?TC) ∧ [X,1]=[?HL,1|?TC] ⇐
    3 × DCI: LA(=)  ↓  {HL/X, TL/[], TC/[]}
compress([],[]) ⇐
    DCI: E1  ↓  {}
□
```

This derivation succeeds. A clause for a new predicate $discCompress_2$ is defined:

```
discCompress2(L,C,HL,TL,TC) ←
                    L=[X],C=[X,1],
                    HL=X,TL=[],TC=[]
```

We continue with clause C_3 for the first *DCI* resolution:

```
compress([X],[X,1]) ⇐
    DCI: C3  ↓  {}
[X]=[?_|?_] ∧ [X]=[?HL|?TL] ∧ compress(?TL,?TC) ∧
[X,1]=[?HL,s(s(?N))|?TTC] ∧ ?TC=[?HL,s(?N)|?TTC] ⇐
```

This derivation fails, and no extraction is performed.

We pursue with P_2, and restart from clause C_1 for the first *DCI* resolution:

```
compress([X,Y],[X,2]) ⇐ X=Y
    NFI: LA(=)  ↓  {Y/X}
compress([X,X],[X,2]) ⇐
    DCI: C1  ↓  {}
[X,X]=[] ∧ [X,2]=[] ⇐
```

This derivation fails, and no extraction is performed.

We continue with clause C_2 for the first *DCI* resolution:

compress([X,Y],[X,2]) ⇐ **X=Y**

NFI: *LA*(=) ↓ {*Y*/*X*}

compress([X,X],[X,2]) ⇐

DCI: C_2 ↓ {}

[X,X]=[?_|?_] ∧ [X,X]=[?HL|?TL] ∧
compress(?TL,?TC) ∧ **[X,2]=[?HL,1|?TC]** ⇐

This derivation also fails, and no extraction is performed.

We continue with clause C_3 for the first *DCI* resolution:

compress([X,Y],[X,2]) ⇐ **X=Y**

NFI: *LA*(=) ↓ {*Y*/*X*}

compress([X,X],[X,2]) ⇐

DCI: C_3 ↓ {}

[X,X]=[?_|?_] ∧ **[X,X]=[?HL|?TL]** ∧ compress(?TL,?TC) ∧
[X,2]=[?HL,s(s(?N))|?TTC] ∧ **?TC=[?HL,s(?N)|?TTC]** ⇐

2 × *DCI*: *LA*(=) ↓ {*HL*/*X*, *TL*/[*X*], *N*/0, *TTC*/[], *TC*/[*X*,1]}

compress([X],[X,1]) ⇐

DCI: P_1 ↓ {}

❑

This derivation succeeds. A new predicate *discCompress*$_3$ is partially defined:

```
discCompress3(L,C,HL,TL,TC,N,TTC) ←
                              L=[X,X],C=[X,2],
                              HL=X,TL=[X],TC=[X,1],
                              N=0,TTC=[]
```

We pursue with P_3, and restart from clause C_1 for the first *DCI* resolution:

compress([X,Y],[X,1,Y,1]) ⇐ X≠Y

DCI: C_1 ↓ {}

[X,Y]=[] ∧ [X,1,Y,1]=[] ⇐ X≠Y

This derivation fails, and no extraction is performed.

We continue with clause C_2 for the first *DCI* resolution:

compress([X,Y],[X,1,Y,1]) ⇐ X≠Y

DCI: C_2 ↓ {}

[X,Y]=[?_|?_] ∧ **[X,Y]=[?HL|?TL]** ∧
compress(?TL,?TC) ∧ **[X,1,Y,1]=[?HL,1|?TC]** ⇐ X≠Y

3 × *DCI*: *LA*(=) ↓ {*HL*/*X*, *TL*/[*Y*], *TC*/[*Y*,1]}

compress([Y],[Y,1]) ⇐ X≠Y

DCI: P_1 ↓ {}

⇐ X≠Y

This derivation succeeds. Another clause for predicate $discCompress_2$ is created:

```
discCompress₂(L,C,HL,TL,TC) ←
                              L=[X,Y],C=[X,1,Y,1],
                              HL=X,TL=[Y],TC=[Y,1],
                              X≠Y
```

We continue with clause C_3 for the first *DCI* resolution:

```
                 compress([X,Y],[X,1,Y,1]) ⇐ X≠Y
                         DCI: C3  ↓  {}
[X,Y]=[?_|?_] ∧ [X,Y]=[?HL|?TL] ∧ compress(?TL,?TC) ∧
                 [X,1,Y,1]=[?HL,s(s(?N))|?TTC] ∧
                   ?TC=[?HL,s(?N)|?TTC]  ⇐  X≠Y
```

This derivation fails, and no extraction is performed.

There is no other property. There are no alternative derivations. So *LA'*(*compress*) is defined as follows, after adding two atoms to *LA*(*compress*):

```
compress(L,C) ⇔
      L=[]      ∧ C=[]
   ∨  L=[_|_] ∧ L=[HL|TL]
                ∧ discCompress₂(L,C,HL,TL,TC)
                ∧ compress(TL,TC)
                ∧ C=[HL,1|TC]
   ∨  L=[_|_] ∧ L=[HL|TL]
                ∧ discCompress₃(L,C,HL,TL,TC,N,TTC)
                ∧ compress(TL,TC)
                ∧ C=[HL,s(s(N))|TTC] ∧ TC=[HL,s(N)|TTC]
```

where the procedures of the new predicates are rewritten as a set Z of logic algorithms:

```
discCompress₂(L,C,HL,TL,TC) ⇔
                      L=[X] ∧ C=[X,1]
                    ∧ HL=X ∧ TL=[] ∧ TC=[]
                 ∨    L=[X,Y] ∧ C=[X,1,Y,1]
                    ∧ HL=X ∧ TL=[Y] ∧ TC=[Y,1]
                    ∧ X≠Y

discCompress₃(L,C,HL,TL,TC,N,TTC) ⇔
                      L=[X,X] ∧ C=[X,2]
                    ∧ HL=X ∧ TL=[X] ∧ TC=[X,1]
                    ∧ N=0 ∧ TTC=[]
```

Suppose that some application-specific heuristics (see Section 13.3.2) suggest that:

- both conditions may be generalized by projection onto their 2nd to 4th parameters;
- the values of the C parameter are irrelevant in both conditions;
- the TL parameter should vary over its entire domain in both conditions.

This transforms Z into Z', which is as follows (after some additional rewriting):

```
discCompress₂(L,C,HL,TL,TC) ⇔
      TL=[]
   ∨  TL=[HTL|_] ∧ HL≠HTL
```

```
discCompress₃(L,C,HL,TL,TC,N,TTC) ⇔ TL=[HTL|_] ∧ HL=HTL
```

If we unfold *LA'*(*compress*) using *Z'*, then we obtain *LA''*(*compress*):

```
compress(L,C) ⇔
      L=[]     ∧ C=[]
    ∨ L=[_|_] ∧ L=[HL|TL]
              ∧ (TL=[]) ∨ (TL=[HTL|_] ∧ HL≠HTL)
              ∧ compress(TL,TC)
              ∧ C=[HL,1|TC]
    ∨ L=[_|_] ∧ L=[HL|TL]
              ∧ TL=[HTL|_] ∧ HL=HTL
              ∧ compress(TL,TC)
              ∧ C=[HL,s(s(N))|TTC] ∧ TC=[HL,s(N)|TTC]   ♦
```

Example 9-5: The logic algorithm *LA*(*firstPlateau*) to be specialized is:

```
firstPlateau(L,P,S) ⇔
      L=[_]          ∧ P=L ∧ S=[] ∧ L=[_]
    ∨ L=[_,_|_]      ∧ L=[HL|TL]
                     ∧ P=[HL] ∧ S=TL ∧ TL=[_|_]
    ∨ L=[_,_|_]      ∧ L=[HL|TL]
                     ∧ firstPlateau(TL,TP,TS)
                     ∧ P=[HL|TP] ∧ S=TS ∧ TP=[HL|_]
```

The corresponding definite program is (after an obvious simplification in C_1):

```
firstPlateau(L,P,S) ←    L=[_],P=L,S=[]                (C1)
firstPlateau(L,P,S) ←    L=[_,_|_],
                         L=[HL|TL],
                         P=[HL],S=TL,TL=[_|_]          (C2)
firstPlateau(L,P,S) ←    L=[_,_|_],
                         L=[HL|TL],
                         firstPlateau(TL,TP,TS),
                         P=[HL|TP],S=TS,TP=[HL|_]      (C3)
```

Finally, let the properties be:

```
firstPlateau([X]  , [X]  , [] )                        (P1)
firstPlateau([X,Y],[X,Y],[] ) ⇐ X=Y                   (P2)
firstPlateau([X,Y],[X]  , [Y]) ⇐ X≠Y                  (P3)
```

The objective is to attempt to prove, by extended execution, that each property P_i is a logical consequence of theory $\mathcal{T}_i$.

Let's start with P_1, and use clause C_1 for the first *DCI* resolution:

firstPlateau([X],[X],[]) ⇐

DCI: C_1 ↓ {}

[X]=[?_] ∧ **[X]=[X]** ∧ **[]=[]** ⇐

$3 \times$ *DCI*: *LA*(=) ↓ {}

❑

This derivation succeeds. A new predicate *discFirstPlateau*$_1$ is partially defined:

discFirstPlateau$_1$(L,P,S) ← L=[X],P=[X],S=[]

We continue with clause C_2 for the first *DCI* resolution:

firstPlateau([X],[X],[]) ⇐

DCI: C_2 ↓ {}

[X]=[?_,?_|?_] ∧ [X]=[?HL|?TL] ∧

[X]=[?HL] ∧ []=?TL ∧ ?TL=[?_|?_] ⇐

This derivation fails, and no extraction is performed.

We continue with clause C_3 for the first *DCI* resolution:

firstPlateau([X],[X],[]) ⇐

DCI: C_3 ↓ {}

[X]=[?_,?_|?_] ∧ [X]=[?HL|?TL] ∧

firstPlateau(?TL,?TP,?TS) ∧

[X]=[?HL|?TP] ∧ []=?TS ∧ ?TP=[?HL|?_] ⇐

This derivation also fails, and no extraction is performed.

We pursue with P_2, and restart from clause C_1 for the first *DCI* resolution:

firstPlateau([X,Y],[X,Y],[]) ⇐ **X=Y**

NFI: *LA*(=) ↓ {*Y*/*X*}

firstPlateau([X,X],[X,X],[]) ⇐

DCI: C_1 ↓ {}

[X,X]=[?_] ∧ [X,X]=[X,X] ∧ []=[] ⇐

This derivation fails, and no extraction is performed.

We continue with clause C_2 for the first *DCI* resolution:

firstPlateau([X,Y],[X,Y],[]) ⇐ **X=Y**

NFI: *LA*(=) ↓ {*Y*/*X*}

firstPlateau([X,X],[X,X],[]) ⇐

DCI: C_2 ↓ {}

[X,X]=[?_,?_|?_] ∧ [X,X]=[?HL|?TL] ∧

[X,X]=[?HL] ∧ []=?TL ∧ ?TL=[?_|?_] ⇐

This derivation also fails, and no extraction is performed.

We continue with clause C_3 for the first *DCI* resolution. See Example 9-2, where the derivation succeeds, and a new predicate *discFirstPlateau*$_3$ is defined:

discFirstPlateau$_3$(L,P,S,HL,TL,TP,TS) ←
L=[X,X],P=[X,X],S=[],
HL=X,TL=[X],TP=[X],TS=[]

We pursue with P_3, and restart from clause C_1 for the first *DCI* resolution:

firstPlateau([X,Y],[X],[Y]) ⇐ X≠Y

DCI: C_1 ↓ {}

[X,Y]=[?_] ∧ [X]=[X,Y] ∧ [Y]=[] ⇐ X≠Y

This derivation fails, and no extraction is performed.

We continue with clause C_2 for the first *DCI* resolution:

```
              firstPlateau([X,Y],[X],[Y]) ⇐  X≠Y
                          DCI: C2   ↓   {}
          [X,Y]=[?_,?_|?_] ∧ [X,Y]=[?HL|?TL] ∧
       [X]=[?HL] ∧ [Y]=?TL ∧ ?TL=[?_|?_]  ⇐  X≠Y
                5×DCI: LA(=)  ↓  {HL/X, TL/[Y]}
                            ⇐  X≠Y
```

This derivation succeeds. A new predicate *discFirstPlateau*$_2$ is partially defined:

```
discFirstPlateau2(L,P,S,HL,TL) ←
                         L=[X,Y],P=[X],S=[Y],
                         HL=X,TL=[Y],
                         X≠Y
```

We continue with clause C_3 for the first *DCI* resolution:

```
              firstPlateau([X,Y],[X],[Y]) ⇐  X≠Y
                          DCI: C3   ↓   {}
          [X,Y]=[?_,?_|?_] ∧ [X,Y]=[?HL|?TL] ∧
                firstPlateau(?TL,?TP,?TS) ∧
   [X]=[?HL|?TP] ∧ [Y]=?TS ∧ ?TP=[?HL|?_]  ⇐  X≠Y
                4×DCI: LA(=)  ↓  {HL/X, TL/[Y], TP[], TS/[Y]}
     firstPlateau([Y],[],[Y]) ∧ []=[X|?_]  ⇐  X≠Y
```

This derivation fails, and no extraction is performed.

There is no other property, nor any alternative derivations. So *LA'*(*firstPlateau*) is defined as follows, after adding three atoms to *LA*(*firstPlateau*):

```
firstPlateau(L,P,S) ⇔
     L=[_]             ∧ P=L ∧ S=[] ∧ L=[_]
                       ∧ discFirstPlateau1(L,P,S)
   ∨ L=[_,_|_]         ∧ L=[HL|TL]
                       ∧ discFirstPlateau2(L,P,S,HL,TL)
                       ∧ P=[HL] ∧ S=TL ∧ TL=[_|_]
   ∨ L=[_,_|_]         ∧ L=[HL|TL]
                       ∧ discFirstPlateau3(L,P,S,HL,TL,TP,TS)
                       ∧ firstPlateau(TL,TP,TS)
                       ∧ P=[HL|TP] ∧ S=TS ∧ TP=[HL|_]
```

where the procedures of the new predicates are rewritten as a set $\mathcal{Z}$ of logic algorithms:

```
discFirstPlateau1(L,P,S) ⇔
               L=[X] ∧ P=[X] ∧ S=[]

discFirstPlateau2(L,P,S,HL,TL) ⇔
               L=[X,Y] ∧ P=[X] ∧ S=[Y]
             ∧ HL=X ∧ TL=[Y]
             ∧ X≠Y
```

```
discFirstPlateau3(L,P,S,HL,TL,TP,TS) ⇔
                    L=[X,X] ∧ P=[X,X] ∧ S=[]
                  ∧ HL=X ∧ TL=[X] ∧ TP=[X] ∧ TS=[]
```

Suppose that some application-specific heuristics (see Section 13.3.2) suggest that:

- the last two conditions may be projected onto their 2nd to 5th parameters;
- the values of the *P* and *S* parameters are irrelevant in all three conditions;
- the *TL* parameter should vary over its entire domain in the last two conditions.

This transforms *Z* into *Z'*, which is as follows (after some additional rewriting):

```
discFirstPlateau1(L,P,S) ⇔
                    L=[_]

discFirstPlateau2(L,P,S,HL,TL) ⇔
                    TL=[HTL|_] ∧ HL≠HTL

discFirstPlateau3(L,P,S,HL,TL,TP,TS) ⇔
                    TL=[HTL|_] ∧ HL=HTL
```

If we unfold *LA'(firstPlateau)* using *Z'*, then we obtain *LA''(firstPlateau)*:

```
firstPlateau(L,P,S) ⇔
     L=[_]            ∧ P=L ∧ S=[] ∧ L=[_] ∧ L=[_]
   ∨ L=[_,_|_]        ∧ L=[HL|TL]
                      ∧ TL=[HTL|_] ∧ HL≠HTL
                      ∧ P=[HL] ∧ S=TL ∧ TL=[_|_]
   ∨ L=[_,_|_]        ∧ L=[HL|TL]
                      ∧ TL=[HTL|_] ∧ HL=HTL
                      ∧ firstPlateau(TL,TP,TS)
                      ∧ P=[HL|TP] ∧ S=TS ∧ TP=[HL|_]          ♦
```

9.5 Future Work

This method can be easily extended to handle negated primitive predicates since they are resolved according to their semantics. Moreover, the constraint that *LA(r)* should be expressed solely in terms of primitive predicates and possibly of the *r/n* predicate can be easily overcome, namely by considering sets of logic algorithms rather than a single logic algorithm.

A more sophisticated extension would be the handling of proofs-by-induction. This requires additional rules of inference, such as those of [Kanamori and Fujita 86] or [Fribourg 93]. Such proofs are sometimes necessary, as shown in [Flener 93].

9.6 Related Work

The research related to our Proofs-as-Programs Method can be separated into two parts: the motivation for the terminology used in naming this method, as well as the discussion of other methods that solve the same (or a similar) problem as the one defined here.

Our Proofs-as-Programs Method is not like the other methods of program extraction from proofs (see Chapter 2), since the program is here extracted from the *unique* final results of *several* proofs, rather than from *multiple* intermediate steps of a *single* proof. What justifies our naming the method as such is a broader interpretation of the proofs-as-programs paradigm: it covers any method of extracting computational contents from a proof.

In terms of methods that solve the same (or a similar) problem as the one tackled by our Proofs-as-Programs Method, there first is the method described by [Smith 82]: given two formulas F and G, the objective is to find the weakest pre-condition P such that G follows from $F \wedge P$. Taking F as the initial logic algorithm, G as the property set, and $F \wedge P$ as the final logic algorithm, this problem is a sub-case of ours, because F, G, P are here sets of formulas. Smith's proofs are performed by natural deduction.

In explanation-based generalization (EBG), there is some research on failure recovery (such as by [Gupta 87]), which is quite similar in spirit to the derivation of weakest pre-conditions.

Another related research is about *logical debugging*, as reported by [Dershowitz and Lee 93]. In the context of logic program debugging, suppose that, upon execution of a test-case, a bug has been discovered, located, and classified as a "missing condition" bug. Their *Constructive Interpreter* adds the missing condition by extracting it from a failed proof that the program satisfies its (complete) specification. Their method seems quite close to ours, except for the used proof-theoretic framework.

The problem of *belief updating from integrity constraints and queries* is introduced by [De Raedt and Bruynooghe 92a] as a generalization of the problems of intensional knowledge-base updating and incremental concept-learning. Given a knowledge-base KB, an integrity constraint theory IT that is satisfied by KB, an integrity constraint IC, and an oracle O that is willing to answer existential and classification queries, the problem of belief updating amounts to finding another knowledge base KB' that satisfies $IT + IC$, and that is obtained by asserting/retracting any clause/fact to/from KB, possibly via asking questions to O. If we abstract away the differences in the chosen languages, this problem statement is very close to the formulation of our Proofs-as-Programs problem: the logic algorithm is replaced by a knowledge-base, properties become integrity constraints, and there is an oracle now. But from these very problem statements, one can also already detect a first major difference: their integrity constraints are incrementally presented and verified, whereas our properties are presented and verified all-at-once. Other main differences lie in the solutions to the two problems. The belief updating problem is solved by an adaptation of Shapiro's *Model Inference System* (MIS, see Section 3.4.1) [Shapiro 82], because integrity constraints are a generalization of examples. Also, integrity constraints are only used for verifying the results of the learning, and not for actually constructing these results. This means that the clause specialization algorithms of *MIS* are still only based on the examples, that is a subset of the provided integrity constraints. The Proofs-as-Programs Method is more powerful in that it actually extracts complex information from properties so as to *constructively* use it in the design of a target logic algorithm.

It is also interesting to directly compare our Proofs-as-Programs Method with MIS [Shapiro 92]. Both "debug" a given statement (logic algorithm, respectively logic program) such that it satisfies a given set of constraints (properties, respectively positive and negative examples), using some theorem proving technique (extended execution, respectively SLD resolution) for the diagnosis. In case of incompleteness (failure to prove a positive constraint), the former adds some atom(s) to some disjunct of the logic algorithm, whereas the latter adds a clause to the logic program. In case of incorrectness (proof of a negative constraint), the latter deletes some clause from the logic program, whereas this case is impossible with the former (there are no negative properties). In case of potential non-termination (failure to prove a constraint within preset resource limits), the latter deletes some clause from the logic program, whereas this case is impossible with the former (by construction, as explained above).

Finally, this technique is related to *abduction* [Kakas *et al.* 92], which plays an important role when the incorporation of incoming information to an existing theory is impossible or inconvenient: for example in deductive databases and knowledge bases, where adding a new piece of knowledge may cause an inconsistency [Bry 90] [Guessoum and Lloyd 90], or in a fault diagnosis, where one is interested in a cause of failure rather than in the failure itself. By abduction, one looks for an explanation of the new knowledge, consistent with the existing theory, and then adds it to the theory. Abductive reasoning is non-monotonic, as many explanations may exist for a given piece of knowledge. Another evidence for non-monotonicity is that explanations of two different pieces of incoming knowledge may contradict each other. In the field of algorithm synthesis, [De Raedt 92] pointed out that MIS actually also performs abduction: in the context of multiple predicate learning, abduced facts are not added to the theory, but rather used as the starting point for a new synthesis phase. The use of abduction in interactive algorithm synthesis from examples is also explored by [Flener *et al.* 94].

9.7 Conclusion

In this chapter, we have presented the Proofs-as-Programs Method, which adds atoms to (and hence specializes) a logic algorithm so that it is complete wrt a set of given properties. The added atoms are extracted from the proof that the initial logic algorithm is already complete wrt these properties.

10 THE MOST-SPECIFIC-GENERALIZATION METHOD

In this chapter, we develop the Most-Specific-Generalization (MSG) Method, which, within a restricted setting, inductively infers a logic algorithm from examples. This method is part of our tool-box of methods for instantiating the predicate-variables of a schema. First, in Section 10.1, we define the concept of most-specific-generalization. Then, in Section 10.2, we state the objective of the MSG Method, and introduce some other preliminary terminology. We proceed by increasing difficulty, and start with the simplest form the problem can take. Thus, in Section 10.3, we first discuss the case where every example is a ground atom. Then, in Section 10.4, we study the case where non-ground examples, called *general examples*, are allowed. General examples have disjunctions and existential variables, and are thus different from properties. Future work and related work are discussed in Section 10.5 and Section 10.6, respectively, before drawing some conclusions in Section 10.7.

10.1 Most-Specific-Generalization of Terms

The concept of most-specific-generalization (msg) was introduced independently by [Plotkin 70] and [Reynolds 70]. We focus on terms and atoms, rather than on wffs.

Definition 10-1: Term s is *less general* than term t (denoted $s \leq t$) iff there is a substitution σ, such that $s = t\sigma$.

The relation $\leq/2$ forms a complete lattice on the term set $\mathcal{T}$ (modulo variable renaming) to which a least element has been added [Lassez *et al.* 87]. The glb operator computes the gci (greatest common instance) of two terms (by a unification algorithm). The lub operator computes the msg of two terms (by an anti-unification algorithm). The msg of two terms thus always exists, and is unique up to variable renaming.

Here follows another, constructive, definition of the concept of msg:

Definition 10-2: Let s and t designate two terms $f(s_1,s_2,\ldots,s_m)$ and $g(t_1,t_2,\ldots,t_n)$, respectively, where $m \geq 0$, $n \geq 0$. The *most-specific-generalization* of s and t, denoted $msg(s,t)$, is defined as follows:

- if $f/m = g/n$, then $msg(s,t) = f(msg(s_1,t_1),msg(s_2,t_2),\ldots,msg(s_m,t_m))$;
- otherwise, $msg(s,t) = inj(s,t)$;

where inj is an injection from $\mathcal{T} \times \mathcal{T}$ into $\mathcal{V}$ (the set of variable symbols).

Example 10-1: The msg of terms $f(a,b,X,Y,X,c)$ and $f(a,c,d,Z,d,b)$ is $f(a,K,L,M,L,N)$.

Definition 10-3: The *most-specific-generalization* of a non-empty set $\mathcal{S}$ of terms, denoted $msg(\mathcal{S})$, is defined as follows:

- $msg(\{t\}) = t$;
- $msg(\mathcal{T} \cup \{t\}) = msg(msg(\mathcal{T}),t)$, where $\mathcal{T}$ is a non-empty set of terms;

where the difference between $msg/1$ and $msg/2$ should be noted.

Definition 10-4: Let s and t designate two atoms $r(s_1,s_2,\ldots,s_n)$ and $r(t_1,t_2,\ldots,t_n)$. The *most-specific-generalization* of s and t, denoted $msg(s,t)$, is the atom $r(m_1,m_2,\ldots,m_n)$, where $<m_1,m_2,\ldots,m_n> = msg(<s_1,s_2,\ldots,s_n>,<t_1,t_2,\ldots,t_n>)$.

The msg of a non-empty set of atoms is defined in the same way as the msg of a non-empty set of terms. The overloading of the *msg* operator (different arities, different types of parameters) should pose no problem to the reader, especially that the different concepts are closely related anyway, and that we only use the msg of atoms with the same predicate symbol.

10.2 Objective and Terminology

Let's close in now on the MSG Method. Intuitively, its objective is to infer a logic algorithm of a predicate *r*/*n*, given a finite set of examples of *r*/*n*.[14] The method should be applicable if the intended relation $\mathcal{R}$ (from which the examples are extracted) can be expressed by a logic algorithm that is defined solely in terms of the =/2 primitive (hence is non-recursive, among others). This is feasible iff, in the intended relation, some parameters are somehow syntactically constructed from some other parameters.

In a first approximation, we suppose that $\mathcal{R}$ is ternary, and that its third parameter is syntactically constructed from its second parameter, while the first parameter may or may not be used in this construction.

Let's illustrate the objective on a sample problem.

Example 10-2: Given the example set:

```
ℰ(pcCompress) = {
        pcCompress(a,[],[a,1])                        (E2)
        pcCompress(b,[b,1],[b,2])                     (E3)
        pcCompress(c,[d,1],[c,1,d,1])                 (E4)
        pcCompress(e,[e,2],[e,3])                     (E5)
        pcCompress(f,[f,1,g,1],[f,2,g,1])             (E6)
        pcCompress(h,[i,2],[h,1,i,2])                 (E7)
        pcCompress(j,[k,1,m,1],[j,1,k,1,m,1])}        (E8)
```

the MSG Method could infer the following version of *LA*(*pcCompress*):

```
pcCompress(HL,TC,C) ⇔
     C=[HL,1|TC]
  ∨  C=[HL,s(s(N))|TTC] ∧ TC=[HL,s(N)|TTC]
```

which is complete wrt $\mathcal{E}$(*pcCompress*) and all "similar" examples. ♦

Let's now formally define what it means for an atom to satisfy the parameter construction constraint mentioned above.

Definition 10-5: An atom $r(t_1,t_2,t_3)$ is *admissible* iff the following conditions hold:

$$cons(t_2) \subseteq cons(t_3)$$
$$vars(t_2) \subseteq vars(t_3).$$

In other word, the constituents of t_2 must be included in the constituents of t_3, where the *constituents* of a term are the constants and variables occurring in that term.

Definition 10-6: A set $\mathcal{A}(r)$ of atoms is *admissible* iff all its atoms are admissible.

Example 10-3: The set $\mathcal{E}$(*pcCompress*) above is admissible.

---

14. In the following, we shall actually distinguish between (ground) examples, as in Definition 6-1, and general examples (to be defined).

We also need a criterion for verifying whether several atoms construct their third parameters from their second parameters in the same way.

Definition 10-7: Let *s*, *t* be two atoms of predicate *r*. Then *s* is *compatible* with *t* iff *msg(s,t)* is admissible. We also say that *s* and *t* are compatible.

Definition 10-8: Let $\mathcal{A}(r)$ be a set of atoms. Then $\mathcal{A}(r)$ is *compatible* iff its atoms are pairwisely compatible.

Example 10-4: Take the data of Example 10-2. Then E_6 is compatible with E_1, because their msg *pcCompress(A,T,[A,1 | T])* is admissible. But E_7 is not compatible with E_2, because their msg *pcCompress(A,[B,s(0) | T],[A,s(M) | U])* is not admissible.

The compatibility relation is reflexive and symmetric, but not transitive. Compatible sets are thus sets over which the compatibility relation is total.

Example 10-5: The atom *r(a,[b],[a,b])* is compatible with *r(c,[d,d],[c,d,d])*, and *r(c,[d,d],[c,d,d])* is compatible with *r(e,[f,g],[e,g,f])*, but *r(a,[b],[a,b])* is not compatible with *r(e,[f,g],[e,g,f])*.

The following theorem is easily proved. It helps in the practical verification of admissibility and compatibility of atom sets.

Theorem 10-1: *Let $\mathcal{A}(r)$ be a non-empty set of atoms. Then:*

(1) *If msg($\mathcal{A}(r)$) is admissible, then $\mathcal{A}(r)$ is admissible;*
(2) *$\mathcal{A}(r)$ is compatible iff msg($\mathcal{A}(r)$) is admissible;*
(3) *$\mathcal{A}(r)$ is compatible iff $\mathcal{A}(r) \cup msg(\mathcal{A}(r))$ is compatible.*

Compatible sets $\mathcal{A}(r)$ of atoms are of great interest, because, by Theorem 10-1, $\mathcal{A}(r)$ and its msg are admissible, and the atoms of $\mathcal{A}(r)$ construct their parameters in the same way as their msg does. In other words, $\mathcal{A}(r)$ can be "collapsed" into a single atom, namely its msg, which "represents" the entire set $\mathcal{A}(r)$.

The following theorem trivially holds:

Theorem 10-2: *Let $\mathcal{A}(r)$ be a non-empty set of (ternary) atoms, and $r(m_1,m_2,m_3)$ be msg($\mathcal{A}(r)$). Then the logic algorithm:*

$$\texttt{r}(X_1,X_2,X_3) \Leftrightarrow X_1=m_1 \wedge X_2=m_2 \wedge X_3=m_3$$

is complete wrt $\mathcal{A}(r)$, and correct wrt all the instances of msg($\mathcal{A}(r)$).

But this theorem is independent of admissibility and compatibility! So what are their roles? We are not interested in synthesizing logic algorithms that cover "too many", if not all, examples beyond the given ones. Intuitively, admissibility and compatibility are thus meant to restrict the covered set, as captured in the following definition.

Definition 10-9: Let $\mathcal{A}(r)$ be a non-empty admissible set of atoms, and $\mathcal{P}(\mathcal{A})$ a partition of $\mathcal{A}(r)$ into compatible subsets. The *natural extension* of $\mathcal{A}(r)$ wrt $\mathcal{P}(\mathcal{A})$ is the set of atoms that match the msg of some element of $\mathcal{P}(\mathcal{A})$.

The constraints on $\mathcal{R}$ can easily be generalized now so as to obtain a larger domain of applicability. Suppose that $\mathcal{R}$ is of arity $n=a+2b$, where $ab\neq 0$, and that its $(a+b+i)^{th}$ parameter is constructed from its $(a+i)^{th}$ parameter, for $1 \le i \le b$, while the first a parameters may or may not be used in these constructions. This generalization covers the particular case above when $a = b = 1$. Definition 10-5 can be changed as follows.

Definition 10-10: An atom $r(any_1, any_2, \ldots, any_a, in_1, in_2, \ldots, in_b, out_1, out_2, \ldots, out_b)$ is *admissible* wrt a and b iff the following two conditions hold:

$$\forall i \in [1,\ldots,b] \;\; cons(in_i) \subseteq cons(out_i)$$
$$\forall i \in [1,\ldots,b] \;\; vars(in_i) \subseteq vars(out_i).$$

The other definitions are unchanged, and both theorems still hold, once adapted.

10.3 The Ground Case

Let's start with the ground case, where all examples are ground atoms (as in Definition 6-1). The problem is stated in Section 10.3.1, and a method to solve it is explained in Section 10.3.2. Its correctness is discussed in Section 10.3.3, and it is illustrated in Section 10.3.4.

10.3.1 The Problem

Formally, the problem can first be posed as follows.
Given:

- a set $\mathcal{E}(r)$ of examples,

such that:

- $\mathcal{E}(r)$ is admissible,

find:

- a logic algorithm $LA(r)$,

such that:

- $LA(r)$ is defined in terms of the =/2 primitive only,
- $LA(r)$ is correct wrt some natural extension of $\mathcal{E}(r)$.

The problem is correctly solved iff the natural extension of $\mathcal{E}(r)$ is the unknown intended relation $\mathcal{R}$. This is of course impossible to verify, so the main issue is to infer a logic algorithm that gives maximal confidence that the problem is correctly solved.

10.3.2 A Method

It seems desirable to infer a logic algorithm that is correct wrt the largest possible natural extension of $\mathcal{E}(r)$. Indeed, a trivial solution would be to partition $\mathcal{E}(r)$ into singletons, and thus create a logic algorithm that is only correct wrt $\mathcal{E}(r)$. This may clearly not be what is intended, because $\mathcal{E}(r)$ is ground and finite. So the "less ground" the msgs of the subsets, the larger the natural extension. And the best way to obtain variables in the msgs of sets of ground atoms is to make these sets as large as possible. So the partition of $\mathcal{E}(r)$ should yield as few subsets as possible, provided they are all compatible. Because of the non-transitivity of the compatibility relation, this is a non-deterministic problem. It can be solved as follows.

First, decompose the graph of the compatibility relation over $\mathcal{E}(r)$ into its connected components. This is a classical graph theory problem, and is done by a depth-first traversal of the graph. The decomposition is unique, and the algorithm is of complexity $O(m+q)$, where m is $\#\mathcal{E}(r)$, and q is the number of edges of the compatibility graph.

Second, partition each connected component into maximal compatible subgraphs (cliques). Non-deterministically retain, for each component, a partition that has the

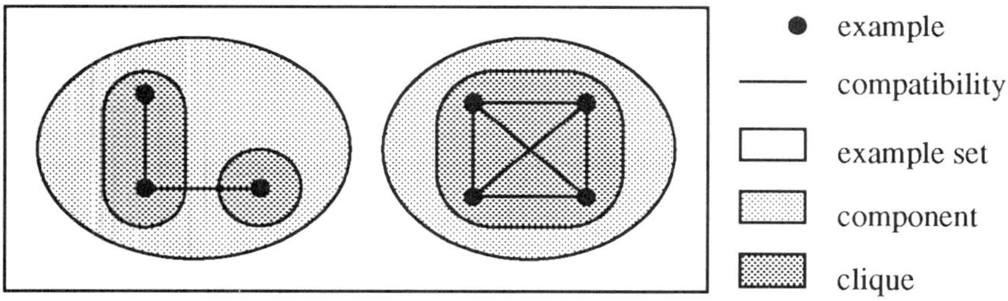

Figure 10-1: MSG Method (ground case): The first two steps

least number of cliques. So far, the algorithm can be graphically illustrated as in Figure 10-1. Note that we could *directly* partition the entire $\mathcal{E}(r)$—rather than its connected components only—into maximal compatible subgraphs. But the chosen approach is justifiable because non-compatible connected components are rather unusual in reality: the components obtained by the first step are often already cliques.

Finally, create a logic algorithm $LA(r)$ from the msgs of the obtained compatible subsets (suppose there are c of them):

$$
\begin{array}{ll}
\mathtt{r}(X_1,\ldots,X_n) \Leftrightarrow & \\
 & X_1=m_{11} \wedge X_2=m_{12} \wedge \ldots \wedge X_n=m_{1n} \\
\vee & X_1=m_{21} \wedge X_2=m_{22} \wedge \ldots \wedge X_n=m_{2n} \\
\vee & \ldots \\
\vee & X_1=m_{c1} \wedge X_2=m_{c2} \wedge \ldots \wedge X_n=m_{cn}
\end{array}
$$

where $r(m_{i1},m_{i2},\ldots,m_{in})$ is the msg of component i $(1 \le i \le c)$, and the X_k $(1 \le k \le n)$ are different variables not occurring in the m_{ij} $(1 \le i \le c,\ 1 \le j \le n)$. The obtained logic algorithm can usually be rewritten more compactly, using equivalence-preserving transformation rules such as elimination of an $X = Y$ atom plus application of the substitution $\{Y/X\}$ to the corresponding disjunct, where Y is an existential variable.

The resulting MSG Method algorithm is thus as follows.

Algorithm 10-1: MSG Method (Ground Case).

(1) Decompose the compatibility graph over $\mathcal{E}(r)$ into its connected components;

(2) Partition each connected component into a least number of cliques;

(3) Create a logic algorithm from the msgs of the obtained cliques.

Note that this algorithm actually also works for atom sets, by virtue of Definition 10-5 and Definition 10-7.

This algorithm is non-deterministic, finite, and never fails. Moreover, the synthesized logic algorithm is non-deterministic in general, and finite, but may fail. For instance, considering Example 10-2, the atom $pcCompress(e,[e,2],X)$ is covered by both disjuncts of the synthesized logic algorithm, namely via the answer substitutions $\{X/[e,3]\}$ and $\{X/[e,1,e,2]\}$.

The computation of the complexity of this algorithm goes as follows. Partitioning a graph into a maximum of k cliques (k being a given constant) is known to be an NP-complete problem [Garey and Johnson 79, page 193]. Hence the union of the first two steps already represents an NP-complete problem, as it requires an iteration over this problem, for $k = 1,\ldots,m$.

10.3.3 Correctness

The following correctness theorem can now be established.

Theorem 10-3: *Let $\mathcal{E}(r)$ be a set of admissible (ground) examples, and LA(r) be the logic algorithm obtained by Algorithm 10-1, using a partition $\mathcal{P}(\mathcal{E})$ of $\mathcal{E}(r)$. Then LA(r) is defined in terms of the =/2 primitive only, and is correct wrt the natural extension of $\mathcal{E}(r)$ wrt $\mathcal{P}(\mathcal{E})$.*

Proof 10-3: Trivial, from Theorem 10-2, Definition 10-9, and Algorithm 10-1. ❑

10.3.4 Illustration

Let's illustrate the described method on some sample problems.

Example 10-6: Take the data of Example 10-2 again. The decomposition is $\{\{E_2,E_4,E_7,E_8\}, \{E_3,E_5,E_6\}\}$. Both components are already compatible, so they need not be partitioned. Their msgs are $pcCompress(A,T,[A,1\,|\,T\,])$ and $pcCompress(B,[B,s(N)\,|\,U], [B,s(s(N))\,|\,U])$. The created logic algorithm effectively is, after rewriting, the one given in Example 10-2.

Example 10-7: Let:

```
ℰ(pcFirstPlateau) = {
                pcFirstPlateau(b,[b],[],[b,b],[])          (E2)
                pcFirstPlateau(j,[j],[k],[j,j],[k])        (E6)
                pcFirstPlateau(m,[m,m],[],[m,m,m],[])}     (E7)
```

and $a = 1$, $b = 2$. All examples are admissible. The decomposition yields one component, namely $\{E_2,E_6,E_7\}$, that is already compatible. The created logic algorithm is:

```
pcFirstPlateau(HL,TP,TS,P,S) ⇔
    HL=A ∧ TP=[A|U] ∧ TS=T ∧ P=[A,A|U] ∧ S=T
```

It may be rewritten as:

```
pcFirstPlateau(HL,TP,TS,P,S) ⇔
    P=[HL|TP] ∧ S=TS ∧ TP=[HL|_]
```

◆

Example 10-8: Let:

```
ℰ(foo) = { foo(a,[],[a])                    (E1)
           foo(b,[c],[b,c])                 (E2)
           foo(d,[e,e],[d,e,e])             (E3)
           foo(f,[g,h],[f,h,g])             (E4)
           foo(i,[j,k,m],[i,k,j,m]) }       (E5)
```

and $a = b = 1$. All examples are admissible. The compatibility graph has one connected component, namely $\mathcal{E}(foo)$ itself, which is not compatible. One of the two (symmetric) possible partitions into cliques is as in Figure 10-2. Whatever the chosen clique partition, the created logic algorithm is:

```
foo(X,Y,Z) ⇔
      X=A ∧ Y=T ∧ Z=[A|T]
    ∨ X=A ∧ Y=[B,C|T]] ∧ Z=[A,C,B|T]
```

◆

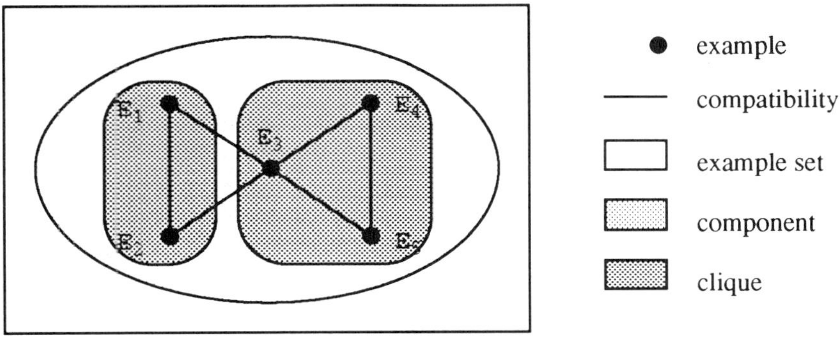

Figure 10-2: MSG Method (ground case): Example

* 10.4 The Non-Ground Case

The groundness assumption on $\mathcal{E}(r)$ is very strong. So we extend the MSG Method to sets $\mathcal{G}(r)$ of not necessarily ground examples, called general examples. The idea is to introduce alternatives in examples. Alternatives are naturally characterized by disjunctions and existential quantifiers.

Definition 10-11: A *general example* of predicate r/n is the existential closure of a disjunction of atoms of predicate r/n.

Note that a single-disjunct general example is different from an atomic property (a property with no body), because properties have universal quantifiers. If there is no ambiguity whether we are referring to an atomic property or a general example, we omit quantifiers.

For ease of notation, a general example $r(\mathbf{P},t_1,\mathbf{Q}) \vee r(\mathbf{P},t_2,\mathbf{Q}) \vee \ldots \vee r(\mathbf{P},t_n,\mathbf{Q})$ is denoted $r(\mathbf{P},\{t_1,t_2,\ldots,t_n\},\mathbf{Q})$, where $t_1, t_2, \ldots, t_n$ are terms, $n > 1$, and $\mathbf{P}, \mathbf{Q}$ are possibly empty vectors of terms. We also allow a recursive use of this convention.

Example 10-9: The general example $append([X],[b],[a,b])$ represents the formula $\exists X\ append([X],[b],[a,b])$. The general example $append(\{[a],[b]\}, \{[c],[d]\}, [a,d])$ represents the formula $append([a],[c],[a,d]) \vee append([a],[d],[a,d]) \vee append([b],[c],[a,d]) \vee append([b],[d],[a,d])$.

Definition 10-12: Given a general example g, the set of *admissible alternatives* of g, denoted $adm(g)$, is defined as follows:

$$adm(g) = \{h \in \mathcal{A} \mid h \text{ is an instance of some disjunct of } g\text{, and } h \text{ is admissible}\}.$$

Definition 10-13: Given a set $\mathcal{G}(r) = \{g_1,g_2,\ldots,g_m\}$ of general examples, the set of *admissible alternatives* of $\mathcal{G}(r)$, denoted $adm(\mathcal{G}(r))$, is defined as follows:

$$adm(\mathcal{G}(r)) = \{\ \{h_1,h_2,\ldots,h_m\} \mid h_i \in adm(g_i)\ \}.$$

Note that the admissible alternatives of a general example (set) are (sets of) atoms, not (sets of) ground examples. Also note that the *adm* relations may be infinite if variables occur in their arguments.

Example 10-10: Let:

```
𝒢(pcPlateau) = { pcPlateau(1,[],A,[b],b)            (G1)
                 pcPlateau(2,[B],B,[c,c],c)         (G2)
                 pcPlateau(3,[C,C],C,[d,d,d],d) }   (G3)
```

and $a = 1$, $b = 2$. Then $adm(G_2)$ contains *pcPlateau*(2,[*c*],*c*,[*c*,*c*],*c*), but not *pcPlateau*(2,[*b*],*b*,[*c*,*c*],*c*), nor *pcPlateau*(2,[*d*],*d*,[*c*,*c*],*c*). ♦

The new problem is stated in Section 10.4.1, and a method to solve it is in Section 10.4.2. Its correctness is discussed in Section 10.4.3, and it is illustrated in Section 10.4.4.

10.4.1 The Problem

Formally, the problem can now be expanded as follows:
Given:
- a set $\mathcal{G}(r)$ of general examples,

such that:
- $\mathcal{G}(r)$ has admissible alternatives,

find:
- a logic algorithm *LA*(*r*),

such that:
- *LA*(*r*) is defined in terms of the =/2 primitive only,
- *LA*(*r*) is correct wrt some natural extension of some element of $adm(\mathcal{G}(r))$.

10.4.2 A Method

The objective is again to produce partitions with the smallest possible number of subsets. This can be done as follows: compute all possible admissible alternatives of $\mathcal{G}(r)$, and partition them using Algorithm 10-1. Select one of the solutions that have the least number of cliques. The resulting extended algorithm is thus as follows.

Algorithm 10-2: MSG Method (Non-ground Case).

(1) Perform Algorithm 10-1 for every element in $adm(\mathcal{G}(r))$, and select a logic algorithm resulting from the least number of cliques.

This algorithm is non-deterministic and NP-complete, as it is based on Algorithm 10-1. It always succeeds, but may be infinite. Moreover, the synthesized logic algorithm is non-deterministic in general, but finite, because Algorithm 10-1 produces such logic algorithms.

If a set *adm*(*g*) is infinite, then the search space must be pruned by applying some heuristics. Thus, given an atom *g* as *r*(*any*,*in*,*out*), where $vars(<in,out>) \neq \emptyset$, we have to bridle the *adm* relation so that, in its search for a substitution σ for *g*, it enumerates a smaller space than the infinite $vars(g) \times \mathcal{T}$, and preferably a finite one. First, this search space can be pruned with type knowledge, such as:
- application-independent type knowledge, e.g. *s*/1 is only applicable to integers;
- application-specific type knowledge, in case type information is given with *g*.

Next, there are some particular cases where the search space is (or may be) reduced, taking advantage of the context:
- if $vars(out) = \emptyset$, then the range of σ is $\mathcal{U}(out)$; we may even first emit the *minimality hypothesis* that the range of σ is restricted to the finite set *cons*(*out*);

- if $vars(in) = \varnothing$, then we may in a first approximation look for the least solution: the *strongly conservative hypothesis* restricts the range of σ to $cons(in)$; otherwise, the *weakly conservative hypothesis* restricts the range of σ to $\mathcal{U}(in)$.

Anyway, the resultant search space may be huge, so we have to be careful in practice to apply this method only when there are few variables in g, less than 3, say. There is no problem of course if the general example is ground, because *adm* then only needs to perform a finite enumeration.

10.4.3 Correctness

The following correctness theorem can easily be proven.

Theorem 10-4: *Let $\mathcal{G}(r)$ be a set of admissible general examples, and LA(r) be the logic algorithm obtained by Algorithm 10-2, using a partition $\mathcal{P}(\mathcal{G}')$ of some element $\mathcal{G}'(r)$ of $adm(\mathcal{G}(r))$. Then LA(r) is defined in terms of the =/2 primitive only, and is correct wrt the natural extension of $\mathcal{G}'(r)$ wrt $\mathcal{P}(\mathcal{G}')$.*

10.4.4 Illustration

Let's illustrate the described method on some sample problems. The first one involves existential variables, while the second involves disjunctions.

Example 10-11: Take the data of Example 10-10 again. If we restrict the functor set to $\{b,c,d\}$, the only element of $adm(\mathcal{G}(pcPlateau))$ is:

```
{ pcPlateau(1,[],b,[b],b)                    (G1')
  pcPlateau(2,[c],c,[c,c],c)                 (G2')
  pcPlateau(3,[d,d],d,[d,d,d],d) }           (G3')
```

The only clique is $\{G_1',G_2',G_3'\}$, and has $pcPlateau(s(N),T,A,[A \mid T],A)$ as msg. The created logic algorithm is, after rewriting, as follows:

```
pcPlateau(HN,TL,TX,L,X) ⇔
                        L=[X|TL] ∧ X=TX ∧ HN=s(N)    ◆
```

Example 10-12: Let:

```
𝒢(pcPermutation) = {
        pcPermutation(a,[],[a])                          (G2)
        pcPermutation(b,[c],[b,c])                       (G3)
        pcPermutation(b,[c],[c,b])                       (G4)
        pcPermutation(d,{[e,f],[f,e]},[d,e,f])           (G5)
        pcPermutation(d,{[e,f],[f,e]},[d,f,e])           (G6)
        pcPermutation(d,{[e,f],[f,e]},[e,d,f])           (G7)
        pcPermutation(d,{[e,f],[f,e]},[e,f,d])           (G8)
        pcPermutation(d,{[e,f],[f,e]},[f,d,e])           (G9)
        pcPermutation(d,{[e,f],[f,e]},[f,e,d])           (G10)
```

and $a = b = 1$. There are $2^6 = 64$ admissible alternatives of $\mathcal{G}(pcPermutation)$: for general examples G_5 to G_{10}, we denote their first alternative by G_i', and their second alternative by G_i''. There are two least partitions, namely $\{\{G_2,G_3,G_5',G_6''\}, \{G_4,G_7',G_9''\}, \{G_8',G_{10}''\}\}$, and $\{\{G_2,G_3,G_5',G_6''\}, \{G_4,G_7',G_9''\}, \{G_8'',G_{10}'\}\}$. For the first partition, the created logic algorithm is as follows:

```
pcPermutation(HL,TP,P) ⇔
      HL=A ∧ TP=T ∧ P=[A|T]
   ∨ HL=A ∧ TP=[B|T] ∧ P=[B,A|T]
   ∨ HL=A ∧ TP=[B,C] ∧ P=[B,C,A]
```

For the second partition, the created logic algorithm is as follows:

```
pcPermutation(HL,TP,P) ⇔
      HL=A ∧ TP=T ∧ P=[A|T]
   ∨ HL=A ∧ TP=[B|T] ∧ P=[B,A|T]
   ∨ HL=A ∧ TP=[B,C] ∧ P=[C,B,A]
```
◆

10.5 Future Work

The MSG Method, as presented here, is sufficient for our future needs. But it may be enhanced along several lines.

First, as of now, the compatibility criterion of Definition 10-10 doesn't prescribe any restrictions on the first a parameters of an $(a + 2b)$-ary atom. This holds because of the statement that they may or may not be involved in the construction of the last b parameters from the middle b parameters. The current compatibility criterion is fine with a large number of applications. But it could be refined so as to include the following restriction: if (some of) the constants or variables of (some of) the first a parameters of atom s are used in the construction of (some of) the last b parameters of s, then the same must happen for atom t. This refinement should enlarge the number of successfully covered applications. Other refinements can be imagined, but the whole framework of correctness definitions and theorems for the MSG Method needs to be proved afresh each time.

Second, the notion of general examples could be extended to the notion of *constrained general examples*. Constraints could indeed be attached to general examples and thus constrain the search for admissible alternatives.

Third, the decomposition of the arity n of predicate r into $a + 2b$ directly results from the applications we have in mind for the MSG Method. But such a restrictive setting may not be suitable for other needs. In order to generalize this setting, we could define the concept of mode, so that we may precisely describe which parameters are constructed in terms of which parameters.

Definition 10-14: Let r be an n-ary predicate symbol. A *mode* m_r for r is a total function from $\{1,2,\ldots,n\}$ into $\{in, in_1, in_2, \ldots, out, out_1, out_2, \ldots, any\}$. If $m_r(i)$ is X, then the ith parameter of r is called an *X-parameter* of r. If $m_r(i)$ is *in or* in_j, then the ith parameter of r is called an *input-parameter* of r. If $m_r(i)$ is *out or* out_j, then the ith parameter of r is called an *output-parameter* of r.

A mode m_r is often written in the more suggestive form $r(m_r(1), m_r(2), \ldots, m_r(n))$. It should be noted that, despite the syntactic similarity, these "construction" modes have nothing to do with the call-modes, such as $r(ground, ground, any)$, that are often found in the logic programming literature. Indeed, our "construction" modes are descriptions of static relationships between parameters, whereas call-modes are descriptions of dynamic states of parameters.

Example 10-13: The mode for *pcPlateau*/5, as defined in Example 10-10, would be *pcPlateau*(in,in_1,in_2,out_1,out_2).

The intuition behind these "construction"-modes is the following. The out_i-parameters must be constructed in terms of the in_i-parameters. The *in*-parameters may or may not be used in the construction of *output*-parameters. The *out*-parameters may or may not be constructed in terms of *input*-parameters. There are no constraints on *any*-parameters. Nothing prevents out_i-parameters to be constructed in terms of in_j-parameters, where $i \neq j$. Nothing prevents out_i-parameters to "invent" constants.

These modes are a possible starting point for a very refined version of the MSG Method, with enhanced admissibility and compatibility criteria.

10.6 Related Work

The related work for the MSG Method can be divided into two categories. First, there is the theoretical research on the concept of msg, and its practical applications. Second, there is research on techniques similar to the MSG Method.

As said earlier, the concepts of msg and anti-unification were introduced simultaneously, but independently, by [Plotkin 70, 71] and [Reynolds 70]. The original motivation is accredited to [Popplestone 70], who suggested that "since unification is useful in automatic deduction by the resolution method, its dual might prove helpful for induction". The main differences between both works are that Plotkin takes a logic-based approach and considers atomic formulas and clauses, whereas Reynolds is more concerned about an algebraic approach and only considers atomic formulas. But their results and msg algorithms are essentially the same.

These early works have spawned a lot of theoretical interest, among which the following studies of term lattices should be noted: [Huet 76] and [Lassez *et al.* 87].

The concepts of msg and anti-unification have naturally generated a lot of practical applications for the machine learning community, and especially from researchers on inductive logic programming (ILP). [Vere 75] infers conjunctive concept descriptions from positive and negative examples, using msgs. He introduces the useful notion of inverse substitution in order to formalize how the term lattice can be traversed "upwards". The problem of learning concept descriptions from negative examples is studied by [Lassez and Marriott 87]. Building on his semantic generalization model (surveyed in Section 7.5), [Buntine 88] suggests the notion of msg of two clauses relative some other clauses.

[Gegg-Harrison 89] extends the computation of msgs to a second-order framework (and improves the complexity of the original algorithms) so as to infer logic program schemas for a logic programming tutor. Simultaneously, but independently, [Tinkham 90] also uses a second-order lattice of logic program schemas so as to efficiently guide an MIS-like system for logic program synthesis from examples.

In terms of alternative techniques to the MSG Method, there is of course the whole literature on empirical learning, and inductive logic programming (ILP), as surveyed in Chapter 3. But it should be noted that the MSG Method only aims at the synthesis of a sub-class of concept descriptions, namely non-recursive algorithms that are implemented in terms of the =/2 primitive only, and whose intended relation, though unknown as a whole, is however known to feature a given dataflow pattern between its parameters. This extremely restrictive setting justifies the non-incremental approach, as well as the highly specialized MSG Method.

The technique of [Vere 75] is quite similar to ours in spirit, as the fundamental notion is the one of msg, and as no recursive concept descriptions are aimed at. But he only aims at conjunctive concept descriptions, whereas our technique is also able to infer disjunctive concept descriptions. Also, the MSG Method is based only on positive examples, and is only set in a first-order logic.

The notion of general example seems to be new. It is not related to noisy examples, because the existence of a correct admissible alternative of a general example is assumed.

10.7 Conclusion

Within a restricted setting, the MSG Method infers, from a finite set of general examples, a non-recursive logic algorithm that is defined in terms of the =/2 primitive only, and that is correct wrt a natural extension of the given examples. The underlying algorithm is non-deterministic.

If the resulting logic algorithm is judged, by whatever application-specific heuristics, to be "not good enough", then the assumption that the examples can be covered by such a logic algorithm must be revised: recursion, or other predicates, or both, might be needed. This requires a more involved method. A possible solution is outlined in Section 14.2.4: it is called the *Synthesis Method*, because it automatically infers a property set of the intended relation (this is possible in some applications), and then uses the entire synthesis mechanism (as described in Part III) in order to infer a logic algorithm that covers the given examples and inferred properties.

So why not immediately use the Synthesis Method? The reason is that both methods tackle *different* classes of problems. The MSG Method and the Synthesis Method are a joint answer to the same overall problem: how to infer, from a finite set of general examples of an unknown relation that is however known to feature a given dataflow pattern between its parameters, a logic algorithm that is correct wrt a natural extension of the given examples. The MSG Method is the "base case" of the answer, because it doesn't look for recursion, and the Synthesis Method is the "structure case" of the answer, because it *does* look for recursion.

Another crucial question that pops up is: Why not use a "classical" concept learner? The reason for not doing so is that a concept learner, in its incremental approach and blind enumeration, doesn't take advantage of the knowledge about the dataflow pattern between the parameters of the intended relation. Concept learners are a reasonable approach if *nothing* is known about the intended relation. But this is not the case here, and more practical methods can thus be developed.

Note that the MSG Method is part of our tool-box for solving sub-problems occurring during synthesis, and not a solution to the overall problem of synthesis from specifications by examples (and properties).

III A LOGIC ALGORITHM SYNTHESIS MECHANISM

Synthesis, in wider philosophical use and generally:
the putting together of parts or elements so as to make a complex whole;
the combination of immaterial or abstract things, or of elements
into an ideal or abstract whole (opposed to analysis).

—*The Oxford English Dictionary*

In this third part, we present a particular logic algorithm synthesis mechanism, designed from the building blocks provided in Part II. Thus, in Chapter 11, we give an intuitive overview of the entire synthesis mechanism, so as to give the reader the feel for its working. Chapter 12 gives full detail about the Expansion Phase of synthesis, that is the first four steps, while Chapter 13 does similarly with the Reduction Phase, that is the remaining three steps. Finally, in Chapter 14, we conclude and evaluate the resulting mechanism.

11 OVERVIEW OF THE SYNTHESIS MECHANISM

In this chapter, we give an intuitive overview of the entire synthesis mechanism, so as to give the reader the feel for its working. Thus, in Section 11.1, we first motivate the desired features of this mechanism. Then, in Section 11.2, we argue for a series of preliminary restrictions of this mechanism, so as to keep the presentation simple until the discussion of its extensions (see Chapter 14). Finally, in Section 11.3, we perform a sample synthesis.

11.1 Desired Features

Considering the state of the art of inductive synthesis from examples (as seen in Chapter 3), we now decide on, and motivate, some desired features of the synthesis mechanism. These decisions are about the specification language, the logic algorithm language, the degree of automation of synthesis, the types of performed reasoning, and the features of the chosen synthesis strategy. In the following, "synthesis system" stands for an implementation of a synthesis mechanism.

Specification Language

We gave a very general definition of specifications by examples and properties in Chapter 6, but postponed the actual decisions about the concrete languages for examples and properties in order to be independent of such decisions for as long as possible. During the course of Part II, various languages have been proposed, according to how much could actually be handled for each notion or method we introduced. Basically, the property language was each time some restriction of normal clauses, the differences lying in whether negation and recursion were allowed or not. The example languages differed in whether negative examples were required or not. In summary:

- in Chapter 6 (specification approach), a sample language was proposed for illustration purposes only;
- in Chapter 7 (synthesis framework), all definitions were language-independent;
- in Chapter 8 (algorithm schemas), there was no concern about specifications;
- in Chapter 9 (Proofs-as-Programs Method), the example language was irrelevant, but properties were constrained to be (possibly recursive) definite clauses;
- in Chapter 10 (MSG Method), the property language was irrelevant, but only positive examples were taken into account, be they ground or general examples.

So we could here simply choose the largest common subset of all the proposed relevant languages. But two additional restrictions can still be made: Are negative examples required? Are recursive properties allowed? Negative examples are usually expected in order to avoid over-generalization. But it can be argued (see Section 14.2.1) that negative information is not required here. Also, although we *could* handle recursive definite clauses, we limit properties to be non-recursive, so as to focus on synthesis from incomplete specifications. Recursion discovery is indeed a major challenge of algorithm synthesis, and a challenge that we want to pick up. So there is no need to give that information away by means of recursive properties. The refined definition of specifications by examples and properties is thus as follows:

Definition 11-1: A *specification by examples and properties* of a procedure for predicate r/n, denoted $EP(r)$, consists of:

- a set $\mathcal{E}(r)$ of positive examples of r (that is, ground atoms whose n-tuples are supposed to belong to the intended relation $\mathcal{R}$);
- a set $\mathcal{P}(r)$ of properties of r (that is, non-recursive definite clauses whose heads are atoms of predicate r).

We thus require multiple, ground, single-predicate, relational, positive-only, pre-synthesis examples that are chosen in a consistent way by a human specifier who knows the intended relation. The predicates used in the properties constitute a partial basis set, and thus a partial conceptual bias for synthesis. For convenience, and as there is no ambiguity in doing so, we drop the universal quantifications of properties. Overall, the specification language is quite expressive and readable. Specifications by examples and properties are usually incomplete, and hence ambiguous, but minimal. There is a danger of internal inconsistency and redundancy in such specifications, though. The synthesis mechanism should be robust to the ordering and choice of examples and properties.

Logic Algorithm Language

We gave a very general definition of logic algorithms in Chapter 4, but postponed the actual decisions about the concrete language for bodies in order to be independent of such decisions for as long as possible. During the course of Part II, various languages have been proposed, according to how much could actually be handled for each notion or method we introduced. In summary:

- in Chapter 6 (specification approach), there is no concern about logic algorithms;
- in Chapter 7 (synthesis framework), logic algorithms were required to be implemented in terms of primitives only; for more specific purposes (see Section 7.2.2 and Section 7.3.2), bodies of logic algorithms were constrained to be in disjunctive normal form (with negation, that is);
- in Chapter 8 (algorithm schemas), all definitions were language-independent;
- in Chapter 9 (Proofs-as-Programs Method), bodies of logic algorithms were constrained to be in prenex disjunctive normal form, though without negation;
- in Chapter 10 (MSG Method), the imposed restrictions were only on target logic algorithms, and hence irrelevant.

So we here simply choose the largest common subset of all the proposed relevant languages. The refined definition of logic algorithms is thus as follows:

Definition 11-2: A *logic algorithm* defining a predicate r/n, denoted $LA(r)$, is a closed well-formed formula of the form:

$$\forall X_1 \ldots \forall X_n \quad r(X_1, \ldots, X_n) \Leftrightarrow B$$

where the X_i are distinct variables, and F is a well-formed formula in prenex disjunctive normal form, without negation. The atom $r(X_1, \ldots, X_n)$ is called the *head*, and B is called the *body* of the logic algorithm.

This definition actually constitutes a partial syntactic bias for the synthesis. As usual, we drop the universal quantifications in front of the heads, as well as any existential quantifications at the beginnings of bodies of logic algorithms. Moreover, we often write logic algorithms in a more compact form, using De Morgan's laws in order to merge disjuncts.

Degree of Automation

With incomplete specifications, it is more realistic to strive for an interactive synthesis mechanism, so as to explicitly disambiguate some situations, rather than have a default iteration over (all) possible choices. The initiative should be on the system's side, because the latter would otherwise slip from the synthesizer category into the design-assistant category. The questions asked to the specifier should be kept simple, the universe of the dialogue being restricted to the specified predicate and the primitive predicates. In other words, predicates that the mechanism invents during the synthesis should not occur in any dialogue, as the specifier is not familiar with them. Also, the language of questions and answers should not be more "complicated" than the actual specification language. This means that the answers could actually be seen as extensions to the initially given specification, so that if the extended specification had been given right away, the synthesis would have been fully automatic. In our case, questions to the specifier could be of the following kinds:

- *classification queries*, such as "is a given ground atomic formula A a positive example of the intended relation $\mathcal{R}$?"; a correct answer is either *yes* (iff the tuple of terms extracted from A belongs to $\mathcal{R}$) or *no* (otherwise);
- *existential queries*, such as "is a given atomic formula A satisfiable in the intended model $\Im$?"; a correct answer is either <*yes*, σ> (iff $A\sigma$ is valid in $\Im$, where σ is a substitution) or *no* (otherwise);
- *universal queries*, such as "is a given atomic formula A valid in the intended model $\Im$?"; a correct answer is either *yes* (iff A is valid in $\Im$) or *no* (otherwise);
- *conditional queries*, such as "under what (conjunctive) condition is a given atomic formula A valid in $\Im$?"; a correct answer is either <*yes*, C> (iff $A \Leftarrow C$ is valid in $\Im$, where C is a conjunction of literals) or *never* (otherwise).

Answers such as "*I don't know*" should also be taken into account. Classification queries are a particular case of universal queries and of existential queries, namely when there are no variables in A. Universal queries are a particular case of conditional queries, namely when C reduces to *true*. Similarly to our assumption about the consistency of specifications with intended relations, we assume that the specifier's answers to queries are noise-free. Note that we talk about questions to a (human) specifier here, and not about the more general problem of asking questions to some oracle. At this level of the discourse, we are not interested in knowing whether a mechanized oracle is queried during synthesis or not.

There is another level of specifier interference during synthesis. Indeed, there is an infinity of algorithms defining a given intended (and computable) relation. For instance, if we only consider divide-and-conquer algorithms, there are design choices to be made about the induction parameter, its decomposition, a well-founded relation over its domain, and so on. A synthesis mechanism should then be able to discover a significant sub-family of algorithms within its search space, one algorithm per combination of taken choices. Given a specification of the *sort*/2 problem, one would thus expect Insertion-Sort, Merge-Sort, Quick-Sort, and so on [Clark and Darlington 80] [Lau 89], and not just one of these algorithms. While the derivability of a large family of algorithms is an impressive (and desired) feature, this may go counter the specifier's expectations, because s/he only needs one algorithm, or because s/he has some understanding of the synthesis mechanism and wants to experiment with some very specific design choices. A synthesis system should thus accept hints about preferences from the specifier, as well as "think aloud" so that the specifier may interfere.

Finally, given some synthesized logic algorithm, how does the specifier continue to interact with the synthesis system? S/he could experiment with the algorithm by executing a logic program derived (Section 4.4) from it, or s/he could directly analyze the algorithm itself (this calls for the invention of meaningful names of system-generated variables and predicates). In either case, an error might be discovered, or maybe even the requirements could change. Debugging techniques can then be invoked at the logic algorithm or logic program level. Ideally, though, the original specification is changed to reflect the corrected/updated requirements, and a new synthesis is performed.

Kinds of Inference

With specifications by examples (which traditionally give rise to inductive synthesis) and properties (which are a particular case of axioms, which traditionally give rise to deductive synthesis), it should be natural to use both inductive *and* deductive inference in the synthesis mechanism, whichever is best suited for each sub-task. Other, obviously less well-founded decisions, would be to do purely inductive synthesis from the examples only, and to use the properties only as integrity constraints in order to reject candidate logic algorithms, or to do purely deductive synthesis from the properties only, and to use the examples only as test-data in order to reject candidate logic algorithms. Moreover, other kinds of inference (such as analogical inference, or abductive inference) could be used as well.

Strategy Criteria

Stepwise synthesis was argued for in Section 7.3 because it allows different methods to be deployed at each step (rather than having a unique method handle a wide variety of different tasks), and because it yields monitoring points where correctness and comparison criteria can be applied (rather than having a unique monitoring point).

Schema-guided synthesis was argued for in Section 8.1 because schemas are an interesting way of incorporating algorithm design knowledge into a synthesis process. Schema-guided synthesis is naturally a stepwise synthesis, as the predicate-variables are not all instantiated at the same time. A most interesting approach was then advocated in Section 8.3, namely to deploy an entire tool-box of predicate-variable instantiating methods, rather than a unique method. In Chapter 9 (Proofs-as-Programs Method) and Chapter 10 (MSG Method), we described two of the more sophisticated methods we have developed so far. Note that these methods are entirely dissociated from specific schemas or predicate-variables.

The divide-and-conquer strategy was presented as an attractive strategy in Section 8.2, because of its diverse applicability, efficient results, and simplicity of application. The chosen approach for developing a synthesis mechanism is thus stepwise synthesis guided by a divide-and-conquer schema.

As a first approximation to this approach, we develop a synthesis mechanism that reflects a hardwired sequence of instantiations of the predicate-variables of (some version of) the divide-and-conquer schema, as well as a hardwired mapping between these variables and the methods of the tool-box. The chosen sequence of steps was presented in Example 8-8; the chosen mapping between steps and methods is presented in the next chapters, as other methods are introduced. The development of a synthesis mechanism that is parameterized on schemas, and that has no fixed sequences of steps or mappings between steps and methods, is considered future research.

Now, what is the chosen strategy for stepwise synthesis? We consider that all the specification information should be available for every inference during synthesis, and that a single run through all synthesis steps is hence sufficient. We thus favor a non-incremental (all-at-once) presentation of examples and properties to the synthesis mechanism. This leads to non-incremental synthesis, which is more "disciplined" than incremental synthesis, where parts of algorithms are continuously designed/debugged/rejected from partial information (which is extracted from an incomplete specification). The drawback of our approach is that we can't use the identification-in-the-limit results that are known for incremental synthesis.

Note the difference between incremental synthesis and the incremental usage of a non-incremental synthesis mechanism: the former continuously debugs a unique algorithm from an increasingly large specification, whereas the latter amounts to presenting increasingly large specifications to a synthesis mechanism that always starts from scratch and generates as many algorithms. The latter approach only makes sense when a specification turns out to be not precise enough. But this amounts to specification augmentation, not to algorithm debugging. A useful generalization of specification augmentation is full-blown specification debugging.

So we adopt the non-incremental synthesis strategy presented in Section 7.3.2, which reflects monotonically decreasing synthesis (and is actually also monotonically increasing, if one also considers the expanded logic algorithms), as well as consistent synthesis. We also strive to make each synthesis step comply with Theorem 7-7.

11.2 Preliminary Restrictions

In order to keep the presentation of the synthesis mechanism simple, we now decide on three preliminary restrictions.

First, regarding the schema underlying the mechanism, we retain version 3 of the divide-and-conquer schema for the theoretical presentation:

```
R(X,Y) ⇔
              Minimal(X)      ∧ Solve(X,Y)
   ∨ ∨1≤k≤c  NonMinimal(X)   ∧ Decompose(X,HX,TX)
                              ∧ Discriminate_k(HX,TX,Y)
                              ∧ (      SolveNonMin_k(HX,TX,Y)
                                    |
                                       R(TX,TY)
                                    ∧  Process_k(HX,HY)
                                    ∧  Compose_k(HY,TY,Y)        )
```

This amounts to the support of binary predicates, single induction parameters, a single minimal form, a single non-minimal form, and non-recursive non-minimal cases.

The support of version 4 (relations of any non-zero arity) is actually a pretty straightforward extension, but the needed vectorizations imply a complication of notations. Some illustrations during the presentation of the synthesis mechanism actually do require version 4, but we assume the reader can easily extrapolate how the theory has to be expanded in order to accommodate them. Version 4 is actually supported by the implementation of the mechanism. The support of any number of minimal or non-minimal forms and of compound induction parameters is considered future research. Note that Section 5.2.2 showed that single minimal forms and non-minimal forms are actually more frequent than one might believe at first sight.

Second, the mechanism should support any inductive types (such as integers, lists, bags, sets, trees, graphs, grammars, and so on) for potential induction parameters, provided their definitions have been made known to it. But whenever concrete datatypes need to be discussed, we arbitrarily restrict the support to lists and integers.

Third, we only aim at the synthesis of single-loop logic algorithms. In other words, we assume that the only "loop" is the one that is achieved in the schema by the recursion on the induction parameter, and that none of the instances of the predicate-variables is defined recursively (possibly as a divide-and-conquer logic algorithm).

11.3 A Sample Synthesis

Instantiating some predicate-variable(s) of a schema is a synthesis step. Our synthesis mechanism is expressed as the following sequence of steps (see Example 8-8):

- Step 1: Syntactic creation of a first approximation;
- Step 2: Synthesis of *Minimal* and *NonMinimal*;
- Step 3: Synthesis of *Decompose*;
- Step 4: Syntactic introduction of the recursive atoms;
- Step 5: Synthesis of *Solve* and the $SolveNonMin_k$;
- Step 6: Synthesis of the $Process_k$ and $Compose_k$;
- Step 7: Synthesis of the $Discriminate_k$.

The chosen, fixed mapping between the synthesis steps and the methods of our toolbox is explained in the next two chapters, where other methods are introduced.

Example 11-1: Let's perform an intuitive overview of these seven steps by illustrating them on the *compress*/2 problem, so that the reader can do some preliminary learning-from-traces before proceeding. Reconsider *EP*(*compress*) as in Example 6-1:

```
ℰ(compress) = { compress([],[])                        (E1)
                compress([a],[a,1])                    (E2)
                compress([b,b],[b,2])                  (E3)
                compress([c,d],[c,1,d,1])              (E4)
                compress([e,e,e],[e,3])                (E5)
                compress([f,f,g],[f,2,g,1])            (E6)
                compress([h,i,i],[h,1,i,2])            (E7)
                compress([j,k,m],[j,1,k,1,m,1]) }      (E8)

𝒫(compress) = { compress([X],[X,1])                    (P1)
                compress([X,Y],[X,2]) ⇐ X=Y            (P2)
                compress([X,Y],[X,1,Y,1]) ⇐ X≠Y }      (P3)
```

The chosen strategy is such that the synthesized logic algorithms progress downwards, while their expansions progress upwards. The synthesis proceeds as follows.

Step 1: Syntactic Creation of a First Approximation

Step 1 creates $LA_1(r)$ by setting its body to *true*. So $LA_1(compress)$ is as follows:

```
compress(L,C) ⇔
     true                                             {E1,...,E8}
```

The set annotation to a disjunct explains which examples are covered by that disjunct. This logic algorithm always holds, and thus covers all given examples.

The expanded version of $LA_1(compress)$, that is $exp(LA_1(compress))$, is as follows:

```
compress(L,C) ⇔
     true    ∧         L=[] ∧ C=[]                        {E1}
               ∨       L=[a] ∧ C=[a,1]                    {E2}
               ∨       L=[b,b] ∧ C=[b,2]                  {E3}
               ∨       L=[c,d] ∧ C=[c,1,d,1]              {E4}
               ∨       L=[e,e,e] ∧ C=[e,3]                {E5}
               ∨       L=[f,f,g] ∧ C=[f,2,g,1]            {E6}
               ∨       L=[h,i,i] ∧ C=[h,1,i,2]            {E7}
               ∨       L=[j,k,m] ∧ C=[j,1,k,1,m,1]        {E8}
```

Note that this expanded version is a mere syntactic translation of the example set.

In the following, we only compute expansions that involve the variables that correspond to parameters in the schema. Also note that the inferences of each Step i (where $i \in \{2,\ldots,7\}$) are actually based on $exp(LA_{i-1}(r))$.

Step 2: Synthesis of Minimal and NonMinimal

An instantiation of the *Minimal* (respectively *NonMinimal*) predicate-variable tests whether the induction parameter is of a minimal (respectively non-minimal) form. These forms must be mutually exclusive over the domain of the induction parameter. Step 2 yields $LA_2(r)$ by first selecting an induction parameter, and then instantiating the *Minimal* and *NonMinimal* predicate-variables by means of a so-called *Database Method*, which here relies on a database of type-specific form-identifying formulas.

For instance, we assume that Step 2 selects L as the induction parameter, identifies it as being of type *list*, and selects the empty list as the (unique) minimal form (which is identified by the atomic formula $L = []$), and the non-empty list as the (unique) non-minimal form (which is identified[15] by the atomic formula $L = [\_|\_]$). $LA_2(compress)$ is thus as follows:

```
compress(L,C) ⇔
      L=[]                                            {E1}
   ∨  L=[_|_]                                         {E2,...,E8}
```

Note the usage of anonymous variables: we are here merely interested in testing of *what* form the induction parameter is, not in knowing *how* it fits this test. This logic algorithm expresses that *compress(L,C)* holds whenever L is either an empty list or a

15. Pseudo-lists, such as $[a|b]$, are actually also identified by this formula.

non-empty list. This is strictly less often than always, as L now has to be a list (or at least a pseudo-list).

The expanded version of LA_2(*compress*), that is *exp*(LA_2(*compress*)), is as follows:

```
compress(L,C) ⇔
        L=[]      ∧          L=[] ∧ C=[]                          {E1}
      ∨ L=[_|_] ∧          L=[a] ∧ C=[a,1]                        {E2}
                      ∨    ...                                    {...}
                      ∨    L=[j,k,m] ∧ C=[j,1,k,1,m,1]            {E8}
```

Note the redundancy between the $L = []$ atoms in the minimal case: one of them is a synthesized atom, whereas the other one is a trailing atom introduced by expansion.

Step 3: Synthesis of Decompose

An instantiation of the *Decompose* predicate-variable deterministically decomposes, in the non-minimal case, the induction parameter, say X, into a vector $\boldsymbol{HX}$ of heads and a vector $\boldsymbol{TX}$ of tails, the tails TX_i being smaller than X according to some well-founded relation. These tails are meant for the recursive computation of the tails TY_i of the other parameter, say Y. Step 3 yields $LA_3(r)$ by instantiating the *Decompose* predicate-variable by means of the *Database Method*, which here relies on a database of type-specific decomposition formulas.

For instance, we assume that Step 3 selects a simple head-tail decomposition of the induction parameter L. This is performed by the atomic formula $L = [HL \mid TL]$. LA_3(*compress*) is thus as follows:

```
compress(L,C) ⇔
        L=[]                                                      {E1}
      ∨ L=[_|_] ∧ L=[HL|TL]                                       {E2,...,E8}
```

Note the redundancy between the instantiations of the *NonMinimal* and *Decompose* predicate-variables. This logic algorithm is thus equivalent to its predecessor.

The expanded version of LA_3(*compress*), that is *exp*(LA_3(*compress*)), is as follows:

```
compress(L,C) ⇔
        L=[]      ∧          L=[] ∧ C=[]                          {E1}
      ∨ L=[_|_] ∧ L=[HL|TL]
                  ∧          L=[a] ∧ C=[a,1]
                         ∧   HL=a ∧ TL=[]                         {E2}
                      ∨    ...                                    {...}
                      ∨    L=[j,k,m] ∧ C=[j,1,k,1,m,1]
                         ∧   HL=j ∧ TL=[k,m]                      {E8}
```

Step 4: Syntactic Introduction of the Recursive Atoms

Now that $\boldsymbol{TX}$ is defined, we can introduce a conjunction of recursive atoms, at the rate of one per TX_i. This introduces a vector $\boldsymbol{TY}$ of tails of Y, at the rate of one per TX_i.

For instance, LA_4(*compress*) is as follows:

```
compress(L,C) ⇔
        L=[]                                                      {E1}
```

```
     ∨ L=[_|_] ∧ L=[HL|TL]
               ∧ compress(TL,TC)                          {E2,...,E8}
```

This logic algorithm expresses that *compress(L,C)* holds iff *L* is either an empty list or a non-empty list whose tail has a compression. As this compression isn't really computed yet, this only amounts to checking whether *L* is a real list (and this hence eliminates pseudo-lists). The expanded version of LA_4(*compress*), that is *exp*(LA_4(*compress*)), is as follows:

```
compress(L,C) ⇔
       L=[]    ∧       L=[] ∧ C=[]                        {E1}
     ∨ L=[_|_] ∧ L=[HL|TL]
               ∧ compress(TL,TC)
               ∧       L=[a] ∧ C=[a,1]
                     ∧ HL=a ∧ TL=[] ∧ TC=[]               {E2}
                   ∨   ...                                {...}
                   ∨   L=[j,k,m] ∧ C=[j,1,k,1,m,1]
                     ∧ HL=j ∧ TL=[k,m] ∧ TC=[k,1,m,1]     {E8}
```

Step 5: Synthesis of Solve and the SolveNonMin$_k$

An instantiation of the *Solve* (respectively *SolveNonMin*$_k$) predicate-variable computes, in the minimal case (respectively the non-recursive non-minimal case), the value of the other parameter *Y* from the induction parameter *X*. Step 5 yields $LA_5(r)$ by using similar methods to those of Steps 6 and 7.

For instance, in case *L* is the empty list, its compression *C* is the empty list as well. This is performed by the atomic formula *C* = []. There is no non-recursive non-minimal case, and hence no need to instantiate some *SolveNonMin*$_k$. LA_5(*compress*) is thus as follows:

```
compress(L,C) ⇔
       L=[]    ∧ C=[]                                     {E1}
     ∨ L=[_|_] ∧ L=[HL|TL]
               ∧ compress(TL,TC)                          {E2,...,E8}
```

This logic algorithm holds strictly less often than its predecessor, as the minimal case is now correctly computed.

The expanded version of LA_5(*compress*), that is *exp*(LA_5(*compress*)), is as follows.

```
compress(L,C) ⇔
       L=[]    ∧ C=[]
               ∧       L=[] ∧ C=[]                        {E1}
     ∨ L=[_|_] ∧ L=[HL|TL]
               ∧ compress(TL,TC)
               ∧       L=[a] ∧ C=[a,1]
                     ∧ HL=a ∧ TL=[] ∧ TC=[]               {E2}
                   ∨   ...                                {...}
                   ∨   L=[j,k,m] ∧ C=[j,1,k,1,m,1]
                     ∧ HL=j ∧ TL=[k,m] ∧ TC=[k,1,m,1]     {E8}
```

Note the redundancy between the $C = []$ atoms in the minimal case: one of them is a synthesized atom, whereas the other one is a trailing atom introduced by expansion.

Step 6: Synthesis of the $Process_k$ and $Compose_k$

An instantiation of a $Process_k$ predicate-variable transforms the heads $\boldsymbol{HX}$ of the induction parameter X into a vector $\boldsymbol{HY}$ of heads of the other parameter Y. An instantiation of a $Compose_k$ predicate-variable computes the other parameter Y from its heads $\boldsymbol{HY}$ (obtained by processing the $\boldsymbol{HX}$) and tails $\boldsymbol{TY}$ (obtained by recursion on the $\boldsymbol{TX}$). Step 6 does this simultaneously, and hence actually looks for an instantiation of a $ProcComp_k$ predicate-variable that computes the other parameter Y from the heads $\boldsymbol{HX}$ and tails $\boldsymbol{TY}$. Step 6 yields $LA_6(r)$ by first invoking the *MSG Method* (see Chapter 10) and assessing its results via some heuristics: if these results are not satisfying, then a so-called *Synthesis Method* (see Section 14.2.4) is invoked.

For instance, in our case the MSG Method is sufficient: it discovers 2 different ways of computing C from HL and TC, so the schema-variable c denoting the number of sub-cases is instantiated with 2. This is actually shown in full detail in Example 10-2 and Example 10-6, where the following instance of *ProcComp* is synthesized:

```
pcCompress(HL,TC,C) ⇔
        C=[HL,1|TC]
    ∨  C=[HL,s(s(N))|TTC]  ∧  TC=[HL,s(N)|TTC]
```

$LA_6(compress)$ is thus as follows:

```
compress(L,C)  ⇔
        L=[]     ∧  C=[]                                     {E1}
    ∨  L=[_|_] ∧  L=[HL|TL]
                 ∧  compress(TL,TC)
                 ∧  C=[HL,1|TC]                   {E2,E4,E7,E8}
    ∨  L=[_|_] ∧  L=[HL|TL]
                 ∧  compress(TL,TC)
                 ∧  C=[HL,s(s(N))|TTC]  ∧  TC=[HL,s(N)|TTC]
                                                       {E3,E5,E6}
```

Note how the splitting of the non-minimal case into 2 sub-cases affects a partitioning of the examples that were covered by the original case. Basically, the added atoms express that the first value of the compression C is necessarily HL, and that the first counter of C is either 1 (in which case the tail of C is simply TC), or an integer $s(s(N))$ strictly greater than 1 (in which case the tail of C is the tail of TC, the first value of TC is also HL, and the first counter of TC is $s(N)$).

The expanded version of $LA_6(compress)$, that is $exp(LA_6(compress))$, is as follows:

```
compress(L,C)  ⇔
        L=[]     ∧  C=[]
                 ∧        L=[]  ∧  C=[]                     {E1}
    ∨  L=[_|_] ∧  L=[HL|TL]
                 ∧  compress(TL,TC)
                 ∧  C=[HL,1|TC]
                 ∧        L=[a]  ∧  C=[a,1]
```

```
                        ∧  HL=a  ∧  TL=[]  ∧  TC=[]                {E2}
                     ∨     L=[c,d]  ∧  C=[c,1,d,1]
                        ∧  HL=c  ∧  TL=[d]  ∧  TC=[d,1]            {E4}
                     ∨     L=[h,i,i]  ∧  C=[h,1,i,2]
                        ∧  HL=h  ∧  TL=[i,i]  ∧  TC=[i,2]          {E7}
                     ∨     L=[j,k,m]  ∧  C=[j,1,k,1,m,1]
                        ∧  HL=j  ∧  TL=[k,m]  ∧  TC=[k,1,m,1]      {E8}
  ∨  L=[_|_] ∧  L=[HL|TL]
                ∧  compress(TL,TC)
                ∧  C=[HL,s(s(N))|TTC]  ∧  TC=[HL,s(N)|TTC]
                ∧          L=[b,b]  ∧  C=[b,2]
                        ∧  HL=b  ∧  TL=[b]  ∧  TC=[b,1]            {E3}
                     ∨     L=[e,e,e]  ∧  C=[e,3]
                        ∧  HL=e  ∧  TL=[e,e]  ∧  TC=[e,2]          {E5}
                     ∨     L=[f,f,g]  ∧  C=[f,2,g,1]
                        ∧  HL=f  ∧  TL=[f,g]  ∧  TC=[f,1,g,1]      {E6}
```

Note that the internal variables *N* and *TTC* do not appear in the expansions.

Step 7: Synthesis of the Discriminate$_k$

An instantiation of the *Discriminate$_k$* predicate-variable tests the values of ***HX***, ***TX***, *Y* in order to see whether *ProcComp$_k$* is applicable. Step 7 yields *LA$_7$(r)* by invoking the *Proofs-as-Programs Method* (see Chapter 9) and generalizing its results via some heuristics.

For instance, in our case the Proofs-as-Programs Method performs as shown in Example 9-4, where the following instances of *Discriminate$_k$* are synthesized ($k = 2,\ldots,3$):

```
discCompress2(HL,TL,C)  ⇔
     TL=[]
  ∨  TL=[HTL|_]  ∧  HL≠HTL

discCompress3(HL,TL,C)  ⇔
     TL=[HTL|_]  ∧  HL=HTL
```

LA$_7$(compress) is thus as follows:

```
compress(L,C)  ⇔
     L=[]     ∧  C=[]                                          {E1}
  ∨  L=[_|_]  ∧  L=[HL|TL]
              ∧  (TL=[]) ∨ (TL=[HTL|_]  ∧  HL≠HTL)
              ∧  compress(TL,TC)
              ∧  C=[HL,1|TC]                          {E2,E4,E7,E8}
  ∨  L=[_|_]  ∧  L=[HL|TL]
              ∧  TL=[HTL|_]  ∧  HL=HTL
              ∧  compress(TL,TC)
              ∧  C=[HL,s(s(N))|TTC]  ∧  TC=[HL,s(N)|TTC]
                                                           {E3,E5,E6}
```

Basically, the added discriminants express that the first sub-case identified at Step 6 is applicable iff *TL* does not start with an element equal to *HL*, and that the second sub-case is applicable iff *TL* does start with an element equal to *HL*.

The expanded version of LA_7(*compress*), that is *exp*(LA_7(*compress*)), is as follows:

```
compress(L,C) ⇔
        L=[]     ∧  C=[]
                 ∧       L=[] ∧ C=[]                          {E1}
    ∨   L=[_|_]  ∧  L=[HL|TL]
                 ∧  (TL=[]) ∨ (TL=[HTL|_] ∧ HL≠HTL)
                 ∧  compress(TL,TC)
                 ∧  C=[HL,1|TC]
                 ∧       L=[a] ∧ C=[a,1]
                     ∧   HL=a ∧ TL=[] ∧ TC=[]                 {E2}
                     ∨   L=[c,d] ∧ C=[c,1,d,1]
                     ∧   HL=c ∧ TL=[d] ∧ TC=[d,1]             {E4}
                     ∨   L=[h,i,i] ∧ C=[h,1,i,2]
                     ∧   HL=h ∧ TL=[i,i] ∧ TC=[i,2]           {E7}
                     ∨   L=[j,k,m] ∧ C=[j,1,k,1,m,1]
                     ∧   HL=j ∧ TL=[k,m] ∧ TC=[k,1,m,1]       {E8}
    ∨   L=[_|_]  ∧  L=[HL|TL]
                 ∧  TL=[HTL|_] ∧ HL=HTL
                 ∧  compress(TL,TC)
                 ∧  C=[HL,s(s(N))|TTC] ∧ TC=[HL,s(N)|TTC]
                 ∧       L=[b,b] ∧ C=[b,2]
                     ∧   HL=b ∧ TL=[b] ∧ TC=[b,1]             {E3}
                     ∨   L=[e,e,e] ∧ C=[e,3]
                     ∧   HL=e ∧ TL=[e,e] ∧ TC=[e,2]           {E5}
                     ∨   L=[f,f,g] ∧ C=[f,2,g,1]
                     ∧   HL=f ∧ TL=[f,g] ∧ TC=[f,1,g,1]       {E6}
```

Note that the internal variables *HTL*, *N*, *TTC* do not appear in the expansions.

The sample synthesis ends here. It can be shown that LA_7(*compress*) is totally correct wrt its intended relation. ♦

Note that Steps 2, 3, 5, 6 are non-deterministic: different logic algorithms can be synthesized upon reconsideration of decisions taken at these steps.

Regarding correctness issues, Steps 2 to 7 are proven to fit the hypotheses of Theorem 7-7. It can be shown that:

$$LA_i(r) \quad \{\ll, \leq\} \quad LA_{i-1}(r)$$

$$exp(LA_i(r)) \quad \{\ll, \not\approx, \cong\} \quad exp(LA_{i-1}(r))$$

where $i \in \{2,\ldots,7\}$.

A careful study of this sample synthesis shows that the synthesis mechanism can actually be decomposed into two phases, an *expansion phase* (covering Steps 1 to 4) and a *reduction phase* (covering Steps 5 to 7). During the former, the expansions are gradually expanding as more variables are introduced. During the latter, the expansions are reduced by partitioning of cases.

12 THE EXPANSION PHASE

Assuming a binary intended relation $\mathcal{R}$, and its corresponding predicate $r/2$, we suppose there is a specification $EP(r)$, whose example set is defined as follows:

$$\mathcal{E}(r) = \{E_1, E_2, \dots, E_m\} = \{\ r(x_1,y_1), r(x_2,y_2), \dots, r(x_m,y_m)\ \}$$

and whose property set is defined as follows:

$$\mathcal{P}(r) = \{P_1, P_2, \dots, P_p\} = \{\ r(s_1,t_1) \Leftarrow B_1,\ r(s_2,t_2) \Leftarrow B_2,\ \dots,\ r(s_p,t_p) \Leftarrow B_p\ \}$$

where the body B_i of property P_i is a conjunction of atoms. As usual in compilation, transformation, or synthesis, we assume that $EP(r)$ is consistent with $\mathcal{R}$: we call this the *consistency assumption*.

Example 12-1: The *firstPlateau*/3 problem is used all along this (and the following) chapter for illustration purposes. We assume that *EP*(*firstPlateau*) is as follows:

```
E(firstPlateau) = {
        firstPlateau([a],[a],[])                    (E1)
        firstPlateau([b,b],[b,b],[])                (E2)
        firstPlateau([c,d],[c],[d])                 (E3)
        firstPlateau([e,f,g],[e],[f,g])             (E4)
        firstPlateau([h,i,i],[h],[i,i])             (E5)
        firstPlateau([j,j,k],[j,j],[k])             (E6)
        firstPlateau([m,m,m],[m,m,m],[]) }          (E7)
P(firstPlateau) = {
        firstPlateau([X],[X],[])                    (P1)
        firstPlateau([X,Y],[X,Y],[]) ⇐ X=Y          (P2)
        firstPlateau([X,Y],[X], [Y]) ⇐ X≠Y }        (P3)
```

In order to keep this chapter self-sufficient, we here repeat the chosen synthesis strategy (see Section 7.3.2), where synthesis is seen as a sequence of f steps:

At Step 1, "create" $LA_1(r)$ such that:

+ $LA_1(r)$ is complete wrt $\mathcal{R}$;
+ $exp(LA_1(r))$ is partially correct wrt $\mathcal{R}$.

At Step i ($2 \le i \le f$), transform $LA_{i-1}(r)$ into $LA_i(r)$ such that:

+ $LA_i(r)$ is a better complete approximation of $\mathcal{R}$ than $LA_{i-1}(r)$;
+ $exp(LA_i(r))$ is a better partially correct approximation of $\mathcal{R}$ than $exp(LA_{i-1}(r))$.

The following theorem (originally Theorem 7-7) indicates a practical way of pursuing this strategy at Steps 2 to f:

Let $LA(r)$ be $r(X) \Leftrightarrow \vee_{1\le j\le m} A_j$ and $LA'(r)$ be $r(X) \Leftrightarrow \vee_{1\le j\le m} A_j \wedge B_j$, where A_j, B_j are any formulas. The following two assertions hold:

(1) *If $LA(r)$ is complete wrt $\mathcal{R}$ and $\mathcal{R}(X) \wedge A_j \Rightarrow B_j$ $(1 \le j \le m)$ then $LA'(r)$ is a better complete approximation of $\mathcal{R}$ than $LA(r)$.*

(2) *If $LA(r)$ is partially correct wrt $\mathcal{R}$ and $A_j \Rightarrow B_j$ $(1 \le j \le m)$ then $LA'(r)$ is a better partially correct approximation of $\mathcal{R}$ than $LA(r)$.*

Indeed, assertion (1) may be applied to the logic algorithms $LA_i(r)$, and assertion (2) may be applied to the logic algorithms $exp(LA_i(r))$, where $2 \le i \le f$.

We also repeat Schema 8-3, that is version 3 of the divide-and-conquer schema:

```
R(X,Y) ⇔
              Minimal(X)      ∧ Solve(X,Y)
   ∨ ∨1≤k≤c  NonMinimal(X)   ∧ Decompose(X,HX,TX)
                              ∧ Discriminatek(HX,TX,Y)
                              ∧ (       SolveNonMink(HX,TX,Y)
                                    |
                                        R(TX,TY)
                                    ∧   Processk(HX,HY)
                                    ∧   Composek(HY,TY,Y)        )
```

Instantiating some predicate-variable(s) of a schema is a synthesis step. The synthesis mechanism is expressed as the following sequence of $f = 7$ steps (see Example 8-8):

- Step 1: Syntactic creation of a first approximation;
- Step 2: Synthesis of *Minimal* and *NonMinimal*;
- Step 3: Synthesis of *Decompose*;
- Step 4: Syntactic introduction of the recursive atoms;
- Step 5: Synthesis of *Solve* and the $SolveNonMin_k$;
- Step 6: Synthesis of the $Process_k$ and $Compose_k$;
- Step 7: Synthesis of the $Discriminate_k$.

The *expansion phase* of synthesis comprises the first four steps of this mechanism. In Section 12.1 to Section 12.4, we give complete descriptions of each of these steps: we state their objectives, describe the used methods, analyze their correctness and progression behaviors, and illustrate them on the *firstPlateau*/3 and *compress*/2 problems.

12.1 Step 1: Syntactic Creation of a First Approximation

A first approximation of the final logic algorithm needs to be "created" so as to establish the applicability of Theorem 7-7.

12.1.1 Objective

According to the chosen strategy, the objective at Step 1 is to "create" $LA_1(r)$ such that:

(1) $LA_1(r)$ is complete wrt $\mathcal{R}$;
(2) $exp(LA_1(r))$ is partially correct wrt $\mathcal{R}$.

The achievement of this objective makes Theorem 7-7 applicable for the next steps.

12.1.2 Method

The safest method to achieve this is to postulate that $LA_1(r)$ is T_r, which is as follows:

```
r(X,Y) ⇔
     true                                        {E1,E2,...,Em}
```

This is always possible, hence Step 1 is fully deterministic (and thus never fails). Step 1 yields a unique case, called the *all-true case*. As usual, the set annotation to a disjunct explains which examples are covered by that disjunct. Now, $exp(LA_1(r))$ is as follows:

```
firstPlateau(L,P,S) ⇔
     true                                                    {E1,…,E7}
```

Logic Algorithm 12-1: LA_1(*firstPlateau*)

```
firstPlateau(L,P,S) ⇔
     true
            ∧     L=[a] ∧ P=[a] ∧ S=[]                        {E1}
               ∨  L=[b,b] ∧ P=[b,b] ∧ S=[]                    {E2}
               ∨  L=[c,d] ∧ P=[c] ∧ S=[d]                     {E3}
               ∨  L=[e,f,g] ∧ P=[e] ∧ S=[f,g]                 {E4}
               ∨  L=[h,i,i] ∧ P=[h] ∧ S=[i,i]                 {E5}
               ∨  L=[j,j,k] ∧ P=[j,j] ∧ S=[k]                 {E6}
               ∨  L=[m,m,m] ∧ P=[m,m,m] ∧ S=[]                {E7}
```

Logic Algorithm 12-2: *exp*(LA_1(*firstPlateau*))

```
r(X,Y) ⇔
     true   ∧     X=x1 ∧ Y=y1                                  {E1}
               ∨  X=x2 ∧ Y=y2                                  {E2}
               ∨  ...                                          ...
               ∨  X=xm ∧ Y=ym                                  {Em}
```

12.1.3 Correctness

We can now prove a theorem establishing that Step 1 is in line with the strategy:

Theorem 12-1: *Step* 1 *achieves the two conditions of its objective*:

(1) $LA_1(r)$ *is complete wrt* $\mathcal{R}$;

(2) *exp*($LA_1(r)$) *is partially correct wrt* $\mathcal{R}$.

Proof 12-1: Let's prove these assertions one by one:

(1) Trivial (by construction).

(2) We obviously have that *exp*($LA_1(r)$) is totally correct wrt $\mathcal{E}(r)$. By the consistency assumption, *exp*($LA_1(r)$) is thus partially correct wrt $\mathcal{R}$. ❑

Note that this proof is independent of $\mathcal{R}$.

12.1.4 Illustration

Let's illustrate Step 1 on the *firstPlateau*/3 and *compress*/2 problems.

Example 12-2: For the *firstPlateau*/3 problem, Step 1 yields LA_1(*firstPlateau*) as in Logic Algorithm 12-1, and *exp*(LA_1(*firstPlateau*)) as in Logic Algorithm 12-2.

Example 12-3: For the *compress*/2 problem, Step 1 yields a logic algorithm and its expansion as in Example 11-1.

12.2 Step 2: Synthesis of *Minimal* and *NonMinimal*

An instantiation of the *Minimal* (respectively *NonMinimal*) predicate-variable tests whether the induction parameter is of a minimal (respectively non-minimal) form.

12.2.1 Objective

The objective at Step 2 is to instantiate the predicate-variables *Minimal* and *NonMinimal* of the divide-and-conquer schema. This amounts to transforming $LA_1(r)$ into $LA_2(r)$ such that it is covered by the following schema:

```
r(X,Y) ⇔
        Minimal(X)
    ∨   NonMinimal(X)
```

where X is the selected induction parameter. This amounts to splitting the all-true case into 2 cases, called the *minimal case* and the *non-minimal case*, respectively. Let *minimal*/1 and *nonMinimal*/1 be the instances. The following objectives of the strategy:

(1) $LA_2(r)$ is a better complete approximation of $\mathcal{R}$ than $LA_1(r)$;

(2) $exp(LA_2(r))$ is a better partially correct approximation of $\mathcal{R}$ than $exp(LA_1(r))$;

and the following integrity constraints of the divide-and-conquer schema:

(3) X is single and of an inductive type;

(4) $X \in dom(\mathcal{R}) \Rightarrow minimal(X) \vee nonMinimal(X)$;

must be satisfied.

12.2.2 Method

This objective can be achieved by the following sequence of tasks:

- Task A: Selection of an induction parameter;
- Task B: Ordering of the examples into a sequence;
- Task C: Partitioning of the example sequence into two sub-sequences;
- Task D: Selection of *minimal*/1 and *nonMinimal*/1.

Let's explain these tasks one by one.

Task A: Selection of an Induction Parameter

Task A is done in the same fashion as in manual logic algorithm construction [Deville 90] (see Section 4.2): the induction parameter must be simple, and of an inductive type. This selection can be automated by type inference from the given examples. In case more detailed specification knowledge is available, the Functionality Heuristic (Heuristic 4-1) and the Directionality Heuristic (Heuristic 4-2) may even be used, the latter being of higher precedence in case they yield contradictory results. A reasonable implementation of this synthesis mechanism would actually even accept preference hints from the specifier. We assume that the uth parameter is selected as induction parameter, where $1 \leq u \leq n$.

Example 12-4: For the *firstPlateau*/3 problem, all parameters are of an inductive type, namely *list*. If we consider the specification of Figure 4-2, both heuristics would point towards L being the "best" induction parameter. Without this extended specification knowledge, a non-deterministic selection of an induction parameter among $\{L, P, S\}$ takes place. We assume that L is effectively selected: its position u is 1.

Task B: Ordering of the Examples

Task B is based on the notion of term-size. As agreed in Section 11.2, this discussion only considers the type-constructors *s*/1 (for integers) and •/2 (for lists).

Definition 12-1: The *size* of a ground term t, denoted $\#t$, is the number of appearances of the outmost type-constructor within t, if t is of an inductive type, and *undefined* otherwise.

Example 12-5: For instance, $\#3 = \#s(s(s(0))) = 3$, because $s/1$ appears thrice in 3. Also, $\#[a,b] = \#\bullet(a, \bullet(b, nil)) = 2$, because $\bullet/2$ appears twice in $[a,b]$. But $\#a = undefined$, because no type-constructor occurs in a.

Definition 12-2: Given an example E of predicate r/n, and an integer position i (where $1 \leq i \leq n$), the *size* of E wrt i, denoted $\#(E,i)$, is the size of the ith parameter of E.

Example 12-6: Considering the examples of $EP(firstPlateau)$, we have $\#(E_1,1) = 1$, and $\#(E_2,1) = \#(E_3,1) = 2$, and $\#(E_4,1) = \#(E_5,1) = \#(E_6,1) = \#(E_7,1) = 3$.

The set $\mathcal{E}(r)$ is now ordered by non-decreasing size of the examples wrt the position u of the selected induction parameter. The result is a sequence $\mathcal{S}$ of examples.

Example 12-7: For the *firstPlateau*/3 problem, with induction on L, the ordered sequence is exactly the one of the given example set: $\mathcal{S} = [E_1,E_2,E_3,E_4,E_5,E_6,E_7]$.

Task C: Partitioning of the Examples

Task C non-deterministically partitions the sequence $\mathcal{S}$ into two sub-sequences $\mathcal{S}_1$ and $\mathcal{S}_2$, such that:

$$\forall E_1 \in \mathcal{S}_1 \ \ \forall E_2 \in \mathcal{S}_2 \quad \#(E_1,u) < \#(E_2,u)$$

The idea is that the examples of $\mathcal{S}_1$ are hypothesized to be of the minimal form, while the examples of $\mathcal{S}_2$ are hypothesized to be of the non-minimal form. Hence the partitioning into 2 sub-sequences, as we agreed upon a total of 2 forms. We call the elements of $\mathcal{S}_1$ the *minimal examples*, and the elements of $\mathcal{S}_2$ the *non-minimal examples*.

Example 12-8: For the *firstPlateau*/3 problem, with induction on L, there are 2 ways of partitioning the example sequence $\mathcal{S}$: either $\mathcal{S}_1 = [E_1]$ and $\mathcal{S}_2 = [E_2,E_3,E_4,E_5,E_6,E_7]$, or $\mathcal{S}_1 = [E_1,E_2,E_3]$ and $\mathcal{S}_2 = [E_4,E_5,E_6,E_7]$. We assume that the first partition is selected.

Task D: Selection of minimal/1 and nonMinimal/1

Task D consists of mechanically extracting *minimal*/1 and *nonMinimal*/1 from a parameterized database. Suppose that the sizes of the examples in $\mathcal{S}_1$ are within the integer interval $[p_1,\ldots,q_1]$, and that the sizes of the examples in $\mathcal{S}_2$ are within the integer interval $[p_2,\ldots,q_2]$. Table 12-1 below shows the used fragment of the database, which only uses primitive predicates (for simplicity, we here restrict it to the situation where $p = p_1 = q_1$ and $p_2 = q_1 + 1$):

Table 12-1: Database of instances of *Minimal*/1 and *NonMinimal*/1

Type of X	*Minimal*(X)	*NonMinimal*(X)
integer	$X = p$	$X > p$
list	$X = [\_,\ldots,\_]$ (p elements)	$X = [\_,\ldots,\_,\_ \mid \_]$ ($> p$ elements)

Type inference from the examples may be used to access the appropriate row of the database. The hypothesis underlying this excerpt of the database is that the examples of sub-sequence $\mathcal{S}_1$ represent *all* the sizes of the minimal form, whereas the examples of sub-sequence $\mathcal{S}_2$ represent only a *prefix* of the sizes of the non-minimal form. This amounts to assuming that q_2 may be safely replaced by $+\infty$. This hypothesis is quite reasonable and covers a huge number of circumstances. Instances reflecting other hypotheses may also be stored in the database. We call such hypotheses the *domain extrapolation hypotheses*. The mechanical instance extraction is thus non-deterministic. The commonality between all instances is that there is only concern about the *size* of the induction parameter, and not about its *value* (hence the presence of anonymous variables in the database). The mentioned hypotheses have an obvious influence upon the formulation of a methodology for choosing "good" examples.

Note that $exp(LA_2(r))$ is as follows:

```
r(X,Y) ⇔
          minimal(X)     ∧   ∨j∈I   X=xj ∧ Y=yj
        ∨ nonMinimal(X)  ∧   ∨j∈J   X=xj ∧ Y=yj
```

where I is the set of indices of the minimal examples, and $\mathcal{J}$ is the set of indices of the non-minimal examples, such that $I \cup \mathcal{J}$ is the integer set $\{1,\ldots,m\}$.

Example 12-9: For the *firstPlateau*/3 problem, with the decisions taken by the previous tasks, we obtain $p = p_1 = q_1 = 1$ and $p_2 = 2 = q_1 + 1$. Following the hypothesis underlying Table 12-1, we assume that the minimal form is [_] (a list of one element) and that the non-minimal form is [_,_ | _] (a list of at least two elements). The instances of *Minimal* and *NonMinimal* thus are $L =$ [_] and $L =$ [_,_ | _], respectively.

Comments

This ends the presentation of the method used at Step 2. Before the discussion of its correctness, a few comments are necessary.

First, note that $L =$ [_] is strictly speaking not an instance of *Minimal*(X). The predicate-variable *Minimal*/1 is rather instantiated to, say, a predicate *minimal*/1, which is defined by the logic algorithm *minimal*(X) $\Leftrightarrow X =$ [_]. It is actually only the renaming substitution $\{X/L\}$ and then the unfolding of *minimal*(L) that bring the atom $L =$ [_] into some logic algorithm for *firstPlateau*/3. So it is only by abuse of language that we may speak of $L =$ [_] as being an "instance" of *Minimal*(X).

Second, it is the very focus on structural aspects of the induction parameter (its size, that is) that makes this database approach possible. If semantic aspects of the induction parameter (its value, that is) also have to be taken into account, then a deductive approach reasoning backwards from instances of all other predicate-variables becomes necessary [Smith 85]. We here clearly separate these aspects: the size of the induction parameter is analyzed at Step 2 for instantiating *Minimal* and *NonMinimal*, and its value is analyzed at Step 7 for instantiating the $Discriminate_k$.

Finally, the methods of tasks A, C, D are non-deterministic, but finite. This means that choice-points are created there, and that the made selections may be reconsidered later, either because synthesis fails, or because synthesis succeeds and the specifier wants more algorithms. Only Task A could possibly fail, namely if there is no parameter of an inductive type. Do not mix up non-deterministic synthesis and a non-deterministic synthesized algorithm. The latter would feature either mutually non-exclusive cases or predicates that are non-deterministic. The logic algorithm synthesized at Step 2 is deterministic, because the two cases are mutually exclusive by construction, and because the introduced predicates are deterministic.

12.2.3 Correctness

We can now prove a theorem establishing that Step 2 is in line with the strategy:

Theorem 12-2: *Step 2 achieves the four conditions of its objective:*

(1) $LA_2(r)$ *is a better complete approximation of* $\mathcal{R}$ *than* $LA_1(r)$;

(2) $exp(LA_2(r))$ *is a better partially correct approximation of* $\mathcal{R}$ *than* $exp(LA_1(r))$;

(3) *X is single and of an inductive type*;

(4) $X \in dom(\mathcal{R}) \Rightarrow minimal(X) \vee nonMinimal(X)$.

* **Proof 12-2:** Let's prove these assertions one by one:

(1) By assertion (1) of Theorem 7-7 and assertion (1) of Theorem 12-1, it suffices to show that:

$$\mathcal{R}(X,Y) \wedge true \Rightarrow minimal(X) \vee nonMinimal(X)$$

in order to prove that $LA_2(r)$ is a better complete approximation of $\mathcal{R}$ than $LA_1(r)$. This statement is actually implied by Point (4) of this theorem, because $\mathcal{R}(X,Y) \Rightarrow X \in dom(\mathcal{R})$ and $F \vee G \Rightarrow F \vee G$.

(2) By assertion (2) of Theorem 7-7 and assertion (2) of Theorem 12-1, it suffices to show that:

$$X = x_j \wedge Y = y_j \Rightarrow minimal(X) \quad (j \in I)$$
$$X = x_j \wedge Y = y_j \Rightarrow nonMinimal(X) \quad (j \in \mathcal{J})$$

in order to prove that $exp(LA_2(r))$ is a better partially correct approximation of $\mathcal{R}$ than $exp(LA_1(r))$. This is achieved by the methods of Tasks B to D.

(3) By the method of Task A, the selected induction parameter is single and of an inductive type.

(4) By the methods of Tasks B to D, *minimal*/1 and *nonMinimal*/1 are mutually exclusive over the domain of the induction parameter within $\mathcal{E}(r)$. If the correct domain extrapolation hypothesis is taken by the method of Task D, then *minimal*/1 and *nonMinimal*/1 are also mutually exclusive over the entire intended domain of the induction parameter. ❑

This proof hinges on the fact that the correct domain extrapolation hypothesis must be taken by the method of Task D. We assume that such is the case. Of course, a reasonable implementation of this synthesis mechanism would include some interaction with the specifier so as to maximize the confidence that everything goes right.

12.2.4 Illustration

Let's illustrate Step 2 on the *firstPlateau*/3 and *compress*/2 problems.

Example 12-10: For the *firstPlateau*/3 problem, Step 2 proceeds as illustrated in the previous six examples. Logic Algorithm 12-3 shows $LA_2($*firstPlateau*$)$, whereas Logic Algorithm 12-4 shows $exp(LA_2($*firstPlateau*$))$.

Example 12-11: For the *compress*/2 problem, Step 2 proceeds as follows. At Task A, both parameters are found to be of an inductive type, namely *list*. If we considered the specification of Figure 4-1, the heuristics would point towards *L* being the "best" induction parameter. Without this extended specification knowledge, a non-deterministic selection of an induction parameter among $\{L, C\}$ takes place. We

```
firstPlateau(L,P,S) ⇔
        L=[_]
    ∨   L=[_,_|_]
```

Logic Algorithm 12-3: *LA*$_2$(*firstPlateau*)

```
firstPlateau(L,P,S) ⇔
        L=[_]
              ∧       L=[a] ∧ P=[a] ∧ S=[]                    {E1}
    ∨   L=[_,_|_]
              ∧       L=[b,b] ∧ P=[b,b] ∧ S=[]                {E2}
                 ∨    L=[c,d] ∧ P=[c] ∧ S=[d]                 {E3}
                 ∨    L=[e,f,g] ∧ P=[e] ∧ S=[f,g]             {E4}
                 ∨    L=[h,i,i] ∧ P=[h] ∧ S=[i,i]             {E5}
                 ∨    L=[j,j,k] ∧ P=[j,j] ∧ S=[k]             {E6}
                 ∨    L=[m,m,m] ∧ P=[m,m,m] ∧ S=[]            {E7}
```

Logic Algorithm 12-4: *exp*(*LA*$_2$(*firstPlateau*))

assume that L is effectively selected: its position u is 1. At Task B, we have $\#(E_1,1) = 0$, and $\#(E_2,1) = 1$, and $\#(E_3,1) = \#(E_4,1) = 2$, and $\#(E_5,1) = \#(E_6,1) = \#(E_7,1) = \#(E_8,1) = 3$. So the ordered sequence of examples is exactly the one of the given example set: $\mathcal{S} = [E_1,E_2,E_3,E_4,E_5,E_6,E_7,E_8]$. At Task C, there are three ways of partitioning this sequence $\mathcal{S}$: either $\mathcal{S}_1 = [E_1]$ and $\mathcal{S}_2 = [E_2,E_3,E_4,E_5,E_6,E_7,E_8]$, or $\mathcal{S}_1 = [E_1,E_2]$ and $\mathcal{S}_2 = [E_3,E_4,E_5,E_6,E_7,E_8]$, or $\mathcal{S}_1 = [E_1,E_2,E_3,E_4]$ and $\mathcal{S}_2 = [E_5,E_6,E_7,E_8]$. We assume that the first partition is selected. At Task D, we obtain $p = p_1 = q_1 = 0$ and $p_2 = 1 = q_1 + 1$. Following the hypothesis underlying Table 12-1, we assume that the minimal form is [] and that the non-minimal form is [_ | _]. The corresponding instances of *Minimal* and *NonMinimal* thus are L = [], and L = [_ | _], respectively. The resulting logic algorithm and its expansion are shown in Example 11-1.

12.3 Step 3: Synthesis of *Decompose*

An instantiation of the *Decompose* predicate-variable deterministically decomposes, in the non-minimal case, the induction parameter X into a vector $\boldsymbol{HX}$ of heads and a vector $\boldsymbol{TX}$ of tails, each tail TX_i being smaller than X according to some well-founded relation. The $\boldsymbol{TX}$ are meant for the computation of the tails $\boldsymbol{TY}$ of the other parameter Y.

12.3.1 Objective

The objective at Step 3 is to instantiate the predicate-variable *Decompose* of the divide-and-conquer schema. This amounts to transforming $LA_2(r)$ into $LA_3(r)$ such that it is covered by the following schema:

```
r(X,Y) ⇔
        minimal(X)
    ∨   nonMinimal(X)∧ Decompose(X,HX,TX)
```

Let *decompose* be the synthesized instance. It is of arity $1+h+t$, where $h = \#\boldsymbol{HX}$ and $t = \#\boldsymbol{TX}$. The following objectives of the strategy:

(1) $LA_3(r)$ is a better complete approximation of $\mathcal{R}$ than $LA_2(r)$;
(2) $exp(LA_3(r))$ is a better partially correct approximation of $\mathcal{R}$ than $exp(LA_2(r))$;
and the following integrity constraints of the divide-and-conquer schema:
(3) $h \geq 0$ and $t \geq 1$;
(4) $X \equiv dom(\mathcal{R}) \wedge nonMinimal(X) \Rightarrow \exists! \boldsymbol{HX}\ \exists! \boldsymbol{TX}\ \ decompose(X,\boldsymbol{HX},\boldsymbol{TX})$;
(5) $\exists$"<" $\forall(decompose(X,\boldsymbol{HX},TX_1,\ldots,TX_t) \Rightarrow \forall i \in \{1,\ldots,t\}\ TX_i$ "<" $X)$;
must be satisfied.

12.3.2 Method

This objective can be achieved by the following sequence of tasks:

- Task E: Selection of a decomposition strategy;
- Task F: Selection of *decompose*/1+*h*+*t*.

Let's explain these tasks one by one.

Task E: Selection of a Decomposition Strategy

Task E consists of selecting one of the three decomposition strategies seen in Section 5.2.2. As a reminder, these strategies are:

- *intrinsic decomposition*: X is decomposed into $h \geq 1$ heads and $t \geq 1$ tails in a manner reflecting the definition of the type of X;
- *extrinsic decomposition*: X is decomposed into $h \geq 0$ heads and $t \geq 1$ tails in a manner reflecting the definition of the type of some other parameter than X, or reflecting the intended relation;
- *logarithmic decomposition*: X is decomposed into $h = 0$ heads and $t \geq 2$ tails of about equal size.

An intrinsic decomposition reflects a well-founded relation selected via the Intrinsic Heuristic (Heuristic 4-3), and an extrinsic or logarithmic decomposition reflects a well-founded relation selected via the Extrinsic Heuristic (Heuristic 4-4). The selection of a strategy is a high-level decision that may significantly affect the complexity of the resulting algorithm (but probably not its existence). A reasonable implementation of this synthesis mechanism would accept a preference hint from the specifier.

If an intrinsic decomposition is selected, then a *decomposition decrement*, denoted d, needs to be selected before proceeding to Task F. This is done by non-deterministically selecting a value within the following integer interval:

$$[\ \#(E_w,u) - \#(E_v,u),\ \ldots,\ \#(E_w,u)\ ]$$

where E_v is the last (largest-sized) example of $\mathcal{S}_1$, and E_w is the first (smallest-sized) example of $\mathcal{S}_2$. The lower bound of this interval represents the size decrease needed to decompose an example of the size of E_v into an example of the size of E_w. The upper bound is justified by the fact that one can at most take away as many elements as there are elements in the smallest non-minimal example. Note that d is thus constrained to be a constant.

Example 12-12: For the *firstPlateau*/3 problem, suppose the intrinsic decomposition strategy is selected, and that the decomposition decrement d is selected to be 1, namely from the interval [1,...,2].

Task F: Selection of decompose/1+h+t

Task F consists of mechanically extracting *decompose*/1+*h*+*t* from a parameterized database. Tables 12-2 to 12-4 below show the used fragments of the database, which only uses primitive predicates (we omit the subscripts i from the HX_i and TX_i in case $h = 1$ or $t = 1$):

Table 12-2: Database of intrinsic instances of *Decompose*/1+*h*+*t*

Type of X	$Decompose(X,\mathbf{HX},\mathbf{TX})$
integer	$add(TX,d,X) \wedge HX=X$
list	$X = [HX_1,\ldots,HX_d \mid TX]$

Table 12-3: Database of extrinsic instances of *Decompose*/1+*h*+*t*

Type of X	$Decompose(X,\mathbf{HX},\mathbf{TX})$
integer	N/A
list	$firstPlateau(X,HX,TX)$ ...
integer-list	$X = [HX \mid T] \wedge partition(T,HX,TX_1,TX_2)$ ...

Table 12-4: Database of logarithmic instances of *Decompose*/1+*h*+*t*

Type of X	$Decompose(X,\mathbf{HX},\mathbf{TX})$
integer	N/A
list	$split(X,TX_1,TX_2)$ ...

Type inference from the examples may be used to access the appropriate row of the database. Note that $exp(LA_3(r))$ is as follows:

```
r(X,Y) ⇔
        minimal(X)      ∧     ∨j∈I     X=xj  ∧ Y=yj
      ∨ nonMinimal(X)   ∧ decompose(X,HX,TX)
                        ∧     ∨j∈J     X=xj  ∧ Y=yj
                                    ∧ HX=hxj  ∧ TX=txj
```

where $\mathbf{hx}_j$ and $\mathbf{tx}_j$ are vectors of witnesses such that $decompose(x_j,\mathbf{hx}_j,\mathbf{tx}_j)$ holds ($j \in \mathcal{J}$).

Example 12-13: For the *firstPlateau*/3 problem, with the decisions of the previous task, the instance $L = [HL \mid TL]$ is extracted from Table 2. This means that $h = t = 1$.

Comments

This ends the presentation of the method used at Step 3. Before the discussion of its correctness, a few comments are necessary.

First, the support of the extrinsic and logarithmic decomposition strategies is quite difficult, as the required knowledge about the intended relation is not available. This apparent drawback may be alleviated however by the observation that the logic algorithms *LA*(*r-int-X*) and *LA*(*r-ext-Y*) are by construction quite similar. Compare

LA(compress) (LA 4-1) and *LA(compress-ext-C)* (LA 5-3), or *LA(compress-int-C)* (LA 5-2) and *LA(compress-ext-L)* (LA 5-1) for illustrations of this observation. In other words, the support of the extrinsic and logarithmic decomposition strategies often doesn't give rise to *new* logic algorithms. This is due to the multi-directionality of logic algorithms: *Compose*(***HY***,***TY***,*Y*) may not only be used in the *composition mode* (***ground***,***ground***,*var*), but also in the *decomposition mode* (***var***,***var***, *ground*). Similarly, *Decompose*(*X*,***HX***,***TX***) may not only be used in the *decomposition mode* (*ground*,***var***,***var***), but also in the *composition mode* (*var*,***ground***,***ground***). However, the constraints (4) and (5) sometimes prevent the reversion of *LA*(*r-int-X*) into *LA*(*r-ext-Y*). Indeed, the decomposition mode of *Compose*(***HY***,***TY***,*Y*) might be non-deterministic. For instance, *efface*(*HY*,*Y*,*TY*), *insert*(*HY*,*TY*,*Y*), *append*(TY_1,[$HY \mid TY_2$],*Y*), and *merge*(TY_1,TY_2,*Y*) may not be used as instances of *Decompose*, but are suitable as instances of *Compose*. Or the decomposition mode of *Compose*(***HY***,***TY***,*Y*) might not reflect a well-founded relation. For instance, $Y = TY_i$ may not be used as an instance of *Decompose*, but is suitable as an instance of *Compose*. Such an instance may appear because *Y* is an auxiliary parameter, or because *Y* would be part of a compound induction parameter for the reversion.

Second, note that the methods of both tasks are non-deterministic, finite, and can never fail. However, the introduced predicates are deterministic in the decomposition mode. This implies that the witnesses $\boldsymbol{hx}_j$ and $\boldsymbol{tx}_j$ are unique. The logic algorithm synthesized at Step 3 is thus deterministic.

Third, the methods used by Steps 2 and 3 could be abstracted into a *Database Method*. This would work as follows: given an example set $\mathcal{E}$, some computations *C*, and a database *DB*, select an entry from *DB* using the key generated by executing *C* on $\mathcal{E}$.

Finally, with an intrinsic decomposition, obvious simplification opportunities arise between *nonMinimal* and *decompose*. However, we never perform these simplifications, so as to present canonical representations of all logic algorithms.

12.3.3 Correctness

We can now prove a theorem establishing that Step 3 is in line with the strategy:

Theorem 12-3: *Step 3 achieves the five conditions of its objective*:

(1) $LA_3(r)$ *is a better complete approximation of* $\mathcal{R}$ *than* $LA_2(r)$;

(2) $exp(LA_3(r))$ *is a better partially correct approximation of* $\mathcal{R}$ *than* $exp(LA_2(r))$;

(3) $h \geq 0$ *and* $t \geq 1$;

(4) $X \in dom(\mathcal{R}) \wedge nonMinimal(X) \Rightarrow \exists! \boldsymbol{HX}\ \exists! \boldsymbol{TX}\ \ decompose(X,\boldsymbol{HX},\boldsymbol{TX})$;

(5) $\exists$"<" $\forall (decompose(X,\boldsymbol{HX},TX_1,\ldots,TX_t) \Rightarrow \forall i \in \{1,\ldots,t\}\ TX_i$ "<" $X)$.

* **Proof 12-3:** Let's prove these assertions one by one:

(1) By assertion (1) of Theorem 7-7 and assertion (1) of Theorem 12-2, it suffices to show that:

$$\mathcal{R}(X,Y) \wedge minimal(X) \Rightarrow true$$

$$\mathcal{R}(X,Y) \wedge nonMinimal(X) \Rightarrow decompose(X,\boldsymbol{HX},\boldsymbol{TX})$$

in order to prove that $LA_3(r)$ is a better complete approximation of $\mathcal{R}$ than $LA_2(r)$. The first statement is trivially true (and we shall omit such statements in the sequel). The second statement is implied by Point (4) of this theorem.

```
firstPlateau(L,P,S) ⇔
        L=[_]
    ∨   L=[_,_|_]           ∧ L=[HL|TL]
```

Logic Algorithm 12-5: $LA_3(firstPlateau)$

```
firstPlateau(L,P,S) ⇔
        L=[_]
                            ∧        L=[a] ∧ P=[a] ∧ S=[]                {E1}
    ∨   L=[_,_|_]           ∧ L=[HL|TL]
                            ∧        L=[b,b] ∧ P=[b,b] ∧ S=[]
                                  ∧  HL=b ∧ TL=[b]                       {E2}
                                ∨    L=[c,d] ∧ P=[c] ∧ S=[d]
                                  ∧  HL=c ∧ TL=[d]                       {E3}
                                ∨    L=[e,f,g] ∧ P=[e] ∧ S=[f,g]
                                  ∧  HL=e ∧ TL=[f,g]                     {E4}
                                ∨    L=[h,i,i] ∧ P=[h] ∧ S=[i,i]
                                  ∧  HL=h ∧ TL=[i,i]                     {E5}
                                ∨    L=[j,j,k] ∧ P=[j,j] ∧ S=[k]
                                  ∧  HL=j ∧ TL=[j,k]                     {E6}
                                ∨    L=[m,m,m] ∧ P=[m,m,m] ∧ S=[]
                                  ∧  HL=m ∧ TL=[m,m]                     {E7}
```

Logic Algorithm 12-6: $exp(LA_3(firstPlateau))$

(2) By assertion (2) of Theorem 7-7 and assertion (2) of Theorem 12-2, it suffices to show that:

$$minimal(X) \wedge X = x_j \wedge Y = y_j \Rightarrow true \quad (j \in I)$$

$$nonMinimal(X) \wedge X = x_j \wedge Y = y_j \Rightarrow$$
$$decompose(X,\mathbf{HX},\mathbf{TX}) \wedge \mathbf{HX} = \mathbf{hx}_j \wedge \mathbf{TX} = \mathbf{tx}_j \quad (j \in \mathcal{J})$$

in order to prove that $exp(LA_3(r))$ is a better partially correct approximation of $\mathcal{R}$ than $exp(LA_2(r))$. The first statement is trivially true. The second statement is implied by Point (4) of this theorem.

(3) The databases used by the method of Task F guarantee that $h \geq 0$ and $t \geq 1$.

(4) The databases used by the method of Task F guarantee that each instance is deterministic.

(5) The databases used by the method of Task F guarantee that each instance reflects decomposition according to some well-founded relation. ❑

12.3.4 Illustration

Let's illustrate Step 3 on the *firstPlateau*/3 and *compress*/2 problems.

Example 12-14: For the *firstPlateau*/3 problem, Step 3 proceeds as illustrated in the previous two examples. Logic Algorithm 12-5 shows $LA_3(firstPlateau)$, whereas Logic Algorithm 12-6 shows $exp(LA_3(firstPlateau))$.

Example 12-15: For the *compress*/2 problem, Step 3 proceeds as follows. At Task E, suppose the intrinsic decomposition strategy is selected. The decomposition decrement d is then necessarily 1, because selected from the interval [1,...,1]. At Task F, the instance $L = [HL \mid TL]$ is extracted from Table 12-2. This means that $h = t = 1$. The resulting logic algorithm and its expansion are in Example 11-1.

12.4 Step 4: Syntactic Introduction of the Recursive Atoms

In the non-minimal case, tails ***TY*** of Y are obtained by recursion on the tails ***TX*** of X.

12.4.1 Objective

The objective at Step 4 is to instantiate the conjunction of recursive atoms of the divide-and-conquer schema. This amounts to transforming $LA_3(r)$ into $LA_4(r)$ such that it is covered by the following schema:

```
r(X,Y) ⇔
          minimal(X)
        ∨ nonMinimal(X)  ∧ decompose(X,HX,TX)
                         ∧ (       true
                                ∨
                                   r(TX,TY)          )
```

This amounts to splitting the non-minimal case into two non-mandatory cases, called the *non-recursive non-minimal case* and the *recursive non-minimal case*, respectively. For convenience, we drop the qualifier "non-minimal" from these two names. Recursion may be useless in the sense that the recursively computed ***TY*** are not needed for the computation of Y. Useless recursion wouldn't affect the correctness of a logic algorithm, though. Its elimination is thus rather a matter of algorithm optimization. The following objectives of the strategy:

(1) $LA_4(r)$ is a better complete approximation of $\mathcal{R}$ than $LA_3(r)$;

(2) $exp(LA_4(r))$ is a better partially correct approximation of $\mathcal{R}$ than $exp(LA_3(r))$;

must be satisfied.

12.4.2 Method

The case splitting and the introduction of a conjunction of recursive atoms into one of the resulting cases are mere syntactic operations, and hence pretty straightforward.

However, the decision whether both cases are necessary involves some computations on the non-minimal examples during the generation of $exp(LA_4(r))$. Recall from Definition 7-25 that exp is actually a ternary operator that expands the disjuncts of a logic algorithm $LA(r)$ wrt some covered examples $\mathcal{E}(r)$ and some oracle $\mathcal{O}(r)$. We agreed on the default usage of the so-called deductive oracle based on the specification $EP(r)$. This oracle is automatable, sound (under the consistency assumption), but not necessarily complete. Other automated oracles can be imagined, performing other types of reasoning on the examples and properties, such as analogical reasoning. A reasonable implementation of this synthesis mechanism would also interact with the specifier, especially when all other oracles yield empty witness sets. Such a *human oracle* is supposed to be sound and complete (under the consistency assumption).

Now, the decision whether both cases are really necessary is achieved by the following sequence of four tasks:

- Task G: Compute $exp(LA_4(r))$ according to some sound oracle $O(r)$;
- Task H: In the non-recursive case, delete every disjunct that is an expansion wrt an example that is also covered by the recursive case. Indeed, every example covered by the recursive case in $LA_4(r)$ is also covered by the non-recursive case (but the converse doesn't hold): this amounts to eliminating unwanted redundancy;
- Task I: In the recursive case, delete every disjunct where the general example $procComp(\langle \mathbf{hx}_j\rangle,\langle \mathbf{ty}_j\rangle,y_j)$ would have no admissible alternatives wrt $a = b = 1$, and expand the non-recursive case wrt the corresponding example E_j. Indeed, if y_j is not somehow constructed in terms of $\mathbf{ty}_j$, then recursion is useless for testing E_j.

This amounts so far to splitting the sequence of examples $\mathcal{S}_2$ (see Step 2) into two complementary (but possibly empty) sub-sequences $\mathcal{S}_{21}$ and $\mathcal{S}_{22}$, such that the examples of $\mathcal{S}_{21}$ are covered by the disjuncts of the non-recursive case, whereas the examples of $\mathcal{S}_{22}$ are covered by the disjuncts of the recursive case. We call the elements of $\mathcal{S}_{21}$ the *non-recursive examples*, and the elements of $\mathcal{S}_{22}$ the *recursive examples.*

- Task J: Take the following decisions:
  - if $\mathcal{S}_{21}$ is empty, then conjecture that recursion *is* necessary for *every* possible example of $\mathcal{R}$, rather than just for those of $\mathcal{E}(r)$, and eliminate the non-recursive case in both $LA_4(r)$ and $exp(LA_4(r))$;
  - if $\mathcal{S}_{22}$ is empty, then conjecture that recursion is *useless* for *every* possible example of $\mathcal{R}$, rather than just for those of $\mathcal{E}(r)$, and eliminate the recursive case in both $LA_4(r)$ and $exp(LA_4(r))$.

If the recursive case is eliminated, then this synthesis mechanism is overkill.

In the following, we assume that the *exp*/3 operator actually executes all of these four tasks, rather than just the first one. Note that $exp(LA_4(r))$ is then as follows:

$$
\begin{array}{llll}
\mathtt{r(X,Y)} \Leftrightarrow & & & \\
 & \mathtt{minimal(X)} & \wedge \quad \vee_{j\in \mathcal{I}} & \mathtt{X=x_j} \wedge \mathtt{Y=y_j} \\
\vee & \mathtt{nonMinimal(X)} & \wedge\ \mathtt{decompose(X,\mathbf{HX},\mathbf{TX})} & \\
 & & \wedge \quad \vee_{j\in \mathcal{K}} & \mathtt{X=x_j} \wedge \mathtt{Y=y_j} \\
 & & & \wedge\ \mathbf{HX=hx_j} \wedge \mathbf{TX=tx_j} \\
\vee & \mathtt{nonMinimal(X)} & \wedge\ \mathtt{decompose(X,\mathbf{HX},\mathbf{TX})} & \\
 & & \wedge\ \mathbf{r(TX,TY)} & \\
 & & \wedge \quad \vee_{j\in \mathcal{L}} & \mathtt{X=x_j} \wedge \mathtt{Y=y_j} \\
 & & & \wedge\ \mathbf{HX=hx_j} \wedge \mathbf{TX=tx_j} \\
 & & & \wedge\ \mathbf{TY} \in \mathbf{ty_j}
\end{array}
$$

where $\mathcal{K}$ is the set of indices of the non-recursive examples, and $\mathcal{L}$ is the set of indices of the recursive examples, such that $\mathcal{K} \cup \mathcal{L}$ is $\mathcal{J}$. The $\mathbf{ty}_j$ are vectors of sets ty_{jk} of witnesses such that $r(tx_{jk},ty_{jki})$ holds for some alternative ty_{jki} of ty_{jk} $(j\in \mathcal{L}, 1\leq k\leq t)$.

Note that the methods of all four tasks are fully deterministic (and thus never fail). Moreover, the logic algorithm synthesized at Step 4 is always deterministic.

12.4.3 Correctness

We can now prove a theorem establishing that Step 4 is in line with the strategy:

Theorem 12-4: *Step 4 achieves the two conditions of its objective:*

(1) *$LA_4(r)$ is a better complete approximation of $\mathcal{R}$ than $LA_3(r)$;*

(2) *$exp(LA_4(r))$ is a better partially correct approximation of $\mathcal{R}$ than $exp(LA_3(r))$.*

* **Proof 12-4:** Let's prove these assertions one by one:

(1) $LA_4(r)$ is trivially equivalent to $LA_3(r)$, hence $LA_4(r)$ is a better complete approximation of $\mathcal{R}$ than $LA_3(r)$.

(2) By assertion (2) of Theorem 7-7 and assertion (2) of Theorem 12-3, it suffices to show that:

$$nonMinimal(X) \wedge decompose(X,\boldsymbol{HX},\boldsymbol{TX}) \wedge$$
$$X = x_j \wedge Y = y_j \wedge \boldsymbol{HX} = \boldsymbol{hx}_j \wedge \boldsymbol{TX} = \boldsymbol{tx}_j \Rightarrow \boldsymbol{r(TX,TY)} \wedge \boldsymbol{TY} \in \boldsymbol{ty}_j \quad (j \in \mathcal{L})$$

in order to prove that $exp(LA_4(r))$ is a better partially correct approximation of $\mathcal{R}$ than $exp(LA_3(r))$. This is trivially true by the very definition of the *exp*/3 operator, provided a sound oracle is invoked. ❑

12.4.4 Illustration

Let's illustrate Step 4 on the *firstPlateau*/3 and *compress*/2 problems.

Example 12-16: For the *firstPlateau*/3 problem, Step 4 proceeds as follows. The case split is performed, yielding a first version of LA_4(*firstPlateau*). Task G computes a first version of *exp*(LA_4(*firstPlateau*)), using the deductive oracle based on *EP*(*firstPlateau*). Note that the full determinism of *firstPlateau*/3 in the mode (*ground,var,var*) makes that the oracle finds a singleton set of witnesses to each query. Task H deletes from the non-recursive case the disjuncts that are expansions wrt the examples E_2 to E_7, because these are also covered by the recursive case. This leaves the expansion of the non-recursive case temporarily empty. Task I deletes from the recursive case the disjuncts that are expansions wrt the examples E_3 to E_5, because these do not lead to the existence of admissible alternatives. The non-recursive case is re-expanded wrt these examples. Task J need not eliminate any case. Logic Algorithm 12-7 is the final version of LA_4(*firstPlateau*), whereas Logic Algorithm 12-8 is the final version of *exp*(LA_4(*firstPlateau*)).

Example 12-17: For the *compress*/2 problem, Step 4 proceeds as follows. The case split is performed, yielding a first version of LA_4(*compress*). Task G computes a first version of *exp*(LA_4(*compress*)), using the deductive oracle based on *EP*(*compress*). Note that the full determinism of *compress*/2 in the mode (*ground,var*) makes that the oracle finds a singleton set of witnesses to each query. Task H deletes from the non-recursive case the disjuncts that are expansions wrt the examples E_2 to E_8, because these are also covered by the recursive case. This leaves the expansion of the non-recursive case empty. Task I doesn't delete any disjuncts from the recursive case, because they all lead to the existence of admissible alternatives. Task J eliminates the non-recursive case. The resulting logic algorithm and its expansion are shown in Example 11-1.

```
firstPlateau(L,P,S) ⇔
      L=[_]
   ∨  L=[_,_|_]         ∧ L=[HL|TL]
   ∨  L=[_,_|_]         ∧ L=[HL|TL]
                        ∧ firstPlateau(TL,TP,TS)
```

Logic Algorithm 12-7: *LA*$_4$(*firstPlateau*)

```
firstPlateau(L,P,S) ⇔
      L=[_]
                        ∧       L=[a] ∧ P=[a] ∧ S=[]             {E1}
   ∨  L=[_,_|_]         ∧ L=[HL|TL]
                        ∧       L=[c,d] ∧ P=[c] ∧ S=[d]
                            ∧ HL=c ∧ TL=[d]                      {E3}
                          ∨     L=[e,f,g] ∧ P=[e] ∧ S=[f,g]
                            ∧ HL=e ∧ TL=[f,g]                    {E4}
                          ∨     L=[h,i,i] ∧ P=[h] ∧ S=[i,i]
                            ∧ HL=h ∧ TL=[i,i]                    {E5}
   ∨  L=[_,_|_]         ∧ L=[HL|TL]
                        ∧ firstPlateau(TL,TP,TS)
                        ∧       L=[b,b] ∧ P=[b,b] ∧ S=[]
                            ∧ HL=b ∧ TL=[b]
                            ∧ TP=[b] ∧ TS=[]                     {E2}
                          ∨     L=[j,j,k] ∧ P=[j,j] ∧ S=[k]
                            ∧ HL=j ∧ TL=[j,k]
                            ∧ TP=[j] ∧ TS=[k]                    {E6}
                          ∨     L=[m,m,m] ∧ P=[m,m,m] ∧ S=[]
                            ∧ HL=m ∧ TL=[m,m]
                            ∧ TP=[m,m] ∧ TS=[]                   {E7}
```

Logic Algorithm 12-8: *exp*(*LA*$_4$(*firstPlateau*))

13 THE REDUCTION PHASE

The *reduction phase* of synthesis comprises the last three steps of the synthesis mechanism. In Section 13.1 to Section 13.3, we give complete descriptions of each of these steps: we state their objectives, describe the used methods, analyze their correctness and progression behaviors, and illustrate them on at least the *firstPlateau*/3 and *compress*/2 problems. More examples can be found in [Flener and Deville 92, 93ab].

13.1 Step 5: Synthesis of *Solve* and the $SolveNonMin_k$

An instantiation of the *Solve* predicate-variable computes, in the minimal case, the value of the other parameter *Y* from the induction parameter *X*. An instantiation of the $SolveNonMin_k$ predicate-variable computes, in the kth sub-case of the non-recursive case, the value of *Y* from the decomposition <***HX***,***TX***> of *X*.

13.1.1 Objective

The objective at Step 5 is to instantiate the predicate-variables *Solve* and $SolveNonMin_k$ of the divide-and-conquer schema. The number *v* of sub-cases of the non-recursive case must also be found. This amounts to transforming $LA_4(r)$ into $LA_5(r)$ such that it is covered by the following schema:

```
r(X,Y) ⇔
              minimal(X)      ∧ Solve(X,Y)
     ∨ ∨1≤k≤v nonMinimal(X)  ∧ decompose(X,HX,TX)
                              ∧ (       SolveNonMink(HX,TX,Y)
                                  ∨
                                        r(TX,TY)                 )
```

The following objectives of the strategy:

(1) $LA_5(r)$ is a better complete approximation of $\mathcal{R}$ than $LA_4(r)$;

(2) $exp(LA_5(r))$ is a better partially correct approximation of $\mathcal{R}$ than $exp(LA_4(r))$;

must be satisfied.

13.1.2 Method

Let's first remember that instances of *Solve*/2 may be defined by fairly complex formulas, including divisions into sub-cases and the corresponding discriminating mechanisms, just as in non-minimal cases. But since this is relatively exceptional, we preferred to keep the schema simple. Rather than excluding such complicated instances of *Solve*/2, we slightly depart from our strict mapping between steps and predicate-variables: this Step 5 synthesizes the actual "solving" part of *Solve*/2, while Step 7 synthesizes its "discriminating" part. For this theoretical discussion, we assume however that this Step 5 does the whole job.

A first idea is to use the MSG Method (see Chapter 10). Note that, in both the minimal and the non-recursive case, *Y* may be totally independent of *X*. Indeed, *Y* could be constructed in terms of:

- all the constituents of X, as in *LA(efface-L)* (LA 5-5), *LA(insert-R)* (LA 5-9), and *LA(permutation-L)* (LA 5-14);
- only some of the constituents of X, as in *LA(member-L)* (LA 5-10);
- all or some of the constituents of X, plus some new constituents, as in *LA(partition-L)* (LA 5-13);
- new constituents only, as in *LA(firstN-N)* (LA 5-7), *LA(parity-L)* (LA 5-12), and *LA(plateau-N)* (LA 5-15).

The idea is then to invoke the MSG Method twice, so as to tune the admissibility parameters a and b according to these construction categories. Remember that for admissible examples of arity $a + 2b$, the last b parameters are constructed from the middle b parameters, while the first a parameters may or may not be used in these constructions. So we first apply the MSG Method on the extracted examples that fall into the first construction category (because the word "all" allows us to fix $a = 0$ and $b = 1$), and we then apply it on all the other extracted examples (where $a = 2$ and $b = 0$).

The synthesis of an instance *solve*/2 of *Solve*/2 may thus be performed by the following sequence of tasks:

- Task K: Extract the example set:

$$\mathcal{E}(solve) = \{\ solve(x_j,y_j)\ \mid\ j \in I\ \}$$

  from $exp(LA_4(r))$;
- Task L: Split $\mathcal{E}$ into two complementary (but possibly empty) sub-sets $\mathcal{E}'$ and $\mathcal{E}''$, such that every example of $\mathcal{E}'$ is admissible wrt $a = 0$ and $b = 1$. The set $\mathcal{E}'$ is relative the minimal examples of r/n where Y is effectively constructed from all the constituents of X, while the set $\mathcal{E}''$ is relative the minimal examples of r/n where Y is not constructed from all the constituents of X;
- Task M: Invoke the MSG Method (namely the ground case) on the set $\mathcal{E}'$ for a=0 and b=1, yielding *LA*(*solve'*), and invoke the MSG Method (again the ground case) on the set $\mathcal{E}''$ for a=n=2 and b=0, yielding *LA*(*solve''*). Admissibility of the provided example sets is achieved in both situations, so the use of the MSG Method is justified. The latter invocation of the MSG Method by construction always discovers a single clique, and may thus possibly miss the appropriate answer;
- Task N: Define *LA*(*solve*) as follows:

```
solve(X,Y) ⇔ solve'(X,Y) ∨ solve"(X,Y)
```

Similarly, the synthesis of the instances $solveNonMin_k/h{+}t{+}1$ of the $SolveNonMin_k/h{+}t{+}1$ may be performed by the following sequence of tasks:

- Task O: Extract the example set:

$$\mathcal{E}(solveNonMin) = \{\ solveNonMin(<\boldsymbol{hx}_j,\boldsymbol{tx}_j>,y_j)\ \mid\ j \in \mathcal{K} \text{ and } \boldsymbol{hx}_j,\ \boldsymbol{tx}_j,\ y_j \text{ appear in } exp(LA_4(r))\ \}$$

  from $exp(LA_4(r))$;
- Task P: Split $\mathcal{E}$ into two complementary (but possibly empty) sub-sets $\mathcal{E}'$ and $\mathcal{E}''$, such that every example of $\mathcal{E}'$ is admissible wrt a=0 and b =1. The set $\mathcal{E}'$ is relative the non-recursive examples of r/n where Y is effectively constructed from all the constituents of the decomposition $<\boldsymbol{HX}, \boldsymbol{TX}>$ of X, while the set $\mathcal{E}''$ is relative the non-recursive examples of r/n where Y is not constructed from all the constituents of $<\boldsymbol{HX},\boldsymbol{TX}>$;

- Task Q: Invoke the MSG Method (namely the ground case) on the set $\mathcal{E}'$ for $a=0$ and $b=1$, yielding *LA(solveNonMin')*, and invoke the MSG Method (again the ground case) on the set $\mathcal{E}''$ for $a=n=2$ and $b=0$, yielding *LA(solveNonMin'')*. Admissibility of the provided example sets is achieved in both situations, so the use of the MSG Method is justified. The latter invocation of the MSG Method by construction always discovers a single clique, and may thus possibly miss the appropriate answer;
- Task R: Define *LA(solveNonMin)* as follows:

```
solveNonMin(HX,TX,Y) ⇔
        solveNonMin'(<HX,TX>,Y)
      ∨ solveNonMin"(<HX,TX>,Y)
```

  which may be re-written as follows:

```
solveNonMin(HX,TX,Y) ⇔ ∨_{1≤k≤v} solveNonMin_k(HX,TX,Y)
```

  hence revealing the value of v, and the instances of the $SolveNonMin_k$.

Every algorithm resulting from the MSG Method is here subjected to an assessment heuristic, so as to figure out whether it may be further generalized. We have identified the following valuable heuristic for *LA(solve)* (similarly for *LA(solveNonMin)*):

* **Heuristic 13-1:** The msg of a singleton clique is not a real generalization, as it is ground. Let $r(x_i,y_i)$ be the example corresponding to such a clique. Some disjunct of *LA(solve)* is thus as follows: $X = x_i \land Y = y_i$. Now, if there is a property $r(s_j,t_j) \Leftarrow B_j$ such that:

(1) $minimal(s_j)$ is provable (where *minimal*/1 is the instance of *Minimal*/1),
(2) $r(x_i,y_i) \le r(s_j,t_j)$ (with substitution σ),
(3) $B_j\sigma$ is provable,

then that disjunct of *LA(solve)* may be semantically generalized (because of (2) and (3)) to $X = s_j \land Y = t_j \land B_j$. This heuristic is justified at the end of Section 13.3.2.

Note that $exp(LA_5(r))$ is as follows:

```
r(X,Y) ⇔
              minimal(X)      ∧ solve(X,Y)
                              ∧    ∨_{j∈I}    X=x_j ∧ Y=y_j
  ∨ ∨_{1≤k≤v} nonMinimal(X)  ∧ decompose(X,HX,TX)
                              ∧ solveNonMin_k(HX,TX,Y)
                              ∧    ∨_{j∈K_k}  X=x_j ∧ Y=y_j
                                            ∧ HX=hx_j ∧ TX=tx_j
  ∨           nonMinimal(X)  ∧ decompose(X,HX,TX)
                              ∧ r(TX,TY)
                              ∧    ∨_{j∈L}    X=x_j ∧ Y=y_j
                                            ∧ HX=hx_j ∧ TX=tx_j
                                            ∧ TY∈ty_j
```

where the $\mathcal{K}_k$ form a partition of $\mathcal{K}$.

The methods of Tasks M and Q are non-deterministic, finite, and never fail, because of the usage of the ground case of the MSG Method. Moreover, the synthesized instances are non-deterministic and finite, for the same reason. The logic algorithm synthesized at Step 5 may thus be non-deterministic, but is certainly finite. All other tasks are fully deterministic. Hence Step 5 never fails.

However, it may happen that the instance of *Solve* or *SolveNonMin* is defined as a full-fledged, possibly recursive, logic algorithm. Different methods need to be applied then. We discuss one such method in Section 14.2.4.

13.1.3 Correctness

We can now prove a theorem establishing that Step 5 is in line with the strategy:

Theorem 13-1: *Step 5 achieves the two conditions of its objective:*

(1) *$LA_5(r)$ is a better complete approximation of $\mathcal{R}$ than $LA_4(r)$;*

(2) *$exp(LA_5(r))$ is a better partially correct approximation of $\mathcal{R}$ than $exp(LA_4(r))$.*

* **Proof 13-1:** Let's prove these assertions one by one:

(1) By assertion (1) of Theorem 7-7 and assertion (1) of Theorem 12-4, it suffices to show that:

$$\mathcal{R}(X,Y) \wedge minimal(X) \Rightarrow solve(X,Y)$$

$$\mathcal{R}(X,Y) \wedge nonMinimal(X) \wedge decompose(X,\boldsymbol{HX},\boldsymbol{TX}) \Rightarrow solveNonMin(\boldsymbol{HX},\boldsymbol{TX},Y)$$

in order to prove that $LA_5(r)$ is a better complete approximation of $\mathcal{R}$ than $LA_4(r)$. However, the second statement is wrong, so assertion (1) of Theorem 7-7 is not applicable to this disjunct. Instead, we may prove the following statement, obtained by applying assertion (1) of Theorem 7-7 to $LA_3(r)$, which is known by assertion (1) of Theorem 12-3 to be complete wrt $\mathcal{R}$:

$$\mathcal{R}(X,Y) \wedge nonMinimal(X) \wedge decompose(X,\boldsymbol{HX},\boldsymbol{TX}) \Rightarrow solveNonMin(\boldsymbol{HX},\boldsymbol{TX},Y) \vee \boldsymbol{r}(\boldsymbol{TX},\boldsymbol{TY})$$

This is of course unprovable in general, because there is no formal definition of $\mathcal{R}$. But the corresponding instance should be proven for each particular synthesis, and this provides thus a criterion to be fulfilled by interaction with the specifier.

(2) By assertion (2) of Theorem 7-7 and assertion (2) of Theorem 12-4, it suffices to show that:

$$minimal(X) \wedge X = x_j \wedge Y = y_j \Rightarrow solve(X,Y) \quad (j \in I)$$

$$nonMinimal(X) \wedge decompose(X,\boldsymbol{HX},\boldsymbol{TX}) \wedge X = x_j \wedge Y = y_j \wedge \boldsymbol{HX} = \boldsymbol{hx}_j \wedge \boldsymbol{TX} = \boldsymbol{tx}_j \Rightarrow solveNonMin_k(\boldsymbol{HX},\boldsymbol{TX},Y) \quad (1 \leq k \leq v)\ (j \in \mathcal{K}_k)$$

in order to prove that $exp(LA_5(r))$ is a better partially correct approximation of $\mathcal{R}$ than $exp(LA_4(r))$. This follows from the correctness of the ground case of the MSG Method (see Theorem 10-3). ❑

This correctness theorem is only applicable to the results obtained *before* application of the assessment heuristics.

13.1.4 Illustration

Let's illustrate Step 5 on a few problems.

Example 13-1: For the *firstPlateau*/3 problem, Step 5 proceeds as follows. Task K extracts the singleton example set:

```
ℰ = { solveFirstPlateau([a],<[a],[]>) }
```

from the minimal disjunct of *exp*(LA_4(*firstPlateau*)). At Task L, the example is found to be admissible wrt a=0 and b=1. So $\mathcal{E}' = \mathcal{E}$ and $\mathcal{E}'' = \emptyset$. At Task M, the MSG Method yields:

```
solveFirstPlateau'(L,<P,S>) ⇔ L=[a] ∧ P=[a] ∧ S=[]
solveFirstPlateau"(L,<P,S>) ⇔ false
```

The first logic algorithm is based on a singleton clique (originating from *firstPlateau*([a],[a],[])), that is example E_1 of $\mathcal{E}$(*firstPlateau*)), and is thus subject to generalization by Heuristic 13-1. Indeed, E_1 is generalized by property P_1 of $\mathcal{P}$(*firstPlateau*), so the generalized logic algorithm is:

```
solveFirstPlateau'(L,<P,S>) ⇔ L=[X] ∧ P=[X] ∧ S=[]
```

At Task N, the instance *solveFirstPlateau*/3 is defined as follows:

```
solveFirstPlateau(L,P,S) ⇔ P=L ∧ S=[] ∧ L=[_]
```

after performing some obvious rewriting.

Similarly, Task O extracts the example set:

```
ℰ = { solveNonMinFirstPlateau(<c,[d]>,<[c],[d]>)
      solveNonMinFirstPlateau(<e,[f,g]>,<[e],[f,g]>)
      solveNonMinFirstPlateau(<h,[i,i]>,<[h],[i,i]>) }
```

from the non-recursive disjuncts of *exp*(LA_4(*firstPlateau*)). At Task P, these examples are found to be admissible wrt a=0 and b=1. So $\mathcal{E}' = \mathcal{E}$ and $\mathcal{E}'' = \emptyset$. At Task Q, the MSG Method yields:

```
solveNonMinFirstPlateau'(<HL,TL>,<P,S>) ⇔
        HL=A ∧ TL=[B|T] ∧ P=[A] ∧ S=[B|T]
solveNonMinFirstPlateau"(<HL,TL>,<P,S>) ⇔
        false
```

The generalization heuristic doesn't apply here. So, at Task R, the instance *solveNonMinFirstPlateau*/4 is defined as follows:

```
solveNonMinFirstPlateau(HL,TL,P,S) ⇔
        P=[HL] ∧ S=TL ∧ TL=[_|_]
```

after performing some obvious rewriting.

Hence, Logic Algorithm 13-1 shows LA_5(*firstPlateau*), whereas Logic Algorithm 13-2 shows *exp*(LA_5(*firstPlateau*)). ♦

Example 13-2: For the *compress*/2 problem, Step 5 proceeds as follows. Task K extracts the singleton example set:

```
ℰ = { solveCompress([],[]) }
```

from the minimal disjunct of *exp*(LA_4(*compress*)). Task L finds the example to be admissible wrt a=0 and b=1. So $\mathcal{E}' = \mathcal{E}$ and $\mathcal{E}'' = \emptyset$. At Task M, the MSG Method yields:

```
solveCompress'(L,C) ⇔ L=[] ∧ C=[]
```

```
firstPlateau(L,P,S) ⇔
      L=[_]            ∧ P=L ∧ S=[] ∧ L=[_]
    ∨ L=[_,_|_]        ∧ L=[HL|TL]
                       ∧ P=[HL] ∧ S=TL ∧ TL=[_|_]
    ∨ L=[_,_|_]        ∧ L=[HL|TL]
                       ∧ firstPlateau(TL,TP,TS)
```

Logic Algorithm 13-1: LA_5(*firstPlateau*)

```
firstPlateau(L,P,S) ⇔
      L=[_]            ∧ P=L ∧ S=[] ∧ L=[_]
                       ∧       L=[a] ∧ P=[a] ∧ S=[]                {E1}
    ∨ L=[_,_|_]        ∧ L=[HL|TL]
                       ∧ P=[HL] ∧ S=TL ∧ TL=[_|_]
                       ∧       L=[c,d] ∧ P=[c] ∧ S=[d]
                             ∧ HL=c ∧ TL=[d]                       {E3}
                          ∨    L=[e,f,g] ∧ P=[e] ∧ S=[f,g]
                             ∧ HL=e ∧ TL=[f,g]                     {E4}
                          ∨    L=[h,i,i] ∧ P=[h] ∧ S=[i,i]
                             ∧ HL=h ∧ TL=[i,i]                     {E5}
    ∨ L=[_,_|_]        ∧ L=[HL|TL]
                       ∧ firstPlateau(TL,TP,TS)
                       ∧       L=[b,b] ∧ P=[b,b] ∧ S=[]
                             ∧ HL=b ∧ TL=[b]
                             ∧ TP=[b] ∧ TS=[]                      {E2}
                          ∨    L=[j,j,k] ∧ P=[j,j] ∧ S=[k]
                             ∧ HL=j ∧ TL=[j,k]
                             ∧ TP=[j] ∧ TS=[k]                     {E6}
                          ∨    L=[m,m,m] ∧ P=[m,m,m] ∧ S=[]
                             ∧ HL=m ∧ TL=[m,m]
                             ∧ TP=[m,m] ∧ TS=[]                    {E7}
```

Logic Algorithm 13-2: *exp*(LA_5(*firstPlateau*))

```
solveCompress"(L,C) ⇔ false
```

The first logic algorithm is based on a singleton clique (originating from *compress*([],[]), that is example E_1 of $\mathcal{E}$(*compress*)), and is thus subject to generalization by Heuristic 13-1. But there is no property in $\mathcal{P}$(*compress*) that generalizes E_1, so no generalization can be performed here. At Task N, the instance *solveCompress*/2 is:

```
solveCompress(L,C) ⇔ C=L ∧ L=[]
```

after performing some obvious rewriting. The resulting logic algorithm and its expansion are shown in Example 11-1. ♦

Example 13-3: During the synthesis of *LA*(*firstN-int-N*), Step 5 proceeds as follows. Task K extracts the example set:

```
𝓔 = { solveFirstN(0,<[], []>)
      solveFirstN(0,<[a],[]>) }
```

from the minimal disjuncts of $exp(LA_4(firstN))$. At Task L, none of these examples is found to be admissible wrt a=0 and b=1. So $\mathcal{E}'' = \mathcal{E}$ and $\mathcal{E}' = \varnothing$. At Task M, the MSG Method yields:

```
solveFirstN'(N,<L,R>)  ⇔  false
solveFirstN"(N,<L,R>)  ⇔  N=0  ∧  L=T  ∧  R=[]
```

At Task N, the instance *solveFirstN*/3 is thus defined as follows:

```
solveFirstN(N,L,R)  ⇔  N=0  ∧  L=_  ∧  R=[]
```

after performing some obvious rewriting. ♦

13.2 Step 6: Synthesis of the $Process_k$ and $Compose_k$

An instantiation of the $Process_k$ predicate-variable transforms, in the kth sub-case of the recursive case, the heads ***HX*** of the induction parameter *X* into a vector ***HY*** of heads of the other parameter *Y*. An instantiation of the $Compose_k$ predicate-variable computes, in the kth sub-case of the recursive case, the parameter *Y* from its heads ***HY*** (obtained by processing the ***HX***) and tails ***TY*** (obtained by recursion on the ***TX***).

13.2.1 Objective

The objective at Step 6 is to instantiate the predicate-variables $Process_k$ and $Compose_k$ of the divide-and-conquer schema. The number *w* of sub-cases of the recursive case must also be found. This amounts to transforming $LA_5(r)$ into $LA_6(r)$ such that it is covered by the following schema:

```
r(X,Y)  ⇔
              minimal(X)       ∧ solve(X,Y)
     ∨ ∨1≤k≤c nonMinimal(X)    ∧ decompose(X,HX,TX))
                               ∧ (      solveNonMink(HX,TX,Y)
                                    |
                                        r(TX,TY)
                                      ∧ Processk(HX,HY)
                                      ∧ Composek(HY,TY,Y)       )
```

where $c = v + w$. The following objectives of the strategy:

(1) $LA_6(r)$ is a better complete approximation of $\mathcal{R}$ than $LA_5(r)$;

(2) $exp(LA_6(r))$ is a better partially correct approximation of $\mathcal{R}$ than $exp(LA_5(r))$;

must be satisfied.

13.2.2 Method

We merge the $Process_k(\boldsymbol{HX},\boldsymbol{HY})$ with the $Compose_k(\boldsymbol{HY},\boldsymbol{TY},Y)$ into $ProcComp_k(\boldsymbol{HX},\boldsymbol{TY},Y)$, so that their instances are synthesized simultaneously. If we isolated the $Process_k(\boldsymbol{HX},\boldsymbol{HY})$, then their only correct instantiations would be defined as:

```
processk(HX,HY)  ⇔  HY=_
```

This would mean that ***HY*** would have to be initialized to a vector of different variables, and without knowing their number *h'*. Moreover, *w* is yet unknown, so we wouldn't know how many of these instances to create. All this would of course complicate the subsequent synthesis of the $Compose_k$. The schema's separation of these predicate-variables is thus rather "academic", but not applicable in practice.

We first hypothesize that all instances of the $ProcComp_k$ are defined in terms of the =/2 primitive only. So we may apply the MSG Method (see Chapter 10). The idea is to initialize the admissibility parameters a and b to h and 1, respectively, as Y is necessarily constructed from $<\mathbf{TY}>$ (which is of length 1), and optionally from $\mathbf{HX}$ (which is of length h). The synthesis of the instances $procComp_k/h+t+1$ of the $ProcComp_k/h+t+1$ may thus be performed by the following sequence of tasks:

- Task S: Extract the general example set:

$$\mathcal{G}(procComp) = \{\, procComp(\mathbf{hx}_j, <\mathbf{ty}_j>, y_j) \mid j \in \mathcal{L} \text{ and } \mathbf{hx}_j, \mathbf{ty}_j, y_j \text{ appear in } exp(LA_5(r)) \,\}$$

  from $exp(LA_5(r))$; [16]
- Task T: Invoke the MSG Method (the non-ground case) on the set $\mathcal{G}$ for $a{=}h$ and $b{=}1$, yielding $LA(procComp)$. Admissibility of the provided general example set is guaranteed by Step 4 (Syntactic introduction of the recursive atoms), so the use of the MSG Method is justified. The search for admissible alternatives of the general examples may be restricted because, by construction, y_j is ground for every general example in $\mathcal{G}(procComp)$, so the minimality hypothesis (see Section 10.4.2) may be emitted;
- Task U: View the synthesized logic algorithm $LA(procComp)$ as follows:

$$\texttt{procComp}(\mathbf{HX}, <\mathbf{TY}>, \texttt{Y}) \Leftrightarrow \vee_{c-w<k\leq v+w}\ \texttt{procComp}_k(\mathbf{HX}, \mathbf{TY}, \texttt{Y})$$

  which reveals the values of w and c, and the instances of the $ProcComp_k$.

Every logic algorithm resulting from the MSG Method is here subjected to some assessment heuristic, so as to figure out whether this method was applicable. This assessment is actually performed on the msgs of the discovered cliques, rather than directly on the produced logic algorithm. We have identified the following valuable heuristic:

Heuristic 13-2: If there are at least as many cliques as properties, then the inferred instances probably only cover the given examples, but not examples with "larger" parameters. The assumption of using =/2 only is thus probably too strong.

This heuristic has an obvious influence upon the formulation of a methodology for choosing "good" examples and properties. In the absence of such "good" specifications, a stronger version of this heuristic would be needed. A heuristic similar to Heuristic 13-1 could be easily defined for $LA(procComp)$.

Example 13-4: During the synthesis of *LA(permutation-int-L)*, the MSG Method is invoked as in Example 10-12. The first result is subject to Heuristic 13-2, because there are "too many" cliques, which lets expect that *LA(pcPermutation)* wouldn't behave as intended on a goal such as *pcPermutation(a,[b,c,d,e,f],R)*. The same holds for the second result. The intended relation for *LA(pcPermutation)* is indeed the one underlying the *stuff*/3 predicate, and thus requires a recursive logic algorithm. We show in Section 14.2.4 how this can be obtained.

Note that $exp(LA_6(r))$ is as follows:

16. Note that the extracted general examples are immediately in shorthand form.

```
r(X,Y) ⇔
            minimal(X)          ∧ solve(X,Y)
                                ∧      ∨j∈I        X=xj  ∧ Y=yj
     ∨ ∨_≤k≤v  nonMinimal(X)    ∧ decompose(X,HX,TX)
                                ∧ solveNonMink(HX,TX,Y)
                                ∧      ∨j∈𝒦k       X=xj  ∧ Y=yj
                                                 ∧ HX=hxj ∧ TX=txj
     ∨ ∨c-w<k≤c nonMinimal(X)   ∧ decompose(X,HX,TX)
                                ∧ r(TX,TY)
                                ∧ procCompk(HX,<TY>,Y)
                                ∧      ∨j∈ℒk       X=xj  ∧ Y=yj
                                                 ∧ HX=hxj ∧ TX=txj
                                                 ∧ TY∈ty'j
```

where the $\mathcal{L}_k$ partition $\mathcal{L}$, and where the elements ty'_{jk} of the $\boldsymbol{ty'}_j$ are subsets of the sets of witnesses ty_{jk} generated at Step 4 (Syntactic introduction of the recursive atoms).

Example 13-5: Let's redo Example 7-13, but with *LA*(*permutation*) now as follows:

```
permutation(L,P) ⇔
      L=[]
   ∨  L=[HL|TL]          ∧ permutation(TL,TP)
                         ∧ efface(HL,P,TP)
```

The expansion of the second disjunct of *LA*(*permutation*) wrt *permutation*([*a*,*b*,*c*],[*c*,*a*,*b*]) and the deductive oracle based on *EP*(*permutation*) is:

$$L = [HL \mid TL] \wedge permutation(TL,TP) \wedge efface(HL,P,TP) \wedge$$
$$(L = [a,b,c] \wedge P = [c,a,b]) \;\wedge\; (HL = a \wedge TL = [b,c] \wedge TP = [c,b])$$

Indeed, if $TL = [b,c]$, then the deductive oracle infers that either $TP = [b,c]$ or $TP = [c,b]$, according to properties P_2 and P_3, respectively. But the *efface*/3 atom only holds for the first answer. ♦

If the result of the MSG Method is rejected (due to Heuristic 13-2), then it is likely that the instance of *ProcComp* is defined as a full-fledged, possibly recursive, logic algorithm. Different methods need to be applied then. We discuss one such method in Section 14.2.4.

Note that the method of Task T is non-deterministic, always succeeds, but may be infinite, because of the non-ground case of the MSG Method. Moreover, the synthesized instances are non-deterministic and finite, for the same reason. The logic algorithm synthesized at Step 6 may thus be non-deterministic, but is certainly finite. All other tasks are fully deterministic. Hence Step 6 never fails.

As the ground case of the MSG Method is much easier, this speaks in retrospect in favor of using the Functionality Heuristic when selecting an induction parameter at Step 2. Indeed, this forces all the $\boldsymbol{ty}_j$ to be ground and unique, so that all the extracted general examples are mere (ground] examples, because all the $\boldsymbol{hx}_j$ and y_j are necessarily ground and unique. This is the best possible situation. The worst possible situation for using the MSG Method is the non-ground case where the parameters of each general example are existential variables. This cannot happen here, because all the $\boldsymbol{hx}_j$ and y_j are necessarily ground and unique. So the worst situation at Step 6 would be the one where the *exp*/3 operator generates a variable for each element of each $\boldsymbol{ty}_j$, because of some "dumb" oracle for *r*/*n*. The MSG Method can still handle such a worst-case situation, as it then enumerates all possible grounding substitutions in its search for admissible alternatives of each general example. This may of course be very time-consuming. The point however is that the oracle used by the *exp*/3 operator is irrelevant, provided it is sound.

13.2.3 Correctness

We can now prove a theorem establishing that Step 6 is in line with the strategy:

Theorem 13-2: *Step 6 achieves the two conditions of its objective:*

(1) *$LA_6(r)$ is a better complete approximation of $\mathcal{R}$ than $LA_5(r)$;*

(2) *$exp(LA_6(r))$ is a better partially correct approximation of $\mathcal{R}$ than $exp(LA_5(r))$.*

* **Proof 13-2:** Let's prove these assertions one by one:

(1) By assertion (1) of Theorem 7-7 and assertion (1) of Theorem 13-1, it suffices to show that:

$$\mathcal{R}(X,Y) \land nonMinimal(X) \land decompose(X,\boldsymbol{HX},\boldsymbol{TX}) \land \boldsymbol{r}(\boldsymbol{TX},\boldsymbol{TY}) \Rightarrow procComp(\boldsymbol{HX},\boldsymbol{TY},Y)$$

in order to prove that $LA_6(r)$ is a better complete approximation of $\mathcal{R}$ than $LA_5(r)$. However, this statement is wrong, so assertion (1) of Theorem 7-7 is not applicable to this disjunct of $LA_5(r)$. Instead, we may prove the following statement, obtained by applying assertion (1) of Theorem 7-7 to $LA_3(r)$, which is known by assertion (1) of Theorem 12-3 to be complete wrt $\mathcal{R}$:

$$\mathcal{R}(X,Y) \land nonMinimal(X) \land decompose(X,\boldsymbol{HX},\boldsymbol{TX}) \Rightarrow solveNonMin(\boldsymbol{HX},\boldsymbol{TX},Y) \lor (\, \boldsymbol{r}(\boldsymbol{TX},\boldsymbol{TY}) \land procComp(\boldsymbol{HX},\boldsymbol{TY},Y)\,)$$

This is of course unprovable in general, as there is no formal definition of $\mathcal{R}$. But the corresponding instance should be proven for each particular synthesis, and this provides thus a criterion to be fulfilled by interaction with the specifier.

(2) By assertion (2) of Theorem 7-7 and assertion (2) of Theorem 13-1, it suffices to show that:

$$nonMinimal(X) \land decompose(X,\boldsymbol{HX},\boldsymbol{TX}) \land \boldsymbol{r}(\boldsymbol{TX},\boldsymbol{TY}) \land X = x_j \land Y = y_j \land \boldsymbol{HX} = \boldsymbol{hx}_j \land \boldsymbol{TX} = \boldsymbol{tx}_j \land \boldsymbol{TY} \in \boldsymbol{ty}'_j \Rightarrow procComp_k(\boldsymbol{HX},\boldsymbol{TY},Y) \quad (c-w < k \leq c)\ (j \in \mathcal{L}_k)$$

in order to prove that $exp(LA_6(r))$ is a better partially correct approximation of $\mathcal{R}$ than $exp(LA_5(r))$. This follows from the correctness of the non-ground case of the MSG Method (see Theorem 10-4). ❑

This correctness theorem is only applicable to the results obtained *before* application of the generalization heuristic.

13.2.4 Illustration

Let's illustrate Step 6 on a few problems.

```
firstPlateau(L,P,S) ⇔
     L=[_]              ∧ P=L ∧ S=[] ∧ L=[_]
   ∨ L=[_,_|_]          ∧ L=[HL|TL]
                        ∧ P=[HL] ∧ S=TL ∧ TL=[_|_]
   ∨ L=[_,_|_]          ∧ L=[HL|TL]
                        ∧ firstPlateau(TL,TP,TS)
                        ∧ P=[HL|TP]  ∧ S=TS  ∧ TP=[HL|_]
```

Logic Algorithm 13-3: LA_6(*firstPlateau*)

```
firstPlateau(L,P,S) ⇔
     L=[_]              ∧ P=L ∧ S=[] ∧ L=[_]
                        ∧     L=[a] ∧ P=[a] ∧ S=[]              {E1}
   ∨ L=[_,_|_]          ∧ L=[HL|TL]
                        ∧ P=[HL] ∧ S=TL ∧ TL=[_|_]
                        ∧     L=[c,d] ∧ P=[c] ∧ S=[d]
                            ∧ HL=c ∧ TL=[d]                     {E3}
                          ∨   L=[e,f,g] ∧ P=[e] ∧ S=[f,g]
                            ∧ HL=e ∧ TL=[f,g]                   {E4}
                          ∨   L=[h,i,i] ∧ P=[h] ∧ S=[i,i]
                            ∧ HL=h ∧ TL=[i,i]                   {E5}
   ∨ L=[_,_|_]          ∧ L=[HL|TL]
                        ∧ firstPlateau(TL,TP,TS)
                        ∧ P=[HL|TP]  ∧ S=TS  ∧ TP=[HL|_]
                        ∧     L=[b,b] ∧ P=[b,b] ∧ S=[]
                            ∧ HL=b ∧ TL=[b]
                            ∧ TP=[b] ∧ TS=[]                    {E2}
                          ∨   L=[j,j,k] ∧ P=[j,j] ∧ S=[k]
                            ∧ HL=j ∧ TL=[j,k]
                            ∧ TP=[j] ∧ TS=[k]                   {E6}
                          ∨   L=[m,m,m] ∧ P=[m,m,m] ∧ S=[]
                            ∧ HL=m ∧ TL=[m,m]
                            ∧ TP=[m,m] ∧ TS=[]                  {E7}
```

Logic Algorithm 13-4: *exp*(LA_6(*firstPlateau*))

Example 13-6: For the *firstPlateau*/3 problem, Step 6 proceeds as in Example 10-7. The resulting logic algorithm is subject to no heuristic. Logic Algorithm 13-3 shows LA_6(*firstPlateau*), whereas Logic Algorithm 13-4 shows *exp*(LA_6(*firstPlateau*)).

Example 13-7: For the *compress*/2 problem, Step 6 proceeds as in Example 10-6. The obtained result is subject to no heuristic. The resulting logic algorithm and its expansion are shown in Example 11-1.

Example 13-8: During the synthesis of *LA*(*plateau-int-N*), the MSG Method is invoked as in Example 10-11. The resulting logic algorithm is subject to no heuristic.

13.3 Step 7: Synthesis of the $Discriminate_k$

An instantiation of the $Discriminate_k$ predicate-variable tests the values of ***HX***, ***TX***, *Y* to see whether $SolveNonMin_k$, respectively $Process_k \wedge Compose_k$, is applicable.

13.3.1 Objective

The objective at Step 7 is to instantiate the predicate-variables $Discriminate_k$ of the divide-and-conquer schema. This amounts to transforming $LA_6(r)$ into $LA_7(r)$ such that it is covered by the following schema:

```
r(X,Y) ⇔
              minimal(X)      ∧ solve(X,Y)
    ∨ ∨1≤k≤c nonMinimal(X)   ∧ decompose(X,HX,TX)
                              ∧ Discriminatek(HX,TX,Y)
                              ∧ (      solveNonMink(HX,TX,Y)
                                  |
                                       r(TX,TY)
                                     ∧ processk(HX,HY)
                                     ∧ composek(HY,TY,Y)        )
```

The following objectives of the strategy:

(1) $LA_7(r)$ is a better complete approximation of $\mathcal{R}$ than $LA_6(r)$;

(2) $exp(LA_7(r))$ is a better partially correct approximation of $\mathcal{R}$ than $exp(LA_6(r))$;

must be satisfied.

Also, Step 7 should be totally independent of the choice of Step 6 to merge the $process_k$ and $compose_k$ predicates.

13.3.2 Method

The bodies of the properties contain explicit information that has not yet been synthesized into the logic algorithms. But this explicit knowledge constitutes the very reason why we augmented example-based specifications with properties. The idea is then to use the Proofs-as-Programs Method (see Chapter 9), as this amounts to "transferring" appropriate variants of atoms from the bodies of properties to the body of a logic algorithm. We thus invoke the Proofs-as-Programs Method with the following *input*:

- use $LA_6(r)$ as the input logic algorithm;
- use $EP(r)$ as the input property set (remember that examples are properties, too);

Indeed, the pre-condition is achieved because $LA_6(r)$ only uses, by Steps 1 to 6, primitive predicates and the *r/n* predicate, and is, by Theorem 13-2, complete wrt $EP(r)$.

- use the following set $\mathcal{H}$ of generalization heuristics:

Heuristic 13-3: From the used divide-and-conquer schema, we know that the parameters of the $discriminate_k$ are ***HX***, ***TX***, and *Y*, so we should *project* [Pettorossi and Proietti 89] the discriminants upon these parameters.

Heuristic 13-4: If parameter *Y* is not an auxiliary parameter (see Section 14.2.2 on how to detect auxiliary parameters), then it is irrelevant for discrimination, and its equality atom may be deleted from the body of every discriminant.

Heuristic 13-5: The parameters ***TX*** and *Y* (the latter only if it is an auxiliary parameter) should range across their entire domains: if necessary, some of their values should be generalized. In our case, this goes as follows:

- if TX_i is an integer and the atom $TX_i = s(s(\ldots s(0)\ldots))$ appears in the last disjunct of a discriminant, then generalize that atom to $TX_i = s(s(\ldots s(N)\ldots))$, where *N* is a new variable; also delete the equality atom involving HX_i;
- if TX_i is a list and the atom $TX_i = [s]$ appears in the last disjunct of a discriminant, then generalize it to $TX_i = [s \mid T]$, where *s* are terms, and *T* is a new variable.

The generalization of *Y* is similar, provided, of course, it is of an inductive type.

The application of the last two heuristics should be interactive and in accordance with the given examples.

The *output* is $LA_7(r)$, and the newly added atoms (compared to $LA_6(r)$) constitute the instances of the $Discriminate_k$ predicates. Note that $exp(LA_7(r))$ is as follows:

```
r(X,Y) ⇔
                minimal(X)         ∧ solve(X,Y)
                                   ∧      ∨j∈I      X=xj  ∧ Y=yj
  ∨ ∨1≤k≤v      nonMinimal(X)      ∧ decompose(X,HX,TX)
                                   ∧ discriminatek(HX,TX,Y)
                                   ∧ solveNonMink(HX,TX,Y)
                                   ∧      ∨j∈𝒦k      X=xj  ∧ Y=yj
                                                  ∧ HX=hxj  ∧ TX=txj
  ∨ ∨c-w<k≤c    nonMinimal(X)      ∧ decompose(X,HX,TX)
                                   ∧ discriminatek(HX,TX,Y)
                                   ∧ r(TX,TY)
                                   ∧ procCompk(HX,TY,Y)
                                   ∧      ∨j∈ℒk      X=xj  ∧ Y=yj
                                                  ∧ HX=hxj  ∧ TX=txj
                                                  ∧ TY∈ty'j
```

As a reminder, Step 7 is supposed to synthesize the "discriminating" part of *Solve*/2. But we assume that the instance *solve*/2 found by Step 5 is unchanged by this Step 7.

Note that the Proofs-as-Programs Method wouldn't need to prove that the examples are logical consequences of the input logic algorithm, as we know that $LA_6(r)$ is already complete wrt $\mathcal{E}(r)$. Moreover, such proofs would result in very specialized discriminants, and hence in the need for considerable generalization afterwards. But the presence of some examples is often necessary within the theories, so that *DCI* may reduce atoms of predicate *r*/*n* in case no property is applicable. The following definition and heuristic capture this:

Definition 13-1: Given a specification and a minimal form, a *property-example* is a minimal example that is a logical consequence of no property.

Example 13-9: The atoms *compress*([],[]) and *length*([], 0) are property-examples. But *platecu*(1,*b*,[*b*]) and *firstN*(0,[],[]) are not property-examples, because they are logical consequences of the first properties of their respective specifications.

Heuristic 13-6: At Step 7, only provide the properties and property-examples of *EP*(*r*) as input property set to the Proofs-as-Programs Method.

Step 7 is deterministic, because of the Proofs-as-Programs Method. It fails iff $LA_6(r)$ is not complete wrt $\mathcal{P}(r)$. This should normally be excluded by the conjunction of assertion (1) of Theorem 13-2 and the consistency assumption. Moreover, nothing can be said about the synthesized discriminants in terms of determinism or finiteness, because nothing is known about the properties.

* We may now justify Heuristic 13-1. When proving the involved property, say P_j, the derivation starting from the clause, say C_i, that is obtained from the generalized minimal disjunct necessarily succeeds, as shown in the following derivation schema:

```
                          r(sj,tj) ← Bj
                  DCI: Ci    ↓    {}
    minimal(sj) & sj=sj & tj=tj & Bj ← Bj
DCI: LA(minimal) and constraint (1)   ↓   {}
              sj=sj & tj=tj & Bj ← Bj
          2×DCI: LA(=), Sim   ↓   {}
                          □
```

Property P_j is thus a logical consequence of the synthesized logic algorithm: the performed generalization is thus legal. Note that the extracted discriminant is redundant with the existing literals of the involved disjunct. If the heuristic hadn't already added the conjunction B_j to that disjunct, then the extracted discriminant would have been B_j.

13.3.3 Correctness

We can now prove a theorem establishing that Step 7 is in line with the strategy:

Theorem 13-3: *Step 7 achieves the two conditions of its objective:*

(1) *$LA_7(r)$ is a better complete approximation of $\mathcal{R}$ than $LA_6(r)$;*

(2) *$exp(LA_7(r))$ is a better partially correct approximation of $\mathcal{R}$ than $exp(LA_6(r))$.*

* **Proof 13-3:** Let's prove these assertions one by one:

(1) By assertion (1) of Theorem 7-7 and assertion (1) of Theorem 13-2, it suffices to show that:

$$\mathcal{R}(X,Y) \wedge nonMinimal(X) \wedge decompose(X,\boldsymbol{HX},\boldsymbol{TX}) \wedge solveNonMin_k(\boldsymbol{HX},\boldsymbol{TX},Y) \Rightarrow discriminate_k(\boldsymbol{HX},\boldsymbol{TX},Y) \quad (1 \le k \le v)$$

$$\mathcal{R}(X,Y) \wedge nonMinimal(X) \wedge decompose(X,\boldsymbol{HX},\boldsymbol{TX}) \wedge \boldsymbol{r(TX,TY)} \wedge procComp_k(\boldsymbol{HX},\boldsymbol{TY},Y) \Rightarrow discriminate_k(\boldsymbol{HX},\boldsymbol{TX},Y) \quad (c-w<k\le c)$$

in order to prove that $LA_7(r)$ is a better complete approximation of $\mathcal{R}$ than $LA_6(r)$. This is of course unprovable in general, because there is no formal definition of $\mathcal{R}$. But the corresponding instance should be proven for each particular synthesis, and this provides thus a criterion to be fulfilled by interaction with the specifier.

(2) By assertion (2) of Theorem 7-7 and assertion (2) of Theorem 13-2, it suffices to show that:

$$nonMinimal(X) \wedge decompose(X,\mathbf{HX},\mathbf{TX}) \wedge solveNonMin_k(\mathbf{HX},\mathbf{TX},Y) \wedge X = x_j \wedge Y = y_j \wedge \mathbf{HX} = \mathbf{hx}_j \wedge \mathbf{TX} = \mathbf{tx}_j \Rightarrow discriminate_k(\mathbf{HX},\mathbf{TX},Y) \quad (1 \le k \le v)\ (j \in \mathcal{K}_k)$$

$$nonMinimal(X) \wedge decompose(X,\mathbf{HX},\mathbf{TX}) \wedge \mathbf{r(TX,TY)} \wedge procComp_k(\mathbf{HX},\mathbf{TY},Y) \wedge X = x_j \wedge Y = y_j \wedge \mathbf{HX} = \mathbf{hx}_j \wedge \mathbf{TX} = \mathbf{tx}_j \wedge \mathbf{TY} \in \mathbf{ty'}_j \Rightarrow discriminate_k(\mathbf{HX},\mathbf{TX},Y) \quad (c-w<k \le c)\ (j \in \mathcal{L}_k)$$

in order to prove that $exp(LA_7(r))$ is a better partially correct approximation of $\mathcal{R}$ than $exp(LA_6(r))$. This follows from the correctness of the Proofs-as-Programs Method (see Theorem 9-2). ❑

This correctness theorem is only applicable to the results obtained *before* application of the generalization heuristics.

13.3.4 Illustration

Let's illustrate Step 7 on the *firstPlateau*/3 and *compress*/2 problems.

Example 13-10: For the *firstPlateau*/3 problem, Step 7 proceeds as in Example 9-5. There are no property-examples, so Heuristic 13-6 only provides the properties of *EP*(*firstPlateau*) as a property-set to the Proofs-as-Programs Method. The applied generalization heuristics are Heuristic 13-3, Heuristic 13-4, and Heuristic 13-5, respectively. Logic Algorithm 13-5 shows $LA_7(firstPlateau)$, whereas Logic Algorithm 13-6 shows $exp(LA_7(firstPlateau))$.

Example 13-11: For the *compress*/2 problem, Step 7 proceeds as in Example 9-4. There is one property-example, namely E_1, so Heuristic 13-6 provides E_1 and the properties of *EP*(*compress*) as a property-set to the Proofs-as-Programs Method. The applied generalization heuristics are Heuristic 13-3, Heuristic 13-4, and Heuristic 13-5, respectively. The resulting logic algorithm and its expansion are shown in Example 11-1.

```
firstPlateau(L,P,S) ⇔
      L=[_]              ∧ P=L ∧ S=[] ∧ L=[_] ∧ L=[_]
   ∨ L=[_,_|_]           ∧ L=[HL|TL]
                         ∧ TL=[HTL|_] ∧ HL≠HTL
                         ∧ P=[HL] ∧ S=TL ∧ TL=[_|_]
   ∨ L=[_,_|_]           ∧ L=[HL|TL]
                         ∧ TL=[HTL|_] ∧ HL=HTL
                         ∧ firstPlateau(TL,TP,TS)
                         ∧ P=[HL|TP] ∧ S=TS ∧ TP=[HL|_]
```

Logic Algorithm 13-5: *LA*$_7$(*firstPlateau*)

```
firstPlateau(L,P,S) ⇔
      L=[_]              ∧ P=L ∧ S=[] ∧ L=[_] ∧ L=[_]
                         ∧       L=[a] ∧ P=[a] ∧ S=[]             {E1}
   ∨ L=[_,_|_]           ∧ L=[HL|TL]
                         ∧ TL=[HTL|_] ∧ HL≠HTL
                         ∧ P=[HL] ∧ S=TL ∧ TL=[_|_]
                         ∧       L=[c,d] ∧ P=[c] ∧ S=[d]
                               ∧ HL=c ∧ TL=[d]                   {E3}
                            ∨    L=[e,f,g] ∧ P=[e] ∧ S=[f,g]
                               ∧ HL=e ∧ TL=[f,g]                 {E4}
                            ∨    L=[h,i,i] ∧ P=[h] ∧ S=[i,i]
                               ∧ HL=h ∧ TL=[i,i]                 {E5}
   ∨ L=[_,_|_]           ∧ L=[HL|TL]
                         ∧ TL=[HTL|_] ∧ HL=HTL
                         ∧ firstPlateau(TL,TP,TS)
                         ∧ P=[HL|TP] ∧ S=TS ∧ TP=[HL|_]
                         ∧       L=[b,b] ∧ P=[b,b] ∧ S=[]
                               ∧ HL=b ∧ TL=[b]
                               ∧ TP=[b] ∧ TS=[]                  {E2}
                            ∨    L=[j,j,k] ∧ P=[j,j] ∧ S=[k]
                               ∧ HL=j ∧ TL=[j,k]
                               ∧ TP=[j] ∧ TS=[k]                 {E6}
                            ∨    L=[m,m,m] ∧ P=[m,m,m] ∧ S=[]
                               ∧ HL=m ∧ TL=[m,m]
                               ∧ TP=[m,m] ∧ TS=[]                {E7}
```

Logic Algorithm 13-6: *exp*(*LA*$_7$(*firstPlateau*))

14 CONCLUSION

In this chapter, we draw some conclusions about the synthesis mechanism presented in the previous two chapters. First, in Section 14.1, we evaluate its current form wrt the objectives. Then, in Section 14.2, we imagine some extensions and list some future work. In Section 14.3, we outline a methodology for choosing "good" examples and properties. A prototype implementation of the synthesis mechanism is being developed: it is called SYNAPSE (*SYNthesis of logic Algorithms from PropertieS and Examples*), and is written in portable Prolog. We discuss its architecture and illustrate its working on some target synthesis scenarios in Section 14.4. Finally, in Section 14.5, we evaluate our synthesis mechanism wrt to some related mechanisms.

14.1 Summary

We have described a logic algorithm synthesis mechanism that is stepwise, guided by a divide-and-conquer schema, non-incremental, monotonically decreasing *and* increasing, as well as consistent. We conjecture that a logic algorithm synthesized at Step 7 is totally correct wrt the intended relation $\mathcal{R}$. Reliability can however not be guaranteed. Moreover, the synthesis mechanism is highly algorithmic and potentially interactive. We have no theoretical results about its power or data-efficiency.

Domain generality and full automation have been sacrificed for the sake of better end-user orientation, and because this is a most reasonable approach with incomplete specifications, where one deliberately admits a gap between the specified relation and the intended relation. Incorporated knowledge sources are the algorithm design knowledge of the divide-and-conquer schema, and the domain knowledge of the typed databases. There is no meta-knowledge and no efficiency knowledge. Whole algorithm families can be synthesized from a single specification, because some synthesis steps are non-deterministic.

Table 14-1 charts a summary of the seven synthesis steps and of their tasks. The columns list (from left to right):

- the name(s) of the instantiated (predicate) variable(s) of version 3 of the divide-and-conquer schema;
- the used method(s) of the tool-box (where *DB* stands for Database Method, MSG_g for the ground case of the MSG Method, MSG_{ng} for the non-ground case of the MSG Method, and *PaP* for the Proofs-as-Programs Method);
- the determinism (minimal and maximal number of possible different answers) of the method underlying each step or task, without the usage of any heuristics; where applicable, a footnote explains under which condition there are no answers, or in what way the heuristics may alter this determinism;
- the time-complexity of the method underlying each step or task, again without the usage of any heuristics;
- the page where the method underlying each step or task is explained.

Empty cells denote non-applicability of a criterion wrt a step or task.

This table shows that all the (predicate) variables of version 3 of the divide-and-conquer schema are instantiated by the synthesis mechanism, using all the methods of the tool-box developed in Part II to do so. Overall, synthesis may fail (for a variety of individual reasons), but it may on the other hand succeed an infinite number of times, yielding as many logic algorithms. The overall mechanism is NP-complete. This is however not dramatic as the number m of examples is usually quite small.

Table 14-1: Summary of the synthesis steps and tasks

		Variable(s)	Method	Answers	Complexity[a]	Page
Step 1				$1-1$	$O(m)$	160
Step 2	Task A			$0-n$ [b]	$O(n)$	162
	Task B			$1-1$	$O(m\ log_2 m)$	162
	Task C			$1-m$	$O(m)$	163
	Task D	*Minimal*, *NonMinimal*	DB	$1-*$	$O(1)$	163
Step 3	Task E			$1-*$	$O(1)$	167
	Task F	*Decompose*	DB	$1-*$	$O(1)$	168
Step 4	Task G			$1-1$	$O(t\ (m+p))$	172
	Task H			$1-1$	$O(m)$	172
	Task I			$1-1$	$O(m)$	172
	Task J			$1-1$	$O(1)$	172
Step 5	Task K Task O			$1-1$ $1-1$	$O(m)$ $O(m)$	176 176
	Task L Task P			$1-1$ $1-1$	$O(m)$ $O(m)$	176 176
	Task M Task Q		MSG_g MSG_g	$1-*$ [c] $1-*$ [d]	NP NP	176 177
	Task N Task R	*Solve*, v, $SolveNonMin_k$		$1-1$ $1-1$	$O(1)$ $O(1)$	176 177
Step 6	Task S			$1-1$	$O(m)$	182
	Task T		MSG_{ng}	$1-\infty$ [e]	NP	182
	Task U	w, c, $Process_k$, $Compose_k$		$1-1$	$O(1)$	182
Step 7		$Discriminate_k$	PaP	$0-1$ [f]	$O(cp^{t+1})$	186
Steps 1 to 7		All variables	Tool-box	$0-\infty$	NP	

a. Where m is the number of examples, p the number of properties, n the arity of r, t the number of recursive atoms, and c the number of non-minimal cases. NP denotes NP-completeness.
b. No answers if there is no parameter of an inductive type.
c. No answers if some heuristic rejects all the results of the MSG Method.
d. No answers if some heuristic rejects all the results of the MSG Method.
e. No answers if Heuristic 13-2 rejects all the results of the MSG Method.
f. No answers if $LA_6(r)$ is not complete wrt $\mathcal{P}(r)$.

Table 14-2 charts a summary of the features of the logic algorithms synthesized at step i. The columns list (from left to right):

- the determinism of the added atoms, given a ground value of the induction parameter, the other parameters being variables;
- the determinism of the synthesized logic algorithm $LA_i(r)$, given a ground value of the induction parameter;
- the characterization of $LA_i(r)$ in terms of correctness and progression; where applicable, a footnote explains under which condition this behavior is achieved;
- the usage (denoted *yes*) or non-usage (denoted *no*) of the property set $\mathcal{P}(r)$;
- the number of cases of $LA_i(r)$, represented as a sum $u+v+w$, where u is the number of minimal cases, v the number of non-recursive cases, and w the number of recursive cases.

This table shows that the instances of the predicate-variables may be defined by algorithms of any kind of determinism. The synthesized logic algorithms $LA_i(r)$ evolve from full determinism ($i = 1$) to determinism ($i = 2...4$) to potential non-determinism ($i = 5...7$), but are always terminating. The logic algorithms $exp(LA_i(r))$ exhibit a non-strict upward progression, starting from a logic algorithm that is totally correct wrt the example set. On the other hand, the logic algorithms $LA_i(r)$ exhibit a possibly strict downward progression, starting from the top logic algorithm. The property set is used by Step 4 (Syntactic introduction of the recursive atoms) and Step 7 (Synthesis of the discriminants). The number of cases of the $LA_i(r)$ evolves from one ($i = 1$) to two ($i = 2...3$) to three ($i = 3...4$) to a sum $1+v+w$ ($i = 5...7$), where v, w are integers. Of course, if it turns out that $w = 0$, then this synthesis mechanism is inadequate.

Table 14-2: Summary of the features of the synthesized logic algorithms

	New atoms	$LA_i(r)$	Correctness and Progression	$\mathcal{P}(r)$	Cases
Step 1	N/A	N/A	$\mathcal{E} \cong exp(LA_1) \leq \mathcal{R} \leq LA_1 = \top$ [a]	no	1
Step 2	$0-1$ $0-1$	$0-1$	$exp(LA_1) \cong exp(LA_2) \leq \mathcal{R} \leq LA_2 \leq LA_1$ [b]	no no	1+1
Step 3	$0-1$	$0-1$	$exp(LA_2) \cong exp(LA_3) \leq \mathcal{R} \leq LA_3 \leq LA_2$	no	1+1
Step 4	N/A	$0-1$	$exp(LA_3) \cong exp(LA_4) \leq \mathcal{R} \leq LA_4 \cong LA_3$ [c]	yes	1+1+1
Step 5	$0-*$ $0-*$	$0-*$	$exp(LA_4) \cong exp(LA_5) \leq \mathcal{R} \leq LA_5 \leq LA_4$	no no	1+1+1 $1+v+1$
Step 6	$0-*$	$0-*$	$exp(LA_5) \cong exp(LA_6) \leq \mathcal{R} \leq LA_6 \leq LA_5$	no	$1+v+w$
Step 7	? – ?	$0-*$	$exp(LA_6) \cong exp(LA_7) \leq \mathcal{R} \leq LA_7 \leq LA_6$	yes	$1+v+w$
Steps 1 to 7	N/A	$0-*$	conjecture: $\mathcal{R} \cong LA = LA_7$	yes	$1+v+w$

a. Under the consistency assumption.
b. If the domain extrapolation hypothesis is correct.
c. If a sound oracle $O(r)$ is used.

We are now in position to analyze which of the challenges of Section 5.3 have been met, and to state how they have been met, respectively why they have not been met:

- *What induction parameter to select?* Task A of Step 2 (Synthesis of *Minimal* and *NonMinimal*) does this non-deterministically by considering all parameters that are of an inductive type, and possibly by using some selection heuristics, or by listening to the specifier's preference hints.
- *How to discover compound induction parameters?* Due to our restriction to version 3 of the divide-and-conquer schema, Task A only considers simple induction parameters. Meeting this challenge is thus considered future research.
- *According to what well-founded relation to decompose the induction parameter?* Step 3 (Synthesis of *Decompose*) does this non-deterministically by considering all predefined decomposition operators (which each reflect some well-founded relation) of a typed database, and possibly by listening to the specifier's hints.
- *Is the mechanism able to design the whole family of possible logic algorithms for a given problem?* This ability is in theory achieved for the family of algorithms that are covered by version 3 of the divide-and-conquer schema. In practice, everything depends on the completeness of the databases used by Steps 2 and 3.
- *How many structural forms are there?* Due to our restriction to version 3 of the divide-and-conquer schema, Task C of Step 2 only considers the distinction between two structural forms, namely one minimal form and one non-minimal form. A generalization of this task is considered future research.
- *What are the structural forms?* Task D of Step 2 non-deterministically selects some domain extrapolation hypothesis and extracts the corresponding predefined forms from a typed database.
- *Into how many sub-cases is each structural case divided?* The progressive discovery of this number is summarized in the last column of Table 14-2.
- *How to discriminate between these sub-cases?* Step 7 (Synthesis of the *Discriminate*$_k$) achieves this by using the PaP Method.
- *How to detect that recursion is useless in some non-minimal sub-cases?* Step 4 (Syntactic introduction of the recursive atoms) creates a non-recursive case if at least one example E_j leads to a non-admissible *procComp*(<$\boldsymbol{hx}_j$>,<$\boldsymbol{ty}_j$>,y_j) atom.
- *How to "invent" or re-use appropriate predicates? How to implement "invented" predicates?* The predicate invention problem is tackled at four points during the synthesis. At Steps 2 and 3, the Database Method re-uses predefined predicates: this amounts to using domain knowledge. At Step 6, the Synthesis Method (see Section 14.2.4 below) invents new composition operators. As of now, there is no method yet of re-using common composition operators. At Step 7, the PaP Method synthesizes discriminants that are in terms of predicates other than *r*/*n*.
- *How to discover which parameters are auxiliary parameters?* Due to our restriction to version 3 of the divide-and-conquer schema, auxiliary parameters are not taken into account. See Section 14.2.2 below on how to achieve this.
- *How to synthesize logic algorithms that are non-deterministic?* Task G of Step 4 is the first—and only—to discover whether the intended relation is non-deterministic given a ground value of the induction parameter and given variables for the other parameters, because the *exp*/3 operator discovers sets of potential values of $\boldsymbol{TY}$ in some non-minimal cases of *exp*($LA_4(r)$). But, in Table 14-2, we observe that $LA_4(r)$ is at best deterministic, and that it is Step 5 that produces the first possibly non-deterministic logic algorithm. Indeed, given a ground value of the induction

parameter, a logic algorithm can only be non-deterministic if it actually unifies Y with some values in several non-mutually-exclusive cases. This is clearly not the case with $LA_4(r)$, where only the induction parameter X is unified with some values. But such is the case with $LA_5(r)$, where the instances of the $SolveNonMin_k$ necessarily do unify Y with some values, and this possibly non-deterministically (because of the MSG Method). Note that the disjunction between the minimal case and the non-recursive case is not an additional source of non-determinism of $LA_5(r)$, because these cases are known to be mutually exclusive (because of Step 2). The non-determinism due to the instances of the $SolveNonMin_k$ might even disappear at Step 7 (Synthesis of the $Discriminate_k$), namely if the added discriminants render these sub-cases mutually exclusive. Step 6 acts in the same way as Step 5: the instances of the $ProcComp_k$ necessarily do unify Y with some values, and this possibly non-deterministically (because of the MSG Method). And the non-determinism due to the instances of the $ProcComp_k$ might also disappear at Step 7, namely if the added discriminants render these sub-cases mutually exclusive. This shows that the discovery of non-determinism and its "synthesis" take place at different moments. They are even totally unrelated events.

- *How to achieve a synthesis that yields logic algorithms that are correct wrt their intentions?* This is impossible to guarantee with specifications by examples and properties. However, the stepwise synthesis framework of Section 7.3.2 and the correctness theorems of the seven synthesis steps clearly identify the critical points, where interaction with the specifier should thus take place.

We also analyze how some of the desired features enumerated in Section 11.1 have been achieved (note that most of them were decisions rather than open questions):

- The *degree of automation* depends on the actual implementation of the synthesis mechanism. Indeed, as it stands, the mechanism is fully automatable. However, there are critical points where interaction with the specifier is safer than blind application of the listed heuristics, however reliable they may seem. The synthesis mechanism is example-driven, and uses the properties at selected moments. This implies that synthesis cannot be done from properties alone. On the other hand, if only examples are provided, or if "not enough" properties are provided, then there should be a lot of interaction with the specifier.
- The *kinds of inference* used during synthesis are inductive inference from the examples (due to the MSG Method), and deductive inference from the properties (due to the PaP Method). The synthesis mechanism is a hybrid of transformational synthesis (due to its stepwise approach), proofs-as-programs synthesis (due to the way discriminants are synthesized), knowledge-based synthesis (due to the divide-and-conquer schema and the databases), bottom-up approximation-driven empirical learning (due to the incomplete properties), and the recurrence relation detection mechanism. But it is not really comparable to the other approaches surveyed in Chapter 3, namely the function merging mechanism (due to the multiple examples) and Shapiro's debugging mechanism (due to the non-incremental approach and the absence of negative examples). The mechanism seems very robust to example ordering (due to its non-incrementality) and example choice.

Note that the expansion phase of synthesis may be likened to *trace generation*, while the reduction phase of synthesis may be likened to *trace generalization*.

14.2 Extensions

Let's now discuss some extensions to the existing synthesis mechanism. First, in Section 14.2.1, we present the problems posed by the introduction of negation in examples, properties, and logic algorithms. In Section 14.2.2, we show how the mechanism can be enhanced to better cope with auxiliary parameters. We then see how the preliminary restrictions of Section 11.2 can be overcome:

- the support of schemas other than version 3 of the divide-and-conquer schema is discussed in Section 14.2.3;
- the synthesis of multiple-loop logic algorithms is discussed in Section 14.2.4, where we describe the Synthesis Method as a complement to the MSG Method;
- the support of inductively defined data-types other than integers and lists is extremely modular: just extend the typed databases with the appropriate instances.

In [Flener 93], we generalize the computational contents of properties, and examine what would be needed to support this. The Future Work sections of the Building Block chapters of Part II constitute other directions for future research.

14.2.1 Negation

In Section 11.1, we have constrained the bodies of logic algorithms and properties to be free of negation, namely because the Proofs-as-Programs Method (which is used by Step 7 of the synthesis mechanism) cannot handle negation. As outlined in Section 9.5, this method could be extended to handle negated atoms that have primitive predicates, which would thus overcome the overall restriction.

Note however that negation is theoretically useless: Horn clause logic is a universal computing formalism (see [Hogger 84] or [Lloyd 87] for accounts of this result). Negation thus doesn't increase the expressive power of Horn clause logic. In practice, however, logic statements are often significantly simplified by the use of negation.

Negative examples (also called *counter-examples*) have been omitted from the specification format adopted in Section 11.1. We are now able to provide the motivation for this decision. Counter-examples are useless in a divide-and-conquer approach, because the relation is "built" from positive examples. And only positive examples can be used in order to "explain" how a specific positive example is "built". Counter-examples could however be used to check whether the synthesized logic algorithm isn't too general compared to the intended relation. This is subject to future research.

Note that if properties could also be equivalence statements rather than only definite clauses, then properties would actually be a generalization of negative examples, because they would then embody conditions about when the intended relation does *not* hold. Most properties are actually equivalence statements. For instance, all properties in the sample specifications of Section 6.2, except for the "informative" property P_2 of *EP*(*efface*), would also be correct if they were equivalences. The current version of the synthesis mechanism would only use the *if* parts of such extended properties in Step 7 for the synthesis of the discriminants. But an extended version performing the above-mentioned over-generalization-check could use the *only-if* parts to infer negative examples, rather than relying on their explicit presence in the specification.

14.2.2 Auxiliary Parameters

Throughout this book, the phrase "auxiliary parameter" keeps popping up. Intuitively, an *auxiliary parameter* is a parameter that has nothing to do with the "inductive nature" of the relation. Note that a parameter is auxiliary for a relation, and hence for all possible logic algorithms for that relation. Logic algorithm synthesis by induction on an auxiliary parameter is obviously a bad idea.

So far, we have completely ignored auxiliary parameters. This is justifiable by the observation that their identification is not necessary at all for correct algorithm design. Indeed, as the logic algorithms of Section 5.2 show, it *is* possible to write algorithms that don't distinguish between auxiliary parameters and "ordinary" parameters. However, the (de)composition of an auxiliary parameter from (into) its heads and tails may look cumbersome because an auxiliary parameter Y and its tail TY are eventually found (at Step 6) to be identical: $Y = TY$. But it is precisely this composition pattern that allows the detection of auxiliary parameters, and their elimination from the decomposition machinery, thus transforming the logic algorithm into a more "graceful" and "natural" version. We call this *late detection*, because it only allows the transformation of the synthesized logic algorithm, rather than a simplification of its actual synthesis process. The appearance of $Y = TY$ in all recursive cases of a logic algorithm is assumed to be the formal definition of the notion of auxiliary parameter.

We should however not forget that just a casual glance at a specification will not always tell whether a parameter is an "ordinary" or an auxiliary one. Things are even more difficult with automated algorithm design, and the surest way is indeed to ignore the potential existence of auxiliary parameters until a transformation phase. But suppose now that knowledge about which parameters are auxiliary parameters *is* available *earlier* during the algorithm synthesis process. It would certainly be helpful to precompile the then-needed transformations into a schema with an explicit consideration of auxiliary parameters. The benefit would be less complex general example sets for the synthesis of the $Process_k$ and $Compose_k$, and hence smaller search spaces. The modified version 4 of the divide-and-conquer schema is:

```
R(X,Y,Z) ⇔
              Minimal(X)     ∧ Solve(X,Y,Z)
   ∨ ∨1≤k≤c   NonMinimal(X)  ∧ Decompose(X,HX,TX)
                             ∧ Discriminate_k(HX,TX,Z)
                             ∧ (    SolveNonMin_k(HX,TX,Y,Z)
                                  |
                                      R(TX,TY,Z)
                                    ∧ Process_k(HX,HY)
                                    ∧ Compose_k(HY,TY,Y,Z)      )
```

where Z is the vector of auxiliary parameters. Note how Y has disappeared from the discriminants: this knowledge is encoded as Heuristic 13-4 at Step 7 (Synthesis of the $Discriminate_k$). This revised schema also calls for a revised admissibility criterion.

Now, how could knowledge about which parameters are auxiliary parameters be available *earlier* during the algorithm synthesis? There are basically two solutions:

- *declaration*: the specifier could declare them as such at specification time;

- *early detection*: at Step 4 (Syntactic introduction of the recursive atoms), a parameter that is not of an inductive type must be auxiliary; this heuristic is sound, but not complete. Other (possibly interactive) heuristics could be elaborated.

These solutions allow faster synthesis and more "natural" synthesized algorithms.

14.2.3 Supporting Other Schemata

The presented synthesis mechanism is guided by version 3 of the divide-and-conquer logic algorithm schema. This preliminary restriction (made in Section 11.2) has considerably simplified the notations needed for the theoretical presentation. The support of version 4 (relations of any non-zero arity) is actually a pretty straightforward extension, because only some additional vectorization is needed. Version 4 is actually supported by the implementation of the synthesis mechanism.

The support of any number of minimal or non-minimal forms and of compound induction parameters is considered future research, as considerable extensions to the already defined tasks need to be developed. Note however that Section 5.2.2 shows that single minimal forms and non-minimal forms are more frequent than one might believe at first sight. As outlined in Section 8.4, there is still a lot of space for designing even more sophisticated divide-and-conquer schemas.

However, version 3 of the divide-and-conquer schema is hardwired into our synthesis mechanism. This results from a hardwired sequence of instantiations of predicate-variables of that schema, as well as from a hardwired mapping between these predicate-variables and the methods of the developed tool-box. Parameterizing the synthesis mechanism on algorithm schemas and tool-boxes would thus be a first step towards supporting schemas reflecting design strategies other than divide-and-conquer.

In other words, a Step 0 would be to select an appropriate schema, and the subsequent steps would be either a hardwired sequence (specific to the selected schema) of applications of methods, or a user-guided selection of variables and methods. Our grand view of algorithm synthesis systems thus is one of a large workbench with a disparate tool-box of highly specialized methods for a set of schemas that covers (as much as possible of) the space of all possible algorithms.

In defense of our hardwiring the divide-and-conquer schema, we should however make the following two remarks. First, the hardwired sequence of predicate-variable instantiations is justifiable by our arguing (see Section 11.3 and Section 12.3.2) that this sequence is probably the only one in the context of logic programming. Second, the hardwired mapping between the predicate-variables and the methods of the tool-box is justifiable by pure common sense.

14.2.4 The Synthesis Method

Within a restricted setting, the MSG Method (see Chapter 10) infers, from a finite set of general examples, a non-recursive logic algorithm defined in terms of the =/2 primitive only, and that is correct wrt a natural extension of the given examples. But if the resulting logic algorithm is judged, by some application-specific heuristic (such as Heuristic 13-2), to be "not good enough", then the assumption that the examples can be covered by such a logic algorithm must be revised: recursion, or other predicates, or both, might be needed. This requires a more sophisticated method.

A possible solution is to automatically infer a property set of the intended relation and then to use an entire synthesis mechanism (such as the one described in the two previous chapters) in order to infer a logic algorithm that is complete wrt the given examples and inferred properties. We here describe such a method, called the *Synthesis Method*, which is specific to the synthesis of the $Process_k$ and $Compose_k$ predicate-variables of the divide-and-conquer schema.

The Synthesis Method assumes that there is a single sub-case of the recursive case ($w=1$), and that $procComp_1(\boldsymbol{HX},\boldsymbol{TY},Y)$, which is hereafter denoted $procComp(\boldsymbol{HX},\boldsymbol{TY},Y)$, is defined by a full-fledged recursive logic algorithm. The synthesis of $LA(procComp)$ may thus be achieved by the following sequence of tasks:

- Task S': Inference of $\mathcal{E}(procComp)$ from $LA_5(r)$ and $EP(r)$;
- Task T': Inference of $\mathcal{P}(procComp)$ from $LA_5(r)$ and $EP(r)$;
- Task U': Synthesis of $LA(procComp)$ from $EP(procComp)$.

Let's explain these tasks one by one, then illustrate them on two sample problems, and finally assess this new method.

Task S': Inference of an Example Set

The inference of an example set would be identical to the method of Task S of Step 6 (Synthesis of the $Process_k$ and $Compose_k$) if the synthesis mechanism were able to handle general examples. Such is however not the case. But we can exploit the fact that the Synthesis Method is only invoked upon "dislike" of the result produced by the MSG Method. Indeed, remember that the non-ground case of the MSG Method proceeds by invoking its other case for every atom set of $adm(\mathcal{G}(procComp))$, and then selecting a "best" solution. So if the logic algorithm resulting from the MSG Method is judged to be "not good enough", then it would be most reasonable to give the corresponding atom-set a "second chance" (provided it is an example-set), rather than to take any other atom-set that corresponds necessarily to a "less good" solution of the MSG Method. Let $\mathcal{E}(procComp)$ be the chosen set.

Task T': Inference of a Property Set

The inference of a property set is based on the observation that the properties of the original predicate are "inherited" by the properties of the *procComp*/3 predicate. This can be formalized as follows.

For every property:

$$r(s_i,t_i) \Leftarrow B_i \qquad (1)$$

such that:

$$nonMinimal(s_i) \qquad (2)$$

$$decompose(s_i,\boldsymbol{hs}_i,\boldsymbol{ts}_i) \qquad (3)$$

where *nonMinimal*/1 is the instance of *NonMinimal*/1 selected at Step 2, and *decompose* is the deterministic instance of *Decompose* selected at Step 3, find variants of examples or body-less properties:

$$r(ts_{ij},tt_{ij}) \qquad (4)$$

and infer the following property of *procComp*:

$$procComp(\boldsymbol{hs}_i,\boldsymbol{tt}_i,t_i) \Leftarrow B_i \qquad (5)$$

This can be justified as follows. By unfolding the head of (1) according to the necessarily unique recursive disjunct of $LA_6(r)$, as it will be, we obtain:

$$nonMinimal(s_i) \wedge decompose(s_i,\mathbf{HS},\mathbf{TS}) \wedge \mathbf{r(TS,TT)} \wedge procComp(\mathbf{HS},\mathbf{TT},t_i) \Leftarrow B_i$$

By (2), (3), and the determinism of *decompose*, this simplifies into:

$$\mathbf{r(ts_i,TT)} \wedge procComp(\mathbf{hs_i},\mathbf{tt_i},t_i) \Leftarrow B_i$$

By (4), this effectively reduces to (5).

Moreover, the resulting properties can often be generalized, for instance by replacing base-case constants by variables. Such a generalization process should be interactive, and should yield new properties that are consistent with the examples.

Task U': Synthesis of LA(procComp)

A logic algorithm *LA*(*procComp*) can now be synthesized from the inferred specification by examples and properties. We use the synthesis mechanism described in the two previous chapters for this. The predicate *procComp* is assumed to be a new primitive.

This completes Step 6, and the synthesis of *LA*(*r*) proceeds to Step 7, where a *true* discriminant is synthesized because the information of the properties of *r*/*n* is "inherited" by the properties of *procComp*, and is thus already accounted for.

Illustration

Let's illustrate the described method on two sample problems.

Example 14-1: The synthesis of *LA*(*permutation-int-L*) leads to the rejection of the first *LA*(*pcPermutation*) that is synthesized by the MSG Method. This was shown in Example 13-4. The Synthesis Method is thus invoked. The specification *EP*(*permutation*) is as in Example 6-4. The logic algorithm LA_6(*permutation*) will be:

```
permutation(L,P) ⇔
        L=[]      ∧ P=[]                                  {E1}
    ∨   L=[_|_] ∧ L=[HL|TL]
                  ∧ permutation(TL,TP)
                  ∧ pcPermutation(HL,TP,P)              {E2-E10}
```

At Task S', the inferred example set is the one corresponding to that first solution of the MSG Method, namely:

```
ℰ(pcPermutation)={pcPermutation(a,[],[a])              (F2)
                  pcPermutation(b,[c],[b,c])           (F3)
                  pcPermutation(b,[c],[c,b])           (F4)
                  pcPermutation(d,[e,f],[d,e,f])       (F5)
                  pcPermutation(d,[f,e],[d,f,e])       (F6)
                  pcPermutation(d,[e,f],[e,d,f])       (F7)
                  pcPermutation(d,[e,f],[e,f,d])       (F8)
                  pcPermutation(d,[f,e],[f,d,e])       (F9)
                  pcPermutation(d,[f,e],[f,e,d]) }     (F10)
```

where example F_i corresponds to example E_i. Note that F_5 and F_6 are "variants". The same holds for F_7 and F_9, and for F_8 and F_{10}. But we cannot eliminate "variants" because we cannot know that *pcPermutation*/3 effectively is a structural-manipulation problem.

At Task T', the inference of a property set goes as follows:

- from property P_1 of $\mathcal{P}(permutation)$:

  $$permutation([X],[X])$$

  infer property Q_1 of $\mathcal{P}(pcPermutation)$:

  $$pcPermutation(X,[],[X])$$

  because example E_1 of $\mathcal{E}(permutation)$ shows that a permutation of [] is [];
- similarly, from property P_2 of $\mathcal{P}(permutation)$:

  $$permutation([X,Y],[X,Y])$$

  infer property Q_2 of $\mathcal{P}(pcPermutation)$:

  $$pcPermutation(X,[Y],[X,Y])$$

  because property P_1 of $\mathcal{P}(permutation)$ shows that a permutation of $[Y]$ is $[Y]$;
- finally, from property P_3 of $\mathcal{P}(permutation)$:

  $$permutation([X,Y],[Y,X])$$

  infer property Q_3 of $\mathcal{P}(pcPermutation)$:

  $$pcPermutation(X,[Y],[Y,X])$$

  because property P_1 of $\mathcal{P}(permutation)$ shows that a permutation of $[Y]$ is $[Y]$.

All three properties could be generalized by replacing all occurrences of the constant *nil* by the same new variable, but this isn't even necessary here.

At Task U', the entire synthesis mechanism is used to synthesize *LA*(*pcPermutation*) from *EP*(*pcPermutation*) as generated by the two previous tasks. Supposing an induction on the second parameter and an intrinsic decomposition thereof, plus a detection that the first parameter necessarily is an auxiliary parameter, the result is:

```
pcPermutation(E,L,R) ⇔
      L=[]      ∧ E=_  ∧ R=[E]                                {F2}
    ∨ L=[_|_] ∧ L=[HL|TL]
                ∧ true
                ∧ E=_  ∧ R=[E|L]                        {F3,F5,F6}
    ∨ L=[_|_] ∧ L=[HL|TL]
                ∧ true
                ∧ pcPermutation(TE,TL,TR)
                ∧ E=TE ∧ R=[HL|TR]              {F4,F7,F8,F9,F10}
```

Note that *EP*(*pcPermutation*) and *LA*(*pcPermutation*) indicate that the underlying problem is the one described in the informal specification of *stuff*/3.

The synthesis of *LA*(*permutation*) proceeds to Step 7 (Synthesis of the *Discriminate*$_k$), where an $LA_7(permutation)$ is found that is equivalent to $LA_6(permutation)$. This resulting logic algorithm for *permutation*/2 is correct, but yields redundant solutions if some element has multiple occurrences in *L*. The usage of *efface*(*HL*,*P*,*TP*), as in *LA*(*permutation-L*) (LA 5-14), which is stronger than *stuff*(*HL*,*TP*,*P*), remedies to such a redundancy. This version may be obtained by our synthesis mechanism if the condition $X \neq Y$ is added to property P_3 of *EP*(*permutation*). ♦

Example 14-2: The synthesis of *LA(compress-int-C)* leads to the rejection of *LA(pcCompress)* as synthesized by the MSG Method. Indeed, the msgs are:

```
pcCompress(A,1,T,[A|T])
pcCompress(A,2,T,[A,A|T])
pcCompress(e,3,T,[e,e,e|T])
```

There are thus as many cliques as properties, and Heuristic 13-2 applies. The Synthesis Method is thus invoked. The specification *EP(compress)* is as in Example 6-1. The logic algorithm LA_6*(compress)* will be:

```
compress(L,C) ⇔
      C=[]          ∧ L=[]                                {E1}
    ∨ C=[_,_|_]     ∧ C=[HC1,HC2|TC]
                    ∧ compress(TL,TC)
                    ∧ pcCompress(HC1,HC2,TL,L)           {E2-E8}
```

where HC_1 is a value and HC_2 is a counter.

At Task S', the inferred example set is the one corresponding to the solution of the MSG Method, namely:

```
ℰ(pcCompress) = {pcCompress(a,1,[],[a])                  (F2)
                 pcCompress(b,2,[],[b,b])                (F3)
                 pcCompress(c,1,[d],[c,d])               (F4)
                 pcCompress(e,3,[],[e,e,e])              (F5)
                 pcCompress(f,2,[g],[f,f,g])             (F6)
                 pcCompress(h,1,[i,i],[h,i,i])           (F7)
                 pcCompress(j,1,[k,m],[j,k,m]) }         (F8)
```

where example F_i corresponds to example E_i.

At Task T', the inference of a property set yields:

```
𝒫(pcCompress) = {pcCompress(X,1,[],[X])                  (Q1)
                 pcCompress(X,2,[],[X,Y]) ⇐ X=Y          (Q2)
                 pcCompress(X,1,[Y],[X,Y]) ⇐ X≠Y }       (Q3)
```

where property Q_i results from property P_i. All properties could be generalized by replacing all occurrences of constant *nil* by a new variable, but this isn't even necessary.

At Task U', the entire synthesis mechanism is used to synthesize *LA(pcCompress)* from *EP(pcCompress)* as generated by the two previous tasks. Supposing an induction on the second parameter, and an intrinsic decomposition, the result is:

```
pcCompress(E,N,L,R) ⇔
      N=s(0)        ∧ E=_ ∧ L=_ ∧ R=[E|L]
                    ∧ (L=[]) ∨ (L=[HL|_]∧HL≠E) {F2,F4,F7,F8}
    ∨ N=s(s(_))     ∧ N=s(TN) ∧ HN=N
                    ∧ pcCompress(TE,TN,TL,TR)
                    ∧ E=TE ∧ L=TL
                           ∧ R=[E|TR] ∧ TR=[E|_]    {F3,F5,F6}
```

Note that *E* and *L* are auxiliary parameters. The synthesis of *LA(compress)* proceeds to Step 7 (Synthesis of the *Discriminate*$_k$), where an LA_7*(compress)* is found that is equivalent to LA_6*(compress)*. ♦

Assessment

The Synthesis Method allows us to overcome the preliminary restriction of Section 11.2 to the synthesis of single-loop logic algorithms only. Indeed, if the instance of *ProcComp* is defined by a full-fledged recursive logic algorithm, then *LA(r)* is a multiple-loop logic algorithm. The synthesis mechanism is thus recursively defined, and there should be no limit to the number of nested loops it could support.

But why not immediately use the Synthesis Method? The reason is that both methods tackle different classes of problems. The MSG Method and the Synthesis Method are a joint answer to the same overall problem: how to infer, from a finite set of general examples of an unknown relation that is however known to feature a given dataflow pattern between its parameters, a logic algorithm that is correct wrt a natural extension of the given examples. The MSG Method is the "base case" of the answer, because it does *not* look for recursion, and the Synthesis Method is the "structure case" of the answer, because it *does* look for recursion.

Note that the instances of *ProcComp* that are synthesized by the Synthesis Method are often one of the following:

- partially evaluated versions of logic algorithms that a human algorithm designer would have (re-)used; for instance, a version of *LA(append)* where the first parameter is always a non-empty list;
- (loop-)mergers of several logic algorithms that a human algorithm designer would have (re-)used; for instance, *LA(pcCompress)* above is the loop-merger of the conjunction used in *LA(compress-int-C)* (LA 5-2):

  $$plateau(N,E,HL) \wedge firstPlateau(L,HL,TL)$$

  which a human algorithm designer would probably even have generalized to:

  $$plateau(N,E,HL) \wedge append(HL,TL,L)$$

  by relaxing, if not "forgetting", the fact that *HL* must be a plateau;
- a combination of the above.

This clearly shows the impeccable precision of automated synthesis.

Other synthesis systems (such as *Cypress* [Smith 85]) are recursively defined, and hence infer their own specifications for appearing sub-problems.

The Synthesis Method is currently too closely entangled with the divide-and-conquer schema, with the synthesis mechanism described in the two previous chapters, and with the objective of Step 6 of that mechanism. In order to make it a full-fledged stand-alone method that can be added to a more general tool-box, some future research is needed to make it schema-independent. It might still rely on the MSG Method for the inference of an example set. But the inference of a property set could probably be made predicate-variable-independent and schema-independent by some theorem-proving task that exploits the integrity constraints of a schema.

Moreover, even the <MSG Method, Synthesis Method> couple isn't the complete answer to the synthesis of instances of the $ProcComp_k$ predicate-variables. Indeed, instances might be defined neither in terms of =/2 only (and hence the MSG Method is inappropriate), nor by recursion (and hence the Synthesis Method is inappropriate).

Example 14-3: A good illustration of this phenomenon is the *minimum(L,M)* problem, which may be defined by the following divide-and-conquer logic algorithm:

```
minimum(L,M) ⇔
      L=[_]            ∧ L=[E] ∧ M=E
   ∨  L=[_,_|_]        ∧ L=[HL|TL]
                       ∧ minimum(TL,TM)
                       ∧ pcMinimum(HL,TM,M)
```

where *pcMinimum*/3 is specified as follows:

pcMinimum(*A*,*B*,*M*) iff *M* is the minimum of *A* and *B*, where *A*, *B*, *M* are integers.

which is defined by the following logic algorithm:

```
pcMinimum(A,B,M) ⇔
      A≤B ∧ M=A
   ∨  A>B ∧ M=B
```

which is clearly not producible by the MSG Method nor by the Synthesis Method. ♦

This shows the need for even more methods to complement the existing ones. Good candidates would be a *Reuse Method* (looking for instances of atoms listed in a database of typical composition predicates), and an *Analogy Method* (looking for analogies between the examples in order to infer instances of the $ProcComp_k$). In the absence of "good" answers, the last straw is to ask the specifier.

14.3 A Methodology for Choosing "Good" Examples & Properties

In Section 6.2, we informally showed how to choose "good" properties, *given* a set of examples. The intuition was that such "good" properties are some form of disambiguating generalizations of the examples. More generally, an investigation of what constitutes a "good" example or a "good" property would lead to the formulation of a methodology for choosing such examples and properties. Following such a methodology should cut down on the time spent on elaborating specifications, possibly reduce to zero the amount of interaction between the specifier and the synthesis system, and diminish the synthesis time, as less examples and properties would have to be handled.

The formulation of such a methodology is of course influenced by the actual language for properties, and by the actual synthesis mechanism. We here stick to the corresponding decisions taken throughout Part III of this book: properties are here non-recursive definite clauses whose heads involve the specified predicate.

There naturally is a nice analogy between such a methodology for choosing examples and the techniques of black-box test-case selection that are used in software validation. For instance, [Goodenough and Gerhart 75] suggest partitioning the domain of an algorithm into a finite number of equivalence classes (that are identified by the characteristics of the parameters of the algorithm), such that the correct behavior of the algorithm on one *representative* of each class will, "by induction", test the entire class, and hence establish the correctness of the algorithm. A more powerful technique is to choose *boundary-case* test-cases of each equivalence class. For instance, rather than picking the empty list and any non-empty list as representatives of a parameter of type *list*, one should pick three lists, of lengths 0, 1, and >1, as its boundary-cases. But both techniques still suffer from the same drawback that they separately consider each characteristic of the parameters for the identification of the equivalence classes. So the idea is to consider all possible causality links between the characteristics of the parameters, and to actually construct a *decision table*, whose columns represent more meaningful equivalence classes, for which boundary-case test-data may then be picked.

The following is a first step towards a methodology for choosing examples and properties. It is not formalized, and is thus reduced to a mere collection of informal guidelines that have been discovered through experimentation with the synthesis mechanism, as well as through our understanding of that mechanism. The methodology assists the specifier in the choice of a minimal set of examples of the intended relation, and in the generalization of these examples into a minimal set of properties of the intended relation $\mathcal{R}$:

(1) Select some inductively defined parameter (let's call it X) among the parameters of predicate r/n. (Note that the synthesis mechanism need not necessarily select the same parameter as the induction parameter.)

(2) Choose examples for each legal size of X up to some size m. Whenever possible, use different constants across the various examples. Make sure that the possible non-determinism of $\mathcal{R}$ (given a ground value of X) is apparent in the examples. The value of m may be determined by co-routining with the next step, but making sure that examples are chosen at least for all boundary-cases.

(3) Generalize into properties, if possible, the examples where X is of a size equal to or less than some integer n, where n is the largest size where this leads to properties without recursion and without redundancy of information. Set m to $n + d$, where d is the decomposition decrement. The most useful generalization technique is the maximally repeated application of the replacing-a-constant-by-a-variable inductive inference rule to an example; this often requires a subsequent specialization by introduction of a body to the resulting unit clause.

This methodology abstracts away the internal apparatus of the synthesis mechanism, but algorithmic and mathematical concepts such as induction parameter, term size, decomposition decrement, and so on, are hard to avoid in its formulation.

Note the interesting role of constants in examples: constants almost act like variables. More precisely, *within* an example, the use of different constants at different positions should reflect non-unifiability of the variables into which these constants could be turned. And the use of the same constant at different positions should reflect unifiability, if not identity, of the variables into which these constants could be turned. However, *across* several examples, the use of different constants at the same positions should reflect their value-irrelevance, and hence unifiability of the variables into which these constants could be turned. But unifiability (if not identity) and non-unifiability are not all there is to say about the variables into which the constants could be turned, because otherwise properties would have no different semantics than the examples they generalize. Indeed, properties have more disambiguating expressive power, in the sense that predicates other than $=/2$ and $\neq/2$ may be used in their bodies.

The methodology for choosing properties, as outlined here and in Section 6.2, shows that it is difficult to find "good" properties without actually having to reject recursive ones. Although being able to craft such recursive properties probably amounts to being able to design the final algorithm, recursive properties should be allowed in specifications, especially as an extreme case of incomplete specifications is a complete specification. Fortunately, our synthesis mechanism *is* able to handle recursive properties: we have only rejected them so as to show that they are *not needed* for successful algorithm synthesis, thus picking up a tougher challenge.

Given our perspective on formal specifications, we would like to call the act of choosing examples and properties an act of *programming by examples and properties*.

14.4 The SYNAPSE System

A prototype implementation of our synthesis mechanism is being developed: it is called SYNAPSE (*SYNthesis of logic Algorithms from PropertieS and Examples*), and is written in portable Prolog. In Section 14.4.1, we discuss its architecture, whereas Section 14.4.2 depicts some target-scenarios of SYNAPSE at-work.

14.4.1 The Architecture of SYNAPSE

The architecture of SYNAPSE is very obvious from the technical details of the underlying synthesis mechanism (see Chapters 12 and 13): synthesis is achieved by a sequence of 7 non-deterministic procedures, each implementing one of the 7 synthesis steps. The implementation is actually based on version 4 of the divide-and-conquer schema, unlike the presentation in this book, which is restricted to version 3. This means that arbitrary n-ary predicates can be handled, rather than only binary ones.

The *input* to the synthesizer is a procedure declaration (consisting of the name of the specified predicate, and the names of the parameters), a set of examples, and a set of properties for that predicate. The theoretical aim of non-deterministically synthesizing all possible algorithms (by iterating over all possible induction parameters and decomposition predicates) is rather undesirable in practice, because the specifier might want to hint at personal preferences for these selections. Synthesis thus always stops at Step 2 (Synthesis of *Minimal* and *NonMinimal*) for letting the specifier select an induction parameter, its minimal form, and its non-minimal form. It also always stops at Step 3 (Synthesis of *Decompose*) for letting the specifier select a decomposition predicate. An entry of the corresponding database that hasn't been selected yet constitutes the default selection. For convenience, synthesis also always stops at Step 4 (Syntactic introduction of the recursive atoms), so that the specifier may declare which parameters are auxiliary parameters. A correct declaration indeed tremendously speeds up the computations at Step 6 (Synthesis of the $Process_k$ and the $Compose_k$). If the declaration is correct, but not complete (in the sense that some, if not all, auxiliary parameters are not declared as such), then synthesis proceeds correctly, but doesn't acquire the maximal possible speed-up. If the declaration is incorrect, then synthesis fails at some later step. The default is that only the parameters of non-inductively defined types are auxiliary parameters. All these optional specifier interactions may be cut off by switching from the default *manual mode* to the *automatic mode*.

The synthesis mechanism does not prescribe any mandatory dialogue with the specifier. But we concluded with the recommendation that any serious implementation of that mechanism should interact with the specifier whenever it applies one of the listed heuristics. The corresponding dialogues have however not yet been fully worked out (according to the guidelines of Section 11.1), and should be the object of future research for extending the current SYNAPSE prototype.

The *output* of the synthesizer is (besides the questions to the specifier) a possibly empty set of successfully designed logic algorithms. Indeed, the non-determinism of some synthesis steps makes the whole synthesis mechanism a non-deterministic mechanism. For debugging purposes, or for otherwise motivated inspections, SYNAPSE may even be switched to the *think-aloud mode*, where it prints out all the taken decisions, as well as all intermediate logic algorithms (of Steps 1 to 6). The default is the *quiet mode*. The printed-out logic algorithms are in canonical representation with respect to (version 4 of) the divide-and-conquer schema. Whereas the universal variables have the names given to them by the specifier in the procedure declaration (and are thus meaningful to the specifier), the existential variables have names invented by the synthesizer. However, the underlying divide-and-conquer strategy suggests a very useful *naming scheme* for these existential variables: the names of the heads (respectively, tails) of some parameter are prefixed by the letter "H" (respectively, "T"), and suffixed by a running number. The synthesized logic algorithms are thus actually in human-readable form, even though a machine-readable form would be sufficient in an ideal automatic programming setting where the output is only executed, but not inspected nor debugged. Logic algorithms are not executable, but they are easily derived into, say, Prolog programs, so that they may be executed and thus tested. However, the synthesized logic algorithms are subject to many transformation and optimization opportunities before they should undergo such an implementation step: SYNAPSE is but a component of the software engineering chain, and should thus not be seen as a stand-alone system.

14.4.2 Target Scenarios for SYNAPSE

We now list a few synthesis scenarios that SYNAPSE is targeted to reproduce. Pending the future extensions of the current prototype, these scenarios may not all already be obtained, but the synthesis mechanism is powerful enough to handle these problems. The used problems range from easy (*plateau*/3) to moderately difficult (*efface*/3) to intricate (*sort*/2). All the given syntheses are in *quiet* and *manual* mode.

Example 14-4: The synthesis dialogue for the *plateau*/3 problem proceeds as follows (the actual dialogue is printed in the `Courier` font: synthesizer output precedes colons, whereas user input follows colons; the default answers to questions are between curly braces; comments on the synthesis are printed in the Times font):

```
Procedure declaration: plateau(N,E,P)
Example:   plateau(1,a,[a])
Example:   plateau(2,b,[b,b])
Example:   plateau(3,c,[,c,c,c])
Example:
Property:  plateau(1,X,[X])
Property:  plateau(2,Y,[Y,Y])
Property:
```

This ends the specification acquisition. Synthesis now starts with the expansion phase (Steps 1 to 4) and asks for the specifier's preferences (because the *manual* mode is *on*):

```
Induction parameter {N}: N
Minimal {N=s(0)}: N=s(0)
```

```
NonMinimal {N=s(s(_))}: N=s(s(_))
Decompose {N=s(TN) ∧ HN=N}: N=s(TN) ∧ HN=N
List of auxiliary parameters {[E]}: [E]
```

The specifier accepts all the default selections. Synthesis now goes fully automatically through the reduction phase (Steps 5 to 7), and yields:

```
   LA(plateau) is
plateau(N,E,P) ⇔
      N=s(0)          ∧ E=_ ∧ P=[E]
   ∨  N=s(s(_))       ∧ N=s(TN) ∧ HN=N
                      ∧ true
                      ∧ plateau(TN,E,TP)
                      ∧ P=[E|TP] ∧ HN=s(s(_)) ∧ TP=[_|_]
```

This logic algorithm is totally correct wrt the intended relation. Quite a few atoms can be simplified away (the last two, for instance). ♦

Example 14-5: The synthesis dialogue for the *efface*/3 problem goes as follows:

```
Procedure declaration: efface(E,L,R)
Example:   efface(a,[a],[])
Example:   efface(b,[b,c],[c])
Example:   efface(e,[d,e],[d])
Example:   efface(f,[f,g,h],[g,h])
Example:   efface(j,[i,j,k],[i,k])
Example:   efface(p,[m,n,p],[m,n])
Example:
Property:  efface(X,[X],[])
Property:  efface(X,[X,Y],[Y])
Property:  efface(X,[Y,X],[Y]) ⇐ X≠Y
Property:
Induction parameter {L}: L
Minimal {L=[_]}: L=[_]
NonMinimal {L=[_,_|_]}: L=[_,_|_]
Decompose {L=[HL|TL]}: L=[HL|TL]
List of auxiliary parameters {[E]}: [E]
LA(efface) is
```

```
efface(E,L,R) ⇔
      L=[_]           ∧ L=[HL] ∧ HL=E ∧ R=[]
   ∨  L=[_,_|_]       ∧ L=[HL|TL]
                      ∧ HL=E
                      ∧ R=TL
   ∨  L=[_,_|_]       ∧ L=[HL|TL]
                      ∧ HL≠E
                      ∧ efface(E,TL,TR)
                      ∧ R=[HL|TR]
```

This logic algorithm is totally correct wrt the intended relation. The main obstacle is the detection that recursion is useless in the second disjunct. ♦

Example 14-6: The synthesis dialogue for the *sort*/2 problem proceeds as follows:

```
Procedure declaration: sort(L,S)
Example:   sort([],[])
Example:   sort([1],[1])
Example:   sort([2,3],[2,3])
Example:   sort([3,2],[2,3])
Example:   sort([4,5,6],[4,5,6])
Example:   sort([4,6,5],[4,5,6])
Example:   sort([5,4,6],[4,5,6])
Example:   sort([5,6,4],[4,5,6])
Example:   sort([6,4,5],[4,5,6])
Example:   sort([6,5,4],[4,5,6])
Example:
Property: sort([X],[X])
Property: sort([X,Y],[X,Y]) ⇐ X≤Y
Property: sort([X,Y],[Y,X]) ⇐ X>Y
Property:
Induction parameter {L}: L
Minimal {L=[]}: L=[]
NonMinimal {L=[_|_]}: L=[_|_]
Decompose {L=[HL|TL]}: L=[HL|TL]
List of auxiliary parameters {[]}: []
LA(sort) is

sort(L,S) ⇔
      L=[]     ∧ S=[]
   ∨  L=[_|_] ∧ L=[HL|TL]
               ∧ true
               ∧ sort(TL,TS)
               ∧ insert(HL,TS,S)

where

insert(E,L,R) ⇔
      L=[]     ∧ E=_ ∧ R=[E]
   ∨  L=[_|_] ∧ L=[HL|TL]
               ∧ HL≥E
               ∧ E=_ ∧ R=[E|L]
   ∨  L=[_|_] ∧ L=[HL|TL]
               ∧ HL<E
               ∧ insert(E,TL,TR)
               ∧ R=[HL|TR]
```

This is the so-called *Insertion-Sort* algorithm. It is non-trivial in the sense that a new predicate, here for convenience called *insert*/3, needs to be invented from scratch. Moreover, this sub-synthesis needs to be done in totally automatic mode, as the specifier is not supposed to be able to answer questions about such invented predicates.

Synthesis then backtracks to the last choice-point (at Step 3 in this case), in its search for alternative logic algorithms:

```
Backtracking...
Decompose {firstPlateau(L,HL,TL)}:
                    L=[HL|T] ∧ partition(T,HL,TL1,TL2)
List of auxiliary parameters {[]}: []
LA(sort) is

sort(L,S) ⇔
      L=[]     ∧ S=[]
   ∨ L=[_|_] ∧ L=[HL|T] ∧ partition(T,HL,TL1,TL2)
               ∧ true
               ∧ sort(TL1,TS1) ∧ sort(TL2,TS2)
               ∧ pcSort(HL,TS1,TS2,S)

where

pcSort(A,L1,L2,R) ⇔
      L1=[]            ∧ R=[A|L2]
   ∨ L1=[_|_]         ∧ L1=[HL1|TL1]
                       ∧ true
                       ∧ pcSort(A,TL1,TL2,TR)
                       ∧ L2=TL2 ∧ R=[HL1|TR]
```

This is the so-called *Quick-Sort* algorithm. It is non-trivial in the sense that a new predicate, called *pcSort*/3, needs to be invented from scratch. It is however obvious that:

```
pcSort(A,L1,L2,R) ⇔ append(L1, [A|L2],R)
```

Again, this sub-synthesis needs to be done in totally automatic mode. Hence, the fact that L_2 actually also is an auxiliary parameter of *pcSort*/3, just like *A*, cannot be declared, and is only detected as such *after* this sub-synthesis has been completed.

Synthesis then backtracks to the last choice-point (again at Step 3 in this case), in its search for alternative logic algorithms:

```
Backtracking...
Decompose {firstPlateau(L,HL,TL)}: split(L,TL1,TL2)
List of auxiliary parameters {[]}: []
LA(sort) is

sort(L,S) ⇔
      L=[]     ∧ S=[]
   ∨ L=[_|_] ∧ split(L,TL1,TL2)
               ∧ true
               ∧ sort(TL1,TS1) ∧ sort(TL2,TS2)
               ∧ merge(TS1,TS2,S)

where

merge(A,B,C) ⇔
      C=[]     ∧ A=[] ∧ B=[]
   ∨ C=[_|_] ∧ C=[HC|TC]
               ∧ (TC=[]) ∨ (TC=[HTC|_] ∧ HC≤HTC)
               ∧ merge(TA,TB,TC)
               ∧ A=TA ∧ B=[HC|TB]
```

```
∨ C=[_|_] ∧ C=[HC|TC]
            ∧ (TC=[]) ∨ (TC=[HTC|_] ∧ HC>HTC)
            ∧ merge(TA,TB,TC)
            ∧ A=[HC|TA] ∧ B=TB
```

This is the so-called *Merge-Sort* algorithm. It is non-trivial in the sense that a new predicate, here conveniently called *merge*/3, needs to be invented from scratch. ♦

14.5 Evaluation

Our synthesis mechanism builds upon a wide variety of ideas found in algorithm design, inductive inference, deductive inference, theorem proving, and so on. Thus, as the sections on related work have shown, specifications by examples and properties (see Chapter 6), the use of algorithm schemas (see Chapter 8), and the use of theorem proving and constructive logics for inferring preconditions (see Chapter 9) are not necessarily new ideas (to algorithm synthesis). But they are here combined in a novel way, and this together with some new results. The main contributions of this book are thus the formulation of a general framework for the stepwise synthesis of logic algorithms (see Chapter 7), the development of a new method for inferring (in a specific setting) non-recursive logic algorithms from examples (see Chapter 10), and the combination of all these ideas for the development of a schema-guided logic algorithm synthesis mechanism from examples and properties (see Chapter 12 and Chapter 13).

In Section 14.5.1, we provide a loose collection of insights into our synthesis mechanism, and in Section 14.5.2 we compare its performance to some related systems.

14.5.1 Insights

The planned use of our synthesis mechanism is for situations where only fragmentary information is available about the intended relation, or where the specifier is unwilling (if not unable) to come up with a more complete description of the intended relation. By the phrase "incomplete specifications", we thus mean specifications where some information about the intended relation is *deliberately* withheld and where the synthesis is expected to *extrapolate*. We thus exclude incomplete specifications in the sense of evolutionary specifications, where one also deliberately withholds some information, but without expecting any extrapolation. The idea there is to gradually refine an algorithm by adding functionalities to its specification.

Although our synthesis mechanism is non-incremental in its handling of the examples and properties, it may of course be used in an incremental fashion by presenting it with increasingly large specifications of the *same* intended relation. In our case, the latter always starts from scratch, for "fear" of missing a possibly more elegant or efficient algorithm by patching the previous one. However, incremental handling of examples and properties need not always amount to a patchwork approach, so this non-conservative attitude is not always justified. Replay information should thus be gathered during synthesis, so as to allow quicker decision-taking during a new synthesis.

With our specification approach, a single problem is specified, and a single logic algorithm is synthesized, at each time. The other predicates used in the specification are assumed to be primitives and to have correct logic algorithms available. This is an assumption that is not made systematically by the machine learning and ILP communities, where multiple related concepts may sometimes be learned simultaneously. Of course, the invention of new sub-problems and the synthesis of logic algorithms therefore (see Section 14.2.4) alleviate this apparent drawback.

Even in programming-in-the-small, it is sometimes necessary to compose several small algorithms of *different* schemas before obtaining an algorithm for the overall problem. In this sense, the solution proposed by this book (namely focus on the divide-and-conquer schema) seems somewhat restricted. However, our vision of a synthesis system as a collection of several schema-dedicated systems or, even better, as a workbench with a schema-driven system coupled to a tool-box of schema-independent methods, shows a way of tackling this restriction. Moreover, there seems to be very little knowledge about how to automate such algorithm decomposition and composition anyway. So this aspect seems a likely candidate for human very-high-level intervention, and our synthesis mechanism should be seen as a component of such a global solution to algorithm synthesis. The here targeted class of algorithms, namely divide-and-conquer algorithms, is a very important and large class.

Another restriction of our synthesis mechanism is that no parameters (such as accumulators) can be introduced to the specified predicate, and that the types of parameters cannot be generalized. For instance, the *reverse(L,R)* problem cannot be generalized into the *reverse(L,R,A)* problem (where *R* is the concatenation of *A* and the reversed list of *L*), although this would lead to a lower complexity algorithm than the so-called naive one. Or the *flatTree(T,L)* problem cannot be generalized into the *flatTree(Ts,L)* problem (where *L* is a list containing the concatenation of the flattened elements of the binary-tree-list *Ts*), although this would lead to a lower complexity algorithm. These generalization processes are called *computational generalization* and *structural generalization*, respectively. The motivation behind such generalization processes is that, somewhat paradoxically, the generalized problem is often easier to implement, and that the resulting generalized algorithm is often of a lesser complexity (for the initial problem) than an algorithm directly designed for this initial problem. Our synthesis mechanism cannot perform such generalizations. However, it seems possible to acquire a specification by examples and properties of the generalized problem by (semi-)automatic derivation from the specification of the initial problem, using generalization schemas. See [Deville 90] for a discussion of such schemas, and for ways of automating the discovery of the needed "eureka".

An extreme case of incomplete specifications are complete specifications! And our synthesis mechanism *is* actually able to handle such complete specifications (such as properties with recursion). However, given a complete specification under the form of a correct definite program, our synthesis mechanism is only likely to rediscover the corresponding logic algorithm if its decomposition predicate is available to it. Pushing the idea of allowing (almost-)complete specifications further, one could even imagine using our synthesis mechanism for some form of "redundant (logic) programming", where the specifier provides examples plus any kind of properties (possibly including a correct definite program), and where synthesis either yields an algorithm or detects an inconsistency within the specification (and is thus unable to design an algorithm).

The use of the logic programming framework, and hence its preference over other programming frameworks (such as the functional, object-oriented, or imperative paradigms), is justified by its enabling a semantic and syntactic continuity from the specification language (definite clauses) to the logic algorithm language (equivalence statements with disjunctive normal form wffs in the right-hand side) to the logic program language (normal clauses, in the case of Prolog). Moreover, especially the PaP Method has a particularly elegant formulation in the logic programming framework.

14.5.2 Comparison with Related Systems

We have no empirical data (synthesis times, example consumption, ...) yet about a comparison between SYNAPSE and its related systems, such as MIS [Shapiro 82], CLINT [De Raedt and Bruynooghe 92b], FOIL [Quinlan 90], or the other model-based systems of the ILP community (see Section 3.4), or the trace-based systems of the LISP community (see Section 3.3). But we may make some predictions by comparing the underlying synthesis mechanisms instead. This requires some analysis first.

The big advantage of ILP systems is their flexibility: literally any logic program can be learned[17] from examples alone. Sometimes, for instance in MIS, the price to pay is however the development of a new clause generator for each new class of programs. The existing systems have greatly varying voraciousness in terms of example consumption, (human) oracle solicitation, and time complexity. But the main point is that their generality of scope is at the same time their limitation. Indeed, these learning mechanisms have no understanding of what they are learning, and the learning process thus often resembles a rather undisciplined patchwork approach. For instance, when MIS (equipped with the eager search-strategy) synthesizes the Insertion-Sort algorithm (including the synthesis of the *insert*/3 predicate), a total of 238 clauses is reported by [Shapiro 82] to be tested before identifying the 5 correct ones. And it must be said that the search space is well-organized. More recent systems have of course improved upon these figures, but the search is still rather blind.

It also appears that these ILP learners are mostly used in what we would like to call the *teacher/learner setting*, where a teacher provides a learner with examples and (almost) exactly the background knowledge that is necessary for successful learning. This requires the teacher to know the targeted logic program, or to at least suspect which predicates might be useful (otherwise, s/he wouldn't be a teacher after all). For instance, in the above-mentioned synthesis of the Insertion-Sort algorithm, the choice of the examples seems to be very much guided by insights about what is wrong with the currently designed algorithm, rather than by what would be universally "good" examples, whatever the obtained sorting algorithm. Or, even worse, the synthesis of the Quick-Sort algorithm is often "forced" by the provision of the *partition*/4 predicate as the only background knowledge to the specification by examples for the sorting problem. The search space is thus pre-enumerated. However, this setting is not always realistic, and the reported performances of the developed learners are greatly biased by it. Indeed, these performances would simply crumble away in what we would like to call the *specifier/synthesizer setting*, where a specifier provides a synthesizer with *any* examples and with *a lot of* background knowledge. In this setting, the synthesizer is expected to come up with algorithms, as the specifier may have no, or little, ideas

17. For ILP systems, we prefer "learning" over "synthesis", as we reserved the latter terminology for the learning of (recursive) algorithms/programs.

about how to do this (otherwise, s/he wouldn't use a synthesizer after all). Constructive induction (predicate invention) is then crucial, rather than an option. If the Quick-Sort algorithm is synthesized from a sorting specification, that's great; and if it's "only" the Insertion-Sort algorithm, that's still fine. Ideally, a whole family of equivalent algorithms should however be synthesized from a given specification.

Although the ILP community has tremendously improved the quality of machine learning research (because the underlying logic framework is much cleaner than most custom-made frameworks, and because of the use of a very small set of inductive inference rules, rather than of a large arsenal of custom-made rules), we recommend breaking up ILP research into several domains. One of these domains is synthesis of recursive logic programs, and is the object of this book. This domain is very important, and is, as shown by Table 3-1, sufficiently more specific than the general one to deserve some very dedicated research. The objective of this separation of concerns is to get a tighter theoretical grip on the learning of the targeted class of concepts (relations in our case), and the introduction of more "discipline" into the learning process.

A few researchers have tackled this lack of "discipline" in the synthesis of recursive logic programs from examples: for instance, [Tinkham 90] and [Sterling and Kirschenbaum 93] investigate the use of schemas to guide synthesis. Curiously, the now virtually defunct research on trace-based synthesis of functional programs from examples [Summers 77] [Biermann 78] did not suffer from such a marked lack of "discipline", even though this research preceded ILP research.

The idea of this book was to introduce "discipline" into the synthesis of recursive logic programs (the chosen sub-domain of ILP), and this by making knowledge available to the synthesizer in a well-structured way. This is clearly within the recent trend of cross-fertilizing empirical and analytic learning. First, algorithm design knowledge is provided by means of an algorithm schema; this aspect is usually missing in ILP research. Second, more algorithm design knowledge is made available by databases of useful instances for some of the predicate-variables of a schema; this is roughly equivalent to the background knowledge used in ILP, but our structured approach doesn't suffer from a performance degradation in the specifier/synthesizer setting. Third, domain knowledge is given by the specifier under the form of properties, which are disambiguating generalizations of examples; this is again roughly equivalent to background knowledge, but our approach directly associates this knowledge to the specified predicate, and thus allows the preservation of such associations.

As a conclusion, our synthesis mechanism has by construction a much smaller scope than the more general ILP systems (recursive logic programs rather than logic programs), but due to the thus possible usage of a very "disciplined" approach based on schema-guidance, and due to the availability of disambiguating properties, it is to be expected that our synthesis mechanism behaves better than ILP systems on the class of recursive logic programs. The improvement should be especially dramatic in the specifier/synthesizer setting. Considering that ILP systems are known to have an example consumption similar to trace-based systems (except for Biermann's system, which often makes do with a single example) and to exhibit an improvement in terms of time complexity over these systems, it is by transitivity also to be expected that our synthesis mechanism improves upon these older systems as well. In other words: SYNAPSE does less, but it does it better!

Appendix: Conventions, Abbreviations, and Symbols

Here follows the complete list of the used typographic conventions, abbreviations, and predefined symbols.

Typographic Conventions

Function-symbols (functors) and predicate-symbols start with a lowercase letter. We often write them out followed by a slash "/" and their arity. Examples are $a/0, f/2, p/3$. Exceptions are some primitive symbols, such as $=/2$, $</2$, $\bullet/2$. Functors of arity 0 are called constants. By abuse of language, we often say predicate instead of predicate-symbol. Variable-symbols, function-variable symbols, and predicate-variable symbols start with an uppercase letter. Examples are X, F, P. An anonymous variable is denoted by an underscore "_". Schema-variable symbols and notation-variable symbols consist of a lowercase letter. Examples are i, j, k, m, n. The distinction with one-letter constants should always be obvious from context. By abuse of language, we often say variable instead of variable-symbol.

Terms and atoms are usually written in prefix notation. If no ambiguity arises, unary terms and atoms are sometimes written without parentheses, whereas binary terms and atoms are sometimes written in infix notation.

A constructed list with head H and tail T is denoted $H \bullet T$, and *nil* denotes the empty list. Another notation for a constructed list with head H and tail T is $[H|T]$, and $[]$ is another notation for the empty list. These alternative notations allow shorthands such as $[H_1,H_2,\ldots,H_n]$ for $\bullet(H_1,\bullet(H_2,\bullet(\ldots,\bullet(H_n,nil)\ldots)))$, and $[H_1,H_2,\ldots,H_n|T]$ for $\bullet(H_1,\bullet(H_2,\bullet(\ldots,\bullet(H_n,T)\ldots)))$, where $n > 0$.

Non-negative integers are successors of the constant zero, which is denoted 0. The sequence of integers is 0, $s(0)$, $s(s(0))$, …, $s^n(0)$, …, where $s/1$ is called the successor functor. Shorthands are 0, 1, 2, …, n, …, respectively.

Variable-symbols, predicate-variable symbols, functors, and predicate-symbols within text paragraphs are written in *Times-italics*. However, entirely formalized paragraphs, such as specifications, (logic) algorithms/programs, are written in `Courier`.

Term vectors and variable vectors of indeterminate but finite length are denoted by **boldface** symbols. Examples are $\boldsymbol{t}$ and $\boldsymbol{X}$. Vectors of vectors of indeterminate but finite length are denoted by **<u>underlined boldface</u>** symbols. Examples are $\underline{\boldsymbol{t}}$ and $\underline{\boldsymbol{X}}$. Given an integer n, an n-tuple of length n is written using angled brackets. An example is $<t_1,t_2,\ldots,t_n>$. Note that an n-tuple is a term, whereas a vector is not a term.

Names of sets or relations start with an uppercase letter, and are written in *Zapf*. An example is $\mathcal{R}$. The predicate symbol corresponding to a relation is the name of the relation, but it then starts with a lowercase letter, and is written in *Times-italics*. For instance, r is the predicate-symbol for relation $\mathcal{R}$. Exceptions are some primitive symbols, such as $=/2$, $</2$, $\in/2$. The complement of a relation has the same name as the relation itself, but crossed out by a slash "/", if the name is a primitive symbol, and $\overline{\text{overlined}}$, otherwise.

The binding of a term t to a variable X is denoted X/t. Substitutions are denoted by Greek lower-case letters. Examples are σ, ρ, θ.

The construct $F[X]$ denotes a wff F whose free variables are $\boldsymbol{X}$. The construct $F[\boldsymbol{t}]$ then denotes $F[\boldsymbol{X}]$ where the free occurrences of $\boldsymbol{X}$ are replaced by the terms $\boldsymbol{t}$. The **boldface** construct $\boldsymbol{r(s,t)}$ denotes a finite conjunction $r(s_1,t_1) \wedge r(s_2,t_2) \wedge \ldots \wedge r(s_n,t_n)$.

The end of a multi-paragraph example is indicated by a black diamond: ♦. The end of a proof is indicated by a quad: ❑. Emphasized and defined words are in *italics*.

Abbreviations

General abbreviations

iff	if and only if
N/A	non-applicable
wrt	with respect to

Scientific abbreviations

DCI	Definite Clause Inference rule
EBG	Explanation-Based Generalization
EBL	Explanation-Based Learning
gci	greatest common instance
glb	greatest lower bound
ILP	Inductive Logic Programming
LA	Logic Algorithm
LP	Logic Program
lub	least upper bound
mgu	most-general unifier
msg	most-specific generalization
NF	Negation-as-Failure
NFI	Negation-as-Failure Inference rule
Sim	Simplification inference rule
SL	Linear resolution with Selection Function
SLD	SL resolution for Definite clauses
SLDNF	SLD resolution with the NF rule
Spec	Specification
SYNAPSE	SYNthesis of logic Algorithms from PropertieS and Examples
wff	well-formed formula
wfr	well-founded relation

Glossary of Symbols

Sets

$\mathcal{A}$	the set of atoms constructed from $\mathcal{Q}$ and $\mathcal{T}$
$\mathcal{B}$	the Herbrand-base (that is the set of ground atoms constructed from $\mathcal{Q}$ and $\mathcal{U}$); $\mathcal{B} \subseteq \mathcal{A}$
$\mathcal{C}$	the set of predefined base-case constants of inductively defined data-types; $\mathcal{C} \subseteq \mathcal{F}$; $\mathcal{C}$ is here assumed to be $\{0, nil\}$
$\mathcal{E}(r)$	a set of examples of predicate r
$\mathcal{F}$	the set of functors
$\mathcal{G}(r)$	a set of general examples of predicate r
$\mathfrak{I}$	the intended interpretation
$\mathcal{I}, \mathcal{J}, \mathcal{K}, \mathcal{L}$	index sets

$\mathcal{L}(r)$	the set of logic algorithms for predicate r; $\mathcal{L}(r) \subseteq \mathcal{W}$
$\mathcal{M}(r)$	the set of possibly infinite logic algorithms for predicate r
$\mathcal{P}(r)$	a set of properties of predicate r
$\mathcal{Q}$	the set of predicate symbols; $\mathcal{Q} \neq \mathcal{F}$
$\mathcal{R}$	the intended relation
$\mathcal{T}$	the set of terms constructed from $\mathcal{F}$ and $\mathcal{V}$
$\mathcal{U}$	the Herbrand-universe (that is the set of ground terms constructed from $\mathcal{F}$); $\mathcal{U} \subseteq \mathcal{T}$
$\mathcal{V}$	the set of variable symbols
$\mathcal{W}$	the set of wff constructed from $\mathcal{A}$ and $\mathcal{V}$
Constants	
f	the number of steps of a synthesis mechanism
m	the number of (general) examples: $m = \#\mathcal{E}(r)$, or $m = \#\mathcal{G}(r)$
nil or []	the empty list
p	the number of properties: $p = \#\mathcal{P}(r)$
ω	infinity
0	the integer zero
$\emptyset$ or { }	the empty set
Functors of arity n, where $n > 0$	
$cons(E)$	the set of constants occurring in expression E
$dom(r)$	the domain of a procedure for predicate r: $dom(r) \subseteq \mathcal{U}$
$dom(\sigma)$	the domain of substitution σ: $dom(\sigma) \subseteq \mathcal{V}$
$funct(E)$	the set of functors occurring in expression E
$msg(s,t)$	the most specific generalization of terms s and t
$\mathcal{P}(\mathcal{S})$	the set of subsets of set $\mathcal{S}$
$range(\sigma)$	the range of a substitution σ: $range(\sigma) \subseteq \mathcal{T}$
$s(i)$	the successor of integer i
$vars(E)$	the set of variables occurring in expression E
$\#\mathcal{S}$	the number of elements of set/vector $\mathcal{S}$, or the size of term $\mathcal{S}$
$H \bullet T$	the list constructed of head H and tail T
$\mathcal{S}_1 \cup \mathcal{S}_2$	the union of the sets $\mathcal{S}_1$ and $\mathcal{S}_2$
$\mathcal{S}_1 \cap \mathcal{S}_2$	the intersection of the sets $\mathcal{S}_1$ and $\mathcal{S}_2$
$\mathcal{S}_1 \setminus \mathcal{S}_2$	the difference of the sets $\mathcal{S}_1$ and $\mathcal{S}_2$
First-order variables of (version 3 of) the divide-and-conquer schema	
X	the induction parameter
Y	the other parameter
$\boldsymbol{HX}$	the heads of X
$\boldsymbol{HY}$	the heads of Y
$\boldsymbol{TX}$	the tails of X
$\boldsymbol{TY}$	the tails of Y
Schema-variables of (version 3 of) the divide-and-conquer schema	
c	the number of sub-cases of the non-minimal case: $c = v + w$
d	the decomposition decrement: $d \geq 1$
h	the number of heads of X: $h = \#\boldsymbol{HX}$
h'	the number of heads of Y: $h' = \#\boldsymbol{HY}$
n	the arity of r

t	the number of tails of X and Y: $t = \#TX = \#TY$
u	the position of the induction parameter within an atom of r/n
v	the number of sub-cases of the non-recursive case
w	the number of sub-cases of the recursive case
Primitive predicates	
$s = t$	term s is unifiable with term t
$s \leq t$	term s is less general than term t; or, according to context: integer s is less than or equal to integer t
$e \in \mathcal{S}$	term e is an element of set $\mathcal{S}$
$\mathcal{S}_1 \subseteq \mathcal{S}_2$	set $\mathcal{S}_1$ is a subset of set $\mathcal{S}_2$
Connectives for logic algorithms, schemas, properties, and implicative goals	
$\forall$	for all (universal quantifier)
$\exists$	there is (existential quantifier)
$\exists!$	there is exactly one (existential quantifier)
$\neg$	not (negation)
$\vee$	inclusive-or
$\veebar$	exclusive-or
$\wedge$	and
$\Rightarrow$	implies
$\Leftarrow$	if
$\Leftrightarrow$	if-and-only-if
$\vee_{a \leq i \leq b} F_i$	$F_a \vee F_{a+1} \vee \ldots \vee F_b$, if $b \geq a$, and *false* otherwise
$\wedge_{a \leq i \leq b} F_i$	$F_a \wedge F_{a+1} \wedge \ldots \wedge F_b$, if $b \geq a$, and *true* otherwise
More conventions for implicative goals	
❑	the empty implicative goal
$?X$	undecided variable X
Y	free variable Y
Connectives for logic programs	
,	and
$\leftarrow$	if
Logic algorithms	
$\bot_r$, $\top_r$	bottom, top of the logic algorithm lattice $(\mathcal{M}(r), \leq)$
$\leq$, $\geq$, $\cong$	is semantically less (more) general than, equivalent to
«, », $\approx$	is syntactically less (more) general than, equivalent to
exp/3	expansion function, relative an example set and an oracle
gen/2	syntactic generalization relation
spec/2	syntactic specialization relation
Meta-logical connectives	
$\models$	Herbrand-logical consequence
$\vdash$	derivability

Precedence Hierarchy (Highest-to-Lowest) of the wff Connectives

$\neg$, $\forall$, $\exists$, $\exists!$

$\vee$, $\veebar$

$\wedge$

$\Leftarrow$, $\Rightarrow$, $\Leftrightarrow$

References

CADE = Conference on Automated DEduction
ICLP = International Conference on Logic Programming
IJCAI = International Joint Conference on Artificial Intelligence
ILP = International Workshop on Inductive Logic Programming
LOPSTR = International Workshop on LOgic Program Synthesis and TRansformation
NACLP = North American Conference on Logic Programming
PLILP = Int'l Symp. on Pgmming Language Implementation and Logic Programming
SLP = Symposium on Logic Programming

[Angluin 84]
D. Angluin. Inductive inference: Efficient algorithms. In [Biermann *et al.* 84a], pp. 503–515.

[Angluin 88]
D. Angluin. Queries and concept learning. *Machine Learning* 2(4):319–342, April 1988.

[Angluin and Smith 83]
D. Angluin and C. H. Smith. Inductive inference: Theory and methods. *Computing Surveys* 15(3):237–269, Sep. 1983.

[Balzer 85]
R. Balzer. A 15 year perspective on automatic programming. In [IEEE-TSE 85], pp. 1257–1268.

[Balzer *et al.* 77]
R. Balzer, N. Goldman, and D. Wile. Informality in program specifications. In *Proc. of IJCAI'*77, pp. 389–397. Also in *IEEE Trans. on Software Engineering* 4(2):94–102, March 1978. Also in [Rich and Waters 86a], pp. 223–232.

[Banerji 84]
R. B. Banerji. Some insights into automatic programming using a pattern recognition viewpoint. In [Biermann *et al.* 84a], pp. 483–502.

[Barker-Plummer 90]
D. Barker-Plummer. Cliché programming in Prolog. In M. Bruynooghe (ed), *Proc. of META'*90, pp. 247–256.

[Barr and Feigenbaum 82]
A. Barr and E. A. Feigenbaum. *The Handbook of Artificial Intelligence*. Morgan Kaufmann, 1982.

[Barstow 79]
D. R. Barstow. An experiment in knowledge-based automatic programming. *Artificial Intelligence* 12(2):73–119, Aug. 1979. Also in [Webber and Nilsson 81], pp. 289–312. Also in [Rich and Waters 86a], pp. 133–156.

[Barstow 84a]
D. R. Barstow. The roles of knowledge and deduction in algorithm design. In [Biermann *et al.* 84a], pp. 201–222.

[Barstow 84b]
D. R. Barstow. A perspective on automatic programming. *AI Magazine* Spring 1984:5–27. Also in [Rich and Waters 86a], pp. 537–559.
[Barstow 85]
D. R. Barstow. Domain-specific automatic programming. In [IEEE-TSE 85], pp. 1321–1336.
[Bates and Constable 85]
J. L. Bates and R. L. Constable. Proofs as programs. *ACM Trans. on Programming Languages and Systems* 7(1):113–136, Jan. 1985.
[Bauer 79]
M. A. Bauer. Programming by examples. *Artificial Intelligence* 12(1):1–21, May 1979. Also in [Rich and Waters 86a], pp. 317–327.
[Bauer *et al.* 89]
F. L. Bauer, B. Möller, H. Partsch, and P. Pepper. Formal program construction by transformations: Computer-aided, intuition-guided programming. *IEEE Trans. on Software Engineering* 15(2):165–180, Feb. 1989.
[Beeson 85]
M. J. Beeson. *Foundations of Constructive Mathematics*. Series of Modern Surveys in Mathematics, Vol. 6, Springer-Verlag, 1985.
[Bergadano and Gunetti 94]
F. Bergadano and D. Gunetti. Inductive synthesis of logic programs and inductive logic programming. In [Deville 94], pp. 45–56.
[Bibel 80]
W. Bibel. Syntax-directed, semantics-supported program synthesis. *Artificial Intelligence* 14(3):243–261, Oct. 1980.
[Bibel and Hörnig 84]
W. Bibel and K. M. Hörnig. LOPS: A system based on a strategical approach to program synthesis. In [Biermann *et al.* 84a], pp. 69–89.
[Biermann 72]
A. W. Biermann. On the inference of Turing machines from sample computations. *Artificial Intelligence* 3(3):181–198, Fall 1972.
[Biermann 78]
A. W. Biermann. The inference of regular LISP programs from examples. *IEEE Trans. on Systems, Man, and Cybernetics* 8(8):585–600, 1978.
[Biermann 83]
A. W. Biermann. Natural language programming. In [Biermann and Guiho 83], pp. 335–368.
[Biermann 84]
A. W. Biermann. Dealing with search. In [Biermann *et al.* 84a], pp. 375–392.
[Biermann 86]
A. W. Biermann. Fundamental mechanisms in machine learning and inductive inference. In W. Bibel and Ph. Jorrand (eds), *Fundamentals of Artificial Intelligence*, pp. 133–169. LNCS 232, Springer-Verlag, 1986.
[Biermann 92]
A. W. Biermann. Automatic programming. In S. C. Shapiro (ed), *Encyclopedia of Artificial Intelligence*, pp. 59–83. John Wiley, 1992. Second, extended edition.

[Biermann and Krishnaswamy 76]
A. W. Biermann and R. Krishnaswamy. Constructing programs from example computations. *IEEE Trans. on Software Engineering* 2(3):141–153, Sep. 1976.

[Biermann and Smith 79]
A. W. Biermann and D. R. Smith. A production rule mechanism for generating LISP code. *IEEE Trans. on Systems, Man, and Cybernetics* 9(5):260–276, 1979.

[Biermann and Guiho 83]
A. W. Biermann and G. Guiho (eds). *Computer Program Synthesis Methodologies*. Vol. ASI-C95, D. Reidel, Dordrecht (NL), 1983.

[Biermann *et al.* 84a]
A. W. Biermann, G. Guiho, and Y. Kodratoff (eds). *Automatic Program Construction Techniques*. Macmillan, 1984.

[Biermann *et al.* 84b]
A. W. Biermann, G. Guiho, and Y. Kodratoff. An overview of automatic program construction techniques. In [Biermann *et al.* 84a], pp. 3–30.

[Biggerstaff 84]
T. J. Biggerstaff. Design directed synthesis of LISP programs. In [Biermann *et al.* 84a], pp. 393–420.

[Boyer and Moore 79]
R. S. Boyer and J. S. Moore. *A Computational Logic*. Academic Press, 1979.

[Bratko and Grobelnik 93]
I. Bratko and M. Grobelnik. Inductive learning applied to program construction and verification. In *Proc. of ILP'*93 (TR IJS-DP-6707, J. Stefan Inst., Slovenia), pp. 279–292.

[Broy 83]
M. Broy. Program construction by transformations: A family tree of sorting programs. In [Biermann and Guiho 83], pp. 1–49.

[Bruynooghe and De Schreye 89]
M. Bruynooghe and D. De Schreye. Some thoughts on the role of examples in program transformation and its relevance for explanation-based learning. In K. P. Jantke (ed), *Proc. of the* 1989 *Int'l Workshop on Analogical and Inductive Inference*, pp. 60–77. LNCS 397, Springer-Verlag, 1989.

[Bry 90]
F. Bry. Intensional updates: abduction via deduction. In D. H. D. Warren and P. Szeredi (eds), *Proc. of ICLP'*90, pp. 561–578. MIT Press, 1990.

[Bundy 88]
A. Bundy. A broader interpretation of logic in logic programming. In R. A. Kowalski and K. A. Bowen (eds), *Proc. of ICLP'*88, pp. 1624–1648. MIT Press, 1988.

[Bundy 92]
A. Bundy. Tutorial notes: Reasoning about logic programs. In G. Comyn, N. E. Fuchs, and M. J. Ratcliffe (eds), *Logic Programming in Action*, pp. 252–277. LNAI 636, Springer-Verlag, 1992.

[Bundy *et al.* 90]
A. Bundy, A. Smaill, and G. Wiggins. The synthesis of logic programs from inductive proofs. In J. W. Lloyd (ed), *Proc. of the ESPRIT Symp. on Computational Logic*, pp. 135–149. Springer-Verlag, 1990.

[Bundy *et al.* 93]
A. Bundy, A. Stevens, F. van Harmelen, A. Ireland, and A. Smaill. Rippling: A heuristic for guiding inductive proofs. *Artificial Intelligence* 62(2):185-253, 1993.

[Buntine 88]
W. Buntine. Generalized subsumption and its applications to induction and redundancy. *Artificial Intelligence* 36(2):149–176, Sep. 1988.

[Burstall and Darlington 77]
R. M. Burstall and J. Darlington. A transformation system for developing recursive programs. *J. of the ACM* 24(1):44–67, Jan. 1977.

[Clark 78]
K. L. Clark. Negation-as-failure. In H. Gallaire and J. Minker (eds), *Logic and Databases*, pp. 293–322. Plenum Press, 1978.

[Clark 79]
K. L. Clark. *Predicate logic as a computational formalism.* TR DOC-79/59, Imperial College, London (UK), 1979.

[Clark 81]
Keith L. Clark. *The synthesis and verification of logic programs.* TR DOC-81/36, Imperial College, London (UK), Sep. 1981.

[Clark and Sickel 77]
K. L. Clark and S. Sickel. Predicate logic: A calculus for deriving programs. In *Proc. of IJCAI'*77, pp. 410–411.

[Clark and Tärnlund 77]
K. L. Clark and S.-Å. Tärnlund. A first order theory of data and programs. In *Proc. of the* 1977 *IFIP Congress*, pp. 939–944. North-Holland, 1977.

[Clark and Darlington 80]
K. L. Clark and J. Darlington. Algorithm classification through synthesis. *The Computer Journal* 23(1):61–65, 1980.

[Clement and Lau 92]
T. Clement and K.-K. Lau (eds), *Proc. of LOPSTR*'91. Springer-Verlag, 1992.

[Cohen and Sammut 84]
B. Cohen and C. Sammut. Program synthesis through concept learning. In [Biermann *et al.* 84a], pp. 463–482.

[Constable *et al.* 86]
R. L. Constable, S. F. Allen, H. M. Bromley, *et al. Implementing Mathematics with the Nuprl Proof Development System.* Prentice Hall, 1986.

[Darlington 81]
J. Darlington. An experimental program transformation and synthesis system. *Artificial Intelligence* 16(1):1–46, 1981. Also in [Rich and Waters 86a], pp. 99–121.

[De Boeck and Le Charlier 90]
P. De Boeck and B. Le Charlier. Static type analysis of Prolog procedures for ensuring correctness. In P. Deransart and J. Maluszynski (eds), *Proc. of PLILP'*90, pp. 222–237. LNCS 456, Springer-Verlag, 1990.

[DeJong and Mooney 86]
G. F. DeJong and R. Mooney. Explanation-based learning: An alternative view. *Machine Learning* 1(2):145–176, 1986.

[De Raedt 92]
L. De Raedt. *Interactive Theory Revision: An Inductive Logic Programming Approach*. Academic Press, 1992.

[De Raedt and Bruynooghe 92]
L. De Raedt and M. Bruynooghe. Belief updating from integrity constraints and queries. *Artificial Intelligence* 53(2–3):291–307, Feb. 1992.

[De Raedt and Bruynooghe 92b]
L. De Raedt and M. Bruynooghe. An overview of the interactive concept-learner and theory revisor CLINT. In [Muggleton 92], pp. 163–191.

[De Raedt and Bruynooghe 93]
L. De Raedt and M. Bruynooghe. A theory of clausal discovery. In *Proc. of ILP*'93 (TR IJS-DP-6707, J. Stefan Inst., Slovenia), pp. 25–40.

[Dershowitz and Lee 93]
N. Dershowitz and Y.-J. Lee. Logical debugging. In [JSC 93], pp. 745–773. Early version, entitled "Deductive debugging", in *Proc. of SLP'*87, pp. 298–306.

[Deville 87]
Y. Deville. *A Methodology for Logic Program Construction*. Ph.D. Thesis, Fac. Univ. Notre-Dame de la Paix, Namur (Belgium), 1987.

[Deville 90]
Y. Deville. *Logic Programming: Systematic Program Development*. Int'l Series in Logic Programming, Addison-Wesley, 1990.

[Deville 94]
Y. Deville (ed), *Proc. of LOPSTR'*93. Springer-Verlag, 1994.

[Deville and Burnay 89]
Y. Deville and J. Burnay. Generalization and program schemata: A step towards computer-aided construction of logic programs. In E. L. Lusk and R. A. Overbeek (eds), *Proc. of NACLP'*89, pp. 409–425. MIT Press, 1989.

[Deville and Flener 94]
Y. Deville and P. Flener. *Correctness criteria for logic program synthesis*. TR, Université Catholique de Louvain (Belgium), 1994. (In preparation.)

[Deville and Lau 94]
Y. Deville and K.-K. Lau. Logic program synthesis: A survey. *J. of Logic Programming, Special Issue on* 10 *Years of Logic Programming*, 1994.

[Drabent *et al.* 88]
W. Drabent, S. Nadjm-Tehrani, and J. Maluszynski. Algorithmic debugging with assertions. In H. Abramson and M. H. Rogers (eds), *Proc. of META'*88, pp. 501–521. MIT Press, 1988.

[Eriksson 84]
L.-H. Eriksson. Synthesis of a unification algorithm in a logic programming calculus. *J. of Logic Programming* 1(1):3-33, June 1984.

[Eriksson and Johansson 82]
A. Eriksson and A.-L. Johansson. Computer-based synthesis of logic programs. In M. Dezani-Ciancaglini and U. Montanari (eds), *Proc. of an Int'l Symp. on Programming*, pp. 105–115. LNCS 137, Springer-Verlag, 1982.

[Feather 87]
M. S. Feather. A survey and classification of some program transformation ap-

proaches and techniques. In L. G. L. T. Meertens (ed), *Program Specification and Transformation, Proc. of the* 1987 *IFIP Congress*, pp. 165–195. Elsevier, 1987.

[Fickas 85]
S. F. Fickas. Automating the transformational development of software. In [IEEE-TSE 85], pp. 1268–1277.

[Flener 93]
P. Flener. *Logic Algorithm Synthesis from Examples and Properties.* Ph.D. Thesis, Univ. Catholique de Louvain, Louvain-la-Neuve (Belgium), 1993.

[Flener and Deville 92]
P. Flener and Y. Deville. Towards stepwise, schema-guided synthesis of logic programs. In [Clement and Lau 92], pp. 46–64.

[Flener and Deville 93a]
P. Flener and Y. Deville. Synthesis of composition and discrimination operators for divide-and-conquer logic programs. In [Jacquet 93], pp. 67–96.

[Flener and Deville 93b]
P. Flener and Y. Deville. Logic program synthesis from incomplete specifications. In [JSC 93], pp. 775–805.

[Flener and Popelínský 94]
P. Flener and L. Popelínský. On the use of inductive reasoning in program synthesis: Prejudice and prospects. In [Fribourg and Turini 94].

[Flener *et al.* 94]
P. Flener, L. Popelínský, and O. Štěpánková. ILP and automatic programming: Towards three approaches. In *Proc. of ILP*'94.

[Follet 84]
R. Follet. Combining program synthesis with program analysis. In [Biermann *et al.* 84a], pp. 91–107.

[Fribourg 90]
L. Fribourg. Extracting logic programs from proofs that use extended Prolog execution and induction. In D. H. D. Warren and P. Szeredi (eds), *Proc. of ICLP*'90, pp. 685–699. MIT Press, 1990. Extended version in [Jacquet 93], pp. 39–66.

[Fribourg 91]
L. Fribourg. Automatic generation of simplification lemmas for inductive proofs. In V. Saraswat and K. Ueda (eds), *Proc. of SLP*'91, pp. 103–116. MIT Press, 1991.

[Fribourg and Turini 94]
L. Fribourg and F. Turini (eds), *Joint Proc. of LOPSTR*'94 *and META*'94. LNCS, Springer-Verlag, 1994. (Forthcoming.)

[Fuchs 92a]
N. E. Fuchs. Hoare logic, executable specifications, and logic programs. *Structured Programming* 13:129–135, 1992.

[Fuchs 92b]
N. E. Fuchs. Specifications are (preferably) executable. *Software Engineering Journal* 7:323–334, Sep. 1992.

[Fuchs 94]
N. E. Fuchs. Private communications, March – August 1994.

[Fuchs and Fromherz 92]
N. E. Fuchs and M. P. J. Fromherz. Schema-based transformations of logic programs. In [Clement and Lau 92], pp. 111–125.

[Garey and Johnson 79]
M. R. Garey and D. S. Johnson. *Computers and Intractability: A Guide to the Theory of NP-Completeness.* W. H. Freeman and Company, 1979.

[Gegg-Harrison 89]
T. S. Gegg-Harrison. *Basic Prolog schemata.* TR CS-1989-20, Duke Univ., Durham (NC, USA), 1989.

[Genesereth and Nilsson 88]
M. R. Genesereth and N. J. Nilsson. *Logical Foundations of Artificial Intelligence.* Morgan Kaufmann, 1988.

[Gold 67]
E. M. Gold. Language identification in the limit. *Information and Control* 10(5):447–474, 1967.

[Goldberg 86]
A. T. Goldberg. Knowledge-based programming: A survey of program design and construction techniques. *IEEE Trans. on Software Engineering* 12(7):752–768, July 1986.

[Goodenough and Gerhart 75]
J. B. Goodenough and S. L. Gerhart. Toward a theory of test data selection. *IEEE Trans. on Software Engineering* 1(2):156–173, June 1975.

[Green 69]
C. Green. Application of theorem proving to problem solving. In *Proc. of IJCAI'*69, pp. 219–239. Also in [Webber and Nilsson 81], pp. 202–222.

[Green and Barstow 78]
C. Green and D. R. Barstow. On program synthesis knowledge. *Artificial Intelligence* 10(3):241–270, Nov. 1978. Also in [Rich and Waters 86a], pp. 455–474.

[Green *et al.* 79]
C. Green *et al.* Results in knowledge-based program synthesis. In *Proc. of IJCAI'*79, pp. 342–344.

[Green and Westfold 82]
C. Green and S. Westfold. Knowledge-based programming self applied. *Machine Intelligence* 10, 1982. John Wiley. Also in [Rich and Waters 86a], pp. 259–284.

[Green *et al.* 83]
C. Green, D. Luckham, R. Balzer, T. Cheatham, and Ch. Rich. Report on a knowledge-based software assistant. In [Rich and Waters 86a], pp. 377–428.

[Grobelnik 94]
M. Grobelnik. Induction of Prolog programs with Markus. In [Deville 94], pp. 57–63.

[Guessoum and Lloyd 90]
A. Guessoum and J. W. Lloyd. Updating knowledge bases. *New Generation Computing* 8:71–88, 1990.

[Gupta 87]
A. Gupta. Explanation-based failure recovery. In *Proc. of the* 1987 *Conf. of the Am. Assoc. for Artificial Intelligence*, Vol. 2, pp. 606–610. Morgan Kaufmann.

[Hagiya 90]
M. Hagiya. Programming by example and proving by example using higher-order unification. In M. E. Stickel (ed), *Proc. of CADE'90*, pp. 588–602. LNCS 449, Springer-Verlag, 1990.

[Hansson 80]
Å. Hansson. *A Formal Development of Programs*. Ph.D. Thesis, Univ. of Stockholm (Sweden), 1980.

[Hansson *et al.* 82]
Å. Hansson, S. Haridi, and S.-Å. Tärnlund. Properties of a logic programming language. In K. L. Clark and S.-Å. Tärnlund (eds), *Logic Programming*, pp. 267–280. Academic Press, 1982.

[Hardy 75]
S. Hardy. Synthesis of LISP functions from examples. In *Proc. of IJCAI'75*, pp. 240–245.

[Hayashi 87]
S. Hayashi. PX: A system extracting programs from proofs. In M. Wirsing (ed), *Formal Description of Programming Concepts*, pp. 399–423. Elsevier, 1987.

[Hayes and Jones 89]
I. J. Hayes and C. B. Jones. Specifications are not (necessarily) executable. *Software Engineering Journal* 4(6):330–338, Nov. 1989.

[Heidorn 76]
G. E. Heidorn. Automatic programming through natural language dialogue: A survey. *IBM J. on Research and Development* 20(4):302–313, 1976. Also in [Rich and Waters 86a], pp. 203–214.

[Henrard and Le Charlier 92]
J. Henrard and B. Le Charlier. Folon: An environment for declarative construction of logic programs. In M. Bruynooghe and M. Wirsing (eds), *Proc. of PLILP'92*, pp. 217–231. LNCS 631, Springer-Verlag, 1992.

[Hill and Lloyd 94]
P. M. Hill and J. W. Lloyd. *The Gödel Report*. MIT Press, 1994.

[Hogger 78]
Ch. J. Hogger. Program synthesis in predicate logic. In D. Sleeman (ed) *Proc. of the AISB/GI Conf. on Artificial Intelligence* (Germany), pp. 22–27. 1978.

[Hogger 81]
Ch. J. Hogger. Derivation of logic programs. *J. of the ACM* 28(2):372–392, 1981.

[Hogger 84]
Ch. J. Hogger. *Introduction to Logic Programming*. Academic Press, 1984.

[Howard 80]
W. A. Howard. The formulae-as-types notion of construction. In J. P. Seldin and J. R. Hindley (eds), *To H. B. Curry: Essays on Combinatory Logic, Lambda Calculus and Formalism*, pp. 479–490. Academic Press, 1980.

[Huet 76]
G. Huet. *Résolution d'équations dans les langages d'ordre* 1,2,...,ω. Thèse de doctorat d'État, Univ. Paris VII, Paris (France), 1976.

[Huet and Plotkin 91]
G. Huet and G. D. Plotkin (eds). *Logical Frameworks.* Cambridge Univ. Press, Cambridge (UK), 1991.

[Huntbach 86]
M. M. Huntbach. An improved version of Shapiro's MIS. In E. Y. Shapiro (ed), *Proc. of ICLP'86*, pp. 180–187. LNCS 225, Springer-Verlag, 1986.

[IEEE-TSE 85]
Special Issue on Artificial Intelligence and Software Engineering (edited by J. Mostow). *IEEE Trans. on Software Engineering* 11(11), Nov. 1985.

[Jacquet 93]
J.-M. Jacquet (ed). *Constructing Logic Programs.* John Wiley, 1993.

[Jantke 89]
K. P. Jantke. Algorithmic learning from incomplete information: Principles and problems. In J. Dassow and J. Kelemen (eds), *Machines, Languages, and Complexity*, pp. 188–207. LNCS 381, Springer-Verlag, 1989.

[Jantke 91]
K. P. Jantke. Monotonic and non-monotonic inductive inference. *New Generation Computing* 8(4):349–360, 1991.

[Jantke and Goldammer 92]
K. P. Jantke and U. Goldammer. Inductive synthesis of rewrite rules as program synthesis. In [Clement and Lau 92], pp. 65–68.

[Johansson 84]
A.-L. Johansson. Using symmetry for the derivation of logic programs. In S.-Å. Tärnlund (ed), *Proc. of ICLP'84*, pp. 243–251.

[Jorge and Brazdil 94]
A. M. Jorge and P. Brazdil. Learning by refining algorithm sketches. *Proc. of the* 1994 *European Conf. on Artificial Intelligence.*

[Jouannaud and Kodratoff 83]
J.-P. Jouannaud and Y. Kodratoff. Program synthesis from examples of behavior. In [Biermann and Guiho 83], pp. 213–250.

[JSC 93]
Special Issue on Automatic Programming (edited by A. W. Biermann and W. Bibel). *J. of Symbolic Computation* 15(5–6), May/June 1993.

[Kakas *et al.* 92]
A. C. Kakas, R. A. Kowalski, and F. Toni. Abductive logic programming. *J. of Logic and Computation* 2(6):719–770, 1993.

[Kanamori 86]
T. Kanamori. *Soundness and completeness of extended execution for proving properties of Prolog programs.* TR ICOT-TR-175, Tokyo (Japan), May 1986.

[Kanamori and Fujita 86]
T. Kanamori and H. Fujita. Formulation of induction formulas in verification of Prolog programs. In J. H. Siekmann (ed), *Proc. of CADE'86*, pp. 281–299. LNCS 230, Springer-Verlag, 1986.

[Kanamori and Seki 86]
T. Kanamori and H. Seki. Verification of Prolog programs using an extension of

execution. In E. Y. Shapiro (ed), *Proc. of ICLP'86*, pp. 475–489. LNCS 225, Springer-Verlag, 1986.

[Kant 83]
E. Kant. On the efficient synthesis of efficient programs. *Artificial Intelligence* 20(3):253–305, May 1983. Also in [Rich and Waters 86a], pp. 157–183.

[Kant 85]
E. Kant. Understanding and automating algorithm design. In [IEEE-TSE 85], pp. 1361–1374. Also in *Proc. of IJCAI'85*, pp. 1243–1253.

[Kant 90]
E. Kant. Automated program synthesis. *Univ. Video Comm.*, Distinguished Lecture Series, Vol. III, 1990.

[Kant and Barstow 81]
E. Kant and D. R. Barstow. The refinement paradigm: The interaction of coding and efficiency knowledge in program synthesis. *IEEE Trans. on Software Engineering* 7(5):458–471, Sep. 1981.

[Kodratoff and Jouannaud 84]
Y. Kodratoff and J.-P. Jouannaud. Synthesizing LISP programs working on the list level of embedding. In [Biermann *et al.* 84a], pp. 325–374.

[Kraan *et al.* 93a]
I. Kraan, D. Basin, and A. Bundy. Logic program synthesis via proof planning. In [Lau and Clement 93], pp. 1–14.

[Kraan *et al.* 93b]
I. Kraan, D. Basin, and A. Bundy. Middle-out reasoning for logic program synthesis. In D. S. Warren (ed), *Proc. of ICLP'93*, pp. 441–455. MIT Press, 1993.

[Lakhotia 89]
A. Lakhotia. Incorporating "programming techniques" into Prolog programs. In E. L. Lusk and R. A. Overbeek (eds), *Proc. of NACLP'89*, pp. 426–440. MIT Press, 1989.

[Lange and Wiehagen 91]
S. Lange and R. Wiehagen. Polynomial-time inference of arbitrary pattern languages. *New Generation Computing* 8(4):361–370, 1991.

[Lassez and Marriott 87]
J.-L. Lassez and K. Marriott. Explicit representation of terms defined by counter examples. *J. of Automated Reasoning* 3:301–317, 1987.

[Lassez *et al.* 87]
J.-L. Lassez, M. J. Maher, and K. Marriott. Unification revisited In M. Boscarol, L. C. Aiello, and G. Levi (eds), *Proc. of the* 1986 *Work. on the Foundations of Logic and Functional Pgmming*, pp. 67–113. LNCS 306, Springer-Verlag, 1987.

[Lau 89]
K.-K. Lau. A note on synthesis and classification of sorting algorithms. *Acta Informatica* 27:73–80, 1989.

[Lau and Prestwich 90]
K.-K. Lau and S. D. Prestwich. Top-down synthesis of recursive logic procedures from first-order logic specifications. In D. H. D. Warren and P. Szeredi (eds), *Proc. of ICLP'90*, pp. 667–684. MIT Press, 1990.

[Lau and Prestwich 91]
K.-K. Lau and S. D. Prestwich. Synthesis of a family of recursive sorting procedures. In V. Saraswat and K. Ueda (eds), *Proc. of SLP'91*, pp. 641–658. MIT Press, 1991.

[Lau and Clement 93]
K.-K. Lau and T. Clement (eds), *Proc. of LOPSTR'92*. Springer-Verlag, 1993.

[Lau and Ornaghi 93]
K.-K. Lau and M. Ornaghi. An incompleteness result for deductive synthesis of logic programs. In D. S. Warren (ed), *Proc. of ICLP'93*, pp. 456–477. MIT Press, 1993.

[Lau and Ornaghi 94a]
K.-K. Lau and M. Ornaghi. A formal view of specification, deductive synthesis and transformation of logic programs. In [Deville 94], pp. 10–31.

[Lau and Ornaghi 94b]
K.-K. Lau and M. Ornaghi. On specification frameworks and deductive synthesis of logic programs. In [Fribourg and Turini 94].

[Lau *et al.* 94]
K.-K. Lau, M. Ornaghi, and S.-Å. Tärnlund. The halting problem for deductive synthesis of logic programs. In P. van Hentenryck (ed), *Proc. of ICLP'94*, pp. 665–683. MIT Press, 1994.

[Lavrač and Džeroski 94]
N. Lavrač and S. Džeroski. *Inductive Logic Programming: Techniques and Applications*. Ellis Horwood (Simon & Schuster), 1994.

[Le Charlier 85]
B. Le Charlier. *Réflexions sur le problème de la correction des programmes*. Ph.D. Thesis (in french), Fac. Univ. Notre-Dame de la Paix, Namur (Belgium), 1985.

[Lichtenstein and Shapiro 88]
Y. Lichtenstein and E. Y. Shapiro. Abstract algorithmic debugging. In R. A. Kowalski and K. A. Bowen (eds), *Proc. of ICLP'88*, pp. 512–531. MIT Press, 1988.

[Lloyd 87]
J. W. Lloyd. *Foundations of Logic Programming*. Springer-Verlag. Second, extended edition, 1987.

[London and Feather 82]
P. E. London and M. S. Feather. Implementing specification freedoms. *Science of Computer Pgmming* 2:91–131, 1982. Also in [Rich and Waters 86a], pp. 285–305.

[Lowry and Duran 89]
M. Lowry and R. Duran. Knowledge-based software engineering. In A. Barr, P. R. Cohen, and E. A. Feigenbaum (eds), *The Handbook of Artificial Intelligence* (Vol. IV), pp. 241–322. Addison-Wesley, 1989.

[Manna 74]
Z. Manna. *Mathematical Theory of Computation*. McGraw-Hill, 1974.

[Manna and Waldinger 77]
Z. Manna and R. Waldinger. The automatic synthesis of systems of recursive programs. In *Proc. of IJCAI'77*, pp. 405–411.

[Manna and Waldinger 79]
Z. Manna and R. Waldinger. Synthesis: Dreams ⇒ Programs. *IEEE Trans. on Software Engineering* 5(4):294–328, July 1979.

[Manna and Waldinger 80]
Z. Manna and R. Waldinger. A deductive approach to program synthesis. *ACM Trans. on Programming Languages and Systems* 2(1):90–121, Jan. 1980. Also in [Webber and Nilsson 81], pp. 141–172. Also in [Biermann *et al.* 84a], pp. 33–68. Also in [Rich and Waters 86a], pp. 3–34.

[Manna and Waldinger 81]
Z. Manna and R. Waldinger. Deductive synthesis of the unification algorithm. *Science of Computer Programming* 1:5–48, 1981. Also in [Biermann and Guiho 83], pp. 251–307.

[Manna and Waldinger 87]
Z. Manna and R. Waldinger. The origin of a binary-search paradigm. *Science of Computer Programming* 9:37–83, 1987.

[Manna and Waldinger 91]
Z. Manna and R. Waldinger. Fundamentals of deductive program synthesis. In F. L. Bauer (ed), *Logic, Algebra, and Computation*, pp. 41–107. Vol. ASI-F79, Springer-Verlag, 1991.

[Martin-Löf 79]
P. Martin-Löf. Constructive mathematics and computer programming. In *Proc. of the* 1979 *Int'l Congress for Logic, Methodology, and Philosophy of Science*, pp. 153–175. Published by North Holland, 1982.

[Michalski 84]
R. S. Michalski. Inductive learning as rule-guided generalization of symbolic descriptions: A theory and implementation. In [Biermann *et al.* 84a], pp. 517–552.

[Mitchell 81]
T. M. Mitchell. Generalization as search. In [Webber and Nilsson 81], pp. 517–542. Also in *Artificial Intelligence* 18(2):203–226, March 1982.

[Mitchell *et al.* 86]
T. M. Mitchell, R. M. Keller, and S. T. Kedar-Cabelli. Explanation-based generalization: A unifying view. *Machine Learning* 1(1):47–80, 1986.

[Mohring 86]
Ch. Mohring. Algorithm development in the calculus of constructions. In *Proc. of the* 1986 *IEEE Symp. on Logic in Computer Science*, pp. 84–95.

[Muggleton 91]
S. Muggleton. Inductive logic programming. *New Generation Computing* 8(4):295–317, 1991. Also in [Muggleton 92], pp. 3–27.

[Muggleton 92]
S. Muggleton (ed). *Inductive Logic Programming*. Academic Press, 1992.

[Muggleton 95]
S. Muggleton. *Foundations of Inductive Logic Programming*. Prentice Hall, 1995. (Forthcoming.)

[Muggleton and Buntine 88]
S. Muggleton and W. Buntine. Machine invention of first-order predicates by

inverting resolution. In *Proc. of the* 1988 *Int'l Conf. on Machine Learning*, pp. 339–352. Morgan Kaufmann, 1988. Also in [Muggleton 92], pp. 261–280.

[Muggleton and Feng 90]
S. Muggleton and C. Feng. Efficient induction of logic programs. In *Proc. of the* 1990 *Int'l Workshop on Algorithmic Learning Theory*. Ohmsha, 1990. Also in [Muggleton 92], pp. 281–298.

[Muggleton and De Raedt 94]
S. Muggleton and L. De Raedt. Inductive logic programming: Theory and methods. *J. of Logic Programming, Special Issue on* 10 *Years of Logic Pgmming*, 1994.

[Neugebauer 93]
G. Neugebauer. The LOPS approach: A transformational point of view. In [Lau and Clement 93], pp. 80–81.

[Nordström *et al.* 90]
B. Nordström, K. Petersson, and J. M. Smith. *Programming in Martin-Löf's Type Theory: An Introduction*. Clarendon Press, Oxford (UK), 1990.

[O'Keefe 90]
R. A. O'Keefe. *The Craft of Prolog*. MIT Press, 1990.

[Partsch and Steinbrüggen 83]
H. Partsch and R. Steinbrüggen. Program transformation systems. *Computing Surveys* 15(3):199–236, Sep. 1983.

[Pettorossi and Proietti 89]
A. Pettorossi and M. Proietti. Decidability results and characterization of strategies for the development of logic programs. In G. Levi and M. Martelli (eds), *Proc. of ICLP'*89, pp. 539–553. MIT Press, 1989.

[Pitt and Valiant 88]
L. Pitt and L. G. Valiant. Computational limits on learning from examples. *J. of the ACM* 35(4):965–984, Oct. 1988.

[Plotkin 70]
Gordon D. Plotkin. A note on inductive generalization. *Machine Intelligence* 5:153–163, 1970.

[Plotkin 71]
G. D. Plotkin. A further note on inductive generalization. *Machine Intelligence* 6:101–124, 1971.

[Popplestone 70]
R. J. Popplestone. An experiment in automatic induction. *Machine Intelligence* 5:203–215, 1970.

[Quinlan 90]
J. R. Quinlan. Learning logical definitions from relations. *Machine Learning* 5(3):239–266, Aug. 1990.

[Reynolds 70]
J. C. Reynolds. Transformational systems and the algebraic structure of atomic formulas. *Machine Intelligence* 5:135–151, 1970.

[Rich and Waters 86a]
Ch. Rich and R. C. Waters (eds). *Readings in Artificial Intelligence and Software Engineering*. Morgan Kaufmann, 1986.

[Rich and Waters 86b]
Ch. Rich and R. C. Waters. Introduction. In [Rich and Waters 86a], pp. *xi–xxi*.

[Rich and Waters 88a]
Ch. Rich and R. C. Waters. Automatic programming: Myths and prospects. *IEEE Computer* 21(8):40–51, Aug. 1988.

[Rich and Waters 88b]
Ch. Rich and R. C. Waters. The Programmer's Apprentice: A research overview. *IEEE Computer* 21(11):10–25, Nov. 1988.

[Rouveirol 91]
C. Rouveirol. Semantic model for induction of first order theories. In *Proc. of IJCAI*'91, pp. 685–690.

[Ruth 78]
G. R. Ruth. Protosystem I: An automatic programming system prototype. In *Proc. of the* 1978 *AFIPS Conf.* Also in [Rich and Waters 86a], pp. 215–221.

[Sammut 93]
C. Sammut. The origins of Inductive Logic Programming: A prehistoric tale. In *Proc. of ILP*'93 (TR IJS-DP-6707, J. Stefan Inst., Slovenia), pp. 127–147.

[Sammut and Banerji 86]
C. Sammut and R. B. Banerji. Learning concepts by asking questions. In R. Michalski, J. G. Carbonell, and T. Mitchell (eds), *Machine Learning: An Artificial Intelligence Approach*, Vol. 2, pp. 167–192. Morgan Kaufmann, 1986.

[Sato and Tamaki 84]
T. Sato and H. Tamaki. Transformational logic program synthesis. In *Proc. of the Int'l Conf. on Fifth-Generation Computer Systems*, pp. 195–201, 1984.

[Sato and Tamaki 89]
T. Sato and H. Tamaki. First-order compiler: A deterministic logic program synthesis algorithm. *J. of Symbolic Computation* 8(6):605–627, 1989.

[Shapiro 82]
E. Y. Shapiro. *Algorithmic Program Debugging*. Ph.D. Thesis, Yale Univ., New Haven (CT, USA), 1982. Published under the same title by MIT Press, 1983.

[Shaw *et al.* 75]
D. E. Shaw, W. R. Swartout, and C. Green. Inferring LISP programs from examples. In *Proc. of IJCAI*'75, pp. 260–267.

[Siklóssy and Sykes 75]
L. Siklóssy and D. A. Sykes. Automatic program synthesis from example problems. In *Proc. of IJCAI*'75, pp. 268–273.

[Sintzoff 93]
M. Sintzoff. Private communication. May 1993.

[Smith 82]
D. R. Smith. Derived preconditions and their use in program synthesis. In D. W. Loveland (ed), *Proc. of CADE*'82, pp. 172–193.

[Smith 84]
D. R. Smith. The synthesis of LISP programs from examples: A survey. In [Biermann *et al.* 84a], pp. 307–324.

[Smith 85]
D. R. Smith. Top-down synthesis of divide-and-conquer algorithms. *Artificial Intelligence* 27(1):43–96, 1985. Also in [Rich and Waters 86a], pp. 35–61.

[Smith 88]
D. R. Smith. *The structure and design of global search algorithms*. TR KES.U.87. 12, Kestrel Inst., Palo Alto, 1988. To appear in *Acta Informatica*.

[Smith 90a]
D. R. Smith. KIDS: A semiautomatic program development system. *IEEE Trans. on Software Engineering* 16(9):1024–1043, Sep. 1990.

[Smith 90b]
D. R. Smith. Algorithm theories and design tactics. *Science of Computer Programming* 14:305–321, 1990.

[Smith 93]
D. R. Smith. Constructing specification morphisms. In [JSC 93], pp. 571–606.

[Smith 94]
D. R. Smith. Synthesis of constraint algorithms. In [Deville 94], pp. 1–9.

[Smith *et al.* 85]
D. R. Smith, G. B. Kotik, and S. J. Westfold. Research on knowledge-based software environments at Kestrel Institute. In [IEEE-TSE 85], pp. 1278–1295.

[Soloway and Ehrlich 84]
E. Soloway and K. Ehrlich. Empirical studies of programming knowledge. *IEEE Trans. on Software Engineering* 10(5):595–609, Sep. 1984. Also in [Rich and Waters 86a], pp. 507–521.

[Steier and Kant 85]
D. M. Steier and E. Kant. The roles of execution and analysis in algorithm design. In [IEEE-TSE 85], pp. 1375–1386.

[Steier and Anderson 89]
D. M. Steier and A. P. Anderson. *Algorithm Synthesis: A Comparative Study*. Springer-Verlag, 1989.

[Sterling and Kirschenbaum 93]
L. S. Sterling and M. Kirschenbaum. Applying techniques to skeletons. In [Jacquet 93], pp. 127–140.

[Summers 77]
Ph. D. Summers. A methodology for LISP program construction from examples. *J. of the ACM* 24(1):161–175, 1977. Also in [Rich and Waters 86a], pp. 309–316.

[Swartout and Balzer 82]
W. R. Swartout and R. Balzer. On the inevitable intertwining of specification and implementation. *Comm. of the ACM* 25:438–440, 1982.

[Takayama 87]
Y. Takayama. Writing programs as QJ proof and compiling into Prolog programs. In *Proc. of SLP'87*, pp. 278–287.

[Tamaki and Sato 84]
H. Tamaki and T. Sato. Unfold/fold transformations of logic programs. In S.-Å. Tärnlund (ed), *Proc. of ICLP'84*, pp. 127–138.

[Tärnlund 78]
S.-Å. Tärnlund. An axiomatic data base theory. In H. Gallaire and J. Minker (eds), *Logic and Databases*, pp. 259–289. Plenum Press, 1978.

[Tinkham 90]
N. L. Tinkham. *Induction of Schemata for Program Synthesis*. Ph.D. Thesis, Duke Univ., Durham (NC, USA), 1990.

[Valiant 84]
L. G. Valiant. A theory of the learnable. *Comm. of the ACM* 27(11):1134–1142, Nov. 1984.

[van Lamsweerde 91]
A. van Lamsweerde. Learning machine learning. In A. Thayse (ed), *From Natural Language Processing to Logic for Expert Systems*, pp. 263–356. J. Wiley, 1991.

[Vere 75]
S. A. Vere. Induction of concepts in the predicate calculus. In *Proc. of IJCAI'75*, pp. 281–287.

[Waldau 92]
M. Waldau. Formal validation of transformation schemata. In [Clement and Lau 92], pp. 97–110.

[Waldinger and Lee 69]
R. J. Waldinger and R. C. T. Lee. PROW: A step toward automatic program writing. In *Proc. of IJCAI'69*, pp. 241–252.

[Waterman *et al.* 84]
D. A. Waterman, W. S. Faught, P. Klahr, S. J. Rosenschein, and R. Wesson. Design issues for exemplary programming. In [Biermann *et al.* 84a], pp. 433–460.

[Webber and Nilsson 81]
B. L. Webber and N. J. Nilsson (eds). *Readings in Artificial Intelligence*. Morgan Kaufmann, 1981.

[Wiggins 92]
G. Wiggins. Synthesis and transformation of logic programs in the Whelk proof development system. In K. Apt (ed), *Proc. of the* 1992 *Joint Int'l Conf. and Symp. on Logic Programming*, pp. 351–365, MIT Press, 1992.

[Wiggins *et al.* 92]
G. Wiggins, A. Bundy, I. Kraan, and J. Hesketh. Synthesis and transformation of logic programs from constructive, inductive proof. In [Clement and Lau 92], pp. 27–45.

[Wile 83]
D. S. Wile. Program developments: Formal explanations of implementations. *Comm. of the ACM* 26(11):902–911, 1983. Also in [Rich and Waters 86a], pp. 191–200.

[Zloof 77]
M. Zloof. Query by example: A data base language. *IBM Systems Journal* 4(16):324–343, 1977.

Subject Index

Symbols

*, any finite integer 72
$\perp_r$, bottom logic algorithm 91
∞, infinity 72
$\mathfrak{I}$, intended interpretation 87
$\mathcal{R}$, intended relation 79
$\models$, logical consequence 18
|, second-order exclusive-or 106
$\equiv$, semantic equivalence 91
$\leq$, semantic generalization 91
$\approx$, syntactic equivalence 92
«, syntactic generalization 92
θ-subsumption 47, 92, 99, 100
T_r, top logic algorithm 91

A

acceptable hypothesis 35
accumulator introduction 19, 45
actual correctness criteria 88–89
actually-computed relation 85
add/3 problem 13
adm/1 operator 139
admissible
  (set of) atoms 134, 136
  alternatives 139
  hypothesis 35
  presentation 34
algorithm 5–6, 41, 46
  See also logic algorithm
  analysis 102
  classification 12
  complexity 5, 109, 212
  construction 6
  design 5–6
    knowledge 11, 53, 113, 214
    strategy 40, 101
  implementation 5–7, 28
  languages 7
  schema 101
  synthesis 6–7, 28, 102
  transformation 5, 28
algorithmic learning 37
algorithmic problems 3
algorithmic synthesis 10
all-at-once presentation 33, 37, 151
all-true case 160
ambiguity, of specifications 7, 17, 32
analytic learning 44, 53, 214
anti-unification 51, 133, 143
append/3 problem 13, 24, 52, 169, 203
application knowledge.
  See domain knowledge
approximation-driven learning 38–39
atomic inductive inference rules 33
atomic transformation rules 18
automated theorem proving 18–19, 23
automatic programming.
  See program synthesis
auxiliary parameter 66, 111, 197
  declaration 197, 206
  detection 197
average/2 problem 111
axiom 18
axiomatic specification 15

B

background knowledge 33, 46, 53, 84
basis set 33, 148
better approximation 94
body, of a logic algorithm 57
body, of a logic algorithm schema 102
break-even point 12, 23

C

canonical representation 102
characteristic hypothesis 35
CHI 22
chunk-wise presentation 33
CIGOL 51
Clam 25–26, 28
classification query 31, 48, 149
CLAUDIEN 52
clause generator 47
CLINT 52
clique 136
compact list 13
compatible (set of) atoms 135

compilation 8, 26
complete presentation 34
complete traversal 71
completeness
  of logic algorithms
    wrt examples 89
    wrt intentions 88
    wrt properties 90
  of oracles 96
  of specifications, wrt intentions 7, 17, 32, 53, 79, 148, 211–212
completeness-preserving progression 94
completion, of a logic program 58, 61
Compose predicate-variable 104, 108, 156, 169, 181–184, 186, 199
compound induction parameter 59, 68, 169, 194
compress/2 problem 13–17, 30–32, 56–62, 64, 75–76, 80, 104, 108, 123–127, 134–138, 152–158, 161–189, 202
computation rule, for *DCI* and *NFI* 118
computational
  contents, of a proof 116, 131
  generalization 212
computed relation 86
concept 31, 41
  classes 34
  description 41, 46
conceptual bias 33
conclusion, of an implicative goal 117
conditional query 149
CONFUCIUS 51
conjecture. *See* hypothesis
conservative learning 38
consistency
  assumption 159, 161, 171, 188, 193
  of examples, wrt intentions 32, 90
  of properties, wrt intentions 90
  of specifications, wrt intentions 90
consistent
  hypothesis. *See* admissible hyp.
  learning 38
  synthesis 93
constituents, of a term 71, 134
constructive
  program verification 4
  rule, of inductive inference 33
  synthesis. *See* proofs-as-pgms syn.
Constructive Interpreter 131
counter, in a compact list 13
counter-example. *See* negative example
cover, of a logic algorithm 102
cover, of an atom 95
Curry-Howard isomorphism 19
Cypress 23, 113, 203

D

Database Method 153–154, 169, 194
data-driven empirical learning 38
data-efficiency, of a learner 38
data-processing problems 3
DCI rule 118–122, 187
dead code 50, 53
Decompose predicate-variable 104, 107–108, 154, 166–170
decomposition decrement 167, 205
decreasing synthesis 93
DEDALUS 21–22
deductive
  inference 18
  oracle 96, 171
  synthesis 17, 114
definite clause inference rule.
    See DCI rule
delOddElems/2 problem 13, 65, 105
derivation schema 120–123, 188
Designer 11
deterministic logic algorithm 72
directionality 56, 61
  heuristic 59, 162
  of axioms 16
  of examples 31
discriminant hypothesis 35
Discriminate predicate-variable 105, 108, 157, 164, 186–189, 197
divide-and-conquer
  schema 109, 197
  strategy 103–104, 109, 150
domain
  checking 59–60

extrapolation hypothesis 164, 193
knowledge 11, 41, 53, 63, 214
downward progression 94

E

early detection, of aux. parameters 198
EBG 44, 131
EBL 19, 44, 53
EBPT 19
efface/3 problem 13, 66, 69, 74, 76, 82, 96, 106, 108, 112, 115, 169, 176, 196, 201, 208
effectiveness, of synthesis 81, 84, 93
efficiency
knowledge 11
of programs 3, 5
of synthesis 19, 46, 81, 84
elems/1 operator 91
empirical learning 31–53, 214
EP systems 41
evolutionary specifications 11, 17, 211
example 29, 33–34, 41
executability, of specifications 7
ExExE 27
existential query 149
exp/3 operator 97, 171–172, 194
expansion
of a conjunction 95–97
of a logic algorithm 97
phase 158, 160–173, 195
explanation-based
generalization. *See* EBG
learning. *See* EBL
exploratory programming 11
expressiveness, of languages 7, 84, 148
extended execution 27, 117
extractive approach 19
extrapolation. *See* prediction
extrinsic
decomposition 71, 168
heuristic 59, 71, 167

F

failure, of a derivation 119
failure, of the PaP Method 121
family of algorithms 12, 101, 149
finite learning 38
finite logic algorithm 72
finite presentation 36
firstN/3 problem 13, 66, 76, 106, 108, 176
firstPlateau/3 problem 13, 15, 29, 56–57, 81, 119–121, 127–130, 138, 159–190, 203
flatTree/2 problem 13, 212
FOIL 52
folding rule 18, 24
formal specification 7–11, 28
free variable 117
fully-deterministic logic algorithm 72
functional form, of axioms 16, 19
functional form, of examples 31, 42
functionality heuristic 59, 162, 183

G

gen/1 refinement operator 92
general example 139
generalization 33–34
heuristics 186
model 99
of terms 133
generalized subsumption 100
GIST 7, 9, 22
GLITTER 22
GOLEM 51
goodness ordering 35
grammatical inference 34
groundness, of examples 31

H

head
of a logic algorithm 57
of a logic algorithm schema 102
of the induction parameter 104, 108
heuristic learning 37
heuristic synthesis 10, 45
heuristics 110, 140
human oracle 171
hypothesis 33
of an implicative goal 117

I

identification 34
  by enumeration 36, 38
  criterion 35
  in-the-limit 35–36
  type 36–38
ILP 46, 51–54, 114, 143
implicative goal 117
increasing synthesis 93
incremental learning 37, 131
incremental synthesis 93
INDUCE 51
induction
  bias 33
  parameter 58, 107, 153–154, 205
    decomposition 71, 167
    selection 59, 162, 183, 194
    traversal 71
inductive
  conclusion 33
  inference 32–33
  synthesis 114
  type 58–59, 107, 152
Inductive Logic Programming. *See* ILP
infinite code 50, 53
infinite logic algorithm 72
informant. *See* oracle
input/output example 31
insert/3 problem 13, 67, 76, 106, 169, 176, 209, 213
insertion-sort algorithm 40, 70, 109, 149, 209, 213
instance 31
  description 31, 33, 41
  of a logic algorithm schema 102
  of a predicate-variable 164
instructor. *See* teacher
intended
  concept 31, 33, 35
  interpretation 87
  model 84
  relation 63, 79, 87
intentions 4–7, 16, 28
interactive learning 37
internal consistency, of specifications 7, 86, 148, 212
interpretative approach 19
intrinsic
  decomposition 71
  heuristic 59, 71, 167
intuitive correctness criteria 87–89
inversion, of resolution 51
iterative learning 37
iterative synthesis 94
ITOU 51

K

KBSA 12
KIDS 23, 113
knowing a concept 31
knowledge 11
  acquisition 11–12, 41

L

language
  continuum 8
  generations 8
  levels 8–9
  of axioms 16
  of examples 31
late detection, of aux. parameters 197
LAWALY / SYN 42
learner 33, 41
learning 32–53
length/2 problem 14–15, 17
LIBRA 22
LINUS 52
LISP 7–8, 21, 42
list/1 problem 14
logarithmic decomposition 71, 168
logic algorithm 28, 56, 148
  See also algorithm
  classification 102
  construction 58, 109
  design 56
  optimization 207
  schema 102
  transformation 61, 207
logic program
  See also program
  derivation 61

schema 27, 50, 112
transformation 62
logic programming 8, 17, 46, 53, 212
logical consequence 18
logical correctness, of algorithms 5–6
Logist 58
loop detection 19
loop merging 111, 203
LOPS 25, 28

M

macroscopic transf. rules 19, 21, 28
MARKUS 50
MARVIN 51
member/2 problem 14–15, 24, 29, 48–50, 67, 76, 106, 176
merge/3 problem 14, 68, 107, 169, 210
merge-sort algorithm 40, 70, 149, 211
meta-knowledge 11
methodology
of example & property choice 204
of example choice 164, 182
of logic algorithm design 58
of logic program development 55
minimal
case 60, 74, 155, 162
example 163
form 60, 163
Minimal predicate-variable 104, 107–108, 153, 161–165
minimality
hypothesis 140, 182
of specifications 7, 148
minimum/2 problem 14, 203
min–max determinism 72
MIS 46–52, 84, 100, 113, 131, 213
MISST 50
mixed presentation 34
Model Inference System. See MIS
model-based synthesis 46
model-driven learning 38
monitoring points 93, 150
monotonic learning 37
monotonic synthesis 93
most-general literal 92
most-general term 92
most-specific-generalization 133, 143
Most-Specific-Generalization Method. See MSG Method
MSG Method 156, 175, 195, 203
ground case 136
non-ground case 139
mult/3 problem 14
multi-directionality 62, 110, 169
multiple-loop logic algorithm 72, 203
multiplicity
of concepts 31
of examples 31
of predicates, in examples 31

N

naive-sort algorithm 101
NatDed 26
natural extension 135
natural language 7–8
Natural Language Computer 9
negation-as-failure inference rule. *See NFI* rule
negative example 29, 196
NFI rule 118–121
non-deterministic logic algorithm 72
non-minimal
case 60, 74, 162
splitting 171
example 163
form 60, 163
NonMinimal predicate-variable 104, 107–108, 153, 161–165, 169
non-recursive
example 172
non-minimal case 74, 105, 155, 171
normalized derivation 119
notation-variable 104
Nuprl 26

O

odd/1 problem 14
one-by-one presentation 33, 37
operational correctness 3–5
oracle 33, 48, 96

order sensitivity 37, 39, 53
ordered/1 problem 14, 16
ordering, of examples 162
Oyster 26, 28

P

PAC-identification 36, 54
PaP Method 116, 157, 186, 194, 195
parameter introduction 111, 212
parity/2 problem 14, 68, 76, 107, 176
partial correctness
 of logic algorithms
  wrt examples 89
  wrt intentions 88
  wrt properties 90
 of specifications, wrt intentions 7
partial-correctness preserving progr. 94
partition/4 problem 14, 69, 76, 106, 176
partitioning, of examples 163
passive learning 37
PECOS 11, 22
Periwinkle 25
permutation/2 problem 14, 16, 69, 76, 83, 96, 104, 141, 176
PHINIX 11, 22
plateau 13
plateau/3 problem 14, 69, 76, 106, 140–141, 176, 203, 207
positive example 29
positive presentation 34, 36
post-condition 16
power, of a learner 38
pre-condition 16, 23, 131
predicate invention 33
prediction 36
preference hint 150, 162, 167, 194, 206
prefix-traversal 71, 74
presentation
 by informant 34
 order, of examples 37
problem classification 3
ProcComp predicate-variable 156, 181–184, 203
procedure declaration 56, 206
Process predicate-variable 104, 108, 156, 181–184, 186, 199
program 3, 5, 6
 See also logic program
 development 4–5
 maintenance 4–5
 optimization 18, 28
 schema 21, 54
 synthesis 5, 18
 testing 4
 transformation 5, 18, 20, 28
 validation 4–5
Programmer's Apprentice 11, 113
programming 3, 8–9
 in-the-large 12
 in-the-small 4, 12, 212
 knowledge 20–21
 languages 7
 methodologies 4
 task 4–5, 12
progression, of synthesis 93
project management 12
Prolog 7–8, 23, 46, 55, 61–62, 207
proof
 by extended execution 117
 by induction 20
 development system 26
 knowledge 20–21
 planning 19–20, 28
Proofs-as-Programs Method. *See PaP Method*
proofs-as-programs synthesis 19–21, 116, 130
property 79
property-example 187
Protosystem I 9
PROW 22
pseudo-list 153, 155
PSI 9, 11, 22

Q

QA3 22
QJ 27
quantifier-free form, of impl. goals 117
Query-by-Example 41

quick-sort algo. 41, 70, 109, 149, 210

R

readability, of languages 7, 84, 148
recursion
  discovery 147
  elimination 75
  introduction 171–173
recursive
  algorithms 54, 109
  examples 172
  logic algorithms 87
  logic programs 214
  non-minimal case 105, 171
  programs 20
  properties 81–83, 120, 205
  specifications 16
  synthesis 203
reduction phase 158, 175–189, 195
redundancy, in specifications 7, 148
redundant code 51, 53
relation 20, 41
relational form, of axioms 16
relational form, of examples 31, 46
relative
  least-general generalization 99
  subsumption 99
reliable learning 38
replay 4–5, 11–12, 17, 19, 211
retrospective program verification 4
reusability 12
reverse/2 problem 14, 43–45, 52, 212
reversibility. *See* multi-directionality
robustness 148, 195

S

SAFE 9, 22
sample-independent ordering 35
scalar 72
schema analysis 102
schema synthesis 102
schema-guided synthesis 21, 110, 214
search
  rule, for *DCI* 118
  space 18–19, 28, 35, 46, 54, 213
    pruning 33, 36, 47, 99, 114, 140
selective rule, of inductive inference 33
semantic
  bias 33
  equivalence, of logic algorithms 91
  generalization, of logic algorithms 91
  manipulation 72
sign, of examples 31
Sim rule 118–121
simple induction parameter 59
simplification rule. *See Sim* rule
single-loop logic algorithm 72
size, of a ground term 163
size, of an example 163
software
  crisis 3
  engineering 3, 9, 12
  life-cycle 4–5
  quality 12
Solve predicate-variable 104, 108, 155, 175–178, 187
SolveNonMin predicate-variable 105, 108, 155, 175–178, 186
sort/2 problem 14, 16, 30, 32, 40, 70, 76, 101, 104, 108–109, 149, 209, 213–214
soundness
  of deductive inference 18
  of inductive inference 33
  of oracles 96
  of synthesis 19
spec/1 refinement operator 93
specification 6–7, 56
  by axioms 15
  by examples 29
  by examples & properties 80, 148
  by traces 42
  elaboration 4–5, 56
  in natural language 9
  languages 7
  maintenance 4–5
  validation 5
specified relation 63, 80, 86
specifier 41
  interaction 110, 165–188, 195, 204
specifier / synthesizer setting 213–214

specifying agent 16, 31
split/3 problem 14, 70, 107, 111
split/4 problem 70, 76
stepwise learning 37
stepwise synthesis 90, 93, 110, 150
strongly conservative hypothesis 141
structural
  case 60, 194
    construction 60
  form 60, 194
    selection 60
  generalization 212
  induction 87
  manipulation 53, 72
stuff/3 problem 14, 69, 201
sub-case 104–107, 194
success, of a derivation 119
success, of the PaP Method 121
sum/2 problem 14, 16–17, 30–32, 83, 87–97
SYNAPSE 206–211
SYNSYS 22
syntactic
  bias 34, 148
  equivalence, of logic algorithms 92
  generalization 99
    of conjunctions 92
    of logic algorithms 92
synthesis 41, 53
  from examples 40
  from traces 42
  strategy 93
Synthesis Method 156, 194, 198, 203
synthesized literal 97
synthesizer 41

T

tail recursion 109
tail, of the induction parameter 104, 108
target language 7
teacher 33, 41
teacher / learner setting 213
theorem 18
theory 18
THESYS 44
tool-box of methods 110, 150, 212
top-down decomposition 109
total correctness
  of logic algorithms
    wrt examples 90
    wrt intentions 58, 88
    wrt properties 90
  of specifications, wrt intentions 7
trace 42
  generalization 42, 195
  generation 42, 195
trace-based synthesis 42, 50, 214
trailing atom 97
Trainable Turing Machine 42
trainer. *See* teacher
trans/1 transformation operator 93
transformation rule 18
transformational implementation 22
transformational synthesis 18–21
type inference 162–163
type knowledge 140

U

undecided variable 117
unfolding rule 18, 24
unification 133
universal query 149
upward progression 94
useless recursion 171, 194

V

value, in a compact list 13
version space 35, 38, 100

W

weakly conservative hypothesis 141
well-founded
  induction 58, 109
  relation 58, 86, 107, 154
    selection 59, 167, 194
Whelk 27–28
wit/1 operator 95
witness 96